2 Edit chart (screen)

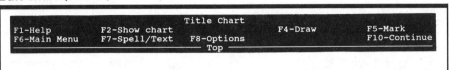

Title Chart

| F1-Help | F2-Show chart | | F4-Draw | F5-Mark |
| F6-Main Menu | F7-Spell/Text | F8-Options | | F10-Continue |

Top

4 File

Get chart	1	Ctrl G
Get template	2	
Apply template	3	
▶ Save chart	4	Ctrl S
Save as template	5	
Save as symbol	6	
Import	7	
Export	8	

7 Import

▶ Import Lotus graph	1
Import Lotus data	2
Import Excel chart	3
Import Excel data	4
Import ASCII data	5
Import delimited ASCII	6
Import dBASE data	7
Import CGM metafile	8

8 Export

▶ Export Professional Write	1
Export CGM metafile	2
Export Encapsulated PostScript	3
Export HPGL plotter file	4
Export PCX bitmap file	5

raphics

F10-Continue

5 Output

▶ Printer 1	1
Printer 2	2
Plotter	3
Film recorder	4
Presentation	5
Presentation list	6
Print chart data	7
Reset spooler	8

6 Presentation

▶ Create presentation	1
Edit presentation	2
Display ScreenShow	3
Get presentation	4
Save presentation	5
Spell check presentation	6

8 Setup

▶ Program defaults	1
Chart default settings	2
Applications	3
Software fonts	4
Printer 1	5
Printer 2	6
Plotter	7
Film recorder	8
Display	9
Input	A
Color palette	B

7 Macros

▶ Select macro file	1
Run macro	2
Record macro	3

Computer users are not all alike.
Neither are SYBEX books.

We know our customers have a variety of needs. They've told us so. And because we've listened, we've developed several distinct types of books to meet the needs of each of our customers. What are you looking for in computer help?

If you're looking for the basics, try the **ABC's** series. You'll find short, unintimidating tutorials and helpful illustrations. For a more visual approach, select **Teach Yourself**, featuring screen-by-screen illustrations of how to use your latest software purchase.

Mastering and **Understanding** titles offer you a step-by-step introduction, plus an in-depth examination of intermediate-level features, to use as you progress.

Our **Up & Running** series is designed for computer-literate consumers who want a no-nonsense overview of new programs. Just 20 basic lessons, and you're on your way.

We also publish two types of reference books. Our **Instant References** provide quick access to each of a program's commands and functions. SYBEX **Encyclopedias** provide a *comprehensive reference* and explanation of all of the commands, features and functions of the subject software.

Sometimes a subject requires a special treatment that our standard series doesn't provide. So you'll find we have titles like **Advanced Techniques, Handbooks, Tips & Tricks**, and others that are specifically tailored to satisfy a unique need.

We carefully select our authors for their in-depth understanding of the software they're writing about, as well as their ability to write clearly and communicate effectively. Each manuscript is thoroughly reviewed by our technical staff to ensure its complete accuracy. Our production department makes sure it's easy to use. All of this adds up to the highest quality books available, consistently appearing on best-seller charts worldwide.

You'll find SYBEX publishes a variety of books on every popular software package. Looking for computer help? Help Yourself to SYBEX.

For a complete catalog of our publications:

SYBEX Inc.
2021 Challenger Drive, Alameda, CA 94501
Tel: (415) 523-8233/(800) 227-2346 Telex: 336311
Fax: (415) 523-2373

Mastering
Harvard Graphics 3 for DOS

Mastering
Harvard Graphics® 3 for DOS®

Glenn H. Larsen
with
Kristopher A. Larsen

SYBEX®

San Francisco • Paris • Düsseldorf • Soest

Acquisitions Editor: David Clark
Editor: Marilyn Smith
Project Editors: Kathleen Lattinville, Barbara Dahl
Technical Editor: Rebecca M. Lyles
Word Processors: Susan Trybull, Ann Dunn, Chris Meredith
Series Designer: Julie Bilski
Chapter Art: Lisa Jaffe
Layout and Paste-up: Lisa Jaffe, Alissa Feinberg
Screen Graphics: Cuong Le
Screen Graphic Artist: Thomas Goudie
Typesetter: Stephanie Hollier
Proofreader: Dina F. Quan
Indexer: Anne Leach
Cover Designer: Ingalls + Associates
Cover Photographer: Michael Lamotte

Library of Congress Card Number: 91-65970
ISBN: 0-89588-870-X

Manufactured in the United States of America
10 9 8 7

This book is dedicated to my mother,
Margaret, for all the love and patience
she gives our family.

- Glenn Larsen

This book is dedicated to my eighth grade
English teacher, John Shea,
who has long served as my mentor.

- Kristopher Larsen

ACKNOWLEDGMENTS

MASTERING HARVARD GRAPHICS 3 WAS A BOOK WE BOTH enjoyed writing, probably because of the many people who contributed to it. Their support, guidance, and professionalism helped mold this book into the finished product you are now holding.

Several people offered guidance during the early stages of this book regarding its content, scope, size, and style. We would like to thank Dianne King, Barbara Gordon, Kathleen Lattinville, and Barbara Dahl at SYBEX for their comments, help, and suggestions. A very special thanks goes to our editor, Marilyn Smith, for the excellent way in which she developed this book.

Our hats are off to the professionals at Software Publishing Corporation for the superior help and support they have given us while writing this book. We would especially like to thank Helen Kendrix, Public Relations Department; Ted Simonides, Product Manager for Harvard Graphics; and Gayle Okumura, Beta Release Coordinator. These professionals provided much of the information for the timely and relevant book you are now reading. Software Publishing Corporation's Technical Support Department helped answer many questions about Harvard Graphics. We would also like to thank Michael Baglietto, Harriet Slatoff, David Cruickshank, Milinda Cohen, Pat Nugent, Brad Bechtel, and Kevin Wineberg for the expert help they provided.

Several people helped develop the SYBEX Enhancement Disk. Michael Gross at SYBEX provided suggestions for transcending the 360-kilobyte limitation of our disk by compressing almost 1 megabyte on it. A special thanks goes to Masterclip Graphics, Inc., for the symbols they provided. Cliff Welles, CEO of Masterclip Graphics, and Keith Money, Senior Vice President of Sales, provided the resources for most of the development of the SYBEX Enhancement Disk.

Much of this book's simplicity results from the efforts of our technical reviewer, Rebecca Lyles, and Peder Larsen, a 14-year-old student. They checked the instructions in this book for clarity and worked on the hands-on sessions, providing suggestions and recommendations.

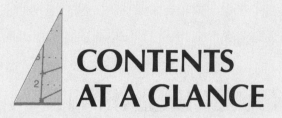

CONTENTS
AT A GLANCE

CONTENTS

Appendices

 **INTRODUCTION**

COMPUTER GRAPHICS HAVE BECOME INCREASINGLY important for persuasive presentations, as they become more accessible to engineers, students, executives, secretaries, educators, salespeople, accountants, and government officials—in short, to anyone who needs to convey information effectively.

This book will help you produce the powerful and effective graphic communication tools you need to reach your audience quickly. Use graphs to get important points across, manage resources, analyze growth, chart sales statistics, and display other data.

IS THIS BOOK FOR YOU?

This book is written for anyone who wants to master Harvard Graphics. It can be used by those with no prior experience with graphics programs, as well as professional computer graphics designers.

Although you do not have to know how to use Harvard Graphics or any other type of presentation software, we do assume that you are somewhat familiar with your computer system. For example, we will not tell you how to turn on your computer, printer, or monitor; nor will you learn how to format your hard disk or install a color graphics board. You will find these subjects fully explained in books devoted to the Disk Operating System (DOS).

You will find that this book complements the Harvard Graphics manual by taking you from making charts to constructing an effective presentation. The book describes chart styles, special effects, and how charts influence your audience. You will learn about Harvard Graphic's quirks and discover tips to increase your productivity.

NEW FEATURES IN HARVARD GRAPHICS 3.0

Software Publishing Corporation added several new features to version 3.0 of Harvard Graphics. One of the major enhancements is the expanded drawing feature, Draw, which now allows you to select options by clicking on icons with your mouse. For example, some of the options added to Draw allow you to add subcharts, animate objects, and use bit-maps and fill patterns in charts.

Harvard Graphics 3.0 also offers three-dimensional bar shapes, such as cylinders and pyramids. Additionally, you can now assign a background drawing, palettes, and font styles to an entire presentation to unify it.

HOW TO USE THIS BOOK

You can begin producing quality graphics without reading *Mastering Harvard Graphics 3* from cover to cover. The first two chapters give you a quick overview of how to use the program. By the end of the second chapter, you will have created several charts.

By the end of Chapter 8, you will be able to create impressive graphics, rivaling those created by graphic artists. You will understand the details of chart construction for any type of chart. In Chapters 9 through 13, you will learn how to automate the chart construction process, design your own charts, unify your charts into a presentation, and transfer data between Harvard and other programs. The appendices provide additional references for using Harvard Graphics, including installation instructions, samples of symbols and templates, and techniques for applying color.

In addition, the inside front cover and first and last pages provide quick references. Refer to the back of the book when you need to refresh your memory about a particular menu option. When you want to see the Harvard Graphics menu structure quickly, just check the inside front cover. It gives you an overview of the menu commands and numbers of the menu options.

The best way to use this book to master Harvard Graphics is to work through each chapter's hands-on practice sessions. You can easily adapt these examples to your own data. Then go on to experiment with different options on your own.

Once you have become familiar with Harvard, you will probably want to keep this book near your computer so that you can refer to it when you are working with commands and features that you use infrequently.

GETTING THE MESSAGES IN THE MARGIN

There are three types of margin notes, each identified by a special symbol, as follows:

 This symbol in the margin denotes any related information about the subject at hand. The note may remind you about something you previously learned or tell you where to look for more information.

 A margin note with this symbol provides tips and shortcuts for using the program— anything that will improve its performance or your understanding of the program's features.

 A note with this symbol tells you to be alert for a potential trouble spot. It explains the problem and offers suggestions for avoiding or resolving it.

USING THE ENHANCEMENT DISK

You can expand your graphics capabilities by installing the SYBEX Harvard Graphics 3 Enhancement Disk bound in the back of this book. This disk gives you superior symbols from Masterclip Graphics, Inc. See Appendices C and F for more information about MasterClips symbols and installing the Enhancement Disk.

A PREVIEW OF THE CONTENTS

Following is a summary of the contents of each chapter and appendix. Use this listing as a guide for where you should start. If you are a beginner, start at Chapter 1. Experienced users can choose their appropriate starting point.

Chapter 1: Introducing Harvard This chapter presents the features of Harvard Graphics. You will learn how to analyze a chart's anatomy and how to select the right chart for your type of data. You will begin to work with the program by configuring your system's output devices, such as your monitor and printer.

Chapter 2: Getting Started This chapter takes you through an accelerated tutorial so you can begin creating simple text, pie, bar, and line charts. You will also learn the essential steps of saving and printing your work. In addition, we discuss when to present printed paper copies, plotted transparencies, and recorded slides to your audience.

Chapter 3: Creating Text Charts In this chapter, you will examine text charts in depth. You will create different types of text charts and use special text-drawing techniques to arrange text in ways that are not possible in standard text charts. You will also learn how to modify your text and check your chart's spelling.

Chapter 4: Creating Pie Charts In this chapter, you will learn how to create an effective pie chart. It discusses methods of presenting your data, including cutting and linking pie slices and fitting more than one pie on your chart.

Chapter 5: Creating Bar and Line Charts This chapter covers how and when to use bar and line charts. You will work with several bar and line chart variations and learn how to use special effects, such as 3D and shadowing, for emphasis.

Chapter 6: Fine-Tuning Your Bar and Line Charts This chapter builds on the previous chapter, showing you how to refine your charts. For example, you will learn how to change the width and style of bars, as well as the characteristics of frames and legends. In addition, you will explore the use of labels, grids, tick marks, and scales.

Chapter 7: Working with Statistics, Calculations, and Formulas This chapter first examines the rudiments of statistics so that you can take full advantage of the program's calculation features. Then you will learn how to use the calculator, formulas, and built-in functions. By using these features, you can sort and analyze your data.

Chapter 8: Creating Organization Charts Internal relationships from family trees to billion-dollar corporation structures can be graphed using an organization chart. This chapter shows you how to design and create charts to illustrate organizational structures.

Chapter 9: Saving Time with the Gallery, Templates, and Macros This chapter discusses the Chart Gallery provided with Harvard Graphics, as well as its extensive template and macro features. Templates provide blueprints for consistently styled charts. Macros automate repetitious tasks for all your charts, streamlining the production process.

Chapter 10: Designing Custom Charts Here you will learn how to design presentation graphics using an assortment of drawing and editing tools. For example, you will practice making a sign that is composed of circles, polygons, and lines. You will also learn how to use the symbols supplied with Harvard Graphics, as well as how to create your own symbols.

Chapter 11: Designing with Draw This chapter shows you how to take full advantage of all the tools available in Draw. You will learn how to use the Draw options to create special effects for highly professional charts.

Chapter 12: Creating Presentations Once you have acquired all the chart-building techniques, you will need to learn how to tie everything together. This chapter describes how to use the program's presentation options to sort your graphs, develop practice cards, and run a computerized show.

Chapter 13: Transferring Information between Harvard and Other Programs In this chapter, you will learn about the importing and exporting methods available for transferring data and charts between Harvard Graphics and other programs, such as Lotus 1-2-3 and dBASE. You will also learn how to set up a template for importing data. The use of the expanded Applications menu is another topic covered in this chapter.

Appendix A: Installing Harvard This appendix covers the basics of installing Harvard Graphics. If you have not yet installed the program on your system, read this appendix before you read Chapter 1, where you will tailor the program more closely to your system.

Appendix B: Supported Devices This appendix lists the printers, plotters, and film recorders that Harvard Graphics supports. If you have any questions about your system's components, check here before you configure the program to them.

Appendix C: Symbols, Symbols, and More Symbols This appendix contains the symbols provided with Harvard Graphics 3.0. It also contains MasterClips art images provided by Masterclip Graphics Inc., which are available on the SYBEX Harvard Graphics Enhancement Disk included with this book. Refer to this appendix when you are looking for a particular symbol to incorporate into a chart or when you seek inspiration for your own drawings.

Appendix D: Touring the Gallery This appendix shows selected templates from the Harvard Graphics Gallery. You can follow the directions under each chart to access that template.

Appendix E: Working with Color and Selecting Palettes This appendix explains how to use color effectively and how to select, edit, and create Harvard Graphics palettes. You can also use this appendix as a guide when printing your charts on a black-and-white or color printer.

Appendix F: Installing the Harvard Graphics Enhancement Disk Follow the directions in this appendix to install the MasterClips symbols and the palette files on the Enhancement Disk that comes with this book.

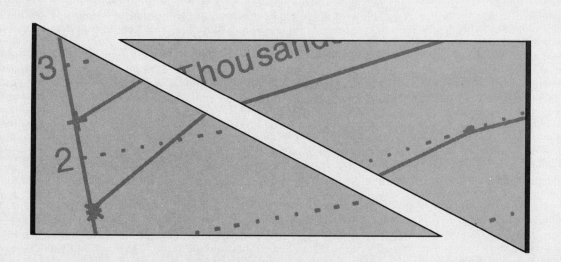

Introducing Harvard

CHAPTER 1

Use Harvard Graphics version 2.0, 2.1, or 2.3 if you have an 8088 computer.

COMPUTERS AND HARVARD GRAPHICS 3.0 HAVE revolutionized presentation graphics. Armed with your 80286, 80386, or 80486 computer and Harvard Graphics 3.0, you can create masterful, aesthetically pleasing graphs in minutes. Added to this arsenal is Harvard's superb drawing program that gives you the flexibility to create highly complex and detailed graphs.

Before computers, graphs were made by gathering stacks of graph paper, a protractor, and a host of other supplies—they took hours to produce. Alternatively, you hired a graphic artist if you lacked the time or skills to produce your own charts. You saw your charts a week later, along with a $500 bill for illustration.

The computer graphics revolution puts sophisticated, powerful tools at your disposal for creating charts easily. Unfortunately, many people lack training in the fundamentals of chart design. They create meaningless graphs that say nothing or make spaghetti graphs that say too much, often because they choose the wrong type of chart for their data. To win in the graphics revolution, you need knowledge; this book helps you gain that knowledge by teaching you how to deliver your messages with charts.

WHY USE GRAPHICS?

Graphics, particularly charts, can quickly communicate your ideas. Showing a visual chart will drive a point home decidedly faster than just describing your point verbally. When you present your ideas rapidly, you conserve both your audience's and your own time. This greater productivity leads to shorter presentations, meetings, and conferences. By stressing and highlighting important ideas, you prevent the audience from misinterpreting your message. Additionally, effective charts project an aura of professionalism. This professional appearance lends credibility to you, your data, and your message. Even if you just use charts for your own analysis, the different perspectives on your data can be invaluable.

There are many reasons for using graphics:

- To disseminate information for organizational action or approval
- To increase your audience's retention of information and impress upon them the value of your presentation
- To streamline your presentations and meetings
- To establish relationships between the data and your ideas that would otherwise be difficult to explain
- To emphasize important ideas
- To prevent misinterpretation of your data or message
- To project a professional image of yourself and your organization
- To add credibility to your presentation

WHY USE HARVARD?

Now that you understand how graphics can be beneficial, we will tell you why you should use Harvard Graphics 3.0 (Harvard, for short): it is easy to use; it takes advantage of the extended or expanded memory in more powerful computers; its files are compatible with other programs; and its many features give you powerful, flexible options. If you're upgrading from Harvard 2.0, 2.1, or 2.2, you'll especially appreciate the many new features in Harvard 3.0.

EASE OF USE

Harvard is easy. As you'll learn in Chapter 2, you can create high-quality graphs in a short period of time. Because Harvard is also intuitive, you can make a selection from a menu and expect to see the functions associated with your choice. If you're stuck, you can reasonably figure out what your options are. If you can't, just use Harvard's built-in Help menus. Harvard is simple enough that beginners can easily construct charts within 20 minutes of installing it.

Creating charts is even simpler when you use an electronic pointing device, such as a mouse. A mouse lets you change a graph rapidly using a point-and-click technique. For example, if you want to change the title of a graph, you point to it on the screen, click a mouse button, and type the new title.

POWER

Harvard 3.0 capitalizes on the advanced features of 80286, 80386, and 80486 computers by using the extended or expanded memory they have available. This means that the complexity of your charts is limited only by the amount of memory installed in your computer.

Taking advantage of extended or expanded memory also optimizes printing by sending the files to a spooler. This allows you to get back to work without waiting for your print job to finish.

COMPATIBILITY

Harvard 3.0 converts 2.x simple list and free-form charts into bullet charts without bullets. Two- and three-column charts are converted into table charts, and multiple charts become drawing charts. Slide show files are converted into presentation files. However, macro files from earlier versions cannot be converted.

You can convert your Harvard 2.x (version 2.0, 2.1, or 2.3) charts into Harvard 3.0 format. Additionally, you can use version 3.0 with the accessory programs Harvard Geographics, ScreenShow Utilities, Business or Military Symbols, and Quick-Charts. You will not need Designer Galleries because it is now incorporated into the Chart Gallery.

You can save your Harvard files in Computer Graphics Metafile (CGM) format. Because CGM files are quickly becoming an industry standard, you will be able to exchange data and graphic files between Harvard and dozens of other programs, such as Ventura Publisher and WordPerfect.

Along with CGM files, you can use bit-mapped files (in PCX or TIF format) with Harvard. The imported images can be modified, scaled, sized, and colored. Export them into Encapsulated PostScript (EPS) format for high-quality output on PostScript printers.

Harvard's importing and exporting capabilities provide you with maximum flexibility in working with symbols, drawings, and charts from other programs. Its ability to display Lotus 1-2-3, Excel, dBASE, and ASCII files simplifies importing data. You can view the file and select the data you want to import into Harvard.

NEW FEATURES

Harvard is an extremely versatile program, which provides dozens of charting options. For example, when creating a text chart, you can choose from a title, bullet, or table (column) chart. Table charts offer a quick way to create text charts with a column-and-row format. You can use the Draw option to add text in free-form style, with different text sizes, colors, placement, styles, and attributes. You can even add pictures or other graphs to your chart, or create a chart from scratch (called a *drawing* chart).

As a general rule, do not use more than 15 to 20 data points in a graph.

You can select from many XY chart (bar, line, and area) options. For example, you can create charts with pyramid- or cylinder-shaped bars, use enhanced 3D options, and set ranges. Up to 1000 data points per series can be entered for most XY charts.

Harvard can perform dozens of built-in calculations and statistical operations on your data. The new version includes a built-in calculator.

In addition to producing charts, Harvard can create slide shows and computer presentations. It has scalable fonts that allow you to vary your type styles. Vibrant color selections are now possible. Harvard's expanded color support includes mixed colors, blended backgrounds, and gradient fills. It is an excellent sign-making program that you can use to print professional bulletins and notices.

Harvard 3.0 even comes equipped with a sophisticated icon-based drawing package. An *icon* is a graphic representation of an executable function. For example, select the box icon when you want to draw a box on your chart. You will also find icons to align, flip, skew, shadow, and rotate objects, as well as edit points on your graphs. Tools such as zoom, rulers, undo, and the scratchpad help you work faster and produce more precise drawings. You will also find the animation feature useful for adding some action to an on-screen presentation.

Handling your presentations is simple with Harvard 3.0's presentation management tools. Use the Presentation option to plan and order your presentation, which can include charts within different subdirectories. Unify your presentations by using a master color palette, title, subtitle, and background drawing, as well as by choosing global presentation options. HGcopy, a Harvard 3.0 utility, enables you to copy your entire presentation and its associated charts onto another drive or directory.

WORKING WITH CHARTS

Not all charts communicate a message. Good charts establish the point you're trying to make quickly, while poor charts fall flat. Just because you used a computer to make a chart doesn't mean it is any good. Figure 1.1 shows a sample pie chart. Would you consider this a useful chart?

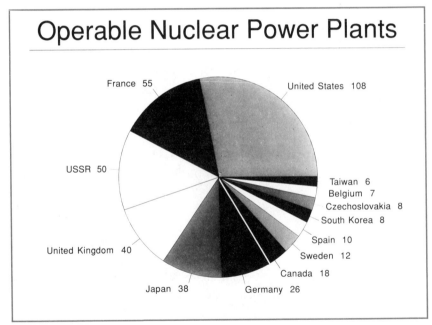

Figure 1.1: One example of a poor presentation chart

I use the terms *graph* and *chart* interchangeably throughout this book.

If you said no, you're right. This pie chart has too many data elements (pie slices). Even though the numbers are there, it is difficult to see that Germany uses almost twice as many power plants as Taiwan and Belgium put together; the relationship is lost. If you can't see relationships among your chart's data, you're probably better off not using the chart. This graph doesn't help the presentation; in this case, the presentation has to help the graph.

Compare the crowded pie chart with the chart shown in Figure 1.2. Using the same data, the revised chart now tells a clear story. Unlike slices in the the cluttered pie chart, the proportional bars in the numbered scale help you see how the number of nuclear plants varies from country to country. There is also a clear message beneath the chart's title that summarizes the central idea.

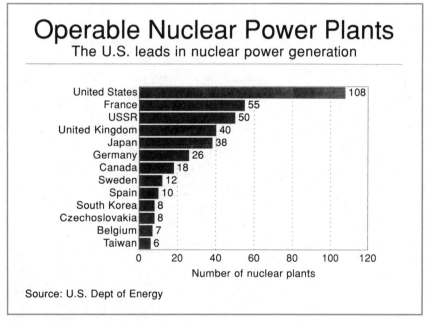

Figure 1.2: A good presentation chart

The difference between these two sample charts illustrates how the type of chart you choose for your data affects their presentation. Like a master artist, you need to blend graphic tools and your ideas carefully. Understanding this is the first step in mastering Harvard Graphics.

EXPLORING THE ANATOMY OF A CHART

When artists learn to draw the human figure, they begin by studying human anatomy. Only then are they able to understand their subjects and portray them realistically. Designing a professional-looking chart is similar. Not until you understand a chart's anatomy can you create an accurate chart.

THE ESSENTIAL ELEMENTS OF A CHART

Although chart types appear strikingly different, they all share some essential elements. Figure 1.3 shows the anatomy of a chart depicting the U.S. national economy from 1986 to 1989. The scale along the left side of the chart represents billions of dollars.

Your charts should always contain a *title*, and we recommend using a *subtitle* as well. Without a title or message, your audience must try to guess what the graph is saying. For example, the graph in Figure 1.3

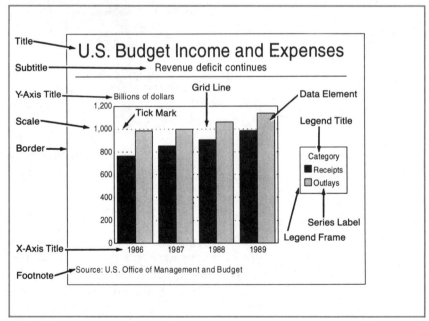

Figure 1.3: Anatomy of a chart

uses this title and subtitle:

U.S. Budget Income and Expenses

Revenue deficit continues

The title uniquely identifies the graph. Adding a subtitle empha-sizes your central idea, saving you presentation time. You have up to three lines for your title and message; we recommend using one title and one subtitle line. This clarifies the chart without cluttering it.

You should always consider using a *footnote*, which is also called a *key* or *reference*, to let your audience know your data source. For example, our U.S. Budget Income and Expenses chart includes the following footnote:

Source: U.S. Office of Management and Budget

Keep a folder of impressive charts. You can use these as models for your own charts.

The members of the audience are more likely to accept the validity of your chart's data if they know where the data came from. How-ever, depending on the composition of your audience, you won't need to include a footnote if you or your organization is the source.

Charts should also include an aesthetic *border*. The border acts like a frame on a painting, keeping the viewer's attention focused on the material inside it. You shouldn't consider your chart complete until it's framed. However, omit a border when you are attaching frames to transparencies (view graphs). The frame acts like a border when you project the chart.

UNDERSTANDING PARTS OF A CHART

There are other parts to a chart's anatomy besides its title, subtitle, footnote, and border. For example, pie charts also include slices. The pie slices are data elements representing the numeric data within your pie. Some graphs, such as line, bar, and area charts, have other parts besides data elements. As you learn more about graphs, you'll see many similarities among them. Refer to the chart in Figure 1.3 to familiarize yourself with the following parts:

- Title: A descriptive heading for the chart

- Subtitle: A distinctive message or brief description of the chart's data

- Footnote: Your source for the data or other explanatory text
- Border: A frame for the chart
- X axis: The horizontal axis of the graph
- X axis title: A title describing the data displayed along the X axis
- Y axis: The vertical axis of the graph
- Scale: The range of numbers or values along the Y axis
- Y axis title: A title identifying the Y-axis scale
- Data element: A number or value used in the chart
- Series: A set of numeric data
- Series label: A label identifying a single series
- Legend title: A label identifying the group of series
- Legend frame: A box around the series labels and legend title
- Grid line: A graphic line showing the intersection of a data element with a value on the scale
- Tick mark: A short, thick line that marks a value on the Y-axis scale

IDENTIFYING THE AXIS, SERIES, AND DATA ELEMENTS

Before you can interpret a graph, you need to understand the differences between the X and Y axes, and a series and a data element. Let's assume that you want to graph the data in Table 1.1.

To start, you need to identify your data for the X axis. When you are making a chart, place your groups along the horizontal X axis. For example, use the X axis for groups such as dates, times, items, places, or names. For the sample table, you would place the years from 1989 to 1992 on the X axis.

Table 1.1: Sample Data: Number of Widget Sales

SALES OFFICE			
YEAR	NEW YORK	CHICAGO	MIAMI
1989	4,567	2,391	1,429
1990	4,987	3,456	2,986
1991	4,852	4,349	2,235
1992	4,920	5,245	2,429

Next define the Y-axis data. The Y axis almost always contains numbers, such as dollars or units. Table 1.1 shows units of widgets ranging from 1,429 to 5,245. When you graph the Y-axis data, Harvard will automatically adjust the scale to the range of 0 to 6,000. You'll find that Harvard does many things automatically to make graphing easier.

The sales figures are data elements, occasionally called data points, points, or just plain elements. For example, the numbers 4,567 and 4,987 are elements showing the number of widgets that the New York office sold.

Look carefully at Table 1.1 and see if you can identify the series. A series is a group or set of elements. It can be a single column, a single pie, a single line, or a group of bars. In Table 1.1, a series is one column. For example, all the numbers in the column under New York belong to the New York series, those under Chicago belong to the Chicago series, and so on.

Now that you know which data will go on the X and Y axes and what Table 1.1's series are, sketch a rough graph of Table 1.1. Then compare your sketch to the graph shown in Figure 1.4.

Harvard's data-entry screen is similar to the form shown in Figure 1.5. You'll find this form handy if you prepare graphs for other people to present. This form was created using Harvard's Draw option. You'll learn more about this limitless option in later chapters.

If you're new to charts, use an organizational form similar to the one shown in Figure 1.5. It helps you recognize the important parts of your graph and streamlines data entry.

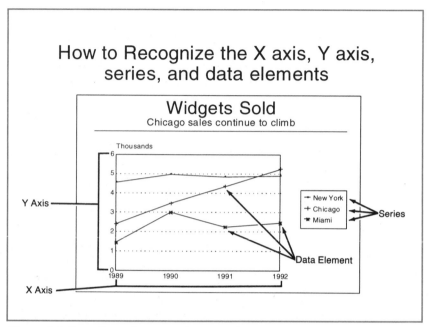

Figure 1.4: Locations of axes, series, and elements

SELECTING THE RIGHT CHART

To present your data well, you need to use the type of graph that suits it. As you saw when you compared Figures 1.1 and 1.2, selecting the wrong graph leads to a poor presentation. You will become more confident about selecting the correct type of graph as you work with the various graphs in later chapters. For now, refer to Table 1.2. It lists each chart type, its most common use, and the chapter in this book that covers that chart.

The following sections introduce some of the more basic types of charts: text, pie, line, bar, organization, and map.

TEXT CHARTS

Typically, most of the data that you'll work with are numbers, which are easily graphed. However, you'll need to use a *text* chart for nonnumeric data. Figure 1.6 shows a text chart that is easy to make.

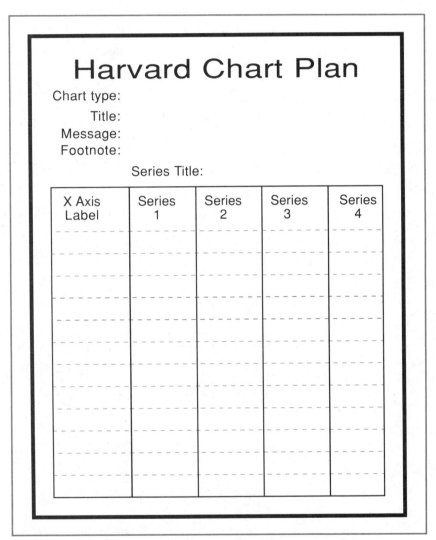

Figure 1.5: Defining and organizing the parts of your graph

With text charts, you can introduce or summarize your presentation to reinforce your main points. By interspersing text charts in your graphics presentation, you can also provide more variety for your audience, which helps to keep them interested in what you have to say.

The best text charts are simple. Keep your lines short by highlighting only the main ideas. If you want to compose complete sentences

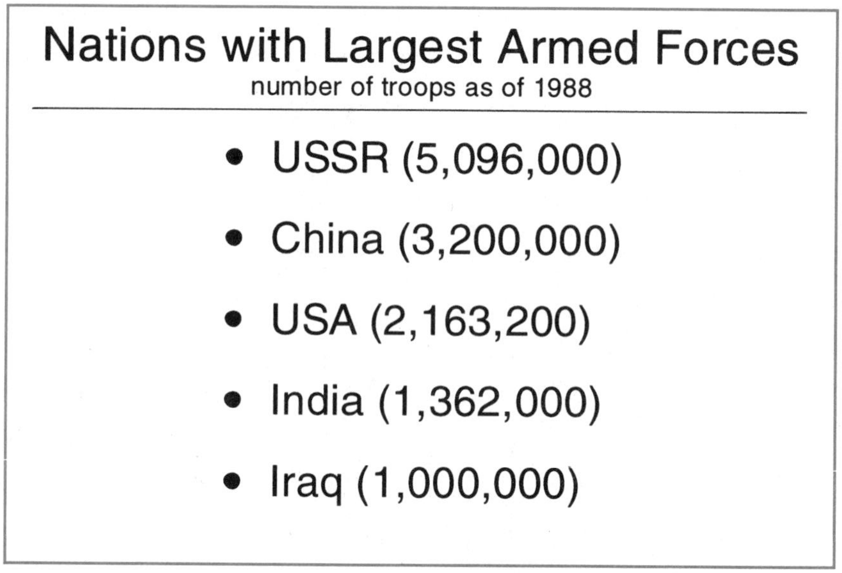

Nations with Largest Armed Forces
number of troops as of 1988

- USSR (5,096,000)

- China (3,200,000)

- USA (2,163,200)

- India (1,362,000)

- Iraq (1,000,000)

Figure 1.6: A sample text chart

Table 1.2: Choosing the Right Chart

TYPE OF CHART	USE	CHAPTER REFERENCE
Text	To highlight your main ideas or present nonnumerical data	3
Range	To show ranges or groups of values	3
Pie	To show parts of a total including ratios, percentages, shares, or quotas at a given point in time	4
Cut Pie	To emphasize an element that is part of a whole; it can also be linked to a column chart to show the components of the slice	4

Table 1.2: Choosing the Right Chart (continued)

TYPE OF CHART	USE	CHAPTER REFERENCE
XY-Line (curve)	To show fluctuations in data over time	5
XY-Line (zigzag)	To illustrate sharp trends and changes over time for frequency, range, and distribution comparisons	5
XY-3D line	To emphasize relationships between series as they vary over time	5
XY-Combination bar and line	To emphasize relationships between series as they vary over time	5
XY-Bar	To illustrate changes or growth over time	5
XY-3D bar	To emphasize magnitude of change or growth over time	5
XY-Cumulative bar	To show increases between consecutive periods	5
XY-Horizontal bar	To rank many similar items or show trends over many time periods	5
XY-Overlap bar	To demonstrate relationships between groups of series	5
XY-Stack bar	To illustrate parts of a total over time, such as sales for several departments	5
XY-Percent bar	To show parts of a whole in percentages at different time periods	5
XY-Dual Y axis (bar or line)	To compare series that have two units or lines of measure, such as dollar amounts and units sold	5

Table 1.2: Choosing the Right Chart (continued)

TYPE OF CHART	USE	CHAPTER REFERENCE
XY-Paired bar	To show correlations between different series using the same X axis, such as the market share between two competitors	5
XY-Deviation bar	To show positive and negative values, such as temperature changes	5
XY-Step bar	To illustrate frequency distributions, ranges, and cumulative totals	5
XY-Point (dot or scatter)	To compare time periods or individual items to establish correlations	5
XY-Trend line	To present statistical trends (and clarify patterns of data)	5
XY-Histogram	To show frequency distribution for two or more series	5
XY-Logarithmic	To demonstrate the percentage or rate of change	5
XY-High/low/close	To show ranges, changes, and values within one time period, such as stock and bond prices	6
XY-Area	To show cumulative totals of several series and changes in volume over time	5
XY-Area with 3D	To emphasize general volume comparisons; not for exact comparisons	5

Table 1.2: Choosing the Right Chart (continued)

TYPE OF CHART	USE	CHAPTER REFERENCE
Organization	To show structure or breakdown of responsibility in an organization	8
Drawing	To illustrate a sequence of procedures or a system	10
Map	To present geographical maps	10

that thoroughly explain your ideas, write a report. Limit your text charts to fewer than ten lines, with no more than seven words to a line. If you try to cram too much into a text chart, your audience will become confused and loose interest.

PIE CHARTS

When you are dealing with simple numeric data, a *pie* chart is one of the easiest graphs to make and understand. Each slice represents an individual part of a particular group. The larger the slice, the greater the percentage of the whole group. In Figure 1.7, for example, the whole pie is the total number of accidental deaths, and its slices are the causes of death, with the corresponding data value and percentage for each cause. (Harvard lets you effortlessly change the data values to percentages.)

A good pie chart is both easy to read and graphically appealing. Although Harvard lets you designate 24 slices, restrain yourself and use 8 slices at most. If necessary, combine some of your smaller slices into one. When there are too many slices, labels run together, and it gets increasingly difficult to compare the sizes of the pie slices.

A useful pie displays only one point in time. For example, you can't use a pie to display two years of corporate financial conditions. The chart just wouldn't make sense. You could, however, use one pie for each time period on the same chart. You can establish any

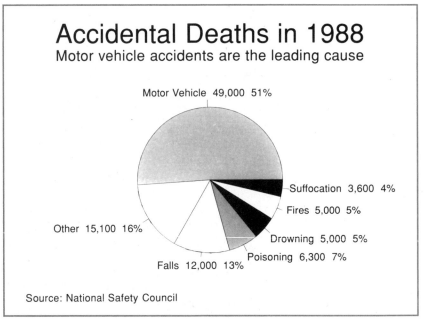

Figure 1.7: A sample pie chart

length of time as a time period: a minute, a day, a year, a decade, and so on.

LINE CHARTS

Unlike a pie chart, a *line* chart shows trends and changes over time. This type of chart is commonly used for frequency distributions, population studies, and range comparisons. For example, Figure 1.8 shows a line chart that is a *frequency distribution*, which counts how many times an event occurred. In this case, the chart counts a group's test scores; four people scored 60, five people scored 62, and so on. (Chapter 7 explains how to use statistics in your charts.)

Notice that the line in Figure 1.8 is smooth and continuous, a *curved* line, which is good for showing trends. The lines which connect data points in Figure 1.9 are straight, or in charting terms, they *zigzag*. This chart's sharp angles emphasize major magnitude differences. When choosing between zigzags and curves, think of what you're trying to say. If you want to show a gradual trend, use the curve. If

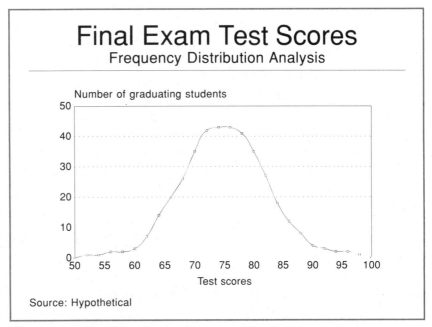

Figure 1.8: A line chart showing frequency distribution

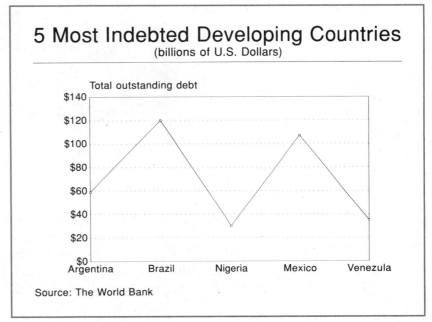

Figure 1.9: A zigzag line chart

you're trying to dramatize fluctuations in your data, however, use the zigzag.

BAR CHARTS

Like a line chart, a standard *bar* chart shows changes over time. However, it is easier for an audience to understand. In fact, it's the first graph students learn to draw in elementary school. Use the standard bar chart when you want to show growth over time and at the same time emphasize differences in mass or size, as in the example in Figure 1.10. To avoid cluttering your bar chart, use 15 bars at most.

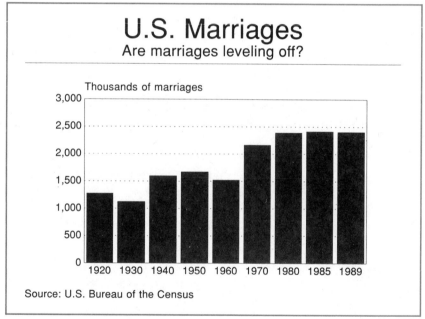

Figure 1.10: A sample bar chart

A *cumulative bar* chart is simply a bar chart with running totals. For example, in Figure 1.11, January's bar displays the sales for that month, while February's bar presents the sales for both January and February. Since the data are cumulated month by month, the last month, December, shows the sales for the entire year.

Figure 1.11: A cumulative bar chart

Cumulative bars are excellent for comparing target objectives with the actual results. Thus, they're often used in graphs showing fund-raising activities and sales goals. You can highlight your goals with illustrative graphic symbols or text.

ORGANIZATION CHARTS

One of the first things a business student learns in college is how to make an *organization* chart, such as the one shown in Figure 1.12. An organization chart breaks down a company's structure, showing who is responsible for what and to whom. Use these charts to show the organization's management to stockholders, creditors, customers, and other people interested in your company.

MAP CHARTS

Map charts are handy when you need to present information organized by state, region, or country. For example, you can show market

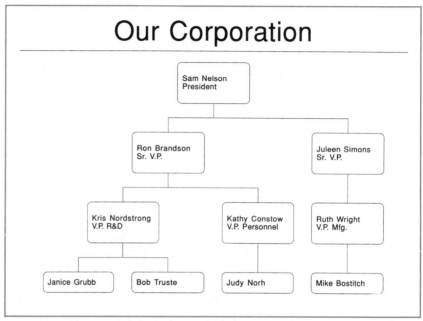

Figure 1.12: A sample organization chart

opportunities on a United States map by coloring states based on their sales volume. Figure 1.13 shows an example of an informative map chart.

GETTING READY TO USE HARVARD

Before buying a mouse, monitor, or printer, read Chapter 2, which describes working with these devices.

Now that you've been introduced to the types of charts you can make with Harvard, let's prepare to start using it. If you haven't already installed Harvard, do so now using the step-by-step instructions in Appendix A. To use Harvard 3.0, you'll need the following hardware and software:

- One hard disk with a minimum of 3.5 megabytes (Mb) of free space (preferably with 10Mb)

- An IBM or compatible 80286, 80386, or 80486 computer with 640 kilobytes (K) or more memory

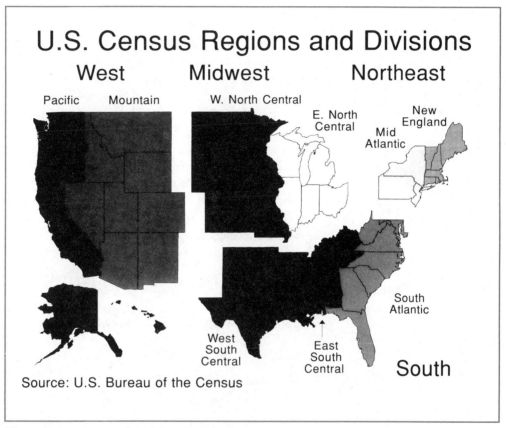

Figure 1.13: A sample map chart showing regions

- A monitor and compatible graphics adapter, preferably a VGA color system (EGA cards must have at least 256K of memory)

- A mouse, preferably one with at least two buttons

- A printer, plotter, film recorder, or other output device

- DOS 3.0 or later (DOS 3.1 or later if using a network)

USING EXPANDED AND EXTENDED MEMORY

The first 640K of memory in your computer is called *conventional memory*. This part of memory is used to load DOS and Harvard.

Harvard needs 438K of this memory for it to run. The memory space between 640K and 1Mb is called *high memory*. When available, it's used to load additional system functions, such as disk and network device support. Of this space, 64K is used by *expanded memory* (EMS) to speed up some operating functions such as storing charting data.

Memory above 1Mb can be EMS, *extended memory* (XMS), or a combination of both memory types. Harvard uses memory above 1Mb for improved performance. For example, this extra memory helps accelerate Harvard's performance when you display, print, and draw charts. Extra memory also accelerates the display of computer presentations and bit-map graphics. We recommend that you use 2Mb of memory or more for improved performance. Harvard Graphics comes with HIMEM.SYS, which you can install to use the extra memory you have available (see Appendix A for installation instructions).

USING HARVARD ON A NETWORK

Networks allow a group of computer users to share computer programs and files. You can run Harvard Graphics on these networks:

- 3Com 3 +
- Novell NetWare/286 or 386
- IBM PC Network
- IBM Token Ring Network

If you plan to use Harvard on a network, make sure your computer is running DOS 3.1 or later and that you install Harvard to use a network. Network software comes with Harvard 3.0, allowing one person to legally use Harvard on the network. Additional concurrent network licenses can be purchased in multiples of one, five, or twenty licenses (concurrent users). For example, if you buy Harvard 3.0 and five user licenses, you're entitled to let any combination of six people use Harvard 3.0 on the network at any given time.

As an alternative, you can set up a non-network installation of Harvard in a separate, private subdirectory of the network that no one else can get to. You must also put the data files in the private directory. This keeps your files and computer safe from failures

If you use Windows 3.0, you probably already have HIMEM.SYS installed.

Don't use Harvard on the network if you haven't installed it for one. Other users on your network can alter your setup and configuration settings.

caused by multiple access. Read your network's manual or consult your network administrator. Each network works differently.

UNDERSTANDING HOW HARVARD USES SUBDIRECTORIES AND PATHS

When you install Harvard on a hard-disk system, it is placed in *subdirectories*. Subdirectories store computer files much like a filing cabinet stores files of papers. This helps keep Harvard's program files organized and away from conflicting software. Table 1.3 shows some of the default subdirectories where Harvard stores files. For example, Harvard stores its main program files in the \HG3 subdirectory and the charts you create in the \HG3\DATA subdirectory. Both the

Table 1.3: Harvard's Subdirectories

SUBDIRECTORY	FILES STORED
\HG3	Stores program files that run Harvard 3.0
\HG3\DATA	Stores the charts and files that you create
\HG3\DRIVER	Stores files needed by specialized equipment such as printers
\HG3\FONT	Contains special font files that enhance lettering styles
\HG3\PALETTE	Holds chart palettes and your customized color palettes
\HG3\GALLERY	Stores predefined templates you can use to create quick charts
\HG3\SYMBOL	Contains symbol files used to illustrate charts
\HG3\EXPORT	Holds files that you export from Harvard, such CGM files
\HG3\IMPORT	Stores imported worksheets and files used to create charts
\HG3\OUTPUT	Holds files that you print to your disk
\HG3\PATTERN	Holds pattern files used to create charts

\HG3 and \HG3\DATA subdirectories are conventions used in Harvard's manual and this book. You can, however, install Harvard and your data files on any subdirectory you choose.

To use the program files in the \HG3 directory, you need to establish a path using the DOS PATH command so your computer can find the Harvard program files. Once the path is set, you can begin using Harvard.

STARTING UP

You can easily run Harvard directly from DOS, either by issuing the commands to change to its directory and start it or through a batch file. If you are using Windows 3.0, you may want to install Harvard as a DOS program in Windows and use that program to run it.

RUNNING HARVARD FROM DOS

One way to run Harvard from DOS is to type the commands in step 3 below each time that you want to start the program. Another, quicker method is to create a DOS batch file that includes these commands, and then use this file to run Harvard automatically. We recommend using a batch file, which you can create by following these steps:

1. Type **C:** and press Enter. Then type **CD** and press Enter. These two commands make sure you are creating the new file in the root directory.

2. Type **COPY CON: HG3.BAT** and press Enter. This sends everything you will enter to the HG3.BAT file.

3. Type **CD\HG3** and press Enter. Then type **HG3** and press Enter. The first command puts you in the \HG3 directory, and the second one starts up Harvard.

4. Type **CD** and press Enter. This final command in your batch file returns you to the root directory when you exit Harvard.

5. Press function key F6, and then press Enter. This puts an end-of-file marker in the file, saves the file, and returns you to the DOS prompt.

After creating this batch file, you can run Harvard from anywhere in your directory system by simply typing **C:\HG3** and pressing Enter.

If you choose not to use a batch file, start Harvard each time by typing

CD\HG3

HG3

pressing Enter after each line.

RUNNING HARVARD FROM WINDOWS

Microsoft Windows is an extremely popular program that allows you to run several programs at one time. If you are using Windows 3.0 or later, you can install Harvard's special program information and icon files in Windows and run Harvard from there.

Follow these steps to add the Harvard files to Windows:

The instructions given here assume that you have some familiarity with Windows. If you need more information, refer to *Mastering Windows 3.0* (SYBEX, 1991) or another guide to using Windows.

1. Select the program group in which you want the Harvard 3.0 icon to appear.

2. Select File, and then choose New from the Program Manager menu bar.

3. When the New Program Object box appears, select Program Item and click on the OK button. The Program Properties box will appear.

4. For Description, type **Harvard 3.0**, and then press Tab.

5. For the Command line option, enter **C:\HG3\HG3.PIF** and click on the Change Icon button. You will see the Select Icon box.

6. At the File Name prompt, type **C:\HG3\HG3.ICO**, and then click on the OK button for both the Select Icon and Program Properties boxes.

This procedure installs Harvard as a DOS program in Windows. You can now start it from Windows by double-clicking on the Harvard icon. However, you should be aware that the Windows mouse will not work with DOS appplications like Harvard 3.0. This means that you will need to load a DOS mouse driver program such as MOUSE.COM. You might want to put the driver in your AUTOEXEC.BAT file so you do not have to remember to load it (see Chapter 2 for details on installing your mouse). Even with the appropriate driver, the mouse will only work when you use Harvard in full-screen mode.

INTRODUCING THE MAIN MENU

Harvard is easy to use. Since Harvard is a menu-driven system, working in it is almost like ordering from a restaurant menu. Start Harvard from DOS by typing **C:\HG3** if you created a batch file, or **CD\HG3**, then **HG3** if you did not. Select the Harvard icon if you are using Windows.

Harvard's opening screen appears, quickly followed by the Main menu, shown in Figure 1.14. The options on the Main menu are summarized in Table 1.4. Many of these options lead to submenus.

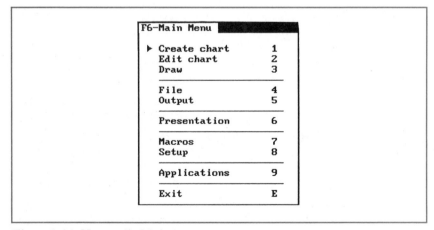

Figure 1.14: Harvard's Main menu

Table 1.4: Main Menu Options

Option	Keystroke	Use	Chapter Reference
Create chart	1	Create new charts	Chapters 2–8
Edit chart	2	Edit the current chart	Chapters 2–8
Draw	3	Add illustrations, drawings, symbols, and bit-mapped images to charts	Chapters 10 and 11
File	4	Get and save chart files	Chapter 2
		Get and save template files	Chapter 9
		Save charts as symbols	Chapter 10
		Import and export Lotus, Excel, ASCII, dBASE, and CGM files	Chapter 13
Output	5	Print, plot, and record your charts and presentations	Chapters 2 and 12
Presentation	6	Create, plan, edit, save, and display presentations, ScreenShows, or HyperShows	Chapter 12
Macros	7	Record, load, or run macros (a series of computer instructions)	Chapter 9
Setup	8	Set default settings in charts, programs, palettes, devices, and fonts	Chapter 1 and Appendix E
Applications	9	Run other application programs or DOS without leaving Harvard Graphics	Chapter 13
Exit	E	Leave Harvard Graphics	Chapter 1

To select a menu option, type the number or letter that is to the right of that option. For example type **1** to choose Create chart or **E** to choose Exit. You can also use the arrow keys or the spacebar to highlight the option and press Enter to select it.

In addition to the ten options on the Main menu, the following five function keys are listed at the top of the screen:

- F1-Help: Displays Help screens describing the courses of action available to you

- F2-Show chart: Displays your current chart
- F6-Main Menu: Displays the Main menu
- F7-Spell check: Checks the spelling on your chart
- F10-Continue: Records the options you have selected

Each screen shows the function keys that can be used from that screen.

GETTING HELP

Harvard provides several types of on-screen help. *Context-sensitive* help is offered in many of Harvard's menus. You will usually see the F1-Help option listed in the top-left corner of the screen. When you press F1, you will get help on how to use the selected menu choice. Press PgDn to see the next Help screen or Esc to exit the Help function.

Harvard's Help Topics Index menu provides information by topic. You can get help on a number of Harvard topics, including technical support by phone. To see the Help Topics Index menu, follow these steps:

You can press F6 to return to the Main menu from many of Harvard's submenus and functions.

1. From the Main menu, press F1 to display the Help screen. Since the Create chart option on the Main menu was selected automatically, a box appears explaining what that option does and describes the options you can choose from it.

2. Press Shift-F1 (press and hold down the Shift key while you press the F1 function key). You will see the Help Topics Index menu, as shown in Figure 1.15.

3. Press the down-arrow key or the spacebar repeatedly until the About Software Publishing Corporation option is highlighted, and then press Enter.

4. When the secondary topics index appears, highlight Technical Support and press Enter. You will see a Help screen describing Harvard's technical support line. Press PgDn to read the entire message (that's where you will find the support telephone number).

5. Press Esc three times to leave the Help system.

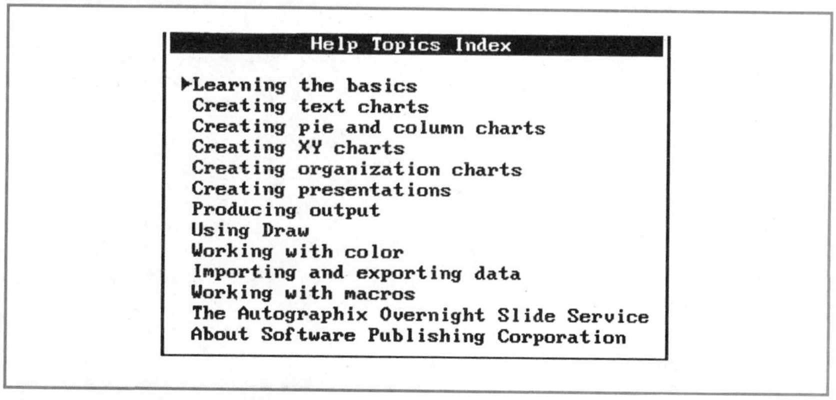

```
┌─────────────────────────────────────────────────────┐
│         ┌───────────────────────────────────┐        │
│         │          Help Topics Index        │        │
│         │ ►Learning the basics              │        │
│         │  Creating text charts             │        │
│         │  Creating pie and column charts   │        │
│         │  Creating XY charts               │        │
│         │  Creating organization charts     │        │
│         │  Creating presentations           │        │
│         │  Producing output                 │        │
│         │  Using Draw                       │        │
│         │  Working with color               │        │
│         │  Importing and exporting data     │        │
│         │  Working with macros              │        │
│         │  The Autographix Overnight Slide Service     │
│         │  About Software Publishing Corporation       │
│         └───────────────────────────────────┘        │
└─────────────────────────────────────────────────────┘
```

Figure 1.15: The Help Topics Index menu

After you become familiar with Harvard, you will be able to use its *speed keys* to quickly select many of its options. For example, in Chapter 2, you will learn that you can retrieve a previously saved chart by pressing Ctrl-G, rather than by selecting File from the Main menu, then choosing Get chart. Another form of help provided by Harvard is the list of speed keys, which is displayed when you press Ctrl-F1. Press Esc when you are finished viewing the speed key list.

CUSTOMIZING HARVARD

Now that you are familiar with the Main menu, you can explore one of its options. Select Setup from the Main menu by pressing **8**. Figure 1.16 shows the Setup menu. Its options let you customize and configure Harvard for your system, as explained in the following sections.

CHANGING THE PROGRAM DEFAULT SETTINGS

Harvard comes with default settings for its options so that you can work with it immediately. Since these defaults are set for a typical system, some of them may meet your needs and some may not. You can change the defaults for screen colors, directories, the color palette, character set, and allocation of memory by choosing the Program defaults option from the Setup menu.

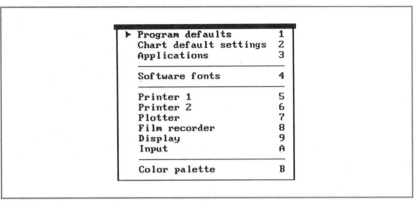

Figure 1.16: The Setup menu

Follow these steps to see if your program default settings are correct (you can make changes if necessary):

Some of the options on the Program Defaults screen are readily understandable; we will discuss the other settings later in the book, when you are more familiar with the program.

1. From the Main menu, type **8** to choose Setup.

2. From the Setup menu, press **1** to display the current program default settings. The Program Defaults screen will resemble the one shown in Figure 1.17.

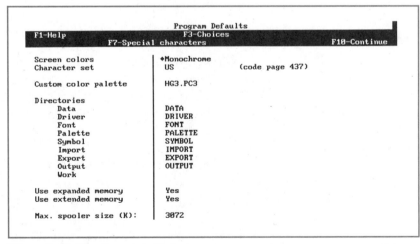

Figure 1.17: The Program Defaults screen

You can select Setup options by pressing F3 and choosing from a list or by pressing the spacebar to cycle through the choices.

3. You will have to change the Screen colors option if you're using a monochrome monitor with a graphics adapter. If you have a Compaq or Toshiba laptop for example, highlight the Screen colors data line and press F3. Next, use the arrow keys to highlight Monochrome and press Enter.

Depending on the character set you select, you might have to change the default chart line spacing, as explained in the next section.

The date and currency formats you use depend on the character set you select. By default, Harvard uses the US character set commonly used in American configurations. Alternatively, you can select a character set from Australia, Belgium, Brazil, Canada (French), Denmark, Finland, France, Germany, Italy, Japan, Netherlands, Norway, Portugal, Spain, Sweden, Switzerland, or the United Kingdom, or use a general multilingual character set.

4. To change the character set, press Tab to highlight the Character set data line. Press the spacebar to cycle through the country choices until you've highlighted the one you want, and then press Enter.

5. To change default directories, move your cursor to the field you want changed and type in the new name. Do this when you need to save files in different subdirectories. For example, Harvard saves data files in the C:\HG3\DATA subdirectory by default. If you wanted to save your files in drive D in a subdirectory called GRAPHS, change the Data field to D:\GRAPHS instead.

6. Press Esc to bypass the memory options for now and return to the Setup menu. Both the expanded and extended memory options should be set to Yes so that you can use this extra memory. Harvard ignores this setting if your computer does not have extra memory, so it doesn't matter if you leave it set to Yes. We also suggest that you leave the maximum spooler size set to 3072. This reduces the time needed to regain control of your computer when printing charts.

CHANGING CHART DEFAULT SETTINGS

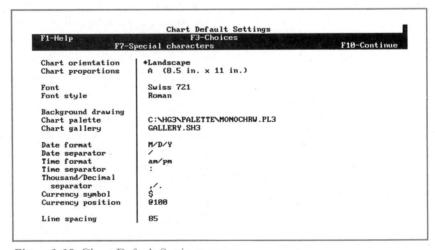

You can easily override the default settings for a particular chart by pressing F8 to select Options while creating or editing the chart.

The other type of default settings you can change are those for the charts you create. The Chart default settings option on the Setup menu allows you to adjust the chart orientation, proportions, fonts, background drawing, palette, character formats, and line spacing.

Use the following steps to check the current default settings for your charts. Press the spacebar or F3 to change the settings if necessary.

1. From the Setup menu, press **2** to select Chart Default settings. You will see the Chart Default Settings screen, shown in Figure 1.18.

2. Press Tab twice to skip the Chart orientation and Chart proportions options. Chart orientation should already be set to Landscape, the orientation in which most of the charts in this chapter were created.

Traditionally, landscape charts are used in 35mm slides, transparencies, and on-line presentations. Remember to change this option to Portrait whenever you want to create a chart that is longer than it is wide (as in Figure 1.5). Portrait orientation is best suited for printed charts you include for reports. Chart proportion should be set to A

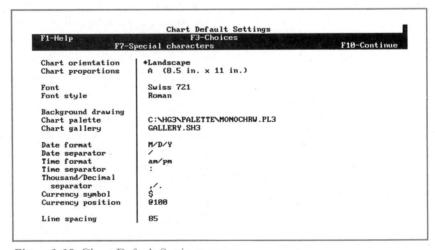

Figure 1.18: Chart Default Settings screen

(8.5 in. × 11 in.) unless you're working with unusual paper sizes or 35mm slides.

The next two options are Font and Font style. The font (lettering style) should be changed first. Then change the default font style, such as bold, italic, or light. You must make the font changes in this order because font styles depend on your selection of fonts. You will learn more about using different fonts in Chapter 3.

3. Press Tab five times to skip the Font, Font style, Background drawing, Chart palette, and Chart gallery options for now. You'll learn about these options later in this book. (If you press Tab too many times and pass the field you want to change on a Harvard screen, you can press Shift-Tab to move backward through the fields.)

Date and currency symbols are stored as character sets, which you select from the Program Defaults screen.

The next eight fields affect character formats. By default, Harvard uses the US character set for the American configuration. It displays $ as the currency value and uses a date format of *M/D/Y*, where *M* is the month, *D* the day, and *Y* the year. You can change to any of the international formats.

4. Move to any of the format options and change them if necessary. Cycle through your choices by pressing the spacebar, or press F3 to select from a list. Change the currency symbol by typing a new symbol, or press F7 to select one from a list. Change the line spacing by entering a new number between 1 and 200. Use 85 for single-spaced lines or 170 for double-spaced lines. You might need to adjust this number depending on the character set you use.

5. Press F10 to return to the Setup menu. Press Esc to return to the Main menu. Read the next section carefully if you have an output device.

CONFIGURING YOUR PRINTER, PLOTTER, AND FILM RECORDER

You need to configure Harvard to work with your output device, which can be a printer, plotter, or film recorder. To do this, you should know the answers to the following questions:

You don't have to worry about version 2.x's VDI drivers for your output devices because direct support is provided within Harvard.

- Is the device a printer, plotter, or film recorder?
- What is its brand name and model?
- Is the device connected to a LPT or COM port?
- If you are using a COM port, what is your communications protocol? Is the baud rate 9600, 4800, 2400, 1200, or 300? Is parity odd, even, or none? Does it use seven or eight data bits, and does it use one or two stop bits?
- Is the device supported by Harvard?

To answer these questions, refer to your computer, your output device, Appendix A of this book, and the Harvard Graphics manuals. You can also check the list of supported devices in Appendix B. If you don't know which port is which, perhaps the following will help guide you.

Computers have a variety of configured ports and assigned device names. For example, a computer's first *printer port* is LPT1, the second LPT2, and the third LPT3. A computer's first *communications port*, also known as a *serial* or *RS-232* port, is COM1, and COM2 is the second.

To determine whether your device is attached to a LPT printer port or a COM serial port, remove the device's cable from the computer. Now look closely at your computer's port. If you see 25 little holes on the port, it's probably a LPT port. If you see either 25 or 9 little pins or wires, you probably have a COM port.

If it is a LPT port and it is attached to the same board as your monitor, it's probably LPT1. You may need to experiment with the port configurations to find one that the device responds to.

To configure your device, follow these steps:

1. From the Main menu, press **8** to display the Setup menu.

2. Select the device you want to configure by choosing one of the following:

   - Press **5** to configure a printer (if you only have one printer).
   - Press **6** to configure a second printer.

- Press **7** to configure a plotter.
- Press **8** to configure a film recorder.

3. Notice that a default device has been selected for you. If you're not using that device, press F3 to list the supported devices. Use PgUp or PgDn to find your device's brand name and model on that list. Devices are listed in alphabetical order.

4. Use the arrow keys to move to and highlight your device's name. Press the F10 key to configure the highlighted device.

5. Press Tab, and then press F3. A list of the possible port configurations will appear. Use the arrow keys to highlight the name of the port connected to your device.

6. If you selected a COM port in step 5, press F4. Check the communications settings and select the appropriate baud rate, parity, data bits, and stop bits. The device will function properly only if these settings are correct.

7. Skip the Default paper size, Use spooler, Quality, Film type and Film size options for now unless you need to change them. You can always override these settings later. Press the F10 key to return to the Setup menu.

CONFIGURING THE SCREEN AND COLOR PALETTE

If you have a VGA monitor and can't see your charts, configure Harvard to EGA. Some VGA cards don't work well with Harvard.

Harvard is intelligent enough to configure your screen display automatically. If you change your video configuration, however, you need to configure it, which is similar to configuring an output device. To do this, press **9** from the Setup menu to select Display, press F3 for a list of options, highlight the type of screen you're using, and press F10 to return to the Setup menu. The new display configuration will take effect the next time you start Harvard.

The Setup menu's Color palette option lets you change how your monitor displays color. It's of little use if you are working with the black-and-white values of a laser or dot-matrix printer. However, if you use a color film recorder, color printer, or a plotter with color pens, you might want to change the palette to match the colors used by your devices. Experiment with Harvard before changing its palette settings. See Appendix E for more information about selecting palettes.

CONFIGURING INPUT DEVICES

If you are using a mouse or a graphics tablet (a CalComp, Kurta, or Summagraphics input device), type **A** to choose the Input option from the Setup menu. Press F3, highlight the name of your device, and then press Enter to select it. If the device is not attached to COM1, press Tab and then the spacebar to cycle through your choices until the correct port is displayed. Press F4 to check the serial port settings, and change them if necessary.

RECONFIGURING HARVARD

You can reconfigure Harvard at any time. If your system changes or if you buy a new output or input device, simply use the Setup menu and select the device to reconfigure. You can also use this procedure if you made an error in your initial configuration.

LEAVING HARVARD

Now that you've installed and configured Harvard, you may want to take a break and exit the program. If you don't want to take a break, read through the instructions for exiting so you'll know how to quit Harvard, and then continue with Chapter 2.

To leave Harvard, do the following:

1. Press the Esc key until you see the Main menu.

2. Type **E** for Exit.

You will return to the DOS prompt. You can now turn off your computer.

SUMMARY

You've covered a lot of ground in this chapter. Not only have you learned the advantages of graphic presentations, but you've seen how to maximize those advantages by using Harvard Graphics.

You've learned how to read and interpret charts. You understand the anatomy of a chart and can show its elements, series, and axes. You're familiar with the differences between pie, line, bar, map, and organization charts.

You have run Harvard Graphics, have become familiar with its Main menu, and customized the program for your system. Finally, you've learned how to exit Harvard.

In the next chapter, you'll learn how Harvard works with a mouse, monitor, and output devices. You'll learn how to use Harvard Graphics and create, save, and print various types of charts.

2

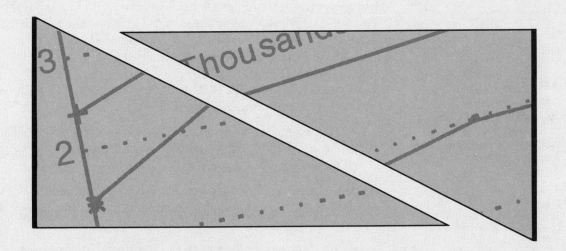

Getting Started

CHAPTER 2

HARVARD IS AN EXCEPTIONALLY EASY PROGRAM TO work with and understand. You can create charts within minutes. Although these charts are simple, they serve as a building block to more complicated charts.

In this chapter, you will get started using Harvard by running its on-line tutorial. Then you will learn how to use the program with input and output devices, such as a mouse and a printer. Finally, you will follow the hands-on steps to produce several types of charts.

GETTING AN OVERVIEW WITH THE ON-LINE TUTORIAL

The on-line tutorial provides a quick overview of Harvard Graphics. This tutorial provides basic instructions for creating and illustrating charts.

Follow these instructions to run the tutorial:

Harvard displays a rotating line in the upper-right corner of the screen when it is busy, such as while loading a program or printing a chart.

1. Type **C:\HG3\HG3TUTOR** and press Enter. You will see a screen prompting you to select your monitor's type.

2. Press **1** to see the tutorial on a VGA monitor, or **2** to see it on an EGA monitor. Be patient if you have a slower computer because this tutorial may take a long time to load.

3. When you see the Harvard Graphics Tutorial menu, with the Introduction option highlighted as shown in Figure 2.1, press Enter.

4. After you read the first page of the tutorial introduction, press the spacebar to see the next page. Continue reading all the introduction screens, pressing the spacebar to see the next one. After the last one, you will be returned to the Harvard Graphics Tutorial menu.

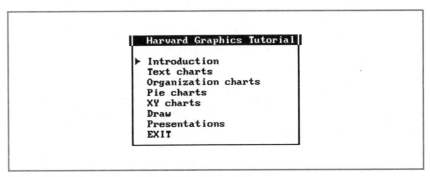

Figure 2.1: The Harvard Graphics Tutorial menu

5. Use the arrow keys to highlight the lesson you are interested in, and then press Enter.

While you are using the tutorial, you can press the spacebar when you want Harvard to fill in the data for you. To stop what you are doing and return to the Harvard Graphics Tutorial menu, press Esc.

6. When you are finished exploring the tutorial lessons, press Esc until you see the Harvard Graphics Tutorial menu. Press the spacebar until the Exit option is highlighted, and then press Enter. You will be returned to the DOS prompt.

Although the tutorial gives you a basic understanding of Harvard, there is much more to learn. Before you begin to create charts, you should know how to interact with the program and which output device to use for your projects.

USING A MOUSE WITH HARVARD

Working with Harvard is easiest when you use both a mouse and the keyboard. Like your keyboard, a mouse is an *input device*; they both send information to the computer. This is different from an output device, such as a printer, which receives information from the computer. To use a mouse, simply push or drag it along your desk and press the buttons to initiate a particular action. For example, you can move the mouse until the mouse cursor is positioned on the menu option you want, and then select it by pressing the left mouse button.

Moving a mouse is more intuitive than typing at the keyboard. When you move the mouse, the pointer on the screen moves in the same direction. Gesturing with a mouse is like moving a pencil to draw a picture. For example, if you're using Harvard's Draw option, you can illustrate your chart with a quick movement of you wrist. In contrast, using the keyboard is slower because it takes a lot of key-presses to move the cursor from one point to another.

BUYING A MOUSE

Your mouse may be one of three types:

- IBM PS/2 direct-connect mouse

- Bus mouse

- Serial mouse

If you use a PS/2 computer, select the IBM mouse. It plugs directly into your computer without requiring a separately installed board or a serial port. Reserve your ports for other devices, such as film recorders, plotters, and printers.

If you're not using a PS/2, you'll need to choose between a bus and a serial mouse. A serial mouse plugs into your computer's serial port; the bus mouse connects to a special board that you install in one of your computer's expansion slots. The type of mouse you select depends on whether you need your expansion slots or your serial ports for other devices. Carefully consider which devices you might later add to your system. For example, if you only have one serial port and plan on installing a plotter, get a bus mouse (providing you have an extra expansion slot in your computer).

Don't buy a one-button mouse because it doesn't offer enough selection capabilities.

When you buy a mouse, make sure it has two or more buttons so it will provide all the selection capabilities you'll need. With a two-button mouse, you can simulate a third button by pressing the two buttons simultaneously.

An alternative to the mouse is the *track ball,* which is a pointing device that is becoming popular. The track ball acts like a mouse but looks like a ball housed in a box. You simply spin the ball in the direction that you want the pointer to move. Its advantage is that you don't need space on your desk to move it around, as you do for a mouse.

INSTALLING THE MOUSE

A *mouse driver* is a software program that tells your computer to check your mouse's input. You install a driver by typing its file name without the extension. For instance, if your driver's file name is MOUSE.COM, you would type **MOUSE** before running Harvard. Alternatively, you can place the command in your AUTOEXEC-.BAT file or include it in the Harvard batch file (HG3.BAT) you created in the last chapter.

Follow these steps to add the MOUSE command to your Harvard batch file:

Use your word processor to edit files and save them as ASCII or DOS text files. Word processors are often easier to use than EDLIN.

1. Type **EDLIN C:\HG3.BAT** and press Enter to run DOS's editor program. An asterisk and an underscore should appear on the screen. If not, make sure you have the editor program (EDLIN.EXE) on your disk. Then change to the directory it is in and repeat the command.

2. Type **1I** and press Enter to turn on EDLIN's insert line mode. You'll know you can add a line to the beginning of your HG.BAT file when you see the line number 1: appear.

3. Type **C:\subdir\MOUSE** (where *subdir* is the name of the subdirectory that your mouse driver is in) and press Enter. If your system uses a driver other than MOUSE.COM, substitute its file name for MOUSE.

4. Press Ctrl-C (press and hold down the Ctrl key while you press the C key). This turns off insert line mode.

5. Type **E** to save the file and return to DOS. If you have trouble with EDLIN, consult you DOS manual.

WORKING WITH THE MOUSE

Start up Harvard so you can practice using the mouse. First, highlight a Main menu option. As the mouse moves across the desk, the cursor or mouse pointer moves across the screen, highlighting different options. If you run out of room on your desk, just pick your mouse up, reposition it, and continue to move it in the desired direction.

On a three-button mouse, the leftmost button selects options, and the rightmost button returns you to the previous menu or screen.

You select an option by pressing the left button on the mouse when the mouse pointer is positioned on top of the menu item or selection you want. The pointer usually looks like a rectangle on the screen. Pressing the right button returns you to the previous menu or screen. In the previous chapter, you used the Esc key to leave the Setup menu. You could have pressed the right mouse button to accomplish the same thing.

To select a function key using a mouse, move the pointer to the list of function keys at the top of the screen and highlight the one you want to use. Then press the left button to access that function. Choosing a function key sometimes displays several pages of options. To move from one page to another, simply click on the down triangle (▼) to move down a page or the up triangle (▲) to move up.

Table 2.1 provides a quick reference to mouse commands and their keyboard equivalents. This book gives instructions for using the keyboard. If you're using a mouse, substitute the appropriate mouse commands for the keyboard instructions.

Once you've finished practicing with the mouse, you can exit Harvard by pressing the right mouse button to return to the Main menu, and then selecting the Exit option.

Table 2.1: Using the Mouse and Keyboard

ACTION	KEYBOARD	MOUSE
Select menu option	Press Enter or F10	Left button
Select setting	Press the spacebar	Left button
Return to previous menu or screen, or cancel an action	Press Esc	Right button
Select function keys	Press F1 to F10	Left button
Drag	Press and hold down the spacebar, use arrow keys to drag, press Enter, and release spacebar	Click left button while moving mouse

USING A GRAPHICS TABLET WITH HARVARD

A *graphics tablet* is a device with a cursor (also called a *puck*) or pen, which lets you draw or trace artwork directly on the screen. With Harvard, you can use a graphics tablet with Harvard's Draw option and on the Color Palettes screen. The Kurta IS/ONE, Summagraphics Summasketch, and CalComp Drawing Board (models 23120-11 and 23180-1) tablets are supported. Table 2.2 summarizes how to use a graphics tablet with Harvard.

Table 2.2: Using a Graphics Tablet

ACTION	KURTA	SUMMAGRAPHICS	CALCOMP
Select menu option	Press yellow or blue button on cursor or press down with pen. With corded pen, press down rapidly.	Press button 1 or 3 on cursor or press down once with pen.	Press button 0 or 2 on cursor or press down once with pen.
Return to previous menu or screen, or cancel an action	Press green or magenta button on cursor or press small round switch on side of pen. With corded pen, press down slowly.	Press button 2 or 4 on cursor or press button on side of pen.	Press button 1 or 3 on cursor.
Drag	Press and hold down yellow or blue button while moving cursor.	Press and hold down button 1 or 3 while moving cursor or press down with pen while moving in any direction.	Press and hold down button 0 or 2 while moving cursor.

HOW YOUR MONITOR INTERACTS WITH HARVARD

Your monitor uses a video card to display your charts. A *video card* is an electronic board installed in your computer that lets your computer send video signals to your monitor. Some video configurations show a better image of your charts than others. It's important for you to understand what to expect on your monitor.

Use a monitor that matches your video card. If you're using a Video Graphics Array (VGA) card, you should also be using an analog monitor. If you're using a monochrome or Hercules Graphics Adapter, you should have a monochrome monitor. The Color Graphics Adapter (CGA) uses a low-resolution red-green-blue (RGB) monitor, while the Enhanced Graphics Adapter (EGA) uses a high-resolution RGB monitor. Video cards aren't interchangeable. For example, you can't use a monochrome video card with a color monitor—it will damage your monitor, video card, or both.

The following are the most common video cards:

- Monochrome, provides text but no graphics, 720 × 350 resolution

- Hercules Graphic Adapter, provides graphics without color, 720 × 385 resolution

- CGA, provides 4 colors, 320 × 200 resolution

- EGA, provides 16 colors, 640 × 350 resolution

- VGA, provides 16 colors, 640 × 480 resolution, or 256 colors, 230 × 200 resolution

You will only get EGA screen resolution for transition effects or animation (discussed in Chapters 11 and 12) when you are using a VGA or Vega Deluxe card.

The resolution of an adapter determines the quality of the monitor display. The EGA video card's resolution, which is 640 × 350, means your monitor can show 640 dots, called *pixels*, across the width of the monitor and 350 pixels down the length. Since the characters and charts that appear on your screen are composed of pixels, the more pixels your screen displays, the sharper its image.

The IBM PS/2 comes with VGA circuitry already installed. VGA produces a superior screen resolution that you will enjoy working with. For other computers, video cards are purchased and installed separately, so they can be of any type. If you are not satisfied with the video card (and monitor) you are using, consider upgrading to a better one. However, avoid using a monochrome card if possible.

If you use a monochrome card other than Hercules Graphics, you will not see graphics on your screen. This means that you will have to print your charts just to see them. In addition, you will not be able to use the Draw option—you can't illustrate a chart you can't see.

If you are using a Vega Deluxe card, select EGA configuration.

If you need to work in color, configure your system with an EGA or a VGA video card and color monitor if possible. If you are using a film recorder that plugs directly into your computer, the quality of your video configuration will affect the quality of your slides. However, higher quality film recorders are not connected to your monitor and can produce images with 2000 to 8000 lines of resolution.

Unlike film recorders, printers aren't affected by a monitor's resolution. In fact, printed output, especially from laser printers, is often better than what you see on your screen.

Now that you are familiar with your monitor and how it affects your printed output, let's explore the output options available to you.

WHICH OUTPUT DEVICE SHOULD YOU CHOOSE?

Usually your choice of output is easy to make. If you only have a printer, you do not have much choice. However, when you have access to a printer, a plotter, and a film recorder, the decision becomes harder.

WHEN TO USE A PRINTER

Some color Post-Script printers produce high-quality charts in paper and transparencies. These tend to be expensive, about $5,000 to $8,000, and it costs about $1 to $2 a copy for supplies.

Use a printer to produce reports, handouts for your presentation, and something for your audience to make notes on. Give your audience a copy or outline of your presentation. Printouts are also useful when you are presenting facts or statistics to small groups of two to ten people.

Printing your data is fast and easy. If you want to produce 3D charts, use a printer because plotters ignore 3D settings. You'll also want a printout if you're going to produce a black-and-white transparency from it.

Note that if you have less than 1Mb of memory in your laser printer, you can print only half of your chart. To print the entire chart, set Harvard to use the Chart size 1/2 option, as discussed later in the chapter.

WHEN TO USE A PLOTTER

Although plotters can't produce 3D charts, they do produce a better-quality output than printers do for most types of charts. However, a plotter can take from 3 to 15 minutes to plot a single graph. Thus, if your presentation contains 12 charts, your plotter (and you) will be busy for up to 3 hours producing them. Because a plotter is so slow, it's not efficient to use it for long presentations to a few people. Nevertheless, a plotter is ideal for making transparencies for overhead projectors.

In its list of symbols, the Harvard manual displays asterisks next to those that can't be produced on plotters.

If you will be addressing an audience of 10 to 25 people, you might consider plotting your color graphs on transparencies for your presentation. You will then be able to project your graphs onto a wall or a screen, and everyone will be able to see them easily. However, consider that transparencies lack the resolution and clarity for large audiences. Use slides when you need to make a presentation to a large group.

WHEN TO USE A FILM RECORDER

For presentations, slides are even better than plotted transparencies. They can be used for an audience of almost any size. The problem with slides is that they're expensive. Outside slide services charge about $10 per slide. If you make your own slides, they cost about $1 each, not including the cost of the equipment, which itself is expensive. An inexpensive recorder, such as the Polaroid Palette, runs for about $2,000 and has a resolution that matches that of the video adapter. The quality of its output is only suitable for small audiences. High-resolution film recorders cost about $8,000.

Now that you know how to use a mouse or graphics tablet with Harvard and understand how your monitor and output devices can affect the appearance of your charts, you are ready to begin creating charts.

CREATING QUICK
AND SIMPLE CHARTS

Harvard provides the Chart Gallery to make it convenient for users to quickly create charts. The Chart Gallery contains sample charts with preset options that you can use as patterns for your own charts. You will learn more about the Gallery in Chapter 9. For now, we will take advantage of it to get started creating text charts without worrying about details.

HANDS-ON: CREATING A TITLE
CHART WITH THE CHART GALLERY

Let's begin with a title chart since presentations themselves usually start with them. Title chart screens are divided into thirds. In general, use the top third of the chart for the title and the center for presenting your topic, message, or name. Use the bottom third for the time, date, and/or location of the presentation.

To create a title chart using the Chart gallery, start Harvard and follow these steps:

1. From the Main menu, type **1** to select the option to create a chart. The Create Chart menu appears, as shown in Figure 2.2.

2. Press **6** to choose the From gallery option. You will see the Gallery menu, shown in Figure 2.3.

3. Press **1** to select text charts and display the choices shown in Figure 2.4.

4. Select Title Chart by pressing **5**.

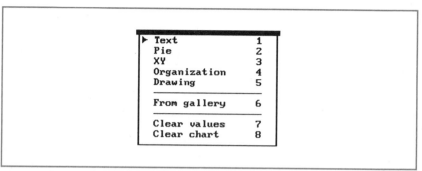

Figure 2.2: The Create Chart menu

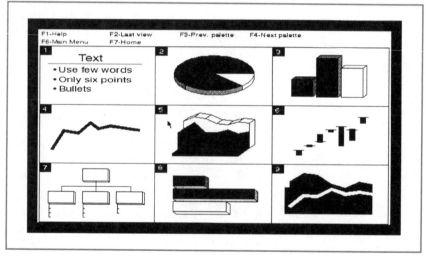

Figure 2.3: The Gallery menu

Remember, to get help on using Harvard, press F1. Return to your chart by pressing Esc from the Help screen.

When you open a Gallery chart, it contains sample data to give you an idea of how to use that type of chart. Before you enter your own text, you must remove the sample text.

5. Press F10 to select the Edit and Clear option. Your cursor should be positioned on the first line of the top section.

6. Type **Mastering Harvard Graphics** on the first line in the top section.

7. Press Enter four times to move the cursor to the first line under *Middle*.

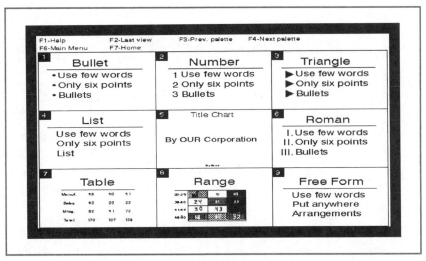

Figure 2.4: The Text Chart Gallery menu

8. Type **Communications** and press Enter.

9. Type **Through** and press Enter.

10. Type **Graphics** and press Enter six times. The cursor will leave the middle section and move to the bottom section of the chart.

11. Type **May 12, 1993** and press Enter.

12. Type **10:30 a.m. in Room 1126**. Your screen should now look like the one shown in Figure 2.5.

13. To view your completed chart, press the F2 key. Your chart will appear on the screen as shown in Figure 2.6.

14. When you are finished admiring your chart, press Esc. You will be returned to where you were in the chart before you pressed F2.

15. Press the F10 key to return to the Main menu.

You've now created your first chart and have viewed it on your screen. Although pressing F10 told Harvard that you finished entering your chart's data, you still need to save the chart.

Title Chart
F1-Help F2-Show chart F4-Draw F5-Mark
F6-Main Menu F7-Spell/Text F8-Options F10-Continue
Top
Mastering Harvard Graphics
Middle
Communications
Through
Graphics
Bottom
May 12, 1993
10:30 a.m. in Room 1126

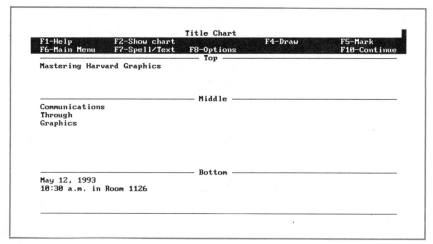

Figure 2.5: Entering text for your title chart

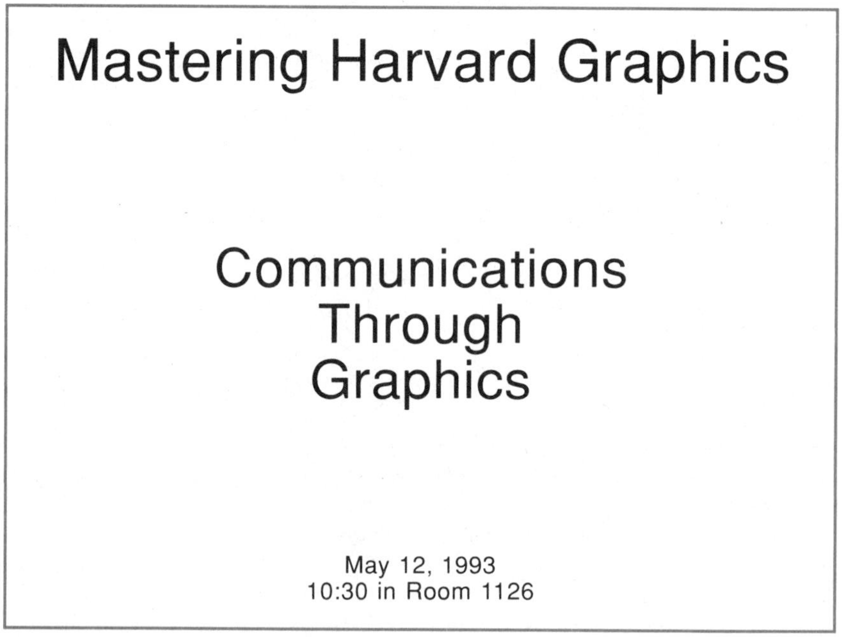

Mastering Harvard Graphics
Communications
Through
Graphics
May 12, 1993
10:30 in Room 1126

Figure 2.6: The completed title chart

HANDS-ON: SAVING YOUR CHART

Unless you save your charts, they will be gone when you quit your current session with Harvard. Save Chart is an option on the File menu. Follow these steps to save the title chart:

1. From the Main menu, press **4** to select the File option and display the File menu.

2. Press **4** to select the Save Chart option. You'll see the Save Chart box, as shown in Figure 2.7. The cursor will be blinking on the line that prompts you to give a file name for your chart.

3. Type **MYTITLE** as the name you want to give to this file, and then press Enter. The cursor advances to the next line, where Harvard has already entered the description for you. By default, Harvard uses the title you typed as the description. You can change the description by simply typing over it. (This will not affect the chart's actual title.)

4. Press Enter three times to keep the default description and settings. Within a few seconds, the file will be saved and you'll return to the Main menu.

Save time by pressing Ctrl-S to save your charts at any time, from the Main menu or from any data-entry screen.

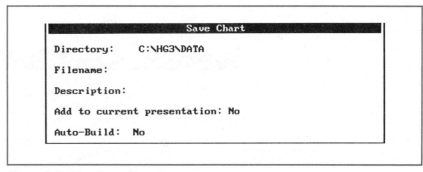

Figure 2.7: The Save Chart box

HANDS-ON: CREATING A LIST CHART WITH THE CHART GALLERY

A simple list chart is nothing more than a bullet chart without the bullets. This chart can list several items, names, or short phrases on separate lines. The lines are automatically centered. As with all Harvard charts, you can include a title, subtitle, and footnote.

1. Press **1** at the Main menu to select the Create chart option.

2. Press **6** at the Create Chart menu to select From gallery.

3. Press **1** to select a text chart, then **4** to choose List.

4. Press F10 to select Edit and Clear. Next, you will see the bullet chart data-entry screen, with the cursor (an underscore) in the Title field at the top of the screen, as shown in Figure 2.8.

5. Type **Simple List Charts** and press Enter.

6. In the Subtitle field, type **Pointers for effective chats** and press Enter. Oops, I think we made a mistake. We dropped the *r*, typing *chats* instead of *charts*.

7. Move the cursor to the *t* in *chats* using the arrow keys. Press the Ins, or Insert, key. Notice that the cursor changes to full-height when insert mode is on. Press **r**, then turn insert mode off by pressing the Ins key again.

8. Press Enter twice to skip the Footnote field and place the cursor on the first line of the list-entry area.

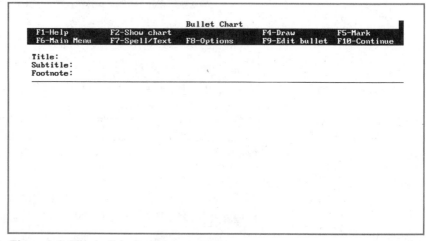

Figure 2.8: The bullet chart data-entry screen

9. Type **Titles are large and bold** and press Enter.

10. Type **Double space for readability** and press Enter.

11. We goofed again by not following our own advice. We've used single-spacing instead of double. Press the up-arrow key once so that you're on the last line you typed. Press Ctrl-Ins (press the Ctrl and Ins keys simultaneously) to insert a blank line between the first and second items. If you wanted to delete the line and start over, you would use Ctrl-Del.

12. Since your cursor is between the two lines, press the down-arrow key three times to start your next double-spaced line.

13. Type **Keep the chart simple** and press Enter twice.

14. Enter the following lines, pressing Enter twice after each line:

    Use subtitles when required

    Use plain text styles

    Abridge your sentences

    Use less than eight lines

    Your screen should now look like Figure 2.9.

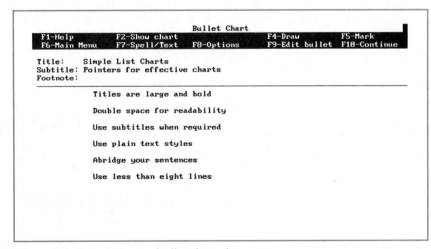

Figure 2.9: Entering your bullet chart data

15. Press the F2 key to view your completed chart. It should look like Figure 2.10. If you are satisfied with the way your chart looks, press Esc until you return to the data-entry screen or the Main menu.

Notice that this time you left the data-entry screen by pressing Esc instead of F10. There are often several ways to execute the same option in Harvard. Whenever possible, we will show you the alternatives, and you can decide which method you prefer. Now you will use another method to save your chart.

16. Press Ctrl-S to save the list chart, and then enter the file name **MYLIST**.

Now that you have created two types of text charts (title and list), we are ready to move onto charts that use numeric data. We will begin with a pie chart. After creating and saving the chart, you will retrieve it and use its data to create bar and line charts.

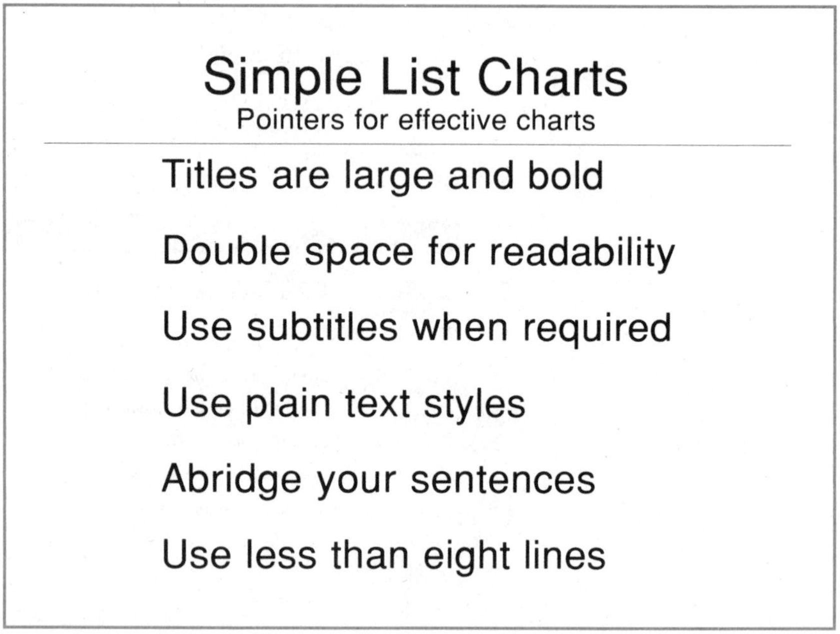

Simple List Charts
Pointers for effective charts

Titles are large and bold

Double space for readability

Use subtitles when required

Use plain text styles

Abridge your sentences

Use less than eight lines

Figure 2.10: Your completed list chart

HANDS-ON: CREATING A PIE
CHART WITH THE CHART GALLERY

The pie chart is one of the easiest types to create and understand. As an example, suppose that you want to graph how a friend distributes his income. You can build a pie chart to divide his total spending into sections and clearly show the distribution.

Follow these steps to create the sample pie chart:

1. Select the Create chart option by pressing **1** from the Main menu. Then press **6** to select the From gallery option.

2. Press **2** to select Pie and display the choices shown in Figure 2.11. Press **1** to select the standard pie chart.

3. Press F10 to select the Edit and Clear option. The pie chart data-entry screen will appear, with the cursor in the Title field.

4. Type **Monthly Spending** for your pie chart's title, and then press Enter.

5. Type **Where's the money going?** in the Subtitle field, and then press Enter four times. This will place your cursor in the first slice's row, under the Label column.

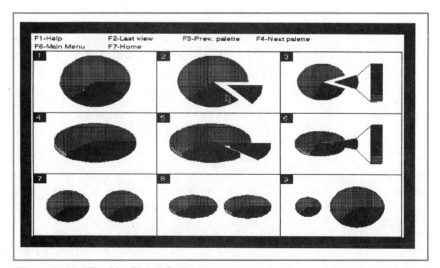

Figure 2.11: The Pie Chart Gallery menu

6. Enter the labels for the pie slice names, pressing Enter after each one:

   Housing

   Food

   Utilities

   Miscellaneous

   Clothing

   Savings

7. Move your cursor to the next column to enter the values for the slices by pressing the Tab key. Move to the first line next to the Housing label by pressing the up-arrow key five times.

8. Add these elements to the Value column by typing each number and pressing Enter:

   1250

   439

   210

   185

   135

   55

Harvard assigns percentages to the values you type. You'll learn more about pie charts and how to change values or percentages in Chapter 4.

9. Press F2 to see your chart. You will see that the Savings and Clothing values overlap, which we will fix by changing their position. Press Esc when you are finished viewing the chart.

The settings made from the pie chart Options menu are discussed in detail in Chapter 4.

10. Press F8 to display the options for pie charts. Then press **9** to choose the Slice percents option and display the Slice Percents box.

11. Press Enter to move the cursor to the Place percents field under the Pie 1 column, and then press the spacebar to choose Adjacent. Your screen should look like Figure 2.12.

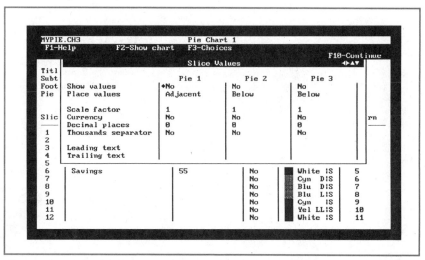

```
MYPIE.CH3                      Pie Chart 1
   F1-Help          F2-Show chart   F3-Choices
                                                        F10-Continue
                              Slice Values                    ◄▶▲▼
Titl
Subt                           Pie 1         Pie 2         Pie 3
Foot   Show values          ◆No           No            No
Pie    Place values         Adjacent      Below         Below

       Scale factor         1             1             1
Slic   Currency             No            No            No                 rn
 ─     Decimal places       0             0             0                  ─
 1     Thousands separator  No            No            No
 2
 3     Leading text
 4     Trailing text
 5
 6     Savings              55            No         ▓ White :S      5
 7                                        No         ▓ Cyn  D:S      6
 8                                        No         ▓ Blu  D:S      7
 9                                        No         ▓ Blu  L:S      8
10                                        No         ▓ Cyn   :S      9
11                                        No         ▓ Yel LL:S     10
12                                        No         ▓ White :S     11
```

Figure 2.12: The Slice Percents box, with Adjacent selected for Place percent

12. Press F2 to display the pie chart, which should look like the one shown in Figure 2.13.

13. Press Esc, then F10 to return to the Main menu.

14. Press **4** to choose File, then **4** again to select Save Chart and enter the name **MYPIE**.

The next chart you'll learn about is the XY bar chart, which is the most flexible pictorial chart you can use in Harvard. For example, you can modify an XY chart to become a vertical bar, percentage, stacked bar, overlapped bar, and even a line graph, as you'll see shortly. Because Harvard provides more options for XY graphs than it does for text and pie charts, it may take you longer to become familiar with the many variations.

The bar graph that you'll create next will borrow its data from the pie chart you just created, MYPIE. By getting the data from the pie chart, you avoid retyping all that information.

HANDS-ON: RETRIEVING A SAVED CHART

To retrieve a saved chart, follow these steps:

To quickly retrieve a chart, press Ctrl-G from the Main menu or a data-entry screen.

1. At the Main menu, press **4** to choose File. This is the same menu you use to save a file.

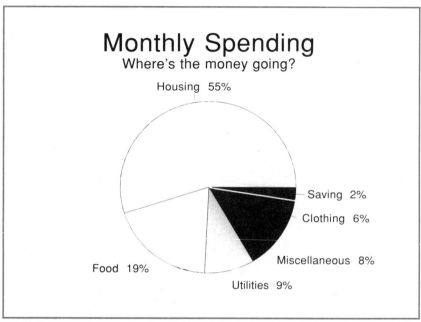

Figure 2.13: The completed pie chart

2. Press **1** to select the Get chart option. A directory appears, showing the files that you saved on the disk. Notice the subdirectory's name above the file names. This tells you where Harvard is looking for your files.

Earlier versions of Harvard use the .CHT extension.

3. Press the down-arrow key until the MYPIE.CH3 file is highlighted. Notice that Harvard automatically added the .CH3 extension to the file name. This way, you'll know that any file ending with a .CH3 extension is a chart file.

4. Once MYPIE.CH3 is highlighted, press Enter or F10. You'll now see this graph displayed on your screen. To get to the Main menu, press Esc twice.

As you've just experienced, retrieving a chart is easy because each chart's name, creation date, type, and description appear in the directory. HG3.DIR is the full name of the file where this directory is stored. Should you ever copy all your chart files to another subdirectory, make sure you include HG3.DIR. Otherwise, you won't see the descriptions of your charts when you want to retrieve one.

After you have retrieved a chart and returned to the Main menu, Harvard automatically uses that chart when you select a menu option that requires a chart. You can tell Harvard not to use it if you want to create a chart from new data.

HANDS-ON: CREATING A BAR CHART FROM EXISTING DATA

Creating our sample bar chart will be quicker because we are borrowing data from the pie chart. Follow these steps to keep the data for the new bar chart:

1. From the Main menu, press **1** to select Create chart, and then press **3** to choose the XY option.

2. From the XY menu, press **4** to select Bar/Line. You will see the Change Chart Type Box, which contains the message

   Keep current data: Yes

3. Press Enter to accept the default Yes. The XY chart data-entry screen appears, and it contains the data from the pie chart data-entry screen, as shown in Figure 2.14.

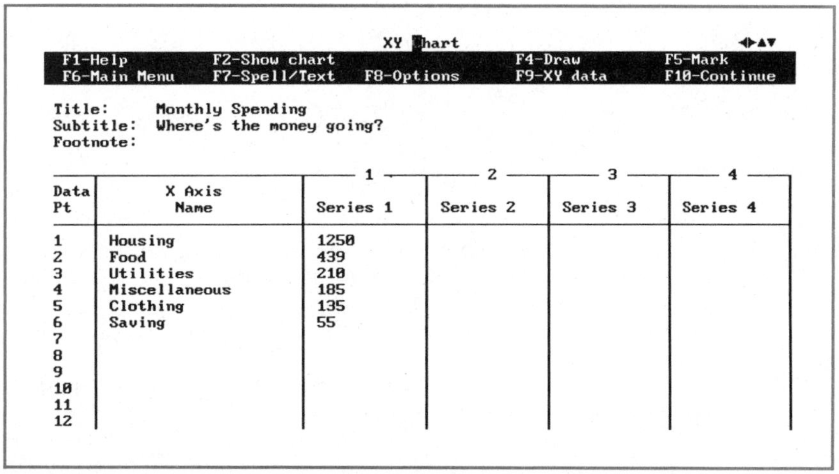

```
                                      XY Chart                          ◆▲▼
         F1-Help           F2-Show chart              F4-Draw       F5-Mark
         F6-Main Menu      F7-Spell/Text   F8-Options  F9-XY data   F10-Continue

         Title:      Monthly Spending
         Subtitle:   Where's the money going?
         Footnote:
         ──────────────────────── 1 ──── 2 ──── 3 ──── 4 ──
         Data    X Axis
         Pt      Name          Series 1   Series 2   Series 3   Series 4

         1       Housing       1250
         2       Food          439
         3       Utilities     210
         4       Miscellaneous 185
         5       Clothing      135
         6       Saving        55
         7
         8
         9
         10
         11
         12
```

Figure 2.14: The XY chart data-entry screen with pie chart data

The labels for the pie slices are now the names of the X-axis points. The value for each point is listed in the Series 1 column (the third column). You can add three more series in the remaining columns.

4. Press F2 to see the new bar chart with the pie chart data, and then press Esc.

Now we will modify the chart by naming the first series and adding a second series, which will contain budget data to help your friend save enough money to buy a computer.

5. Move your cursor to the Series 1 column by pressing the Tab key three times.

6. Type **Spent**, and then press the Del key three times.

7. Move to the Series 2 column by pressing the Tab key. Press Ctrl-Del to clear the line, and then type **Budget**.

8. Move to the first row in the Budget column by pressing Enter.

9. Type the following budget figures, pressing Enter after each number:

   1000

   420

   200

   200

   120

   334

Figure 2.15 shows the completed XY chart data-entry screen. Each number is the second series data for the X-axis point in the same row. For example, 120 is the budgeted amount for Clothing, which is the fifth X-axis point.

10. Press the F2 key to view your graph. Notice that the X-axis labels run together. Press Esc. Let's correct this problem.

11. Press F8 to see the XY chart options. Then press **2** to choose Text attributes.

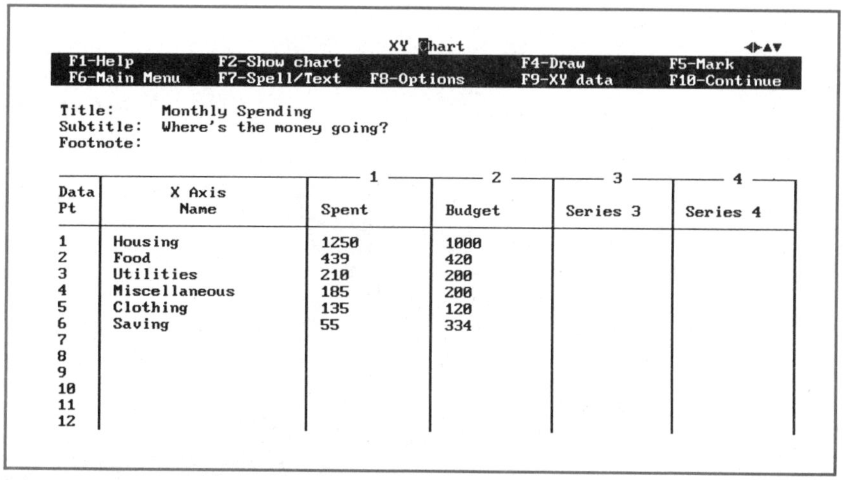

Figure 2.15: The completed bar chart data-entry screen

The settings made from the XY chart Options menu are described in Chapter 5.

12. Choose the For labels option by pressing **2**. You will see the Text Attributes Labels box.

13. Press Tab two times to move to the Alignment column next to the X axis labels field, and then press the spacebar twice to change the option to Angled.

14. Press F2 to view your graph, which should look like Figure 2.16. Press Esc to continue.

15. Press Ctrl-S to save the chart, giving it the name **MYBAR**.

HANDS-ON: CREATING A LINE CHART

The only difference between a Harvard bar chart and line chart is that the X-axis points in a line chart series are connected by a line rather than shown as separate bars.

In the following steps, you will reuse our bar chart data and create a line chart:

1. From the Main menu, press **1** to create a chart, and then press **3** to choose the XY option.

2. Select the Line option by pressing **5**.

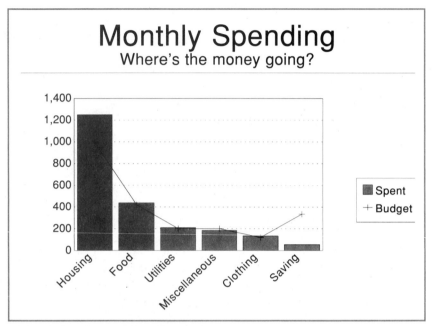

Figure 2.16: The completed bar chart

3. When the Change Chart Type box appears, select Yes to keep the same data.

4. Press F8 to select Options, and then press **7** to select Legend and display the Legend Options box.

5. Press the down-arrow key three times, and then press the spacebar twelve times to change the appearance of the legend box. This gives the legend box a drop shadow.

6. Press Esc, and then press F8 to see the line chart options again.

7. Press **1** to display the Titles/Footnotes box. Then press Enter to move to the Y1 axis title field.

8. Type **Dollars spent**, and then press Esc to leave the Titles/Footnotes box.

9. Press F2, and you will see that the X-axis labels run together, as they did in the bar chart. Press Esc to return to the data-entry screen.

10. Press F8, then **2**, then **2** again to display the Text Attributes Labels box.

11. Press Tab twice to reach the Alignment column next to the X axis labels field, press the spacebar twice to change the setting to Angled, and then press F10.

12. To add currency symbols to the chart, press F8 and type **A** to display the Format Options box. Press Tab once to move to the Y Axis column, press the down-arrow key twice to reach the Currency field and then press the spacebar to change the setting to Yes. Press Esc to return to the data-entry screen.

13. Press F2 to see the completed chart, which should look like Figure 2.17, and then press F10 to return to the Main menu.

14. Press **4** to choose File, then **4** again to choose Save Chart, and name the chart **MYLINE**. If you saved it under the previous name, MYBAR, you would replace the bar chart.

⊙ If you save a new chart that graphs data from another chart under the same name as the chart the data came from, you will overwrite the old chart.

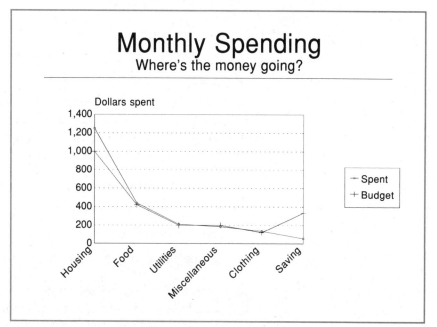

Figure 2.17: The completed line chart

CORRECTING YOUR ERRORS

When you use Harvard, it's likely you will make mistakes. As you saw when you made your simple list chart, it is usually simple to correct errors, provided you know which keys to press. Error correction is a simple two-step process: you move the cursor to the error, and then correct it by deleting, replacing, or inserting characters.

You use the Tab, Shift-Tab, and arrow keys to move around on the chart, just as you would a menu. Harvard uses the keystrokes common to many word processors. Table 2.3 summarizes the keys you will need to correct your errors. You can also correct spelling errors automatically, as you'll learn in Chapter 3.

When you press the left-arrow key on the first character of your line, the cursor moves to the end of the previous line. Similarly, if you press the right-arrow key at the end of a line, you'll move down to the beginning of the next line.

PRINTING YOUR CHARTS

After you have created and saved your charts, you will want to print them. You may choose to send your charts to a printer, plotter, or film recorder. The following sections describe each of these output options.

DOUBLE-CHECKING YOUR CHART

Regardless of which output device you choose, you should look your chart over before printing it. Doing this saves time and money. Each mistake you make can cost you up to $10 just for the materials, plus it takes extra time to reprint the chart.

Before printing your graph, check the following:

- Is all the text there? (Long lines may be truncated.)
- Is your spelling correct?
- Are your message and title clear?
- Is the chart simple and easy to understand?

Remember that you retrieve a chart by using the Main menu's File option. When you return to the Main menu and choose the Output option, Harvard uses the chart you just retrieved.

Table 2.3: The Cursor-Movement and Editing Keys

KEY	ACTION
Up arrow	Moves cursor up one line
Down arrow	Moves cursor down one line
Left arrow	Moves cursor one space to the left
Right arrow	Moves cursor one space to the right
Tab	Moves cursor to the next column or field
Shift-Tab	Moves cursor to the previous column or field
Home	Moves cursor to the line's first item
End	Moves cursor to the line's last item
Ctrl-left arrow	Moves cursor one word to the left
Ctrl-right arrow	Moves cursor one word to the right
Ctrl-up arrow	Moves cursor up one line
Ctrl-down arrow	Moves cursor down one line
Backspace	Deletes the character to the left of the cursor, moving the cursor back one space
Del	Deletes the character at the cursor
Ins	Switches character insertion mode on and off
Ctrl-Del	Deletes a line on the screen or clears a chosen selection
Ctrl-Ins	Inserts a line on the screen

PRODUCING PRINTER OUTPUT

Since you used the Main menu's Setup option in Chapter 1 to configure Harvard for your printer, it should be ready to be used.

To practice printing a chart, follow these steps:

1. Press Ctrl-G, highlight MYLINE.CH3, and press Enter to retrieve the line chart.

2. Press Esc twice to return to the Main menu, and then press **5** to choose Output and display the Output menu, shown in Figure 2.18.

3. Press **1** to choose the Printer 1 option. You will see the Output to Printer box, as shown in Figure 2.19.

The Output to Printer box lists the device and port you have configured, as well as six options. We will examine these options shortly. For now, we will accept all the default settings to quickly print the chart.

4. Make sure that your printer is turned on and is on-line, and then press F10.

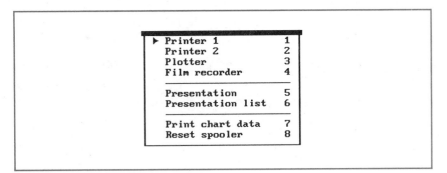

```
       ┌─────────────────────────┐
    ▶  │ Printer 1            1   │
       │ Printer 2            2   │
       │ Plotter              3   │
       │ Film recorder        4   │
       ├─────────────────────────┤
       │ Presentation         5   │
       │ Presentation list    6   │
       ├─────────────────────────┤
       │ Print chart data     7   │
       │ Reset spooler        8   │
       └─────────────────────────┘
```

Figure 2.18: The Output menu

```
       ┌──────────────────────────────────────┐
       │           Output To Printer          │
       ├──────────────────────────────────────┤
       │ Device          Apple LaserWriter Plus│
       │ Port            LPT1                   │
       │ Quality         ◆Draft                 │
       │ Paper size      A  (8.5 in. x 11 in.)  │
       │ Chart size      Full                   │
       │ Copies          1                      │
       │ Output to disk  No                     │
       │ Output filename C:\HG3\OUTPUT\         │
       └──────────────────────────────────────┘
```

Figure 2.19: The Output to Printer box

You will know that Harvard is busily working on your print job when it displays the Printing box, which contains the message

Press Esc to cancel

Depending on your choice of printing options and your printer, your chart will be printed in 10 seconds to 3 minutes, and the Printing box will remain on the screen. If you change your mind and decide not to print the chart, press Esc. After your print job is finished, you will be returned to the Main menu.

Many of the output options affect presentations. As you will learn later in the book, you can assign a group of charts to a presentation and print all of them at once.

PRINTING OPTIONS You can adjust the settings for the options in the Output to Printer box as necessary. When an option has several settings, use the arrow keys to highlight the one you want to use and press the spacebar to change it, type in a new value, or press F3 to see a list of choices.

Select from the following printing options:

Press F2 to preview your chart on the screen before printing it. The display shows how your chart will look on white paper without color.

- Quality: Choose from three printing modes, Draft, Medium, and High. Draft mode prints your charts quickly, but they have a rough appearance. With Medium mode, your charts look better but take longer to print. The High mode can be painfully slow, but it produces the best-looking charts. Note that some printers can work in only one or two printing modes. For example, your printer many only be able to print in Draft or High mode, and it will use High mode when you select Medium.

- Paper Size: Choose the type of paper you are using. Your choices include None, A (8.5 in. × 11 in.), A4 (210mm × 297mm), and Legal (8.15 in. × 14 in.).

- Chart Size: Select the size of your graph and the position it will occupy on the paper. Full size takes the entire page; half size takes up only half the sheet of paper.

- Copies: Enter the number of copies you want to print. Harvard will output as many as you want.

To print an output-to-disk file, at the DOS prompt, type **COPY filename.PRN**, where *filename* is the name you assigned to the output file. Depending on your system configuration, you may need to substitute LPT1, LPT2, LPT3, COM1, or COM2 for PRN.

- Output to Disk: Choose this option to send the chart file to a disk rather than to the printer. Later, you can print the chart from the disk without using Harvard.

- Output Filename: Change the default name if you are saving the chart to disk. When you press Enter after this option, Harvard will start printing the chart.

If your printer is not ready when you press Enter, you will see the error message

Output device is not ready
Press (Enter key) to continue; Esc to Cancel

Check to make sure that you have turned on your printer and that the on-line light is on. Also make sure that the printer cables are attached properly and the printer has paper. If you are still having problems, press Esc to cancel the print job and try reconfiguring your printer as discussed in Chapter 1. Otherwise, press Enter to continue when your printer is ready.

PRODUCING PLOTTER OUTPUT

If you want to output your chart to a plotter, press **3** from the Output menu. You will see the Output to Plotter box, shown in Figure 2.20. This box provides the same options as the Output to Printer box, described in the previous section.

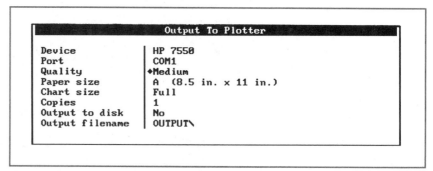

```
┌─────────────────────────────────────────────────────────┐
│  ┌─────────────────────────────────────────────────┐    │
│  │              Output To Plotter                  │    │
│  │ Device          HP 7550                         │    │
│  │ Port            COM1                             │    │
│  │ Quality         ◆Medium                         │    │
│  │ Paper size      A  (8.5 in. x 11 in.)           │    │
│  │ Chart size      Full                            │    │
│  │ Copies          1                               │    │
│  │ Output to disk  No                              │    │
│  │ Output filename OUTPUT\                          │    │
│  │                                                 │    │
│  └─────────────────────────────────────────────────┘    │
└─────────────────────────────────────────────────────────┘
```

Figure 2.20: The Output to Plotter box

The only plotter option that has a different effect is Quality. As with a printer, you can select from Draft, Medium, and High mode. However, unlike the printer's settings, the Medium and High mode for plotters produce proportional spacing. This means that each letter has a particular width assigned to it. For example, the letter *M* might take up five proportional spaces, while the letter *i* might use only one space. Proportional spacing makes your charts easier to read.

The Quality setting for plotters functions as follows:

- Draft: No proportional spacing, patterns instead of solid colors, stick-like lettering only, no text attributes

- Medium: Proportional spacing, stick-like lettering, colors filled in (including color text), no additional text attributes

- High: WYSIWYG (what you see is what you get) plotting

PRODUCING FILM RECORDER OUTPUT

To ouput your charts to a film recorder, press **4** from the Output menu to display the Output to Film Recorder box, shown in Figure 2.21. You can set the following options:

- Quality: Choose from High, Medium, and Draft mode.

- Film Type: The settings you can select from will vary according to the type of film recorder you are using.

- Film Size: The film size selections will also vary depending on your film recorder.

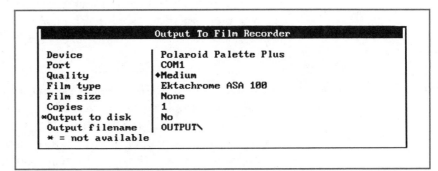

Figure 2.21: The Output to Film Recorder box

- Copies: Enter the number of copies you want to produce, up to 999.

- Output to Disk: Although it is listed on the screen, you cannot use this option with a film recorder.

- Output Filename: You can choose to enter a file name for your chart.

PRODUCING CHART DATA

The Print chart data option on the Output menu allows you to print the values you used to create the graph. The printout includes the X-data labels, the names of the series, and the elements used in the series.

For example, if you printed the MYBAR chart you created earlier in the chapter using the Print chart data option, your output would resemble Figure 2.22.

	Spent	Budget
Housing	1250	1000
Food	439	420
Utilities	210	200
Miscellaneous	185	200
Clothing	135	120
Savings	55	334

Figure 2.22: Printing a bar chart with the Print chart data option

SUMMARY

You now have a basic understanding of how Harvard works, and you have practiced using it. You learned how Harvard works with a mouse and your video display, and have explored your output options.

You can now start producing your own graphs and experimenting with the options that are available. In the next chapter, we will examine more complicated charts. You'll learn how to create artistic text charts using bullets and graphics. You'll also learn how to change the size, style, and colors of your text characters, check your spelling automatically, and how to use text charts in presentations. You're well on your way toward mastering Harvard.

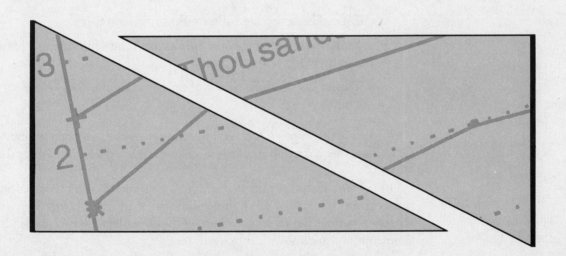

Creating Text Charts

CHAPTER 3

AS YOU LEARNED IN CHAPTERS 1 AND 2, PICKING THE right chart to convey your message is essential. You'll want to use text charts to convey messages, break up repetitive displays of graphs, and build anticipation. Remember that your text chart must be able to stand on its own merit without the benefit of illustrations.

UNDERSTANDING YOUR TEXT CHART CHOICES

You use the Text Chart menu (press **1** from the Main menu, then **1** again) to specify the type of text chart you want to create. You can choose from the following options:

- Title: Use to create presentation title charts
- Bullet: Use to group and emphasize related items, or create a simple list (without bullets)
- Table: Use to create columnar lists and charts showing ranges

Each chart type has a limit to the number of lines you can enter: 16 lines for a title chart, 48 lines for a bullet chart, and 24 lines for a table chart.

In the last chapter, you learned how to make a title chart, which introduces or outlines your presentations. You also learned how to create a simple list (a bullet chart without bullets), which provides information quickly with little fanfare.

When you use a bullet chart with bullets, the bullet's bold appearance grabs your audience's attention, emphasizing the items in your list. You use bullets to group related information. However, you should not overuse bullets in your presentations, or your text charts (and your presentation) will become monotonous.

To align table chart numbers with decimals along their decimal points, press F8, choose Column, and change Number alignment to Decimal.

Table charts are ideal for displaying short phrases or phrases mixed with numeric values, such as financial figures. Consider carefully, however, whether a pictorial graph might be better for your numeric data. Often, you can place a table to present alphanumeric data, and then follow it with a pictorial chart showing the data's relationships. You can also place an overlay of color shading on your values to show ranges, using Harvard's Range option. Do this to show the relationships of the figures displayed in your table.

DESIGNING EFFECTIVE TEXT CHARTS

Besides choosing the right type of text chart for your message, you also need to design it well. Your chart's design affects your audience's perception of you and your organization.

There is also a lesson to learn from the mail-order industry. The next time you sift through your junk mail, look at those with quality stationery, illustrative brochures, and professional designs. Although the company might operate from a garage, the effective design of its literature may suggest a large, efficient organization. Similarly, if your chart is neat, orderly, and intelligible, your audience will perceive you, your organization, and your presentation more favorably.

Consistency is the most important element of a design. If you use a border in one chart, all your charts in the presentation should have borders. Likewise, use the same font for all your graphs. Your presentation, particularly its logo and graphic design, should be consistent with your organization's other presentations. Frequent changes give viewers the impression of a disorganized organization.

ADJUSTING YOUR CHART'S APPEARANCE

You can easily change the design and look of your charts through the Appearance Options box, shown in Figure 3.1. Press F8 to display the options for text charts, and then choose Appearance to see

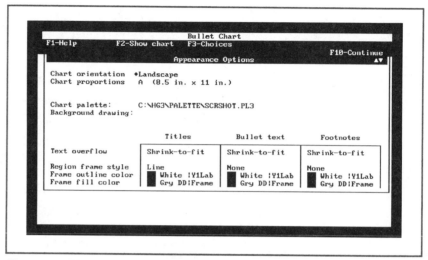

Figure 3.1: The Appearance Options box

the options box. From here, you can change the following chart features:

- Chart orientation
- Chart proportions
- Chart palette
- Background drawing
- Text overflow
- Region frame styles and colors

You'll learn about palettes as you progress through this book. The following sections explain the other appearance options.

CHANGING THE ORIENTATION

All the charts you have created so far have a landscape orientation, which is the default setting. Like landscape paintings, these charts are wider than they are long. Conversely, portrait-oriented charts are longer than they are wide, as shown in the top-left box of Figure 3.2.

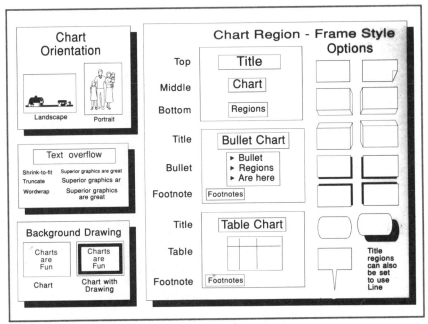

Figure 3.2: Adjustments made through the Appearance Options box

Use the Portrait setting for long lists, forms, and detailed flow or organization charts.

The first field of the Appearance Options box lets you change the chart orientation. Press the spacebar to toggle between Landscape and Portrait.

CHANGING THE PROPORTIONS

If you're working on a chart with unusual proportions, select a chart proportion size that is equal to or smaller than the size you are using.

You can use the Chart proportion field in the Appearance Options box to set the proportional size of a chart so that it corresponds to the output medium proportions. This allows you to see how the chart will appear in its final form. For example, set Chart proportion to A (8.5 in. × 11 in.) when you are creating charts to be printed on standard-size paper. If you are creating slides, set Chart proportion to 35mm slide (24mm × 36mm).

This option works the same as changing the chart proportions through the Chart default settings option on the Setup menu (discussed in Chapter 1), except that only the current chart is affected.

Use it to change the proportions of the individual chart you are working on without having to reset your configuration.

USING BACKGROUND DRAWINGS

Design a back-
ground drawing
using Harvard's Draw
option, which is discussed
later in the chapter.

A background drawing is a chart that includes a border, logo, symbols, or other illustrations and serves as a backdrop to the main chart. You output a background drawing and a chart as a single chart. In the Background Drawing field in the Appearance Options box, type the complete path and file name of the chart you want to use as the background drawing.

Harvard supplies three chart files that contain background drawings with different borders: FRAME0.CH3, FRAME1.CH3, and FRAME2.CH3. For example, if you want to use the FRAME1 chart as your background drawing, and it is stored in Harvard's default data subdirectory, you would enter

C:\HG3\DATA\FRAME1.CH3

in the Appearance Options box.

Remember, do not
place borders on
charts that will be pre-
sented as framed trans-
parencies because the
edge of the paper or
plastic serves as a border.
Also, some film recorders
will cut off parts of your
borders.

Using background drawings is an efficient way to give all your charts a uniform border. When you find a border that you would like to include on most of your charts, you can put it (and any other items you want on every chart) in a drawing chart, and then make that chart the default background drawing. To set a default background drawing, use the Chart default settings option on the Setup menu, enter the chart's name in the Background drawing field, and press F10. Each new chart you create will now be merged with that background drawing.

FRAMING CHART REGIONS

Harvard assigns regions to the charts you create. Figure 3.2 shows the different regions defined for text charts, as well as the frame styles you can select to emphasize them. In fact, Figure 3.2 is an example of a drawing chart with four regions, which each have a shaded frame.

You might want to use regions to emphasize your chart's title. You can give frames outline and fill colors to make them stand out even more. Select the frame style for each region from the Appearance Options box.

ADJUSTING TEXT OVERFLOW

When the text you enter as a line on your chart is too long to fit on a single line, by default, Harvard will shrink it to fit.

You can change the way text overflow is handled by choosing one of the other Text overflow options in the Appearance Options box: Truncate, which chops off the characters that don't fit, or Wordwrap, which wraps the characters down to the next line. These options are also illustrated in Figure 3.2.

To force a line of text to word wrap, press Ctrl-Enter to insert a line feed.

MAKING YOUR CHARTS READABLE

One important element of a readable chart is the placement of the text on it. For example, Figures 3.3 and 3.4 show two charts with the same text. Although their text is identical, one chart is unattractive and unreadable, and the other is more appealing and easier to read.

There are three errors in the chart shown in Figure 3.3. First, it uses all capital letters, which gives it a harsh, angular look. Second, the lines aren't double-spaced, which makes them run together. Third, because the chart isn't enclosed in a frame, the viewer's attention is more likely to wander.

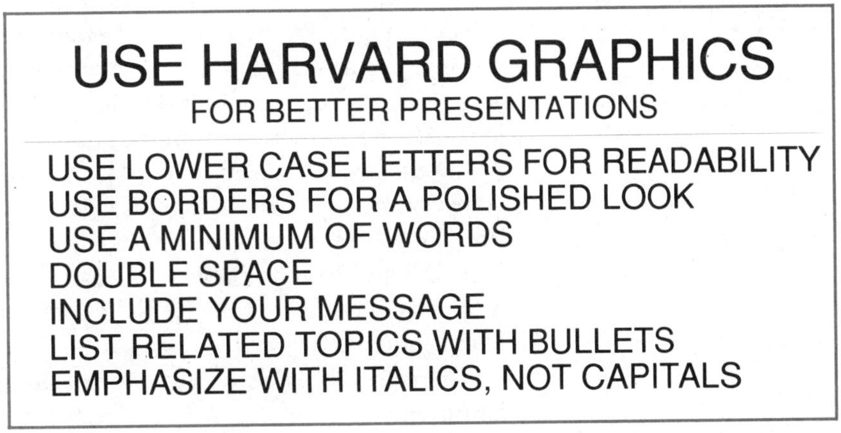

USE HARVARD GRAPHICS
FOR BETTER PRESENTATIONS

USE LOWER CASE LETTERS FOR READABILITY
USE BORDERS FOR A POLISHED LOOK
USE A MINIMUM OF WORDS
DOUBLE SPACE
INCLUDE YOUR MESSAGE
LIST RELATED TOPICS WITH BULLETS
EMPHASIZE WITH ITALICS, NOT CAPITALS

Figure 3.3: A text chart with poor text placement

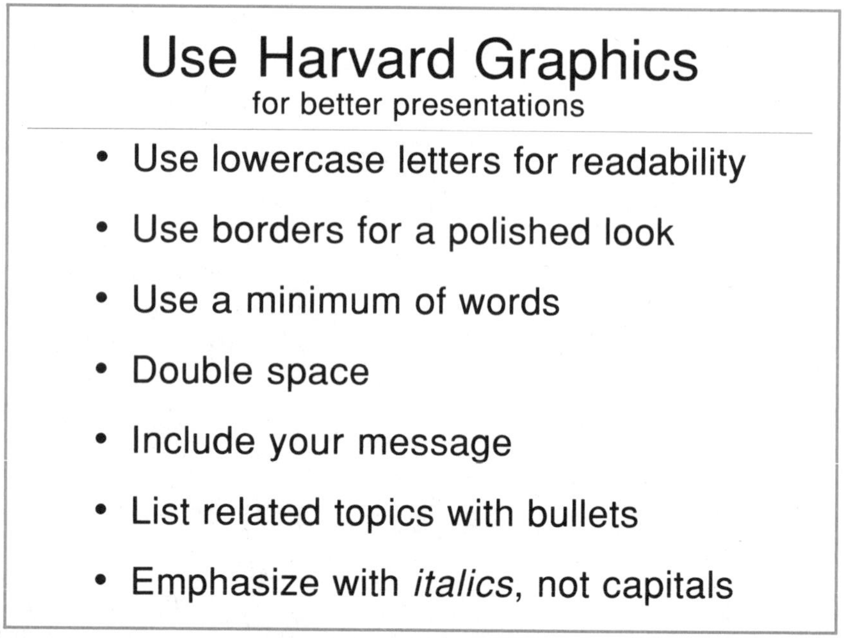

Use Harvard Graphics
for better presentations

- Use lowercase letters for readability

- Use borders for a polished look

- Use a minimum of words

- Double space

- Include your message

- List related topics with bullets

- Emphasize with *italics*, not capitals

Figure 3.4: A text chart with good text placement

On the other hand, the chart in Figure 3.4 is readable because it uses both uppercase and lowercase letters and the text is double-spaced. Its border and bullets focus the audience's attention on its contents.

When you're creating color charts, the colors you use will also affect their readability. Almost 10 percent of the population is color blind or has difficulty distinguishing between red and green. Refrain from using these colors as more than minor elements in your design. For example, if you create a chart that uses red for negative numbers, someone in the audience may see those numbers in another color and think they're positive. Add parentheses or minus signs to further identify negative values.

Another point to keep in mind is that charts aren't the place to flaunt your vocabulary. Charts should be short and precise in meaning. This isn't, however, an excuse for abbreviating terms your audience isn't familiar with. You probably won't cause confusion by using NASA, but not everyone knows that DPM stands for Department of Personnel Management.

There are a number of options you can use to sculpt each text character the way you want it. You can easily set the font or text characteristics to achieve a professional look. The following sections describe how fonts, text attributes, and special characters affect your chart's readability.

SELECTING FONTS AND TEXT STYLES

Although you should keep your charts consistent in their design, you also want to help your audience focus on the key parts of each chart's message. One way to do this is by changing the appearance of important words. You can emphasize text by changing its font, outlining, shadowing, slanting, subscripting, superscripting, underlining, or by changing its size and color.

Harvard's default font style is Swiss 721, but you can choose from ten fonts in various styles, as shown in Figure 3.5. The Swiss 721 font is a good choice for most of your text because it is boldfaced and can be read easily.

To apply attributes to your text, press F5 to select the Mark option and highlight the first letter you want to change. Then use the arrow keys to mark the letters or words, or press Shift-F5 to highlight an entire line. Next, press F10 to display the Marked Text Options box, as shown in Figure 3.6. Move the cursor to highlight the option you want to apply to the marked text, and then press the spacebar to toggle between options, or press F3 to select from a list. To change the text size, type in the size that you want to use.

Be careful when you are changing the attributes of your text charts—you don't want to have too many different text styles in your chart, or your audience will become distracted and may have trouble reading your chart easily. In general, we recommend changing only two or three attribute styles in a chart. For example, stick with one font style and use italics or slants to emphasize words or parts of your chart.

HARNESSING SPECIAL CHARACTERS

For some of your text charts, you may need to include special characters, such as the pi symbol (π) or the English pound sign (£), which are not on your keyboard. Figure 3.7 lists the special characters that you can use with the default Swiss 721 font, along with the codes to produce

If you have trouble seeing the Gothic font when you print in High mode, try printing in Medium mode.

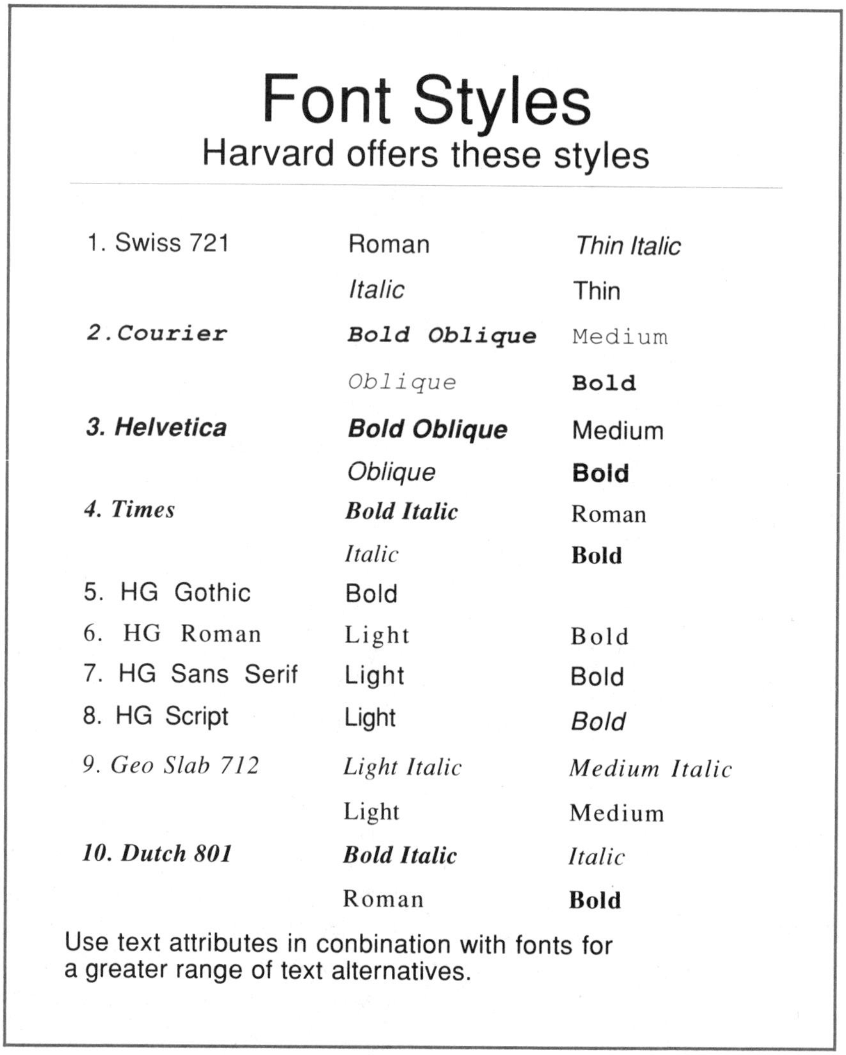

Font Styles
Harvard offers these styles

1. Swiss 721	Roman	*Thin Italic*
	Italic	Thin
2. Courier	**Bold Oblique**	Medium
	Oblique	**Bold**
3. Helvetica	**Bold Oblique**	Medium
	Oblique	**Bold**
4. Times	**Bold Italic**	Roman
	Italic	**Bold**
5. HG Gothic	Bold	
6. HG Roman	Light	Bold
7. HG Sans Serif	Light	Bold
8. HG Script	Light	*Bold*
9. Geo Slab 712	*Light Italic*	*Medium Italic*
	Light	Medium
10. Dutch 801	***Bold Italic***	*Italic*
	Roman	**Bold**

Use text attributes in conbination with fonts for
a greater range of text alternatives.

Figure 3.5: Examples of available fonts and styles

them. You can use these special bullet, currency, mathematical, and international characters in any type of Harvard chart, not just text charts.

To enter a special character, place the cursor where you want that character to appear, and then press and hold down the Alt key while

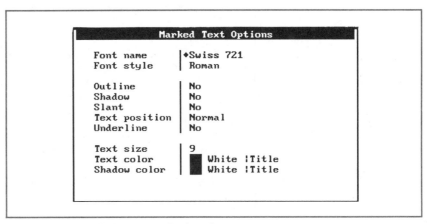

Figure 3.6: The Marked Text Options box

typing its code (see Figure 3.7) using the keys on the numeric keypad (not the ones above the letter keys on the keyboard). When you release the Alt key, the special character will appear.

You can also view a list of special characters on the screen and select a character from it. Press Ctrl-B to see the special characters list. Use the PgDn and PgUp keys to move through the pages in the list. When you see the special character you want to insert in your chart, use the arrow keys to highlight it, and then press Enter to place it in the chart (at the cursor's position when you pressed Ctrl-B).

Note that although you can display the character on the screen, your printer may not be able to print it. Check your printer manual to determine which special characters it supports.

If you change the font or font style after entering special characters, they may disappear. Changing to another character set (different from the one you set up Harvard to work with) can also affect the special characters you entered. Always double-check your charts for accuracy.

WORKING WITH BULLET CHARTS

In this section, you will create a bullet chart. Then you will learn how to create build charts and modify a chart's bullets or layout.

HANDS-ON: CREATING A BULLET CHART

Start Harvard and follow these steps to create the sample bullet chart shown in Figure 3.8:

1. Press **1** from the Main menu, then **1** again to select the Text option and display the Text Chart menu.

Special Characters
in Swiss 721 Roman Font

10 (line feed)	144 É	162 ó	180 ┤	220 ▄
126 ~	145 æ	163 ú	186 ‖	223 ▀
128 Ç	146 Æ	164 ñ	187 ╗	230 μ
129 ü	147 ô	165 Ñ	188 ╝	241 ±
130 é	148 ö	166 ª	191 ┐	242 ≥
131 â	149 ò	167 °	192 └	243 ≤
132 ä	150 û	168 ¿	193 ┴	244 ¶
133 à	151 ù	170 ¬	194 ┬	245 §
134 å	152 ÿ	171 ½	195 ├	246 ÷
135 ç	153 Ö	172 ¼	196 ─	247 ≈
136 ê	154 Ü	173 ¡	197 ┼	248 °
137 ë	155 ¢	174 «	200 ╚	249 ▶
138 è	156 £	175 »	201 ╔	250 •
139 ï	157 ¥	176 ▒	207 ¤	251 √
140 î	158 Pt	177 ▓	217 ┘	252 *
141 ì	159 ƒ	178 ▦	218 ┌	253 −
142 Ä	160 á	179 │	219 █	254 ■
143 Å	161 í			

Figure 3.7: Special characters available in the Swiss 721 font

2. Press **2** to choose the Bullet option. The bullet chart data-entry screen will appear, with the cursor in the Title field, as shown in Figure 3.9.

3. Type **Text Attributes in Harvard** and press Enter. The cursor will advance to the next line, where you'll enter the subtitle.

Text Attributes in Harvard
Select from a variety attributes

- Swiss 721 in Roman is the text

- Outline looks like this

- Shadow looks like this

- *Slant looks like this*

- There are two text positions
  - This is subscript
  - This is superscript

- <u>Underline looks like this</u>

Figure 3.8: Sample bullet chart

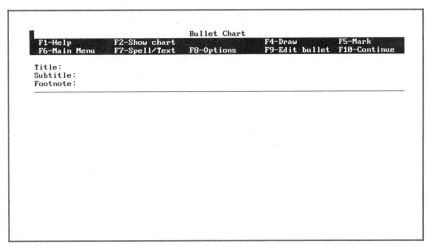

Figure 3.9: The bullet chart data-entry screen

4. Type **Select from a variety of attributes** and press Enter twice to move the cursor to the body of your chart. You'll now see a bullet on the screen, with the cursor a few spaces

to the right of it. You're ready to enter the first bulleted item.

5. Type **Swiss 721 in Roman is the text type** and press Enter. You won't see a bullet appear on the next line because you only pressed Enter once. (Harvard requires bulleted lines to be double-spaced, but you can add single-spaced subtopics with a different bullet character.)

6. Press Enter again to move to the next line and type **Outline looks like this**.

7. To change this line's attribute, press Shift-F5 to select the entire line. Press F10 to display the Marked Text Options box.

8. Use the arrow keys to move the cursor to the Outline field and press the spacebar to change the default to Yes.

9. Press Esc to return to the data-entry screen.

10. Press Enter twice to add another bullet, and then type **Shadow looks like this**. Press Shift-F5, then F10. Highlight the Shadow field using the arrow keys and press the spacebar to change the default to Yes. Press Esc to return to the data-entry screen.

In Harvard, Slant is sometimes used in place of an italic style.

11. Press Enter twice to add a new bullet and type **Slant looks like this**. Press Shift-F5, then F10. Highlight the Slant field and change it to Yes. Press Esc to return to the data-entry screen.

12. Press Enter twice, type **There are two special text positions,** and press Enter once.

13. To add a sub-bullet, press Ctrl-B to access the special characters list. Press the down-arrow key five times, and then press Enter to select and insert the dash as a sub-bullet. Leave the cursor on this line.

14. Press the spacebar twice to leave some space between the bullet and your text and type **This is subscript**.

15. Use the arrow keys to position the cursor under the first *s* in *subscript*. Press F5, then the right-arrow key eight times to

select the word. Press F10 and highlight the Text position field. Press the spacebar once to change the default setting to subscript, and then press Esc.

16. Press Enter to move down one line, press Ctrl-B, make sure that the dash is highlighted, and then press Enter to add another sub-bullet.

17. Press the spacebar twice to leave some space between the bullet and your text and type **This is superscript**. Mark the word *superscript*, and then press F10. Move down to the Text position field and press the spacebar twice to change the position to superscript.

18. Press Enter twice and type **Underline looks like this**. Press Shift-F5, then F10. Move to the Underline field, press the spacebar to change the setting to Yes, and then press Esc.

19. Save your bullet chart as **MYBULLET** using the Save Chart option on the File menu, and then print it using the Output option.

Refer to this chart, which should resemble Figure 3.8, to see what the marked text options look like. Because this chart provides examples of various text attributes, it contains more styles than you would normally include in a well-designed chart.

CREATING SUSPENSE WITH BUILD CHARTS

One way to keep your audience's attention is to build anticipation with a series of text charts that build on each other. For example, if you were giving a marketing presentation on Harvard, your bullet chart listing the text attributes in Harvard could be divided into a series of build charts rather than presented all at once. You would start with a chart that contains just the first bulleted item, then show the second chart listing the first item plus the next one, and continue presenting the other bulleted items one at a time by building on the previous charts.

It takes time to create a series of six individual build charts. Fortunately, Harvard provides an autobuild feature that makes a full list into a series of charts for you. You create the final chart and save it as an Auto-Build chart.

Follow these steps to make MYBULLET into a series of build charts:

1. Retrieve the MYBULLET file and press Ctrl-S to display the Save box.

2. Press Enter until your cursor is positioned on the Auto-Build field, press the spacebar to change the entry to Yes, and press Enter. You will see the Auto-Build Bullet Chart box.

The Build type field in the Auto-Build Chart box has three options: Sequential, Highlighted, and Both. The Both option, the default, shows the current item and the previous ones, with the current item highlighted. The Sequential option displays the current item and the previous items. The Highlighted option shows all the items in each build chart but highlights the current one. For a true build chart series, keep the Build type option set to Both.

3. Press F10 to save the autobuild series.

You must print each chart made with the Auto-Build option separately.

Harvard creates and saves the five build charts for you while leaving your original intact. They will be named MYBULLET.CH3, MYBULLE1.CH3, MYBULLE2.CH3, and so on. You can print the original and autobuild charts as you would regular charts.

You can create autobuild charts from any type of text chart: title, bullet, or table. Just change the Auto-Build field to Yes when you save the text chart and set the options in the Auto-Build box, if necessary.

CHANGING BULLET SHAPES, SIZES, COLORS, AND POSITIONS

In addition to modifying the text's appearance in your charts, you can change the bullets themselves as well. To do this, press F8 to access the Options menu, and then press **5** to display the Bullets Options box, shown in Figure 3.10. The Bullet type field should be

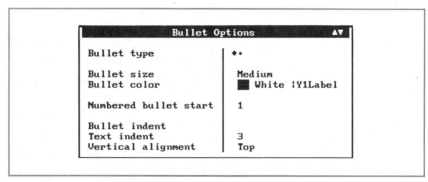

Figure 3.10: The Bullet Options box

highlighted. Press the spacebar until you see the type of bullet you want, or press F3 to select from a list of bullet types.

The other options in the Bullet Options box allow you to change the size (Small, Medium, or Large) and color of your bullets, and to adjust the indentation and vertical alignment of the text in your bullet charts. Figure 3.11 illustrates the choices for bullets. Press the spacebar after you highlight the option you want to change, or press F3 to select from a list of choices.

After you select bullet options, press Esc to return to the data-entry screen. All the bullets will be changed to conform to your selections. If you chose bullets 1. or I., the bullets will be replaced by arabic or roman numerals. You can change the starting number for these types of bullets by entering a new number in the Numbered bullet start field in the Bullet Options box.

Selecting from the Bullet Options box changes all the bullets in the chart. If you want to selectively edit one bullet, move your cursor to the line containing the bullet and press F9 to display the Edit Current Bullet box. Choose from the options in this box to change the bullet type, size, and color for the selected bullet line.

WORKING WITH TABLE CHARTS

Building a table chart is a quick and easy way to arrange text in neat columns. The steps you follow to create this type of chart are similar to those for creating other text charts. In this section, you will

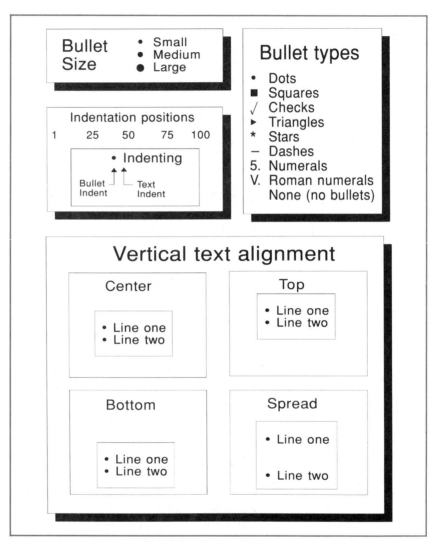

Figure 3.11: Bullet options for types, sizes, indentation, and alignment

In general, use only whole numbers in table charts. Round fractional numbers so they look better in the columns and are easier to read.

create a three-column chart. You can create table charts with up to twenty-four columns.

By default, Harvard automatically adjusts the size and alignment of your chart's rows and columns. Columns are left aligned when they contain text, and they are right aligned and decimal-point aligned when they contain numbers.

HANDS-ON: CREATING A TABLE CHART

In the following steps, you will create the table chart shown in Figure 3.12.

1. From the Main menu, press **1** to select Create chart, press **1** to choose Text, and press **3** to select Table. The table chart data-entry screen will appear, as shown in Figure 3.13. Notice that each column has a blank header area where you type the description for the column.

2. Type **Ocean Areas and Depths** for the title and press Enter.

3. Type **for the world's largest bodies of water** for the subtitle and press Enter.

4. Type **Depth in feet** for the footnote and press Enter.

5. You'll now see the cursor in the first column header area. Type **Name** as the column header, and then press Tab to move to the next header.

Ocean Areas and Depths
for the world's largest bodies of water

Name	Sq. Miles	Avg. Depth
Pacific Ocean	64,186,300	12,925
Atlantic Ocean	33,420,000	11,730
Indian Ocean	28,350,500	12,598
Arctic Ocean	5,105,700	3,407
South China Sea	1,148,500	4,802
Caribbean Sea	971,400	8,448
Mediterranean Sea	969,100	4,926
Bering Sea	873,000	4,926
Gulf of Mexico	582,100	5,297
Sea of Okhotsk	391,100	3,192

Depth in feet

Figure 3.12: Sample three-column table chart

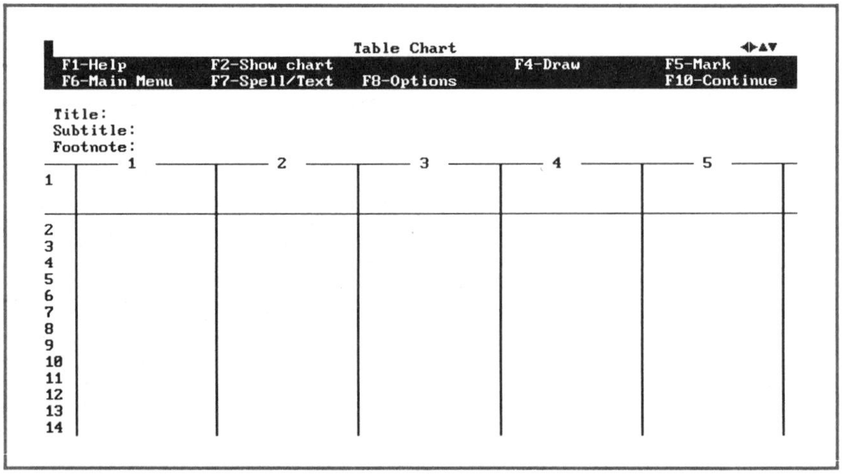

Figure 3.13: The table chart data-entry screen

6. Type **Sq. Miles** and press Tab.

7. Type **Avg. Depth**, press Enter twice, and press Shift-Tab twice to move to the first column's data area.

8. Type the following values in the Name, Sq. Miles, and Avg. Depth columns. Press Tab to move to the next column, and press Enter after each line. Don't worry about aligning your numbers because Harvard does it for you.

As you type in the ocean names, some of you text will scroll out of view to the left, but don't worry—the complete names will appear on the chart.

Pacific Ocean	'64,186,300	12925
Atlantic Ocean	'33,420,000	11730
Indian Ocean	'28,350,500	12498
Arctic Ocean	'5,105,700	3407
South China Sea	'1,148,500	4802
Caribbean Sea	'971,400	8448
Mediterranean Sea	'969,100	4926
Bering Sea	'873,000	4893
Gulf of Mexico	'582,100	5297
Sea of Okhotsk	'391,100	3192

Once you use the single quotation mark to treat a number as text, continue using it for all the numbers in that column or they won't align properly.

You're probably wondering why you typed the ' in front of the second column values. Unfortunately, Harvard displays table chart numbers above 9,999,999 in scientific notation, even when you set Harvard to use standard notation. The single quotation mark (') tells Harvard to treat the following numerals as text values. Since these numbers become text characters, you must type in the comma because you cannot set a thousands separator for text values.

9. Press F8 and type **6** to display the Column Options box, shown in Figure 3.14.

10. Move the cursor to the Text alignment field in Col 2 and press **R** for right alignment. Press Tab and then **R** to set Col 3 to use right alignment as well.

11. Move to the Thousands separator field, and in Col 3, change the setting to Yes.

12. Press F2 to see your chart; it should resemble Figure 3.12. When you're finished, press Esc until you return to the data-entry screen.

13. Save your chart as **MYTABLE.CH3**.

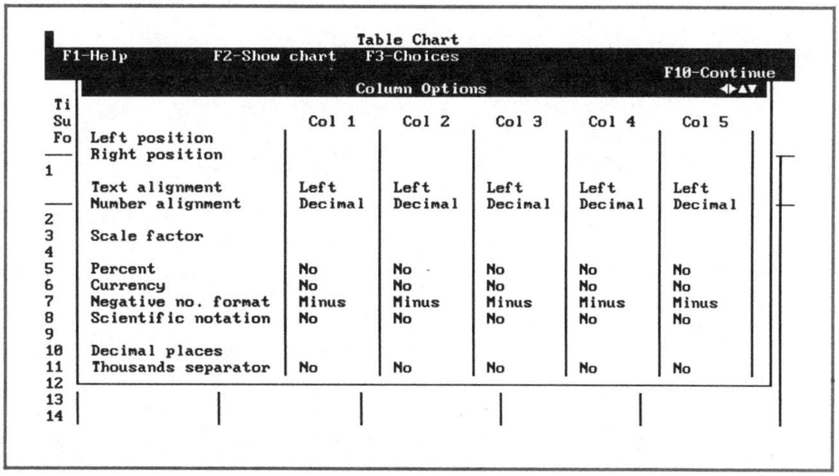

Figure 3.14: The Column Options box

MODIFYING COLUMN FORMAT, ALIGNMENT, AND SCALE

In the previous section, you used the Column Options box to change the text alignment in two columns and set the thousands indicator to appear in a column. As you saw, this box contains quite a few options for fine-tuning your table charts.

You can select from left, center, right, spread, and decimal (for numbers) alignment; choose minus or parentheses as a negative number format; and display numbers with a percent symbol, dollar sign, in scientific notation, or with a thousands separator. The effects of these options are illustrated in Figure 3.15.

Another option in the Columns Option box is Scale factor. If you want the numbers in a column divided by a scale factor, enter the value for the factor under the appropriate column. For example, instead of entering the large numbers in the second column of our table chart as text (so they wouldn't be put in scientific notation), you could have entered them as numbers, and then set column 2 to a scale factor of 100. Then the number 64,186,300, for example, would appear as 641,863. If you are using a scaling factor, don't forget to note it in the column heading, as in *Sq. Miles (in Thousands)*.

The Left position and Right position choices at the top of the box can be used in conjunction with other options to adjust the column spacing, as explained in the next section.

Always note the scale factor in your table chart; otherwise, the numbers will be misinterpreted.

CHANGING COLUMN OR ROW SPACING

To change the column or row spacing on your chart, you must first access the Table Options box and turn off automatic table sizing. Then set the column positions in the Column Options box, or the row positions in the Row Options box. Follow these general steps to adjust the column or row spacing in a table chart:

1. Press F8 from the table chart data-entry screen to access the Options menu, and then press **5** to display the Table Options box, shown in Figure 3.16.

2. In the Automatic table sizing field, press the spacebar to change the setting to No. Press Esc to return to the data-entry screen.

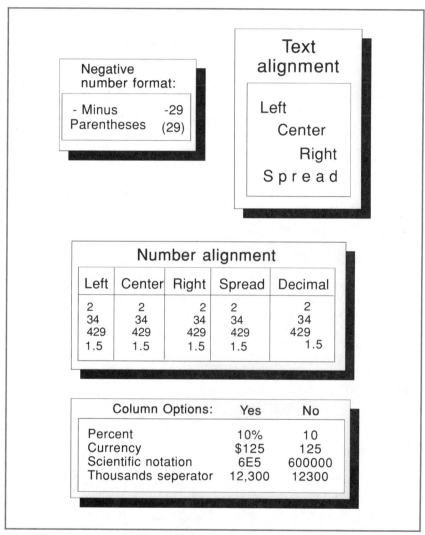

Figure 3.15: Effects of Column Options box settings

3. Press F8 to access the Options menu again.

4. Change the column or row spacing as follows:

 • To adjust the column spacing, press **6** to access the
 Column Options box, and type new values, from 0 to
 100, for the left and right starting positions of the

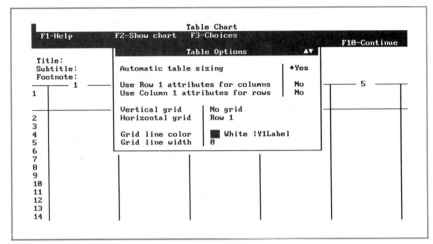

Figure 3.16: The Table Options box

columns you want to adjust. The starting positions are measured from the extreme left side of your chart, the 0 position, to the extreme right edge, the 100 position. Figure 3.17 illustrates some left and right positions.

- To adjust the row spacing, press **7** to access the Row Options box. Enter new values, from 0 to 100, for Top position and Bottom position to set the positions for each row to be changed. Position 0 is at the extreme top of the chart, and position 100 is at the very bottom.

5. Press F10 to return to the data-entry screen.

To ensure that all the text in the table is a consistent size, set Text overflow to Truncate. You can then adjust the size of the text in the table until it fits properly.

Changing the column or row spacing for a chart can affect the text in the table. Figure 3.18 illustrates how the Text overflow settings (in the Appearance Options box) can change the text appearance when you turn off automatic table sizing. You should always check the chart's appearance by pressing F2 after changing its spacing. You might find that some columns are truncated and that the text is in mixed sizes.

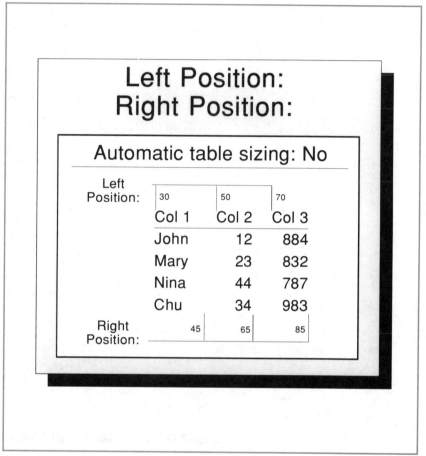

Figure 3.17: Setting column positions

CHANGING GRIDS
AND TABLE TEXT ATTRIBUTES

The Table Options box also contains options for changing the table grid's appearance and applying text attributes to entire columns or rows. As illustrated in Figure 3.19, you can set a horizontal grid, a vertical grid, or both for individual columns and rows or for all of them. By combining horizontal and vertical grids, you can have horizontal and vertical lines on your chart.

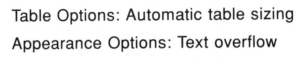

Table Options: Automatic table sizing

Appearance Options: Text overflow

Automatic table sizing: Yes
Text overflow: Truncate

	On Hand
Disk Drives	4
VGA Monitor	6
Laser Printer	2

Automatic table sizing: Yes
Text overflow: Shrink-to-fit

	On Hand	On Order
Disk Drives	4	0
VGA Monitor	6	2
Laser Printer	2	3

Automatic table sizing: No
Text overflow: Truncate

	On Hand	On Order
Disk Drives	4	0
VGA Monitor	6	2
Laser Printer	2	3
Super 1029 Ma	0	2

Automatic table sizing: No
Text overflow: Shrink-to-fit

	On Hand	On Order
Disk Drives	4	0
VGA Monitor	6	2
Laser Printer	2	3
Super 1029 Mainframe	0	2

Figure 3.18: Changing row or column spacing can affect text

To quickly apply text attributes to all the rows or columns in a table chart, first use the Mark option (press F5) to change the attributes of the text in the first column or row, and then use the Table Options box to set the same attributes for the rest of the rows or columns.

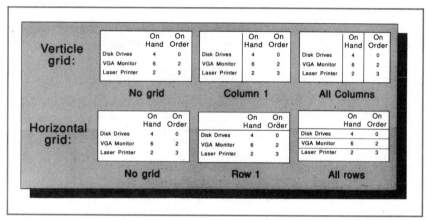

Figure 3.19: Using grids on table charts

Set Use Row 1 attributes for columns to Yes when you want all the rows in your chart to have the same attributes. For example, if the first row in column 1 is italic, all rows in column 1 will be set to italic. If the first row in column 2 uses red text, all rows in that column will be displayed in red.

Set Use Column 1 attributes for rows to Yes when you want the text in the rows to use the attributes set in column 1. For example, if row 5 in the first column is underlined, then row 5 will be underlined in all columns.

When both Use Row 1 attributes and Use Column 1 attributes are set to Yes, Harvard ignores the row settings and uses only the column 1 attributes.

CHANGING THE TEXT SIZE

You may find that the text in your table chart is too big or small to fit properly in the columns. You can change the size of the text through the Text Attributes box. Press F8 to display the Options menu, then 2 to see the default settings for the size, color, alignment, font, and font style, as shown in Figure 3.20.

Harvard allows only one size setting for the text in the body of your chart.

To change the size of your text, place the cursor on the appropriate field in the Size column and enter a new number, ranging from 0 to 100 (including decimals). Compare the different text sizes listed in Figure 3.21 with the inch ruler in that figure. Actual text sizes may vary depending on your output device and printing choices, so differences in text sizes are relative. For example, size 8 is always twice the height of size 4, regardless of which output device you use.

```
                              Table Chart
   F1-Help            F2-Show chart   F3-Choices
                                                          F10-Continue
                              Text Attributes                  ▲▼

                        Size        Color      Alignment  Font Name    Font Style
        Title           9        █ White !Ti   Center     Swiss 721    Roman
  −     Subtitle 1      5        █ White !Su   Center     Swiss 721    Roman
  1     Subtitle 2      5        █ White !Su   Center     Swiss 721    Roman

  −     Table           7        █ White !Te   Left       Swiss 721    Roman
  2
  3     Footnote 1      3.5      █ White !Fo   Left       Swiss 721    Roman
  4     Footnote 2      3.5      █ White !Fo   Left       Swiss 721    Roman
  5     Footnote 3      3.5      █ White !Fo   Left       Swiss 721    Roman
  6
  7     Legend title    3.5      █ White !Y1   Center     Swiss 721    Roman
  8     Legend labels   3.5      █ White !XL   −          Swiss 721    Roman
  9
 10  │           │            │          │            │
 11  │           │            │          │            │
 12  │           │            │          │            │
 13  │           │            │          │            │
 14  │           │            │          │            │
```

Figure 3.20: The Text Attributes box

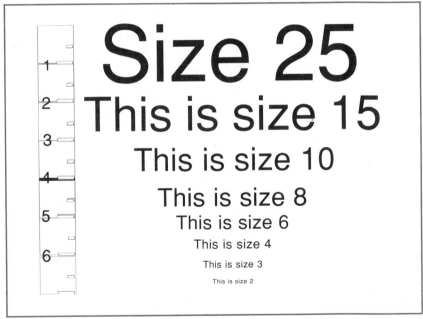

Figure 3.21: The relative text sizes in Harvard

Try changing your chart's Table text size from Harvard's default to 4 and then press F10 to return to the data-entry screen. Press F2 to view your chart and see how the different size looks. You can also use Table 3.1 to determine the right size for your chart's text. Note that

Table 3.1: Chart Text Size Guide

LANDSCAPE			PORTRAIT			
NUMBER OF CHARACTERS	SINGLE SPACING	DOUBLE SPACING	SIZE	NUMBER OF CHARACTERS	SINGLE SPACING	DOUBLE SPACING
6	2	1	**35**	5	3	2
7	2	1	**30**	6	3	2
10	3	1	**25**	7	4	2
12	3	2	**20**	9	5	3
17	3	3	**15**	12	6	4
25	6	4	**10**	18	9	6
32	8	5	**8**	23	11	7
42	11	6	**6**	29	15	9
48	13	8	**5**	36	18	11
58	16	10	**4**	43	22	13
60	21	13	**3**	60	30	18
60	32	18	**2**	60	44	24
60	48	24	**1**	60	48	24

the table is only an approximate guide because Harvard uses proportional spacing, which can vary the number of characters per line. The smallest size listed in the table matches Harvard's limit of 48 lines and 60 characters.

To use Table 3.1, count the number of characters, including spaces, in the longest line of the chart, and then count the number of lines. Look in the table, under the appropriate orientation (landscape or portrait) and find the size that fits both your chart's spacing and number of characters. Set the Size option for Table in the Text Attributes box to this size, and then view the chart. If your lines are still too long, consider splitting them into two lines. If you have too many lines, consider paring down the current chart's contents or creating a second chart.

Be careful when selecting small type sizes. Don't use sizes smaller than 4, or your audience won't be able to read the chart. If your text is smaller than size 8, be sure to double-space it for maximum readability.

Not all the space on a chart is in a printable area. Because Harvard reserves a small margin up to 1 inch around your chart, all your text may not be printed, even though you see some additional space on the paper. The type of printer you use affects the printable area of your chart.

If you are not using a title or subtitle in your chart, you can capture the additional space at the top of your chart by changing its line size to 0.

PUTTING RANGES IN YOUR TABLE CHART

Use Harvard's Range options when you want to emphasize or group ranges of values in your table chart. Figure 3.22 shows an example of a chart that uses shading to group ranges of sales figures. By highlighting ranges, you make it easier for the audience to compare the values.

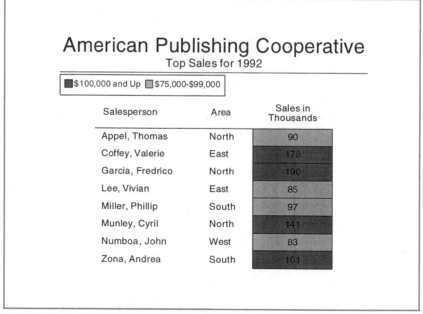

American Publishing Cooperative
Top Sales for 1992

■$100,000 and Up □$75,000-$99,000

Salesperson	Area	Sales in Thousands
Appel, Thomas	North	90
Coffey, Valerie	East	178
Garcia, Fredrico	North	190
Lee, Vivian	East	85
Miller, Phillip	South	97
Munley, Cyril	North	141
Numboa, John	West	83
Zona, Andrea	South	101

Figure 3.22: A sample table chart with ranges

You define ranges through the Range Options box. Follow these general steps to set up ranges in a table chart:

1. Press F8 to access the Options menu, and then press **8** to select Range and display the Range Options box, shown in Figure 3.23.

2. Press **Y** to change the Use ranges field to Yes, and then press Enter.

3. You can press Enter at the Show values field and leave the default Yes, which shows the numbers in the column, or press the spacebar to select No, which removes the numbers and shows only the shading, and then press Enter.

4. The choices for the Use color field are Cell or Values. The Cell option colors the whole *cell*, or the block in which the number appears, and Values colors only the number. Press the spacebar to toggle between the options. (Figure 3.22 uses the Cell setting.)

5. Move to the line under Legend, and type a descriptive range value. In Figure 3.22, the first description is *$100,000 and Up*.

You provide more information to your audience by leaving Show values set to Yes; they will see both the shading that represents the values and the actual numbers.

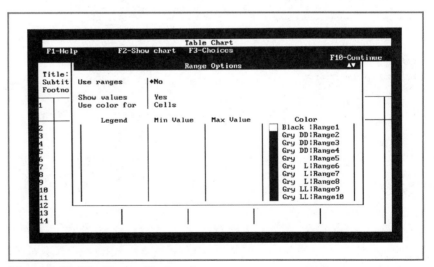

Figure 3.23: The Range Options box

6. Move to the Min Value column and type the lowest value for the range (it should match the legend description). For the sample chart, the minimum value is 100.

7. In the Max Value column, enter the highest value for the range. In Figure 3.22, the maximum value is 200.

8. Move to the Color column and press F3 to select from a list of colors for the range. Highlight your choice and press Enter.

9. Repeat steps 5 through 8 for each range you want to define in the table chart.

10. Press F10 to return to the data-entry screen.

11. Press F8, then **9** to display the Legend Options box. The cursor will be on the Show legend field.

12. Press **Y** to choose Yes and place a descriptive legend on the table chart. You will learn about the legend options in Chapter 5. For now, press F10 to accept the default settings and return to the data-entry screen.

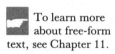 When necessary, convert numeric entries to text by preceding them with a single quotation mark (') to ensure that they are not converted into ranges.

WORKING WITH FREE-FORM TEXT USING DRAW

To learn more about free-form text, see Chapter 11.

The Draw option is one of Harvard's best features because it provides almost limitless capabilities. You can add text, letters, and special characters anywhere you like and in whatever size or attribute you desire. You can even use different text sizes in the chart's body, and on the same line if you like.

To use the Draw option with a text chart, just type in that chart's title and subtitle in its data-entry screen. Then you can create the rest of the chart using the Draw option's Add command.

HANDS-ON: ADDING CUSTOMIZED TEXT TO A CHART

Although you probably didn't know it when you bought this book, you also get a free certificate of accomplishment as a Harvard Master without any additional cost—all you have to do is design it.

Follow these steps to begin creating the certificate chart shown in Figure 3.24:

1. From the Main menu, press **1**, then **1**, then **2** to choose a bullet chart and display the bullet chart data-entry screen.

2. Type **Harvard Master** in the Title field and press Enter.

3. To change the size of the title line, press F8 to access the Options menu, and then press **2** to select the Text attributes option.

4. Move to the Title field in the Size column and change the setting to 14.

5. Press Tab three times to move to the Font Name column, and then press the spacebar until the name HG GOTHIC appears.

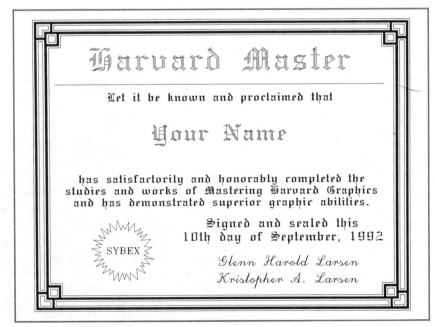

Figure 3.24: Your Harvard Master certificate

6. Press PgDn to move to the Appearance Options box. Make sure the Chart orientation is set to Landscape. If it is not, move to Chart orientation and press the spacebar.

7. Press Esc to leave the Text Attributes box and return to the data-entry screen.

Now that you have set up your chart, you are ready to add its body text with the Draw option.

You might find displaying a ruler on the screen is helpful while you are creating the diploma. From the Draw screen, press F8, then **3**, and change the Show rulers setting to Yes. Press F10 to continue.

8. Press F4 to select the Draw option from the data-entry screen. You can also choose Draw from the Main menu by pressing **3**. You will see the Draw screen, as shown in Figure 3.25.

9. Using the arrow keys, move the pointer (the Draw cursor) to the Text tool (with the letters Abc) in the right column and press Enter. The cursor may change shapes as you move it around the Draw screen. Also, the default settings for Draw may have been reset if you or someone else already used this option. You might have to peek ahead to

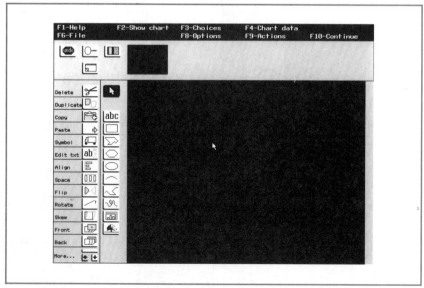

Figure 3.25: The Draw screen

Chapter 10 to learn about the basics of Draw if you have trouble creating your diploma.

10. Move the pointer to the Font field and press the spacebar. Then move the cursor up to the HG GOTHIC option and press Enter.

11. Move the pointer onto the edit screen. The pointer will become a cross-hairs shape. Now move the cross-hairs cursor until it is about $1/2$ inch under the letter *H* in *Harvard* and press the spacebar.

12. Move the cross-hairs cursor straight across the screen until you are under the letter *r* in the word *Master*. Next, move the cursor down until the width of the rectangle is about $1/2$ inch and press Enter. A box for entering text appears.

13. Type **Let it be known and proclaimed that**.

14. Press Esc to exit the text box. Notice that Harvard automatically centered your text within the box.

15. Move up to the small slider bar on the top of the screen, position the pointer over the right-arrow box, and press the spacebar until the size is set for 10.

16. Move back onto the edit screen and position the cross-hairs cursor about $1/4$ inch under the *L* of *Let* and press the spacebar.

17. Move the cursor across the screen until it is positioned under the second *t* in the word *that*, and then move the cursor down about 1 inch and press Enter.

18. Type in your name and press Esc.

19. Move the cursor up to the ruler and change the size setting back to 5.

20. Return the cursor to the edit screen, position it about $1/2$ inch under your name on the far-left edge of the screen, and press the spacebar.

21. Move the cursor across the screen to the far-right edge, move it down about 2 inches, and press Enter.

22. Type the following sentences in the text box that appears, pressing Enter after each line.

    has satisfactorily and honorably completed the

    studies and work of Mastering Harvard Graphics

    and has demonstrated superior graphic capabilities

23. Press Esc, and then move the cursor up to the ruler and change the size to 5.5.

24. Starting on the right edge of the edit screen, about 1 inch under the last line you typed, move the cross-hairs cursor over 5 inches and then down about ¾ inch, and then press Enter.

25. Type the following lines, pressing Enter after each one. Replace *number* with the day number, as in 10th if today is the tenth of the month. Replace *month, year* with the current month and year, as in January 1992.

    Signed and sealed this

    number **day of** *month, year*

26. Press Esc, and then move the cursor back up to the ruler and change the size to 6. Also, change the font to HG SCRIPT.

27. Add another text box. Start the box on the right edge of the screen, about a ¼ inch under the date line, and move it to the left until the cross-hairs cursor is positioned under the starting point of the date line. Then move the cursor down about 1 inch and press Enter.

28. Type **Glenn Harold Larsen**, press Enter, type **Kristopher A. Larsen**, and then press Esc.

Now that you have entered the text using the Draw option, you are ready to continue and add the other elements.

HANDS-ON: ADDING SYMBOLS TO YOUR CHART

Now you will see how easy it is to add a graphic symbol to a chart. You will use the Draw option's commands to create the "official seal."

1. Select the Symbol tool in the left column, and then choose
    the Get icon the menu that appears.

2. Move the cursor to the file called STARS1.SY3. This file
    contains the starburst that you will use on the certificate.

3. Press Enter to use the highlighted file. Your screen should
    look like the one shown in Figure 3.26.

4. Move the cursor to the box whose symbol looks like the one
    in Figure 3.24, press Enter to highlight it, press F10, and
    then press Esc. The box that appears on your chart is
    where Harvard proposes that you place the symbol.

5. Move to the center of that box and press and hold down the
    spacebar. Using the arrow keys, position the symbol, refer-
    ring to Figure 3.24 as a guide.

6. After you have positioned the starburst, change the text size
    to 4 and the style to ROMAN.

7. Make a text box, type **SYBEX**, and press Esc twice. Move

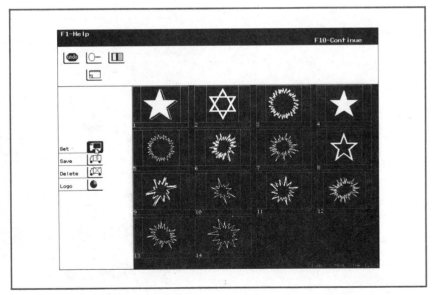

Figure 3.26: Selecting a symbol

the cursor to the center of the text box and press the spacebar. A four-tipped arrow will appear. Using the arrow
keys, move the text box into the center of the starburst.

HANDS-ON: ADDING THE BORDER

The only item left to add to your chart is the border. Follow these
steps:

1. Choose the Symbol tool and then select the Get icon.

2. Move the cursor to BORDER.SY3. You will see the screen
   shown in Figure 3.27, showing the border styles in this file.

3. Move the pointer to the border shown in the bottom-left
   corner, press the spacebar to highlight the Name field for
   this border, press Esc, and press F10. The border will
   appear on your chart.

4. Move the pointer to the middle of the border and press the
   spacebar. Now, using the arrow keys, move the bottom-left

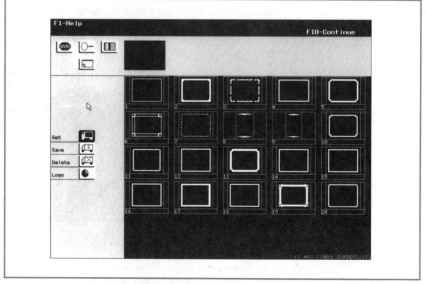

Figure 3.27: Choosing a border

corner of the border down to the bottom-left corner of the screen and press Enter.

5. Move the pointer up to the upper-right corner of the frame surrounding the border and place the pointer precisely on the handle at this corner. Press the spacebar. The pointer should turn into a two-headed arrow. Use the arrow keys to move the upper-right corner of the border up to the upper-right corner of the screen, and then press Enter.

CORRECTING ERRORS
WITH THE DRAW OPTION

Always save your chart before deleting items. You may delete too much or change your mind.

If you find a mistake when you check over your chart, you can correct it easily. To remove an error, use the Draw option's Delete command. Return to the Draw screen by pressing **3** from the Main menu. Move the pointer to the object that you want to delete and press Enter. Harvard will place a thin frame around the object. Next, move the cursor to the Delete button, press the spacebar, and then press Enter.

If your text or symbol is correct but in the wrong place, you can move it instead of deleting it. To move an object, place the pointer on it and press Enter to select it. Then press the spacebar and use the arrow keys to move the object to the proper location.

CHECKING YOUR SPELLING

You're not finished with the certificate yet. You should always check to see if your spelling is correct. Even if they are not apparent to you, your audience will catch your spelling errors. It's better to let Harvard find them instead. The spelling checker will also find repeated words, such as *the the*. However, it won't find text or numbers with improper punctuation, such as *15,00*.

To use Harvard's spelling checker, press **2** to select Edit chart from the Main menu, and then press F7 to choose Spell/Text. You will see the Spell/Text menu, as shown in Figure 3.28.

If you misspelled any words, Harvard will display them one at a time on the screen. Even if you spelled everything in your certificate

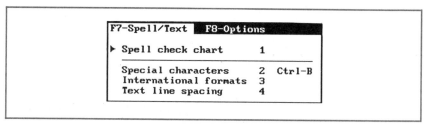

Figure 3.28: The Spell/Text menu

correctly, Harvard will display some of the proper names and tell you that they are not in the dictionary, as shown in Figure 3.29. You can then take one of the following actions:

- If Harvard presents a word that is correct but is also one you probably will not use again, press Enter or **1** to continue checking the text.

- If the word is correct and you will use it frequently, you can add it to Harvard's dictionary by highlighting the Add option and pressing Enter. Harvard will continue checking the text, and it will never flag that word again in any of your charts.

- If the word is misspelled, highlight the Type correction option and retype it correctly, or highlight the Select a suggested spelling option to have Harvard list possible corrections and choose one of the suggested words.

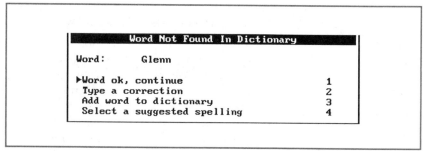

Figure 3.29: Harvard reports a word not found in its dictionary

When the entire chart has been checked, you will see the message

Spell check complete

Press Esc twice to return to the Main menu. Then you can save your chart as **DIPLOMA** using the Save Chart option on the File menu, and print it using the Output option.

SUMMARY

You have learned how to create all the types of text charts, and you know how their design affects you, your organization, and the charts' contents.

In addition to creating bullet, table, and build charts and adding free-form text with the Draw option, you have learned how to check the spelling of your charts, which helps ensure that each completed chart is professional-looking.

In Chapter 4, you will learn how to master the creation of pie charts. You will find that many of the techniques you learned in this chapter can be applied to pictorial charts, since you will often add text to them.

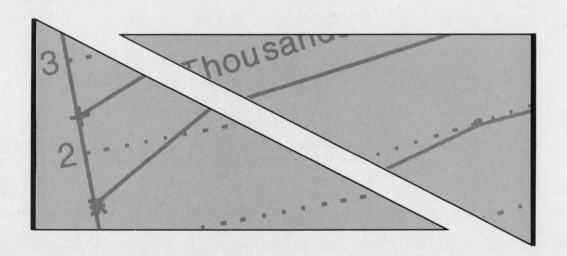

Creating Pie Charts

CHAPTER *4* _____

A PIE CHART PRESENTS THE ELEMENTS IN A SINGLE series as wedges in a circle, or slices in a pie. When used with the appropriate data and design, they can be very informative and attractive. In Chapter 2, you created a pie chart using the Chart Gallery. In this chapter, you will learn how to design your own pie charts.

_____ *WHEN TO USE A PIE CHART* _____

Pie charts are ideal for showing percentages of a whole, such as how each division in an organization contributes to the total of sales. Each slice of pie is a data element in the series—the whole pie. Pie charts are useful for illustrating the following types of data:

- Sales income
- Expense and budget breakdowns
- Market shares
- Population components
- Ratios

Once you decide to present your data in a pie chart, consider whether several pies will work better than just one. Remember that you cannot have more than one series in a single pie. For example, you might want to design a chart with two pies, each showing a different year's financial data. Then your audience will be able to see the changes in percentages from one year to the next.

Although you can place up to six pies in a single chart, too many pies will clutter up the chart. Also, it is not a good idea to place more than seven slices in a single pie.

After you choose the number of pies, you need to decide which type of pie chart to use. You can choose between a cut, proportional, linked, or 3D pie chart. The following sections describe these variations.

FOCUSING ATTENTION ON A SLICE

You can cut a slice from a pie to emphasize its data. For example, if you are designing a pie for a company's sales, you may want to pull out the slice for the division with the highest sales percentage.

Cut only one or two slices from a pie. Otherwise, the chart will look cluttered and it will be difficult for your audience to compare the elements.

LINKING PIES AND PERCENTAGE BARS

You may want to use a pie chart but find that you have too many data elements—the sizes of the resulting pie slices would be difficult to compare, and their labels would run together. To get around this problem, you can create a chart within a chart by treating a cut slice as both part of the whole series and as its own series. As you can see in Figure 4.1, the cut slice links the pie's elements to the data elements on the percentage bar.

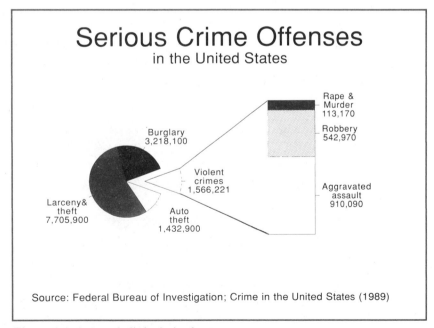

Figure 4.1: A sample linked pie chart

Your information will be clearer if you use a pie and a percentage column in a linked chart.

When linking charts, you can choose to have the cut slice's chart displayed as either a pie or percentage bar. We suggest using a percentage bar to display the linked graph; otherwise, it could take your audience a while to figure out that the two pies aren't two separate series.

BEWARE OF PROPORTIONAL PIE CHARTS

Although you can use two or more pies in your graph to show their relative value, you may unintentionally deceive your audience. For example, Figure 4.2 contains a proportional pie chart showing the relative sales of a bakery's pies. On a daily basis, it markets and sells twice as many apple pies as it does blueberry pies. Thus, the apple pie in Figure 4.2 should be twice as big as the blueberry pie. Do you think it is?

If your answer is no, you're mistaken but not alone. For many people, it's difficult to determine circular proportions because they

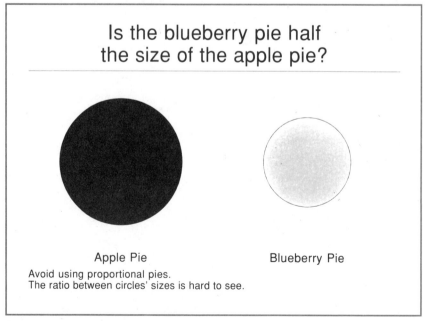

Figure 4.2: A proportional pie chart

You want your charts to be easily understandable, so avoid comparing pie sizes.

think in terms of linear distance. Mathematically, the apple pie is twice the area of the blueberry pie, just what it should be.

Worse yet for your audience is a proportional pie chart that has a percentage bar or one that uses 3D effects. Because these elements do not have similar shapes, the information you are trying to present is lost.

WORKING WITH 3D EFFECTS

Even though they are interesting to look at, 3D pie charts can mislead your audience. Figure 4.3 shows a pie that is evenly divided in half. However, because the closer half is lighter than the other half (a trick for showing perspective), it may look larger.

Don't let artistic style distort your charts. A chart's primary function is to inform. Style is always secondary to meaning.

Because a 3D perspective in a pie chart can be confusing, refrain from using this option in your pie charts. Otherwise, your chart's credibility may be questioned.

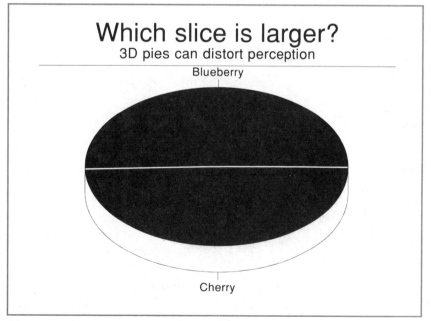

Figure 4.3: Creating a 3D effect in your pie charts

DESIGNING EFFECTIVE PIE CHARTS

Ideally, your charts should be both accurate and artistically appealing. Your audience will be captured by an attractive graph and will, therefore, understand its message quicker—provided its message is clear.

PLACING THE ELEMENTS

You should arrange your data from the largest element to the smallest, unless you want to emphasize a particular element. Your most important element should start at the 3 o'clock position on the pie. The other elements should progress in importance in a counterclockwise direction, with each subsequent slice a lighter color. Fortunately, Harvard does this for you automatically, so you do not have to worry about slice placement unless you rearrange the slices (using the Sort slice option, described later in the chapter).

SELECTING CHART PATTERNS

The patterns on a pie chart can affect its readability drastically. For example, after looking at the patterns in Figure 4.4 for a while, you will think that the lines waver. You may even see little circles moving about. This illusion is known as the *moire effect*. You will usually see it on pop-art calendars or posters (which are about the only places it belongs).

If you use seven or fewer slices in your pie chart (as we recommend), you can choose patterns that don't create this effect. However, if you have more slices, you will run out of good combinations and may have to start using pop-art patterns.

The patterns in the printed output may not match the ones you see on the screen.

Appendix E shows some of the palettes available with Harvard 3.0. The palette you select affects the shading and patterns used by your output device. By default, Harvard uses the HG3.PL3 palette, shown in Figure 4.5 (for standard printers) or Figure 4.6 (for PostScript printers or plotters). It contains 12 patterns, numbered from 0 to 11.

When printing your pie charts with slices, you will notice that Draft mode shows wider lines with greater spacing, which adds to the moire effect. High mode's better quality makes finer lines, minimizing the pop-art look.

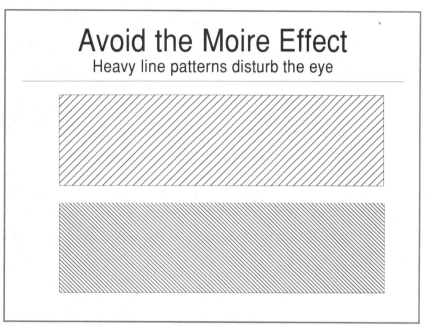

Figure 4.4: Harvard patterns can create a moire effect

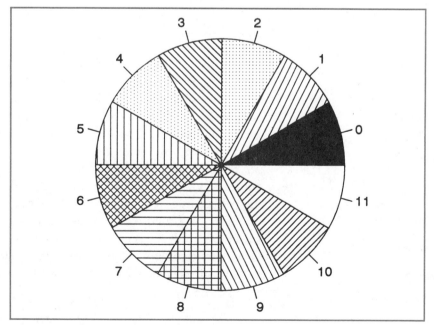

Figure 4.5: Default HG3.PL3 patterns on a standard printer

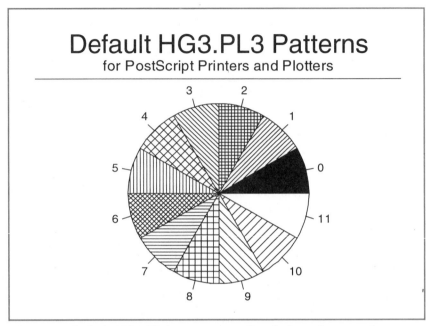

Figure 4.6: Default HG3.PL3 patterns on a PostScript printer or plotter

SELECTING COLORS

When you display charts on your color monitor or print them on a color printer, plotter, or film recorder, you have a wide range of colors to choose from in addition to the 12 patterns. Harvard automatically assigns a color to each pie slice, but you can select other colors, as explained later in the chapter.

The colors you see on the monitor and the shading that your output device uses will vary according to the palette you select and the output device itself. Color numbers are keyed to parts of the chart, such as the title, text, series1, and so on. As you change palettes, new colors are assigned to the color number and the chart part that it's keyed to. Table 4.1 shows color numbers, codes, and the chart parts they affect. Remember that colors and code names can vary, but the color numbers and chart parts they affect remain the same.

Palettes like HG3.PL3 look good in color but produce poor black and white (B&W) printed copies. Conversely, the MONOB&W.PAL palette produces better B&W output but looks terrible in color. Appendix E explains how to create your own palette.

Table 4.1: Harvard's Selection of Colors

COLOR NUMBER	CODE	CHART PART
1	Title	Chart title
2	Subtitle1	Subtitle, first line
3	Subtitle2	Subtitle, second line
4	Text	Main text in chart
5	TextHigh	Highlighted text (used in autobuilds)
6	TextDim	Dimmed text (used in autobuilds)
7	footnote	Footnote text
8	XLabel	X-axis label
9	Y1Label	Y1-axis label
10	Y2Label	Y2-axis label
11	Xtitle	X-axis title
12	Y1Title	Y1-axis title
13	Y2Title	Y2-axis title
14	Frame	Frame and legend outlines
15	FrameBkg	Frame fill color
16	Bullet	Bullets in text charts
17	BulletDm	Bimmed bullets (used in autobuilds)
18	Lines	Lines in organization charts, and in linked pies
19	Shadow	Shadows for 3D charts
20	Legend	Legend fill color
21	Series1	Series 1 (used in pie and XY charts)
22	Series2	Series 2 (used in pie and XY charts)
23	Series3	Series 3 (used in pie and XY charts)
24	Series4	Series 4 (used in pie and XY charts)

Table 4.1: Harvard's Selection of Colors (continued)

COLOR NUMBER	CODE	CHART PART
25	Series5	Series 5 (used in pie and XY charts)
26	Series6	Series 6 (used in pie and XY charts)
27	GoalY1	Goal zone in Y1 axis
28	GoalY2	Goal zone in Y2 axis
29	Draw1	Used for drawing
30	Draw2	Used for drawing
31	Draw3	Used for drawing
32	Outlines	Outlines in series
33	Range1	Ranges for table charts
34	Range2	Ranges for table charts
35	Range3	Ranges for table charts
36	Range4	Ranges for table charts
37	Range5	Ranges for table charts
38	Range6	Ranges for table charts
39	Range7	Ranges for table charts
40	Range8	Ranges for table charts
41	Range9	Ranges for table charts
42	Range10	Ranges for table charts
43–64	Custom	Unassigned

Figure 4.7 shows a sample pie chart produced using the default HG3.PL3 palette. Palette color names often combine the color, intensity, and code. For example, Blue D | Series 2 means a dark blue color that fills the second slice in a pie chart. Intensity values include the following:

- DD for darkest
- D for dark

Be careful to check how the color selections print in black-and-white charts. For example, you can't distinguish between Series 5 and 6 in Figure 4.7.

- L for light
- LL for lightest

The darker colors dominate the chart and should be reserved for elements you want to emphasize. Use lighter colors for less important elements. Rather than displaying many colors, consider using one or two colors with patterns in your charts. Combining colors and patterns also helps to differentiate colors that don't show enough contrast.

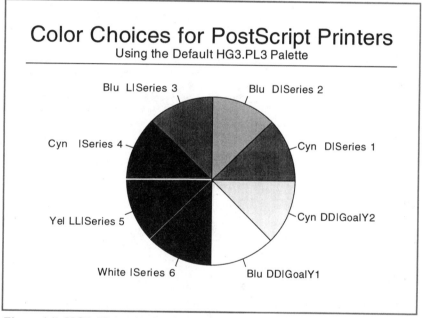

Figure 4.7: HG3.PL3 colors printed in black and white (B&W)

WORKING WITH PIE CHARTS

Creating a pie chart is a little different than creating a text chart. When you choose Text from the Create Chart menu, you see another menu from which to select the type of text chart. When you choose Pie, the pie chart data-entry screen appears immediately. You create the chart first, and then choose the enhancements.

CH. 4

Always use percent-
age figures in your
pie charts. Adding dollar
amounts, however, is
optional.

To create a pie chart, press **1** from the Main menu, then **2** from the Create Chart menu. This displays the first pie chart data-entry screen, labeled Pie Chart 1, as shown in Figure 4.8.

Enter a title, subtitle, footnote, and labels, as you did for the sample pie chart in Chapter 2. You can enter up to 22 characters for each label. Type the numeric values for the labels in the Value column. For example, you might enter the label Payroll and the value $105,600 for a pie chart showing company expenses.

When you set the Cut Slice column to Yes for a slice, it will be extracted from the pie, as explained earlier in the chapter. The two other columns, Color and Pattern, contain Harvard's default settings, which you can change as described shortly.

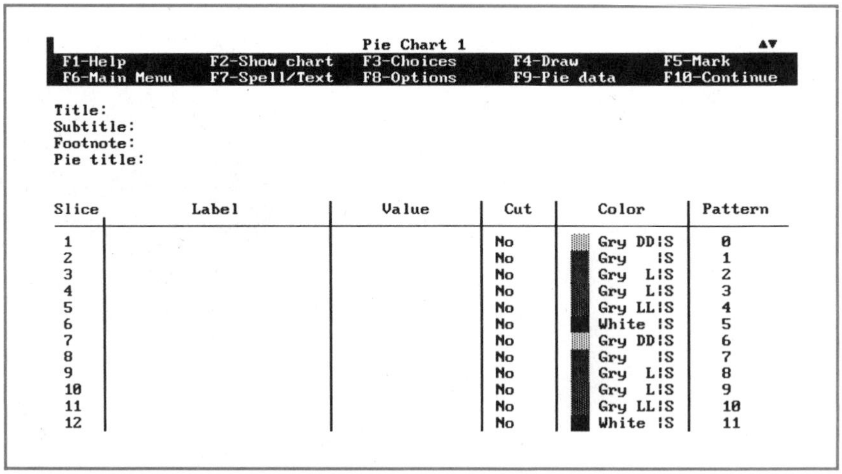

```
                            Pie Chart 1                             ▲▼
   F1-Help         F2-Show chart   F3-Choices     F4-Draw        F5-Mark
   F6-Main Menu    F7-Spell/Text   F8-Options     F9-Pie data    F10-Continue

 Title:
 Subtitle:
 Footnote:
 Pie title:


 Slice       Label              Value        Cut     Color      Pattern

   1                                         No    ▓ Gry DD!S      0
   2                                         No    ▓ Gry    !S     1
   3                                         No    ▓ Gry  L!S      2
   4                                         No    ▓ Gry  L!S      3
   5                                         No    ▓ Gry LL!S      4
   6                                         No    ▓ White !S      5
   7                                         No    ▓ Gry DD!S      6
   8                                         No    ▓ Gry    !S     7
   9                                         No    ▓ Gry  L!S      8
  10                                         No    ▓ Gry  L!S      9
  11                                         No    ▓ Gry LL!S     10
  12                                         No    ▓ White !S     11
```

Figure 4.8: The pie chart data-entry screen

DELETING, INSERTING AND MOVING PIE SLICES

You can easily edit and rearrange pie slices on the data-entry screen, as follows:

- To remove a slice, place the cursor in the slice's row and press Ctrl-Del.

- To insert a slice, place the cursor in the row where you want to add the slice and press Ctrl-Ins.

- To move a slice to a new position, move the cursor to its row, and then press Ctrl-up arrow to move the slice up a row, or Ctrl-down arrow to move it down a row.

After you modify your chart, be sure to press F2 to check its readability. You may need to reassign colors or patterns to the slices if the original ones are not right for the new order.

PLACING SEVERAL PIES ON ONE CHART

As mentioned earlier, you can enter data for up to six pies on one chart. Figure 4.9 shows examples of charts showing from one to six pies.

The first screen displayed when you choose Pie from the Create Chart menu is for the data for the first pie in the chart, as indicated by the title at the top of the screen, Pie Chart 1. To enter data for a second pie, press Ctrl-PgDn. The next screen's title is Pie Chart 2, and the data you enter here will be used for the second pie. Continue pressing Ctrl-PgDn to enter data for pies 3 through 6. Press Ctrl-PgUp to return to the previous pie's data-entry screen.

CUSTOMIZING YOUR PIE CHARTS

You can customize your pie charts by using the selections on the Options menu, shown in Figure 4.10. To display this menu, press F8 from the pie chart data-entry screen.

The Text Attributes option on this menu works the same as the one on the text chart's Options menu, as explained in Chapter 3. The only difference is that you have extra lines for the titles and labels.

The other options for pie charts are described in the following sections.

CHANGING SLICE PATTERNS AND COLORS   By default, your pie slices are colored, not patterned. If you want to use patterns for

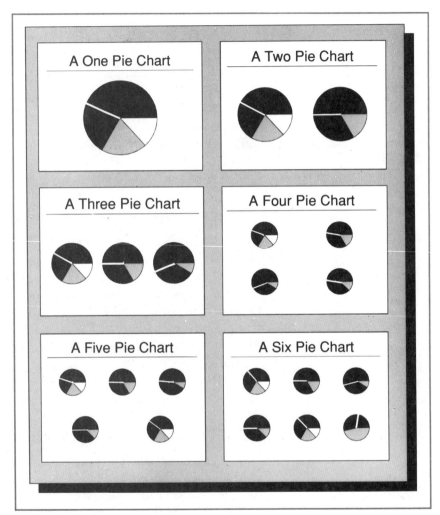

Figure 4.9: Creating one to six pies

your slices, press F8 from the data-entry screen, and then choose Style from the Options menu. This displays the Style Options box, shown in Figure 4.11.

Move the cursor to the Slice fill style field and press F3 to list the options Color, Pattern, or Both. If you have a black-and-white printer and monitor, set Slice fill style to Pattern. If you have a color monitor and a black-and-white printer, use the Both option (for colored patterns). You must set the Slice fill style for each chart.

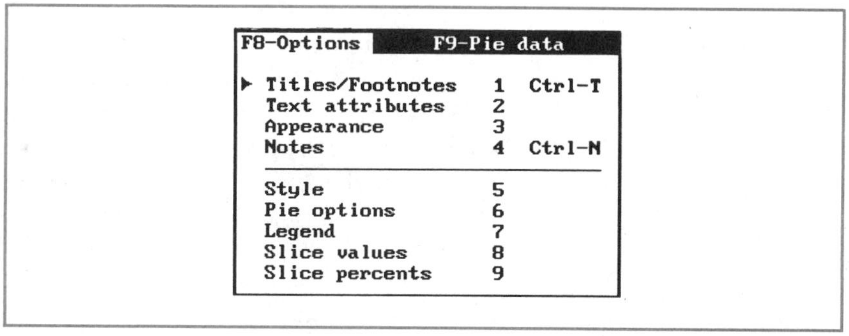

```
┌─────────────────────────────────────────┐
│  ┌───────────────┬──────────────────┐    │
│  │ F8-Options    │   F9-Pie data    │    │
│  ├───────────────┴──────────────────┤    │
│  │▶ Titles/Footnotes    1   Ctrl-T  │    │
│  │  Text attributes     2           │    │
│  │  Appearance          3           │    │
│  │  Notes               4   Ctrl-N  │    │
│  │  ─────────────────────────────   │    │
│  │  Style               5           │    │
│  │  Pie options         6           │    │
│  │  Legend              7           │    │
│  │  Slice values        8           │    │
│  │  Slice percents      9           │    │
│  └──────────────────────────────────┘    │
└─────────────────────────────────────────┘
```

Figure 4.10: The pie chart Options menu

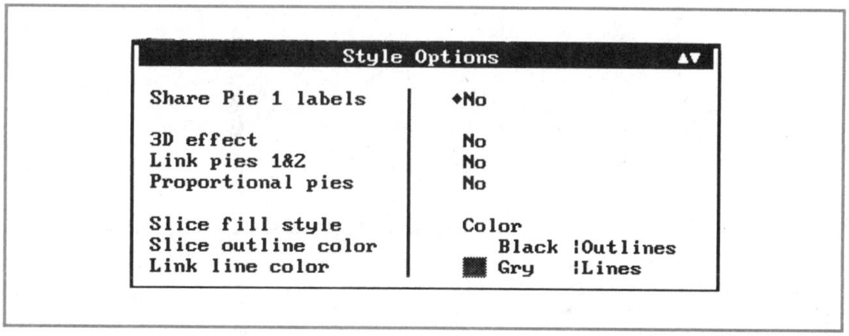

```
┌───────────────────────────────────────────────┐
│   ┌──────────────────────────────────────┐     │
│   │         Style Options            ▲▼  │     │
│   │                                      │     │
│   │  Share Pie 1 labels    ◆No           │     │
│   │                                      │     │
│   │  3D effect             No            │     │
│   │  Link pies 1&2         No            │     │
│   │  Proportional pies     No            │     │
│   │                                      │     │
│   │  Slice fill style      Color         │     │
│   │  Slice outline color       Black !Outlines │
│   │  Link line color       ■ Gry   !Lines│     │
│   └──────────────────────────────────────┘     │
└───────────────────────────────────────────────┘
```

Figure 4.11: The Style Options box

For the best color or pattern effects, work from dark to light. Fluctuating between dark and light makes it difficult to see pie shading differences.

Although the F3-Choices option is always on the pie chart data-entry screen, you can only use it in the Color column. It will not work in the Pattern column.

If you want to change the default pattern for a slice after choosing to use patterns, press F10 to return to the data-entry screen and use the arrow keys to move to the row for that slice. Then press the Tab key to move the cursor to the Pattern column and replace the pattern number with the number of the pattern you want to use (see Figure 4.5 or 4.6).

You do not need to go through the Options menu to change a slice's color. To change a color, move to the Color column on the data-entry screen and press F3. A list of available colors will appear. Highlight the color you want to use and press Enter.

Through the use of color, you can create build pie charts, similar to text build charts (although there is no autobuild feature for pie charts). On the first build chart, hide all your slices except the first one. You hide slices by assigning them background colors. On the second pie chart, show only two slices, and so on until all your pie slices are revealed.

CHOOSING A PIE CHART STYLE The other settings in the Style Options box establish the style for the chart. As discussed earlier in the chapter, you should decide which style fits your data before you create the pie chart. After entering the data, select the variation you want from the Style Options box. Use the arrow keys to move to the different fields, and press the spacebar to toggle between Yes and No.

You can combine the Proportional style with either the 3D or Link style. Additionally, you can combine the 3D effect with the Link style. Figure 4.12 shows the effects you can achieve with the selections in the Style Options box.

Using the Proportional style with the 3D style usually distorts the pie and makes it harder to understand.

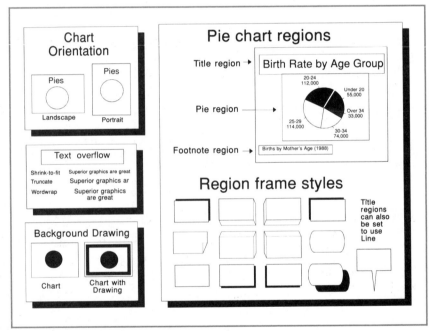

Figure 4.12: Changing your pie chart's style

The Titles/Footnotes and Notes options are also available on the text chart Options menu. Press F8 from the text chart data-entry screen and then select one of these options to add extra lines of text or enter notes.

ADDING AND CHANGING TITLES AND FOOTNOTES Choose Titles/Footnotes from the Options menu to edit or enter line of text for titles, subtitles, footnotes, and legend titles. This option displays the Titles/Footnotes box, shown in Figure 4.13. Each line holds 100 characters. You can also display the Titles/Footnotes box by pressing the Ctrl-T speed key from the data-entry screen.

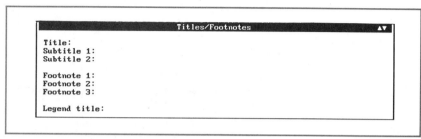

Figure 4.13: The Titles/Footnotes box

Set the Appearance options before you enter data. If you type the data first and then set the Appearance options, the chart might not appear as you intended.

ADJUSTING THE CHART'S APPEARANCE The Appearance option on the pie chart Options menu is similar to the text chart Appearance option, which is described in Chapter 3. The main difference is how the regions are defined in the chart. Figure 4.14 illustrates the effects of the settings in the pie chart Appearance Options box.

ADDING NOTES Select Notes from the Options menu (or use the Ctrl-N speed key) when you want to record a note. The Notes box, shown in Figure 4.15, will appear. You can enter a note of up to 11 lines, with 60 characters per line, for your chart.

Print the notes separately or with your charts to remind yourself of important information. This way, you can plan your presentation while creating your charts. Note that you can print notes only for charts included in presentations. See Chapter 12 for more information.

FORMATTING PIE CHARTS

The other selections on the pie chart Options menu are useful for formatting your pie charts, as described in the following sections. After you select one of these options and display its choices, move to the one you want to use with the Tab, Shift-Tab, and arrow keys, and then use the spacebar to cycle through the options or insert a number.

You will notice that there is a column for each pie. To format a chart with just one pie, make the changes in the Pie 1 column and forget about the other columns. For a two-pie chart, make the changes in the Pie 1

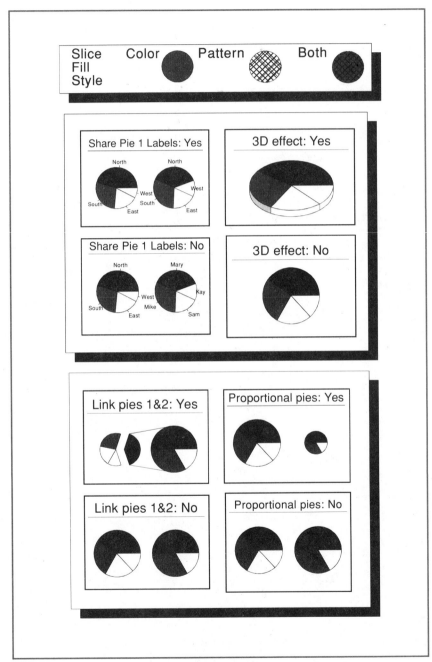

Figure 4.14: Effects of pie chart Appearance Options box settings

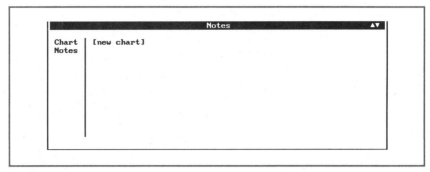

Figure 4.15: The Notes box

and Pie 2 columns. You will need to adjust the settings in the appropriate column for each pie you want to affect. Press Tab to move forward through the pie columns; use Shift-Tab to move backward.

MAKING ADJUSTMENTS WITH THE PIE OPTIONS

Select Pie from the pie chart Options menu to display the Pie Options box, shown in Figure 4.16. Here, you set whether you are creating a pie or column chart. The box also has options for sorting your slices, setting the 3D slice depth, and controlling the display of labels and pointers. If you are creating a chart with several pies, you can set separate options for each pie. For example, in a three-pie chart, you can set the labels so that they only appear on two of the pies.

```
┌─────────────────────────────────────────────────────────────────────┐
│                          Pie Options                          ◆►▲▼   │
│                    Pie 1            Pie 2            Pie 3            │
│   Show pie        ◆Yes             Yes              Yes              │
│   Show as          Pie             Pie              Pie              │
│                                                                      │
│   Pie size         100             100              100              │
│   Starting angle   0               0                0                │
│                                                                      │
│   Sort slices      No              No               No               │
│   Slice pointer    Short           Short            Short           │
│   3D slice depth   30              30               30               │
│                                                                      │
│   Show slice labels Yes            Yes              Yes              │
└─────────────────────────────────────────────────────────────────────┘
```

Figure 4.16: The Pie Options box

Select from the following pie options:

- Show Pie: Sets the display of the selected pie. Use this option to hide a pie if you do not want to show all the pies in a chart with multiple pies.

- Show As: Displays your series as either a pie or column. Use the Column setting for Pie 2 in a linked-pie chart.

- Pie Size: Sets the size of the pie. Enter a number from 1 to 100. Larger numbers make bigger pies. However, keep in mind that the larger the pie, the more likely the labels for thin pie slices will run together. Experiment with your pie's size to balance these two extremes. You cannot use this option to set different sizes for pies in the same chart. Harvard will ignore the Pie size setting for all pies except Pie 1.

Try changing the starting angle to prevent pie slice labels from running into each other.

- Starting Angle: Sets a starting angle for your first slice. Choose a number from 0 to 359. Starting angle 0 is at the 3 o'clock position, angle 90 is at 12 o'clock, angle 180 is at 9 o'clock, and angle 270 is at 6 o'clock. Keep your most important pie slice between the 0 and 90 angle, because this is the area viewers will focus on.

- Sort Slices: Sorts pie slices from the largest to the smallest, which can give a degree of order to jumbled pies. However, it's better to enter the data in the order you want it presented so that you do not disrupt the graduation of the slices' color or patterns. Because the slices are sorted by their rows on the data-entry screen, whatever values you set in their Color or Pattern column remain with them. To keep the same order of patterns or colors, you can reassign the pattern or color values after you sort the slices.

- Slice Pointer: Sets the length of the line that runs from the label to the pie slice (the pointer). Choose None (for no pointer), Short, Medium, or Long.

- 3D Slice Depth: Sets the thickness of the 3D pie. Enter a number from 0 to 100, with 100 producing the thickest slices.

In general, you should enter pie chart labels either on the data-entry screen or create your own labels with the Draw option. Do not present a pie chart without any labels at all.

- Show Slice Labels: Sets the display of slice labels. Use this option to hide your labels if they are running together and you want to create labels inside the slices with the Draw option.

Figure 4.17 illustrates some of the effects of the settings in the Pie Options box.

ADDING A LEGEND TO A PIE CHART

Legends duplicate the labeling function by showing the description and colors or patterns used in the pie. You may want to show a legend instead of labels when you have several pies on a chart or many slices in a pie. The audience might find it easier to read the larger legend than each tiny label pointing to a slice.

To display a legend, choose Legend from the Options menu. You will see the Legend Options box, shown in Figure 4.18. Change the Show legend setting to Yes.

Figure 4.19 shows the positions you can assign to your legend. To change the default position, move the cursor to the Legend location field and press the spacebar to cycle through the 12 positions. You can also change the Legend frame style setting by using the spacebar to cycle through the styles. You will learn more about legends in the chapters about XY charts.

ADJUSTING SLICE VALUES

You can fine-tune the way that the numbers appear on your pie chart by choosing Slice values from the Options menu. This displays the Slice Values box, as shown in Figure 4.20, which contains the following options:

When you are working with thin slices, place the values next to your labels to keep each slice's value and label separate from the others.

- Show Values: Controls whether or not the numeric values of pie slices appear.

- Place Values: Places the numeric values below or next to the label, or inside the pie slice itself. If you choose Inside placement, be sure that dark patterns don't obscure the value (you can't see black numbers on a black pattern).

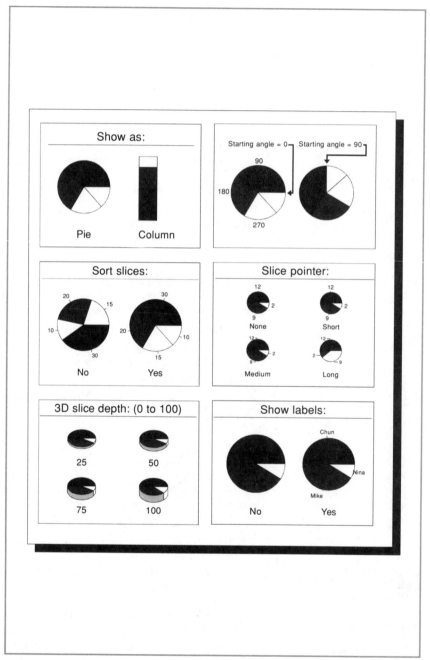

Figure 4.17: Effects of the Pie Options box settings

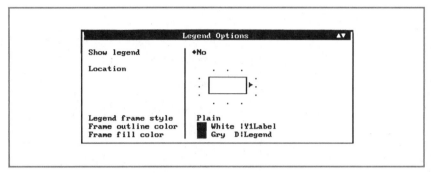

Figure 4.18: The Legend Options box

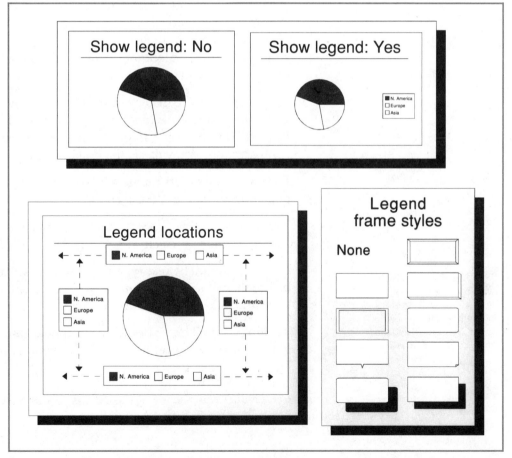

Figure 4.19: Effects of the Legend Options box settings

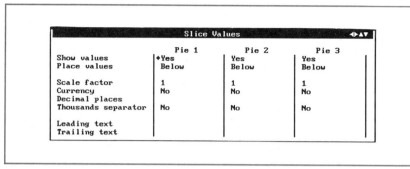

Figure 4.20: The Slice Values box

- Scale Factor: Divides the value by the number entered. For example, if you enter 100 for the scale factor, the number 1000 will appear on the chart as 10. Don't forget to include a line in the chart's footnote to tell the audience about the scale factor, or they may be misled by the values.

- Currency: Sets the display of the data as monetary values, using the monetary symbol you established when you configured Harvard (see Chapter 1). If you are using the U.S. configuration, you will see the dollar sign ($).

- Decimal Places: Sets the number of decimal places to appear in the values on the chart.

- Thousands Separator: Sets the display of a comma to separate thousands in pie chart values, as in 2,000,000.

- Leading Text: The text typed in this field will appear before the values. For example, you could enter *approx.* to have it appear before values, as in approx. 5.

- Trailing Text: The text typed here appears after the values. For example, you could enter *yearly* to identify annual figures.

If you want to include a special character in your leading or trailing text, you can press Ctrl-B to select from the special characters list.

Figure 4.21 illustrates some of the effects of the Slice Values box settings.

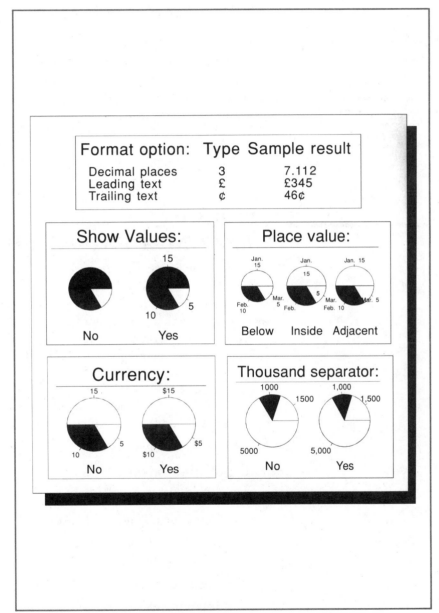

Figure 4.21: Effects of the Slice Values box options

SETTING SLICE PERCENTS

Showing both the values and percents in a pie chart can be confusing. If you must show both, set either Place value or Place percent to Inside.

Choosing Slice percents from the Options menu displays the Slice Percents box, which is similar to the Slice Values box, but it has fewer selections. Change the Show percents setting to Yes to display percentages for the slice values. For Place percents, you can choose to place the percentages below or next to the label, or inside the pie slice.

The other Slice Percents box settings—Decimal places, Leading text, and Trailing text—serve the same purpose as they do in the Slice Values box. Figure 4.22 shows some examples of the effects of the settings.

HANDS-ON: CREATING A TWO-PIE CHART

You'll now create a chart with two pies using several of the options you've read about in this chapter. You're going to make the chart shown in Figure 4.23, which compares the two parts of a financial balance sheet. Because total assets equal total liabilities and capital, the assets are presented in one pie and the liabilities and capital are shown in the other. Start creating your chart by following these steps:

1. Press **1** at the Main menu to select the Create chart option. Then press **2** to select the option for creating a pie chart. The Pie Chart 1 screen will appear.

2. Type the following lines in the Title and Subtitle fields:

   Warby Corporation's

   1991 Balance Sheet Analysis

3. In the Pie title field, type **Assets**.

4. In the Label and Value columns, type these label names and values for the first pie chart:

Fixed Assets	92200
Investments	49800
Current Assets	46500
Good Will	15000

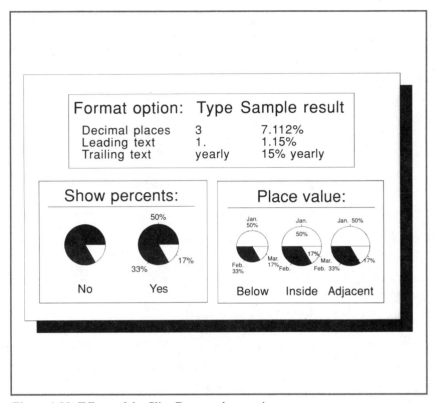

Figure 4.22: Effects of the Slice Percents box settings

Most financial charts compare both actual dollar values and percentages, so you'll show both in this chart. This means that for maximum readability, you'll have to put either the values or percentages within the pie slices and rearrange the patterns so that the numbers inside the pies are readable. You'll use patterns 4, 5, 3, and 6 to present your first four elements in order from darkest to lightest (see Figures 4.5 and 4.6).

5. Press Tab to move the cursor to the first row under the Pattern column, change the first slice's pattern from 0 to 4, and press Enter. Change the Investments slice's pattern from 1 to 5 and press Enter. Change the third slice's pattern to 3 and press Enter. Change the fourth slice's pattern from 3 to 6.

6. Press Ctrl-PgDn to enter the data for the second pie. The Pie Chart 2 screen will appear.

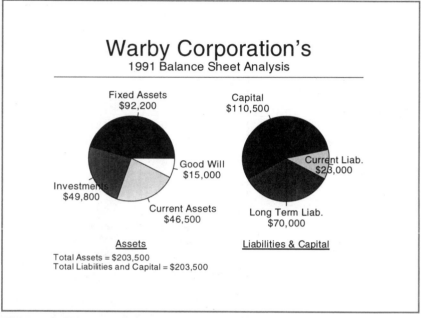

Figure 4.23: The sample two-pie chart

7. Type **Liabilities & Capital** in the Title field, and then enter the following data in the Label, Value, and Pattern columns:

Capital	110500	4
Long Term Liab.	**70000**	**5**
Current Liab.	**23000**	**3**

8. Press F8 to display the Options menu, and then press **1** to access the Titles/Footnotes box.

9. Move to the Footnote 1 field, type **Total Assets = $203,500**, and press Enter. Add a second line to your footnote by typing **Total Liabilities and Capital = $203,500**.

10. Press Esc to return to the Pie Chart 2 screen.

11. Move to the Pie title field and press Shift-F5 to highlight the field. Then press F10, move to the Underline option, and press the spacebar to select Yes.

You had just enough space to type that last line. If you didn't, you could have continued typing the footnote on a third line, or you could have used Draw to add text.

12. Press Esc, then Ctrl-PgUp to return to the Pie Chart 1 screen.

13. Move to the Pie title field, press Shift-F5, press F10, move to the Underline option, press the spacebar to select Yes, and then press Esc.

14. You have entered most of the components for the two-pie chart. See how it looks so far by pressing the F2 key.

It doesn't look very good, does it? The first pie's Current Assets label collides with the second pie's Long Term Liab. label. To correct this, you can shorten the labels, change their starting angles, or make each pie smaller. In this case, the pie labels can't be shortened without affecting their readability, so you will rotate the slices.

15. Press Esc to return to the data-entry screen. Then press F8 and select Pie options. Move to the Pie 2 column and change the Starting angle setting to 13. This rotates the second pie's starting angle just enough to prevent its text from mixing with the first pie's.

16. Press F2 again and see if the text looks better now. Press Exc, and then press PgDn twice to move to the Slice Values box.

17. Change the Thousands separator setting to Yes (by pressing the spacebar) for both the Pie 1 and the Pie 2 columns.

18. Since the chart shows dollar amounts, move the cursor to the Currency option and select Yes in both the Pie 1 and the Pie 2 columns. Press Esc to return to the data-entry screen.

19. You have finished customizing the chart. Now press F7 to check the spelling in it.

20. For a last check, press F2 to view your chart. It should look like the one shown in Figure 4.23. If everything is correct, press Esc.

21. After correcting any errors, press Ctrl-S to save the chart as **WARBY**, and then print it in High mode using the Output option on the File menu.

SUMMARY

You have now explored the use of pie charts. You learned how to emphasize important elements and choose the pie chart that will best present your data. You are also starting to become familiar with combining colors and patterns in your charts.

In this chapter, you have been working with only one data series. In the next chapter, you'll learn how to create charts using two or more series.

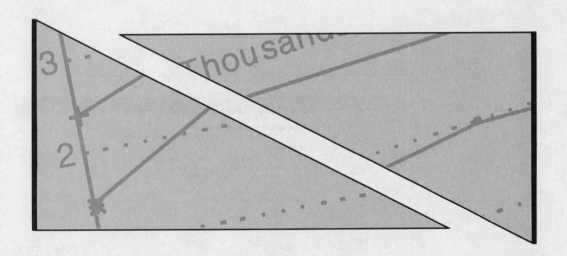

Creating Bar and Line Charts

CHAPTER 5

WITH HARVARD'S XY CHART OPTIONS, YOU CAN create various types of bar and line charts in a wide variety of styles. As always, you need to examine your data and objectives carefully when selecting your bar or line chart's type and style.

SELECTING AN XY CHART TYPE

When you're designing an XY chart, your first decision is which type of chart to use. To select an XY chart type, press **1** from the Main menu, and then press **3** to choose XY from the Create Chart menu. The XY menu, shown in Figure 5.1, displays the following choices:

- Bar
- Stacked bar

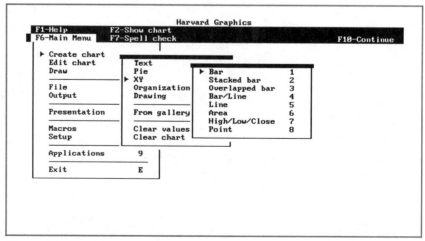

Figure 5.1: The XY menu

- Overlapped bar
- Bar/Line
- Line
- Area
- High/Low/Close
- Point

Figure 5.2 shows how each of these types of charts displays the data.

You can display 1000 values per series—more than you should ever need.

Harvard lets you display up to 16 series in a chart. Remember, each series is composed of one or more data elements. However, you should limit your chart to fewer than 4 series to prevent it from appearing cluttered. If your data is complex, consider using several charts.

WHEN TO USE A BAR CHART

As you learned in Chapter 2, bar charts are the simplest for audiences to understand. Use them to show volume and simple time comparisons. You can group bars together to compare data elements of different series. For example, the bar chart in Figure 5.2 shows four groups containing a data element (bar) from each of the series. You shouldn't have more than 12 to 15 bars in your chart. This means that if you arrange your data into five series, you can compare at most three groups of data elements from those series.

Along with a simple bar chart, which you created in Chapter 2, you can choose from the following bar chart types:

- Stacked Bar Chart: Stacked bars are used to show parts of the total over time, such as sales for several departments. Data that is suitable for a multiple pie chart usually is also appropriate for a stacked bar chart. In fact, the rules for good pie charts are also applicable to stacked bar charts.

- Overlapped Bar Chart: When you want to demonstrate the relationships between groups of series, use an overlapped bar chart, which stresses relationships between series more than a simple bar chart does.

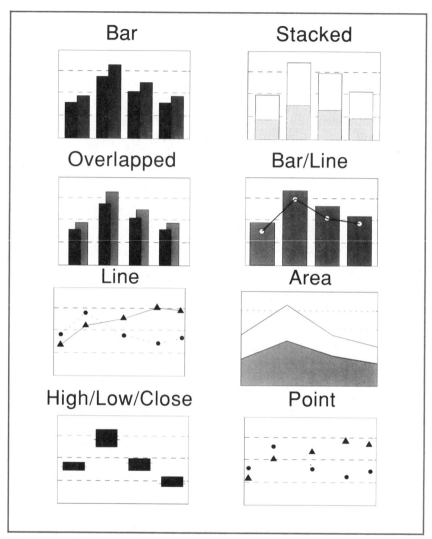

Figure 5.2: Choosing a chart type to fit your data

MIXING SERIES TYPES WITH BAR/LINE CHARTS

Use a bar/line chart to help distinguish different types of data on the same chart. For example, in a chart showing product sales versus product costs, you could use bars to show the sales and a line to show the cost of goods.

You can include a trend line or average line with bars to clarify the pattern or trend for your data. For example, you could create a series of bars to show a corporation's sales over a 12-month period, and then copy the sales data to a second series to display a trend line. The bars show the changes in sales from month to month, and the trend line shows whether overall sales are up or down. You could also include an average line to show the average sales volume.

WHEN TO USE A LINE CHART

An area chart also shows data fluctuations; however, it emphasizes volume rather than changes.

You can include a larger number of elements in a line chart than you can in a bar chart. For example, 50 years of statistical data would make a bar chart too cluttered, while the same data in a line chart would be easy to understand.

Although each line, which is a series, can contain many data elements, limit the number of series you display. Using more than five series in a line chart will make it very difficult to read.

Both normal (zigzag) and curved lines show the amount of change from one data point to another. Although you can easily identify the data fluctuations by looking at the zigzag line's angles and height, the curved line is better for displaying gradual changes or general trends, as in frequency distributions. See Chapter 2 for a discussion of zigzag versus curved lines

Harvard provides a variety of different line chart types from which to choose: trend, average, step line, exponential, log regression, and power regression.

As mentioned in the previous section, a trend chart shows the direction toward which the data elements are moving over time. Use it to make sense out of fluctuating or scattered data. When you choose this type of chart, Harvard averages the series' data to make a straight line, which is known as the *best-fit line*. Trend lines have the same advantages and limitations as curved lines.

Step lines are good for illustrating frequency distributions, ranges, and cumulative totals. The angular lines simulate stair steps.

The average, exponential, log regression, and power regression types show statistical functions in the line chart. Harvard computes these statistics automatically from the data you enter.

WHEN TO USE AN AREA CHART

Area charts combine lines with patterns or colors to indicate volume. Like a stacked bar chart, an area chart shows several series stacked on top of one another. The top line in the area chart shows the cumulative total of all the series.

Use an area chart for a single series when you want to emphasize changes in its data. You can also use a line chart for a single series, although a line chart doesn't stress the overall pattern as much as an area chart does. However, its data values are easier to pinpoint. (See Figure 5.2 to compare an area chart with a line chart.)

When you create an area chart, work from dark to light so your darkest patterns will be on the bottom of the stack and the lightest on top. This prevents the layered series from looking top heavy. Also, to minimize distortion, you should place the series with the greatest fluctuation on the top of the stack.

Once you have found a good color and pattern combination in an area chart, save it as a template for others.

WHEN TO USE A HIGH/LOW/CLOSE CHART

Traditionally, you'll find high/low/close charts used for stock market data, such as changes in bond quotes over several months. However, you can use these charts for more than just security transaction data. They are ideal for presenting such information as income levels by job classification, or price comparisons of competing products. In fact, any data that shows ranges and averages is a candidate for high/low/close charts.

Unlike in bar and line charts, the values shown in high/low/close charts don't usually start at 0. This means you can change the starting value for the X axis without distorting the data.

Close refers to the final or ending prices for a given time period.

WHEN TO USE A POINT CHART

Use a point chart, which is also called a *scatter* or *dot* chart, to show correlations between two or three series of values. Point charts are often used to graph statistical analyses. Each series can contain up to 1000 data points if you use a numeric or time-based X axis.

Consider adding a trend line to show the pattern between a series' scattered points, as many people find it difficult to compare groups of dots. Make sure your audience is familiar with point charts before you present them.

SELECTING A CHART STYLE

After you've determined the type of chart you're going to create, consider whether the data is suitable for a special style. You select chart styles from the Style Options box. To access this box, press F8 to display the XY chart Options menu, shown in Figure 5.3, and then choose Style. You will see the options shown in Figure 5.4.

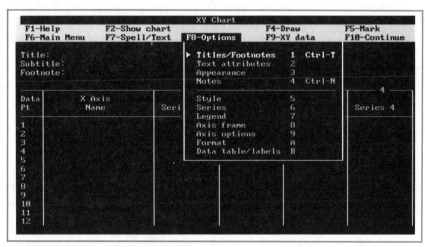

Figure 5.3: The XY chart Options menu

⊙ Some variations distort data. For example, if you use the Overlap and 3D options together in a bar chart, the value 7 will be graphed as 6¼.

To make selections from the Style Options box, highlight the setting you want to change, and then press F3 to choose from a list or press the spacebar to cycle through the choices. You can change any of the Style Options box settings for your XY charts. For example, you can choose another bar style for a line chart to achieve different line effects.

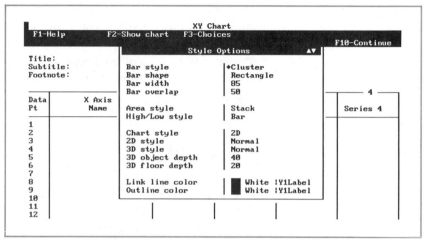

Figure 5.4: The Style Options box

CHOOSING A BAR STYLE

By default, bar charts are in the Cluster style. You can change to another style by changing the setting for Bar style in the Style Options box. You can sometimes change a chart's type by changing its style. For example, selecting the Bar style for a high/low/close chart will make that chart a bar chart.

You can choose from the following bar styles:

The Cluster and Overlap options work only with bar charts.

- Cluster: With this style, the data elements are grouped together, which makes it easier to compare several series' data elements. The Cluster style setting doesn't affect line, trend, curve, or point chart types.

- Overlap: In this style, the bars are clustered into groups and they overlap one another within the groups. When you use the Overlap style, make the series with the smaller values the first ones so that the shorter bars in the overlapping groups are in front of the larger ones. Otherwise, the smaller series' bars will be obscured by the previous series' bars.

- Stack: This style works like a pie in that it shows the parts within a whole. Use the Stack style to show data that you would need six or seven pies to represent. Order your series from largest to smallest. This way, the dominant elements are on the bottom of the stacks, which balances them. To emphasize the bottom elements, give them your chart's darkest color or pattern.

- 100%: When you use this style with the Stack option, each stack is the same size, giving it a value of 100 percent while showing each of its parts as a percentage. This style emphasizes the differences between the percentages within the stacks. It shows percentages (not values) along the Y1 axis.

- Step: Charts in this style look like staircase steps. Changes in the data are shown in 45-degree angles. The Step style emphasizes mass and volume in frequency distributions. Step style charts, or *histograms,* are for audiences familiar with statistical graphs. They are most often used in technical presentations.

- Paired: This style is also called a *sliding bar* graph. Use it to show correlations between different types of data in a dual-axis graph. For example, you can present the number of personnel working in a division on the left side of the Y axis and the dollars generated on the right side. To use this style, you must also use the Series Options box to set up a second Y axis for the chart, as described in the next section.

Figure 5.5 illustrates each of the bar chart styles.

USING BAR ENHANCEMENTS

When used correctly, bar enhancements can make your charts more informative and attractive. However, they can also distort the chart's data if they are not used correctly. In the 2D style field of the Style Options box, you can select from the following enhancements for a 2D bar chart (when the Chart style field is set to 2D):

- Normal: Disables all enhancements (the default setting). If you do not want to use any chart enhancements, leave the 2D style field set to Normal.

The bottom-left chart in Figure 5.5 shows a poor example of a Step style chart. Histograms should graph only one series.

Distinguish each paired element by matching the colors of the Y-axis labels to those of the bars' elements.

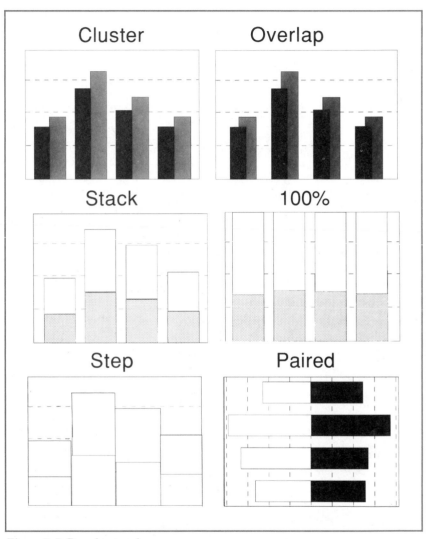

Figure 5.5: Bar chart styles

When printing in black and white don't use pattern 1 (solid) in your bar chart if you have selected the Shadow enhancement. You might not see the shading differences between the shadow and the black bars in printed charts.

- Shadow: Adds a dimension to your charts by placing a black edge on the right side of the bars to create a shadowed effect. The Shadow enhancement works best with the Cluster, Paired, Stack, and 100% styles.

- Link: Draws lines between bars to connect the elements in a series. The line's angle helps show how the series changes from one element to the next. Because Stack and 100% bar charts focus on the changes between the elements within the bars and not between the bars, use the Link enhancement with these types of charts to compare the elements in a series.

- Horizontal: Flips the bars to the Y axis, so they are horizontal rather than vertical. Use this enhancement when your chart shows a single series containing fewer than 16 bars, particularly if your X-axis labels are long (the labels will not run together as they would in a vertical chart). If possible, rank the data in numerical order for a horizontal chart. It's easier to make comparisons when the bars are arranged from smallest to largest or vice versa.

Figure 5.6 illustrates the various enhancements you can select for 2D charts.

A horizontal line chart is difficult to read. Use the Horizontal enhancement for bar charts only.

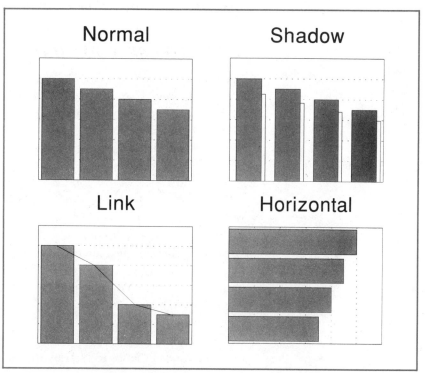

Figure 5.6: 2D Normal, Shadow, Link, and Horizontal effects

The only selection you can make for a 3D style chart (when the Chart style field in the Style Options box is set to 3D) is Horizontal, as illustrated in Figure 5.7. Using 3D charts is discussed in the next section.

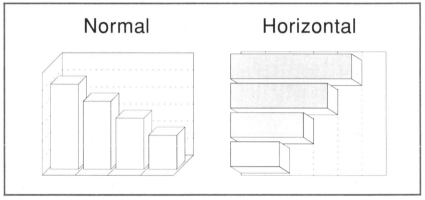

Normal   **Horizontal**

Figure 5.7: 3D Normal and Horizontal effects

WHEN TO USE A 3D CHART

Plotters ignore the 3D option.

A 3D chart emphasizes the differences in your data but often misrepresents their values. As you can see in the examples in Figure 5.8, it's difficult to identify the value for each element in a 3D chart. With the 3D style, two identical data elements may seem to have different values if one is closer to the audience than the other. Furthermore, the members of your audience might not know that the back edge of the bar identifies its value.

The order in which you enter your series is important when you are using a 3D style. If you're not careful, a series with large values can hide a smaller valued series. Always enter your 3D data so the series with the smallest values are placed in the Series 1 column. The series with the largest values should be placed in the last series column you'll use. You can use the @COPY or @EXCH function to reorder your series column. You will learn more about these functions later in this chapter.

Use 3D when general relationships are of interest. Don't use 3D if you want your audience to identify the values for the data. Ideally, you

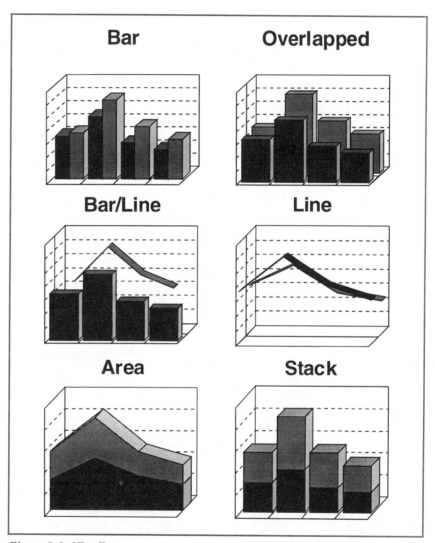

Figure 5.8: 3D effects

should use 3D only when you want to emphasize a single series. You can't select the Paired bar style for a 3D chart.

The Bar shape field in the Style Options box affects only 3D charts. Use it to display 3D bars shaped as rectangles, pyramids, octagons, or cylinders. Figure 5.9 shows the styles you can select for 3D bar shapes.

When you use pyramid-shaped bars, the values appear smaller than they actually are because of the tapering of the pyramid.

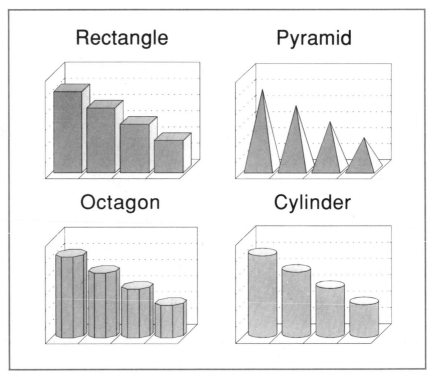

Figure 5.9: Bar styles for 3D charts

USING AREA AND HIGH/LOW/CLOSE CHART STYLES

The 3D enhancement holds the same dangers in area charts as it does in bar and line charts—your data values are distorted and it's difficult to read the scale.

When you create an area chart, it is in the Stack style by default. You can use the Area style field in the Style Options box to change to an Overlap or 100% style area chart. However, we do not recommend using the Overlap style for an area chart because it can be misleading—viewers might misinterpret the overlap as a stacked style.

Your style options for high/low/close charts are limited. For example, you can't select patterns for your series. However, you can change the setting in the High/Low style field in the Style Options box to Bar, Area, or Error bar.

Figure 5.10 illustrates the styles you can select for area and high/low/close charts.

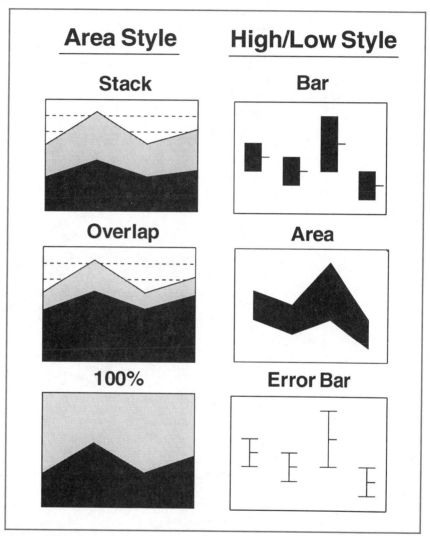

Figure 5.10: Styles for area and high/low/close charts

USING OTHER XY CHART VARIATIONS

The other choices on the XY chart Options menu allow you to create cumulative, dual-axis, and logarithmic charts. The following sections describe these chart variations.

SHOWING CUMULATIVE TOTALS   Rather than displaying a series as individual element values, you can display them cumulatively as running totals or year-to-date amounts. The top chart in Figure 5.11 shows a standard bar chart, and the bottom shows the same data graphed as cumulative totals.

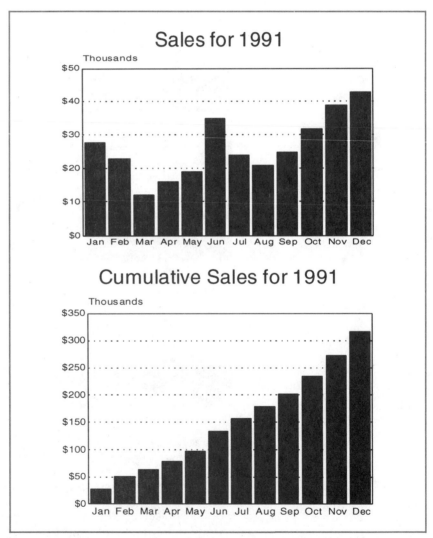

Figure 5.11: Cumulative chart versus standard bar chart

Cumulative is a poor choice for high/low/close charts because they are difficult to understand when their data is presented as totals.

To show cumulative totals, press F8 and select Series from the XY chart Options menu. This displays the Series Options box, as shown in Figure 5.12. Move your cursor to the Cumulative field in the column for the series you want compounded and change the setting to Yes. Be sure to let your audience know that your chart shows cumulative totals by noting it in your chart's title, subtitle, or footnote.

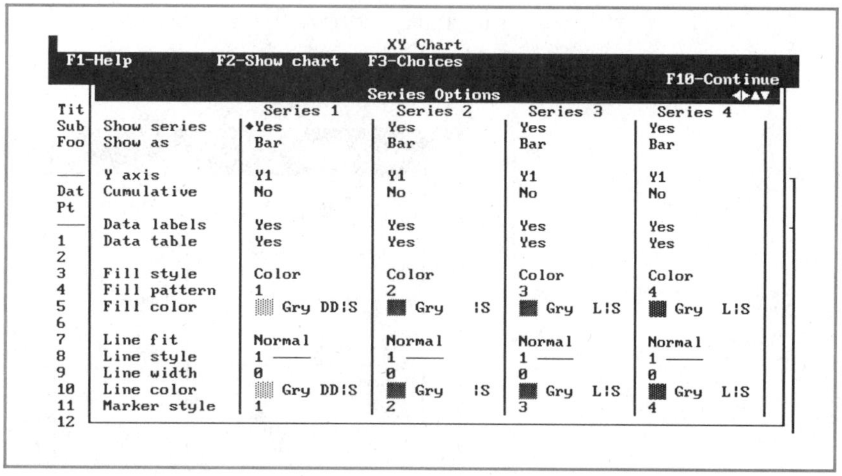

```
                                        XY Chart
    F1-Help              F2-Show chart  F3-Choices
                                                              F10-Continue
                                         Series Options             ◄►▲▼
  Tit                   Series 1        Series 2       Series 3      Series 4
  Sub   Show series     ◆Yes            Yes            Yes           Yes
  Foo   Show as         Bar             Bar            Bar           Bar

  ───   Y axis          Y1              Y1             Y1            Y1
  Dat   Cumulative      No              No             No            No
  Pt
  ───   Data labels     Yes             Yes            Yes           Yes
  1     Data table      Yes             Yes            Yes           Yes
  2
  3     Fill style      Color           Color          Color         Color
  4     Fill pattern    1               2              3             4
  5     Fill color      ▓ Gry DD¦S      ■ Gry   ¦S     ■ Gry  L¦S    ■ Gry  L¦S
  6
  7     Line fit        Normal          Normal         Normal        Normal
  8     Line style      1 ─────         1 ─────        1 ─────       1 ─────
  9     Line width      0               0              0             0
  10    Line color      ▓ Gry DD¦S      ■ Gry   ¦S     ■ Gry  L¦S    ■ Gry  L¦S
  11    Marker style    1               2              3             4
  12
```

Figure 5.12: The Series Options box

Use the Series 2 column for your most important series and make it the Y2 series in a Paired bar chart. You can further emphasize it by giving it a dark color or pattern.

ADDING A SECOND Y AXIS   You can give an XY chart two Y axes so that it has two separate scales—one on the right side of the chart and the other on the left side.

The Y axis field in the Series Options box can be set to either Y1 (the default value) or Y2. To display a series on the right side of the graph, change its setting in the Y axis field to Y2 by pressing the spacebar. The Y1-axis scale will be displayed on the left side of the graph, and the Y2-axis scale will appear on the right side.

Because a dual-axis chart is difficult to read, use the Paired style with it so that the two series are easier to distinguish from each other. Since this chart style is complicated, it's a blessing that Harvard won't let you make a 3D dual-axis chart.

Unless you and your audience are familiar with log charts, don't use them.

SHOWING CHANGE WITH A LOGARITHMIC CHART Logarithmic charts display the data's degree or rate of change as opposed to its values. These charts are used to lessen the effect of wide variations in the data presented. They are used most often to graph technical and scientific data and are not common in business presentations.

To make your chart logarithmic, choose Axis from the Options menu to display the Axis Options box, shown in Figure 5.13. In the Scale type field, change the setting from Linear to Log. For a traditional logarithmic chart, set only the Y axis to Log.

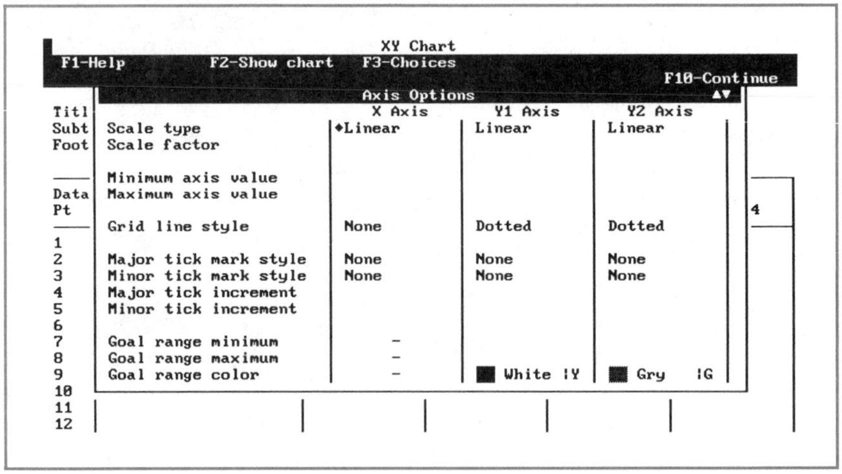

Figure 5.13: The Axis Options box

SHOWING NEGATIVE VALUES WITH A DEVIATION CHART Another type of XY chart you can create is a deviation chart, which shows negative values. For example, you may use negative values if you are working with temperatures or loss of income.

You can select the Stack style to present a negative and a positive series together.

You do not have to select an option or change a setting to create a deviation chart. When you place a minus sign (–) in front of any one value on the XY chart data-entry screen, Harvard will automatically turn your graph into a deviation chart.

SETTING UP XY CHARTS

After you choose a chart type from the XY menu, the X Data Type box appears, with the cursor in the X data type field, as shown in Figure 5.14. You use this box to tell Harvard what type of data you're plotting across the X axis.

SELECTING AN X-AXIS DATA TYPE

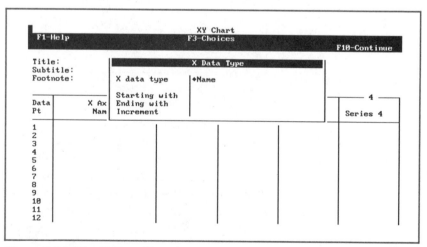

The default X-axis data type is Name. To select another data type, press the letter that represents the data type you want to use. For example, if you want to compare yearly financial figures, press **Y** for Year. You can also press F3 to select a data type from a list (press PgDn to see the complete list). After selecting your X-axis data type, press Enter.

Next, Harvard prompts you for the Starting with value for your data. Table 5.1 shows the formats you can use for each X data type. Enter the starting value and press Enter. For example, if you selected a year data type, you could choose 1980 for the starting year.

Harvard then prompts you for the Ending with value for your data. Type the ending value and press Enter. For example, you could type 1992 as the year for the ending value.

Finally, the cursor moves to the Increment field. Specify how many numbers or months to skip. If you want the complete range intact, press Enter without typing an increment. Otherwise, type a number and press Enter.

If you want to use Name (the default setting) for your X-axis data type, just press F10. The box will disappear, and you can begin creating your chart. You will have to type your X-axis labels on the data-entry screen.

The X data type default setting, Name, ignores increment values and includes all X-axis labels.

Figure 5.14: The X Data Type box

Table 5.1: Valid starting, editing, and increment values

X DATA TYPE	VALID FORMATS	VALID INCREMENTS
Day	Sunday	None
Week	1	2, 3, etc.
Month	Jan	2, 3, etc.
Quarter	1	2
	First	2
	Q1	2
Year	1992	2, 3, etc.
	92	2, 3, etc.
Month/Day	Jan 1	2, 3, etc.
	1/1	2, 3, etc.
Month/Yr	Jan 92	2, 3, etc.
	1/92	2, 3, etc.
Qtr/Yr	First 92	2
	1/92	2
	1/1992	2
Time	1 AM, 12 PM	2 ... 60 (min)
	1:00, 24:00	2 ... 60 (min)
Number	1	2, 3, etc.

The XY chart data-entry screen will appear. If you selected the Name data type, you will have to type your X-axis labels. For other data types, Harvard automatically fills in the X-axis labels for you.

If you made a mistake in setting your X-axis data type or decide to change to another type, press the F9 key to display the XY Data menu, shown in Figure 5.15. Then press **1** to choose Set X data type or **2** to select Quick X entry and reenter the X-axis data type information.

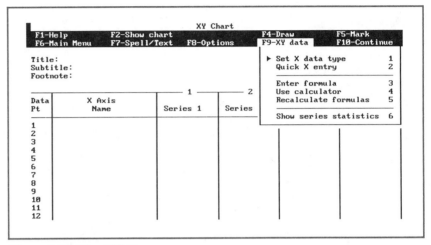

Figure 5.15: The XY Data menu

ADDING TEXT AND VALUES

If you are familiar with scientific notation, use it to enter large numbers quickly. For example, 5E7 equals 50,000,000. The E, which stands for exponent, tells Harvard to shift the decimal point seven places to the right. Knowing scientific notation is also useful if you have to edit large numbers that Harvard has converted into this format.

Once you return to the XY chart data-entry screen, you can enter the title, subtitle, footnote, and your data, just as you did in Chapter 2. You can type up to 100 characters for each line for the title, subtitle, and footnote.

You can add more than 12 data elements for each series. After you fill in the first 12 rows, press PgDn. On the next screen that appears, enter 12 more elements. You can continue to press PgDn and enter more elements, up to a maximum of 1000 for each series. Move to each previous group of elements by pressing the PgUp key.

You can also enter up to 16 data series, although the data-entry screen shows columns for only Series 1 to Series 4. To add more series, move your cursor to the Series 4 column and press Tab (or use your mouse to click on the ▶ triangle on the top-right side of your screen). When you press Tab, a Series 5 column appears. Press Tab again to display a Series 6 column, then again to see a Series 7 column, and so on. Press Shift-Tab to return to the previous column.

REARRANGING ROWS OF ELEMENTS

On the XY chart data-entry screen, you can easily add, delete, or move rows of data elements, as follows:

- To delete a row of elements, move the cursor to that row and press Ctrl-Del.

- To insert a row at the cursor's position, press Ctrl-Ins.

- To move a row of elements, position the cursor on the row to be moved and press Ctrl-up arrow to move the row up, or Ctrl-down arrow to move the row down.

MANIPULATING COLUMNS

Remember to press F2 to view your graph and check the order of your series.

The order in which you enter your series on the XY chart data-entry screen is usually determined by the type of chart you are creating. For example, you enter your series with the smallest values first if you are creating an overlapped bar chart; you enter the series with the largest values first when you want to create a stacked bar chart. If you change the chart type, you may have to reorder your series.

You can use the Enter formula option on the XY Data menu to rearrange your columns of data instead of retyping them. Move to the column you want to change and press F9 to display the menu, then type 3 to choose Enter formula. In the formula box, type a formula using one of Harvard's built-in functions, as follows (replace the n in the command with the number of the series column):

@CLR	Erases a column
@COPY(#n)	Copies a column
@EXCH(#n)	Switches two columns
@MOVE(#n)	Moves a column

For example, suppose you change your 3D bar chart to a stacked bar chart. You now want to switch your largest column (Series 4) with your smallest column (Series 1). To switch the columns, begin by moving the cursor to the first column, since you want Series 1 to receive the values in Series 4. Next, press F9 and choose Enter formula from the XY Data menu. In the Enter Formula box, type @EXCH(#4) and press Enter. The 4 tells Harvard which column you're switching with the current column. Since the cursor is in column 1, Harvard exchanges column 1's data with column 4's. None of the other columns are changed.

Always start your formulas with @. Also remember to use the number sign (#) in front of the column number and to place parentheses around the # and column number. Chapter 7 provides more information about using formulas with Harvard.

HANDS-ON: CREATING XY CHART VARIATIONS

In the following steps, you will explore some of the XY chart variations. While constructing the charts, you'll also get to practice using scientific notation, which is a handy shortcut for entering large numbers.

Our chart will show the totals of book sales by category, comparing sales to males and females. The X axis will show the types of books, and the Y axis will represent people. To create the chart, follow these steps:

1. From the Main menu, press **1**, then **3**, then **1** to select Bar. The X Data Type box will appear, with the default setting of Name in the X data field.

2. Since we are using book categories on the X axis, press F10 to accept Name as the data type. The XY chart data-entry screen will appear.

3. Type **Sales of Books by Category** for the title, **by sex (1991 averages)** for the subtitle, and **Source: American Publishing Cooperative (fiction)** for the footnote.

4. Move to the X Axis Name column and type the following labels:

Fiction

General (press Ctrl-B and Enter) **Nonfiction**

Biography

Poetry

Children's

By pressing Ctrl-Enter before entering an X-axis label, you tell Harvard to display it on the line below the other X-axis labels. Use this technique to prevent labels on your charts from running together.

5. To enter the number of male and female unit sales in each of the five book groups, type the following data in the Series 1 and Series 2 columns:

Series 1	Series 2
95900	51200
30000	30900
30300	44000
14900	13800
12600	7400

6. Move the cursor to the Series 1 column and replace Series 1 by typing **Male.** Then move to Series 2 and change it to **Female.**

7. You've now created a clustered bar chart, which is the default type. Press F2 to view it. Figure 5.16 shows what your chart should look like.

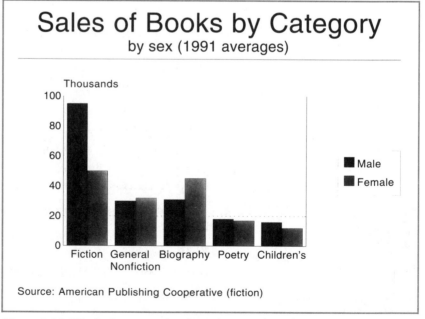

Figure 5.16: Displaying your data in a clustered bar chart

8. Return to the Main menu and use the File option to save this chart under the name **BOOKS**.

9. To make a variation of the chart you just saved, return to the Main menu and press **2** to select the Edit chart option. The XY chart data-entry screen that appears contains the previous chart's data.

10. Press Ctrl-T to display the Titles/Footnotes box and change the subtitle to **by sex (1991 percentages)**. Then press F10 to continue.

11. Press F8, type **5**, and press F3 to see a list of bar styles in the Style Options box.

12. Highlight and select 100% in the Bar style field and press F10 to continue.

13. Press F2 to see your percentage chart, which should look like the one shown in Figure 5.17. Because you changed the bar style, the graph now shows the percentages of males

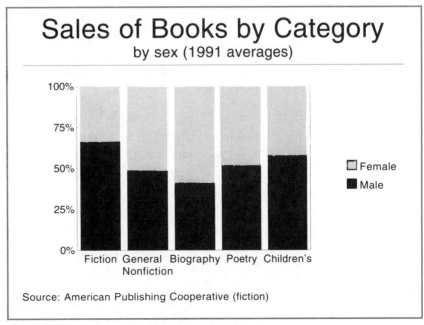

Figure 5.17: Displaying your data in a 100% chart

and females for each major book group instead of the average numbers.

14. Return to the Main menu and save your chart as **PERCENT**.

15. Press **2** to select the Edit chart option. Again, you'll see the data that you previously used.

16. Press Ctrl-T to display the Titles/Footnotes box and change the subtitle back to **by sex (1991 averages)** and press F10.

17. To make Female the Y2 series, press F8 and type **6** to display the Series Options box. Move to the Series 2 column and press the spacebar in the Y axis field. Press F10 to continue.

18. From the data-entry screen, press F8, type **5**, and press F3 to select a new bar style. Highlight and select Paired for the Bar style field and press F10.

19. Press F2 to see your paired bar chart, which should look like the one shown in Figure 5.18.

Paired charts are best for showing dissimilar types of data, such as dollars and units, but you can use them for similar data types as well. Make the data you want to emphasize the Y2 series.

You can experiment on your own with the other styles and enhancements. Refer to the sample charts earlier in this chapter and try to duplicate their effects, and try the other variations as well. You will see that some variations present data better than others.

HANDLING GRAPHING PROBLEMS

After you have chosen the chart variation that best represents your data, you may still encounter graphing problems. This section identifies several problems and provides some suggestions on how to correct or minimize their effects.

AVOIDING OVERLAPPING X-AXIS LABELS

If your X-axis labels are too long and can't be shortened, there are several ways to prevent them from running together:

- Place all or part of long labels on a second X-axis line by pressing Ctrl-Enter before typing it, as you did in the previous section.

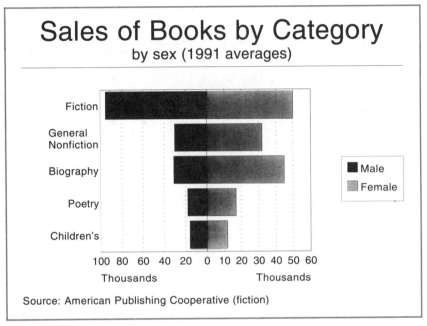

Figure 5.18: A paired bar chart

Avoid using a vertical X axis for labels with text because they are difficult to read in a vertical orientation.

Use symbols rather than text for axis labels whenever appropriate. Just set the Data labels field for each series in the Series Options box to No, and use Draw to add the symbols.

- If your chart is oriented vertically, set the 2D or 3D style in the Style Options box to Horizontal. Your X-axis labels may fit along the vertical axis.

- Change the angle of the axis labels by setting the Alignment field in the Text Attributes Labels box, shown in Figure 5.19, to Vertical or Angled. (Press F8, then **2**, then **2** from the data-entry screen; move to the Alignment field; and press V for Vertical or A for Angled.)

- Change the size of the text used for the X-axis labels by setting the X labels field in the Text Attributes Labels box to a smaller number. (Move the cursor to the X labels field and type a smaller type size number, such as 2.5, in the Size column.)

- Hide the labels (set the Data labels field in the Series Options box to No), and then use the Draw option to enter and position the text for your labels.

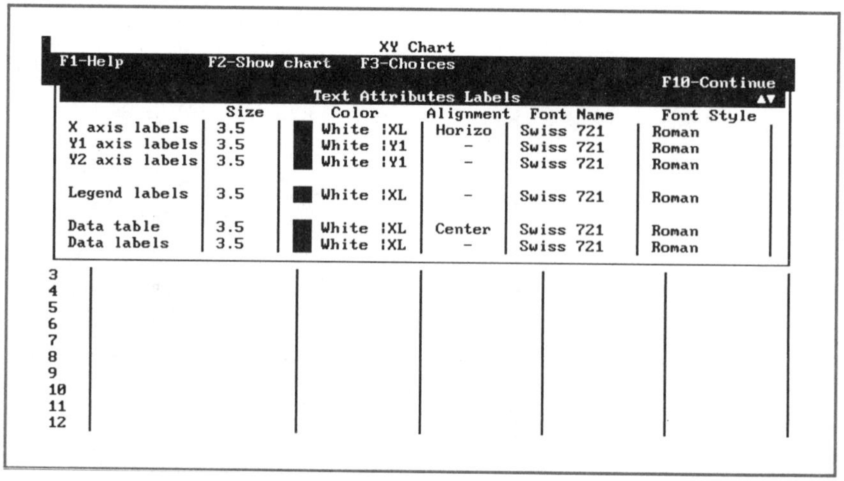

```
                            XY Chart
F1-Help           F2-Show chart   F3-Choices
                                                  F10-Continue
                     Text Attributes Labels                ▲▼
                Size        Color     Alignment  Font Name    Font Style
X axis labels   3.5      █ White !XL   Horizo    Swiss 721    Roman
Y1 axis labels  3.5      █ White !Y1     -       Swiss 721    Roman
Y2 axis labels  3.5      █ White !Y1     -       Swiss 721    Roman

Legend labels   3.5      ■ White !XL     -       Swiss 721    Roman

Data table      3.5      ■ White !XL   Center    Swiss 721    Roman
Data labels     3.5      ■ White !XL     -       Swiss 721    Roman
3
4
5
6
7
8
9
10
11
12
```

Figure 5.19: The Text Attributes Labels box

ADJUSTING FOR LOPSIDED, UNVARYING, OR MISSING DATA

Some other common graphing problems arise when your data is not balanced or too balanced, or some values are missing.

ADJUSTING LOPSIDED DATA If one of your series is much larger than the others, differences between the smaller series will be harder to see because of the way Harvard plots data. For example, if one of the bars in a bar chart has a value of 240 and the remaining bar values are all less than 20, the Y-axis scale will go up to 250, making the smaller bars look like they are the same size.

You can correct this by entering another value for the data that is very different than the rest. For example, in the example above, you would give the large bar a value of 30 on the XY chart data-entry screen. It will still be larger than the other bars, and viewers will be able to see differences in the other bars' values. Use the Draw option to add text and place the real values above each bar. To make it clear that the large bar doesn't show the real value, call attention to its number (240) by adding an arrow symbol to point to it.

When you need to show the precise values of all your data, choose Data Table/Data Labels from the Options menu. This displays the

Some people feel that data that is lopsided or shows little fluctuation should be left as is to accurately reflect the relationships. Others feel that data occasionally needs to be adjusted to clarify the information being presented.

box shown in Figure 5.20. Set the Show data labels field to Yes. The amounts will then be displayed above the bars or next to the data points on the lines, as illustrated in Figure 5.21.

GRAPHING DATA SHOWING LITTLE CHANGE One way to show the variations in data with values that do not cover a wide range is to start your Y axis with a value other than 0. To change the axis starting value, choose Axis from the Options menu to display the

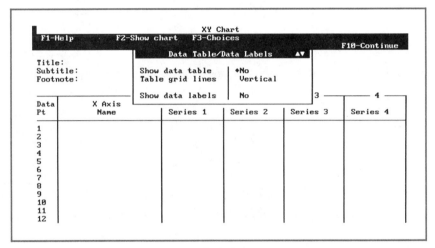

Figure 5.20: The Data Table/Data Labels box

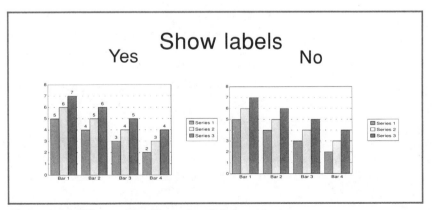

Figure 5.21: Effects of the Show data labels setting

Axis Options box and enter your new starting value in the Minimum axis value field in the Y Axis column.

DEALING WITH MISSING DATA When working with certain types of values, such as those for chronological data, you may occasionally be missing data. For example, you might have the data for 1988, 1990, and 1991 but not 1989. The best solution is to skip the missing data and include a footnote to explain that the missing figures are unavailable.

CREATING ACCURATE CHARTS

As you know, your data needs the right type of chart to be presented well without distortion. However, the data must be accurate, or your graph won't tell the complete story. You may have to factor in several types of data. For example, you might conclude from a graph of your company's sales by division that the most productive division has the greatest sales. However, you might see a different story if you divide your sales data by the number of employees within each division. You might find that a smaller division generates more sales per employee than the larger division.

ADJUSTING FOR INFLATION

Suppose you want to show how your sales company has been doing over a period of years. It would be misleading to merely plot a line of total sales. Instead, you need to correct your data for changes in the inflation rate for the product. This is done by using the appropriate price index published yearly by the government and dividing the sales totals by the index figure called the *deflator*. The resulting annual figures can then be plotted to show the real quantitative trend.

To get an idea of how the deflator rate varies, look at Figure 5.22, which shows Consumer Price Index deflators from 1947 to 1990. This table uses 1982 to 1984 as the base years, meaning an average dollar during this period is worth a dollar, while later years' dollars are worth less than a dollar. You can refer to this chart for your own data when you need deflators.

Consult an almanac, the *Annual Economic Report to the President,* or the *Statistical Abstract of the United States* for other deflators.

Consumer Price Index (CPI)

1947-90 annual averages for all urban consumers

Year	CPI	Factor	Year	CPI	Factor
1947	22.3	4.4843	1982	96.5	1.0363
1950	24.1	4.1494	1983	99.6	1.0040
1955	26.8	3.7313	1984	103.9	0.9625
1960	29.6	3.3784	1985	107.6	0.9624
1965	31.5	3.1746	1986	109.6	0.9124
1970	38.8	2.5773	1987	113.6	0.8803
1975	53.8	1.8587	1988	118.3	0.8453
1980	82.4	1.2136	1989	124.0	0.8065
1981	90.9	1.1001	1990	128.7	0.7770

Source: U.S. Bureau of the Census

Figure 5.22: Consumer Price Index (CPI) and deflator factors

You can enter dollars and deflators directly into the data-entry screen by using Harvard's built-in calculator, as described in Chapter 7, or by using calculation functions to compute the deflators for the values you enter. You'll try the latter method in the next hands-on session.

SHOWING THE DATA TABLE

You can design pictorial charts to offer a graphic presentation of numbers and use text charts to show precise numbers. If you want to do both in the same chart, you can include a *data table,* which lists the values of the series and elements, on your XY chart. The data table will appear beneath the X axis.

To add the data table to your chart, press F8 to access the Options menu, and then choose Data Table/Data Labels. Set the Show data table field to With chart. Then set the Table grid lines field to Vertical, Horizontal, or Both to show the precise values within a frame.

Select None if you want to display the data without the frame. Figure 5.23 illustrates the effects of the data table settings.

To change the data table's text size, press F8, then **2**, then **2** to display the Text Attributes Labels box. Then enter another size in the Data table field.

Another alternative is to turn an XY chart into a text table chart. To do so, retrieve the XY chart you want to convert, select Create chart from the Main menu, choose Text, and then select Table. Choose Yes when Harvard asks if you want to keep the data values. The data for your XY chart will then be used to create the table chart.

You may want to create a chart that shows a table as an XY chart and display it as a data table without the chart, rather than using a text table chart. This way, you can use the built-in calculator and formula functions.

HANDS-ON: GRAPHING ADJUSTED DATA

You'll now create the line chart shown in Figure 5.24, which shows unadjusted sales data and sales data adjusted with deflators

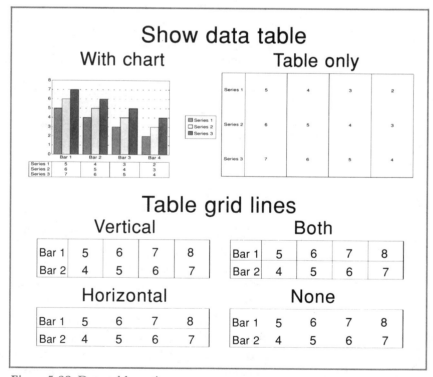

Figure 5.23: Data table options

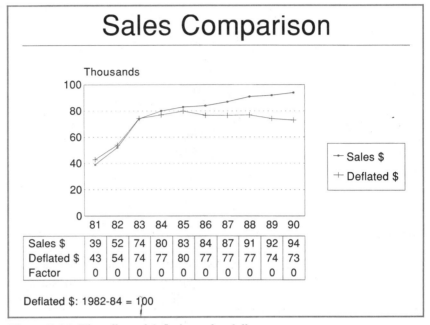

Figure 5.24: The effect of deflating sales dollars

(taken from Figure 5.22). Here are the steps to follow:

1. From the Main menu, press **1**, then **3**, then **5** to create a line chart. The X Data Type box will appear.

2. Press **Y** to change the X data type from Name to Year, and then press Enter. Type **81** as the value for the Starting with field and press Enter again. Type **90** in the Ending with field and press F10. The data-entry screen will appear, with the X-axis labels already filled in.

3. Type the following text for your title and footnote:

   Sales Comparisons

   Deflated \$: 1982-84 = 100

4. To change the Series 1 title, move your cursor to the Series 1 field, type **Sales \$**, and press Enter.

5. Enter the following figures in the Sales $ column for the years 1981 to 1990:

   39000

   52000

   74000

   80000

   83000

   84000

   87000

   91000

   92000

   94000

6. Move the cursor to the Series 2 column and replace the label by typing **Deflated $**. You'll use a calculation to fill in the values for the second series, so now move on to Series 3.

7. Press Tab to move to the Series 3 label, type **Factor**, and press Enter.

8. Enter the following deflator figures for 1981 to 1990 in the Factor column:

   1.1001

   1.0363

   1.004

   .9625

   .9624

   .9124

   .8803

   .8453

   .8065

   .777

9. Move the cursor to the Series 2 column for Deflated $, press F9, and type **3** to insert a formula.

If you need to enter a large number, such as 122000/3.2222, you could type it in scientific notation format, as in 123E3/3.222.

10. Type **(#1)*(#3)** and press Enter. This tells Harvard to multiply the rows in column 1 by those in column 3. The results are automatically calculated and placed in column 2.

11. Press F8 and type **6** to display the Series Options box. Move the cursor to the Show series field for the Series 3 column and set it to No. Now the deflator factors will not appear on the chart.

12. Move the cursor to the Data table field for the Series 3 column and set it to No (so that the deflators do not appear in the data table you will include on the chart), and then press F10.

13. Press F8 and type **B** to display the Data Table/Data Labels box. Set Show data table to With chart. The chart will now include a data table below the X axis.

The settings in the XY chart Format Options box are similar to those in the pie chart Format Options box, which are described in Chapter 4.

14. Press PgUp to display the Format Options box, shown in Figure 5.25. Move your cursor to the Decimal places field in the Y1 Axis column and enter **0** to set the number of decimal places displayed to zero. Then press F10.

15. Save your chart as **DEFLATED** and then print it. It should look like the one shown in Figure 5.24.

	Format Options		▲▼
	X Axis	Y1 Axis	Y2 Axis
Show axis labels	◆Yes	Yes	Yes
Percent	No	No	No
Currency	No	Yes	No
Scientific notation	No	No	No
Decimal places		2	
Thousands separator	Yes	Yes	Yes
Leading text			
Trailing text			

Figure 5.25: The Format Options box

HANDS-ON: CREATING
A HIGH/LOW/CLOSE CHART

Most XY charts are similar, and you use the same options and procedures to create and edit them. However, the high/low/close chart shows the data differently and provides fewer choices for variations.

In the following steps, you will create the high/low/close chart shown in Figure 5.26, which graphs investment information (one of the most common uses of this type of chart).

Figure 5.26: The sample high/low/close chart

1. From the Main menu, press **1**, then **3**, then **7** to choose High/Low/Close. When prompted, type **N** and press Enter so you do not keep the current data.

2. In the X Data Type box, press **M** to select Month as the data type. Next, specify **Jan** for the Starting with field and **Dec** for the Ending with field. Press F10 to continue. The data-entry screen will appear, listing the months in the X

Axis Month column and with the High, Low, Close, and Open series already filled in for the first four series.

3. Type the following title and subtitle:

American Publishing Cooperative

1991 Monthly Stock Prices

4. Enter the values for the three series in the High, Low, and Close columns as shown in Figure 5.27. If you also wanted to show the opening values for the stock each month, you could enter them in the Open column.

5. Press F2 to see how your chart looks. The High and Low series have the same legend—an outlined rectangle. Press Esc to return to your chart.

6. To adjust the legend titles, move to the High series label on the top of the second column and change it to **High/Low**. Press Tab and delete the Low label by pressing the space-bar over it.

7. Press F8 and type **A** to display the Format Options box. Set the Currency field in the Y1 Axis column to Yes to display the Y1-axis values as currency. To use two decimal places for cents, type **2** in the Decimal places field in the Y1 Axis column. Then press F10.

8. To move the legend, press F8, and type **7** to display the Legend Options box. Set the Placement field to Inside, and then press F10.

9. Save the completed chart as **MYHIGH**. It should look like the one shown in Figure 5.26.

You have probably realized by now that one of Harvard's strengths is its consistency. Learning about one chart type's options gives you the skills for working with another type of chart.

SUMMARY

In this chapter, you learned about the different chart variations that you can produce by using the XY chart options. You learned

```
 MYHIGH.CH3                          XY Chart                              ◄►▲▼
  F1-Help          F2-Show chart                  F4-Draw         F5-Mark
  F6-Main Menu     F7-Spell/Text   F8-Options     F9-XY data      F10-Continue

 Title:      American Publishing Cooperative
 Subtitle:   1991 Monthly Stock Prices
 Footnote:

 ────────────────────────── 1 ──────── 2 ──────── 3 ──────── 4 ───────
 Data       X Axis
 Pt         Month            High/Low                 Close      Open

 1       Jan              7          6.5        7
 2       Feb              7.75       6.5        7.25
 3       Mar              7          6.5        6.75
 4       Apr              6.75       6.25       6.75
 5       May              8          5          6.5
 6       Jun              10         7.75       8
 7       Jul              12         9.25       10
 8       Aug              11         10         11
 9       Sep              11.5       9.75       11.25
 10      Oct              11         10         10.5
 11      Nov              11.25      9.75       10.5
 12      Dec              12.5       11         11.75
```

Figure 5.27: High/low/close chart data

how to select the most appropriate chart type and enhancements for your data, as well as how to manipulate and move your series columns to show your data in the best order.

The problems of graphing are now familiar to you, and you know some steps you can take to correct them. You have also practiced creating accurate charts by incorporating variables such as inflation into your data.

In the next chapter, you'll learn how to refine your XY charts to produce the exact effects you want.

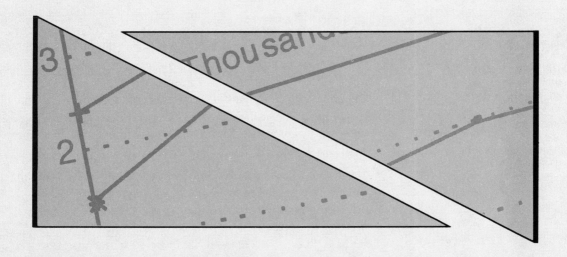

6

Fine-Tuning Your Bar and Line Charts

CHAPTER 6 _____

WHEN YOU HAVE VERIFIED THE ACCURACY OF YOUR
data and chosen the best chart type, style, and enhancements, your
chart conveys your message effectively. In the previous chapter, you
learned how to add some enhancements to your XY charts. In this
chapter, you will learn how to use XY chart options to refine your
charts further.

CUSTOMIZING THE BARS

In Chapter 5, we discussed the main settings in the XY chart Style
Options box (accessed by pressing F8 from the data-entry screen and
choosing Style). The other Style Options settings can be used to customize the bars in your chart, as follows:

If your chart has
many elements,
your bars will end up
looking like sticks, no
matter how much you
adjust the Bar width
setting. In this case,
choose another type of
chart, such as line, or
split the bars between
two charts.

- Bar Width: Enter a number between 1 and 100—representing the percentage of available space—to change the width of
  the bars in your chart. Choose a number that will make your
  bars wider than the space separating them. You can adjust
  the bar width in 2D and 3D charts, but not in bar charts in
  the Step style (because the step bar doesn't have spaces
  between its columns). Figure 6.1 shows how a bar chart looks
  with bar width settings of 25, 50, and 75.

- Bar Overlap: Enter a number between 1 and 100 (representing the percentage of available space, as in bar width) to
  adjust the amount of space that the bars extend into one
  another in a bar chart with the Overlap style. This style
  stresses differences between bar lengths; setting Bar overlap to
  a number between 60 and 75 emphasizes further differences.
  You will need to experiment with this setting—if the bars
  overlap too much, they will be hard to distinguish from each
  other. You can also use this option to change the spacing in

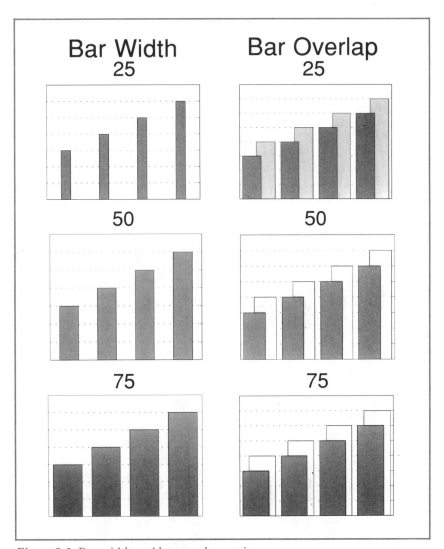

Figure 6.1: Bar width and bar overlap settings

3D bar charts. Figure 6.1 also shows the effects of Bar overlap settings of 25, 50, and 75.

- 3D Object Depth: To change the distance between series. in a 3D chart, enter a number from 1 to 100. Set the 3D object depth to a high number to increase the depth of the

The amount of available space is determined by the number of series and elements your chart has. For example, if you choose Overlap for the Bar style setting and set Bar overlap to 50, 50 percent of the bar will overlap onto the next bar.

objects, which in turn decreases the space between the rows of bars. A smaller object depth lets you see bars that may be hiding behind larger ones. Unfortunately, this also tends to distort your graph. Figure 6.2 illustrates the effects of setting the 3D object depth to 25, 50, and 75.

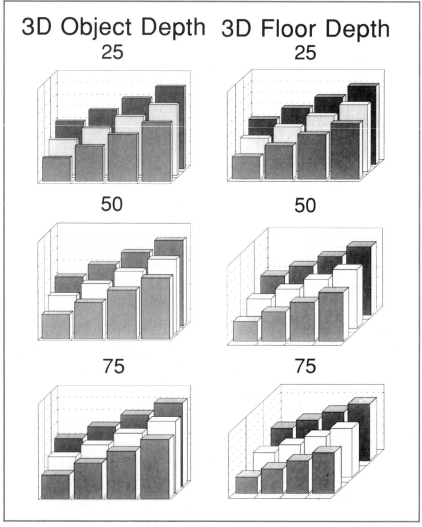

Figure 6.2: 3D object depth and floor depth settings

- 3D Floor Depth: Enter a number from 0 to 100 that represents the percentage of space you want to use to change the size of the floor (the platform for the elements) in a 3D chart. Figure 6.2 includes examples of the effects of setting the floor depth to 25, 50, and 75.

- Link Line Color: To change the color of the link line that is used when the 2D chart style is set to Link, press F3 in the Link line color field. Use the arrow keys to select a color and press Enter.

- Outline Color: The outline color is the color of the thin line used to draw the bars. It provides a subtle uniformity to all the series in the chart and can help to delineate the different series. To change the colors for the bar outlines in a chart, press F3 in the Outline color field, choose a color, and press Enter.

CHANGING THE AXIS FRAME

The *axis frame* is the border around the XY graph in the chart. By default, Harvard uses a full frame. You can change the frame's style, outline color, and fill color through Axis Frame box. To display this box, press F8 and select Axis frame from the Options menu. Then adjust the settings as follows:

Although many graphic artists prefer to use a full frame to focus the viewer's attention on the graph, others consider frames unnecessary frills that distract from the data and purpose of the chart. If you subscribe to the no-frills viewpoint, set Frame style to XY or X, and also change the Frame fill color to Background to provide some definition to the XY graph.

- Frame Style: Set the axis-frame style to Full, XY, or X. Although you can also choose Y or None, we don't recommend these settings because your bars will look like they are floating. Figure 6.3 illustrates the effects of the Frame style settings.

- Frame Outline Color: To change the color of the axis frame's outline, move the cursor to the Frame outline color field, press F3, highlight a color, and press Enter. The grid lines and tick marks in the chart will also be in the color you assigned to the frame.

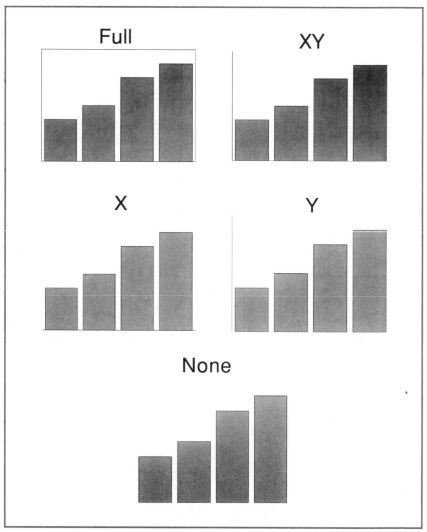

Figure 6.3: Effects of the Frame style settings

Contrasting colors can be quite effective. For example, use light foreground colors such as white, yellow, green, or light blue for bars and lines against dark background colors like black or dark blue. You can also use dark foreground colors against a light background.

- Frame Fill Color: To change the axis frame's fill color, move the cursor to the Frame fill color field and either press F3 and choose from a list or press the spacebar to cycle through your color choices.

REFINING THE LEGEND

When you have more than one series, a legend helps viewers read your chart. As you have learned in previous chapters, you can change the settings for the legend through the Legend Options box. Press F8 from the data-entry screen and select Legend to adjust the following settings:

- Show Legend: By default, this field is set to Yes so that a legend appears on your XY chart. You will probably want to change it to No when you create a chart with only one series. Also, you might want to set Show Legend to No and label each series with your group directly using Draw, so that your audience will absorb the information more quickly, without searching for the legend.

If you do place the legend inside the frame, make sure that it doesn't distract from the data or cover important bars or lines.

- Placement: By default, Harvard displays legends outside the frame. To position the legend within the graph's frame instead, move the cursor to the Placement field and press **I** to select Inside. (Type **O** to place the legend outside the graph frame).

- Location: You can select from 12 positions for the legend, as shown in Figure 6.4. The rectangle in the Legend

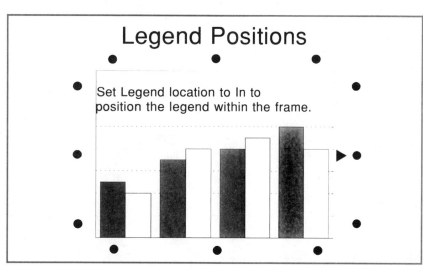

Figure 6.4: Positioning your legend

Options box represents the axis frame, and the three dots on each of its sides represent the potential locations for your legend. The triangle points to the default location. To change it, press the spacebar until the triangle points to the location you want to use. Choosing a dot from the top or bottom of the rectangle for the Location changes the axis frame from square to rectangle, as illustrated in Figure 6.5, and the X-axis labels are more likely to run into one another.

You can use the Appearance Options box settings to put frames around the chart region to further enhance the axis-frame style. You can select region frames like those shown in Figure 6.6.

- Legend Frame Style: By default, Plain is selected for Legend frame style, which places a single line around your legend. This is suitable for legends that appear inside the axis frame. You can choose from the other styles shown in Figure 6.6. Selecting another style, such as Shadow, for a legend that is outside the frame gives your legend an attractive border and directs attention to it. You can also select None to have your legend appear without a frame.

- Frame Outline Color: As with the axis frame, you can change the color used for the legend frame. To change a color, move

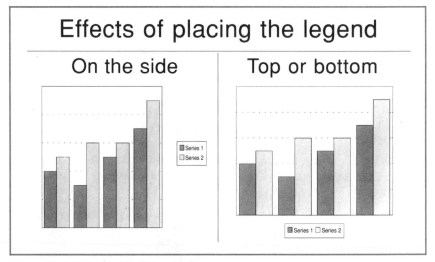

Figure 6.5: Effects of Position settings

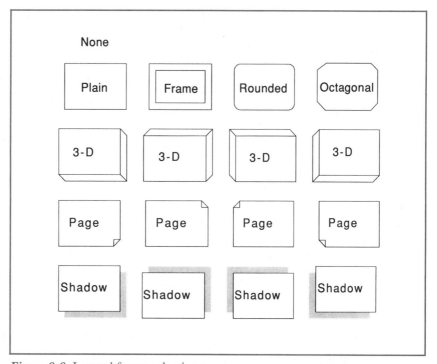

Figure 6.6: Legend frame selections

the cursor to the Frame outline color field and press F3 to choose from a list or press the spacebar to cycle through the color choices.

- Frame Fill Color: To change the fill color for the legend frame, move the cursor to the Frame fill color field and press F3 to select from a list of colors or press the spacebar to cycle through the choices.

ADJUSTING GRID LINES AND TICK MARKS

Grid lines and tick marks help your audience identify the values of your chart's elements. You change these items through the settings in the Axis Options box, accessed by pressing F8 and choosing Axis from Options menu.

USING GRID LINES

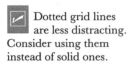 Dotted grid lines are less distracting. Consider using them instead of solid ones.

In the Grid line style field of the Axis Options box, you can set grid lines to appear on the Y axis, X and Y axes, or X axis. You can also turn off the grid lines altogether by choosing None. The styles you can select between are Dotted or Solid. Figure 6.7 illustrates the effects of the grid line settings.

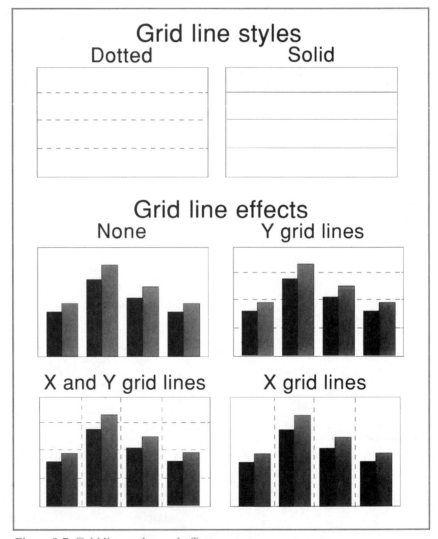

Figure 6.7: Grid line styles and effects

Although you can tell Harvard to create grid lines for the X, Y1, and Y2 axes, only do so when they are absolutely necessary for determining the values of elements. You might even want to remove all the grid lines (set Grid line style to None) and label the elements directly with Draw. You should also remove all grid lines when you create a dual-axis chart because they are confusing to the viewer.

⊙ Some plotters draw grid lines through bars.

Use Y-axis grid lines when you're not labeling elements. Figure 6.7 shows how horizontal Y-axis grid lines make it easier to read bar and line values when the Y axis scale covers a wide range of numbers. Use both X- and Y-axis grid lines when both axes contain wide ranges of numbers. X-axis grid lines by themselves usually have little value.

Note that grid lines are essential on a 3D chart to enable the audience to determine the values of the elements.

SETTING THE STYLE OF TICK MARKS

Tick marks are short, thick lines along the X and Y axes that can protrude from either side of the frame. *Major tick marks* have long lines and point to labels aligned along the axis frame. *Minor tick marks* are shorter lines and serve as incremental markers between major tick marks. Use tick marks by themselves or with grid lines to help your audience determine the values of data elements.

In the Axis Options box, you can change the tick marks through the Major tick mark style and Minor tick mark style settings. The choices are None, Out, In, and Both, as illustrated in Figure 6.8.

If you have many X-axis and Y-axis labels, select Out for the X-axis and Y-axis Major tick mark settings. Tick marks along the outside edge of the frame point to the labels they represent.

You should try to maintain a consistent tick mark style in your charts. For example, set the X-axis and Y-axis tick mark style to In, Out, or Both for all your charts.

⊙ Do not enter commas as thousands separators when setting chart specifications. Harvard automatically converts the commas you type in numeric values to decimals.

SETTING TICK MARK INCREMENTS

The increments between your tick marks can be set to a number from 0 to 9,999,999 (or up to 9.9999E + 30 if you enter the increment in scientific notation). To set the increment, move the cursor to the

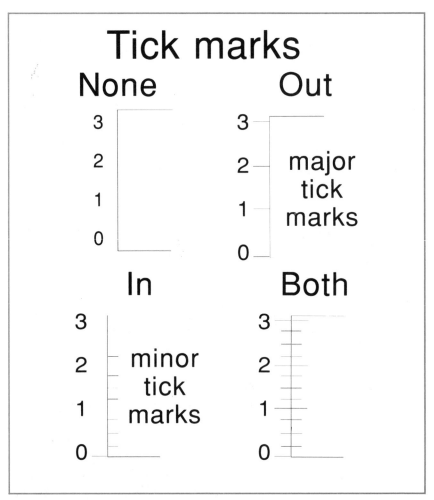

Figure 6.8: Tick mark styles

Major tick increment or Minor tick increment field in the Axis Options box and enter the new value.

The Major tick increment value you enter for the X axis sets the number of labels that are displayed along the X axis. For example, if you type 2 in the Major tick increment field, the chart will include only every other label. Use a minor tick mark increment to show the position of the unmarked labels. Figure 6.9 shows the effects of the tick mark

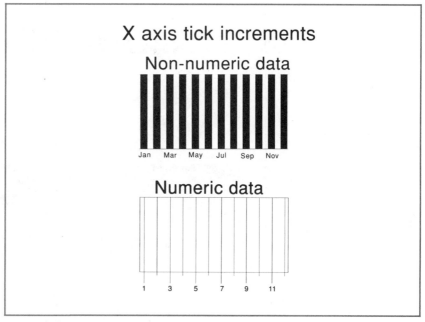

Figure 6.9: X-axis tick increment settings

increment settings. Note that any Major tick increment value will be ignored when the X-axis data type is set to Name.

SETTING GOAL RANGES

You can set a range on your charts to represent goals for your values. For example, you could create a sales chart showing the organization's goals as a shaded rectangle stretching behind your series and across the X axis, as shown in Figure 6.10.

Three options in the Axis Options box are used to show a goal range:

- Goal range maximum
- Goal range minimum
- Goal range color

Set an X-axis goal to call attention to a group of X-axis labels and their values. For example, you might want to highlight your division's elements from the rest of your organization by putting a goal range on your section of the X axis.

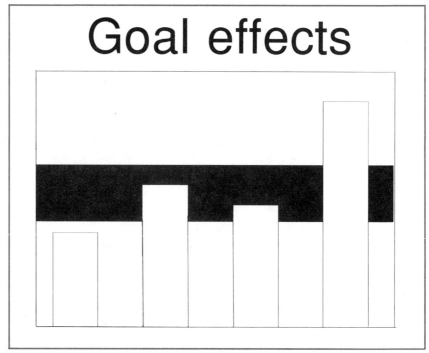

Figure 6.10: Setting a goal range

Type the values for the starting and ending range in the Goal range minimum and Goal range maximum fields. The value you type must be higher than your lowest data element in order for the goal to be displayed. Use the Goal range color field to change the shading of the goal rectangle.

REFINING THE SCALE AND AXES RANGES

The scale and ranges of values are important factors in the effectiveness of a chart. As you learned in earlier chapters, you set the scale type and factor and the axes ranges through the Axis Options box (press F8 from the data-entry screen and choose Axis). Your Scale type choices are Linear, the default, and Log, for logarithmic charts (usually used only in technical presentations). The following sections describe in more detail the effects of using different scale factors and adjusting the beginning and ending values of the X or Y axis.

USING SCALE FACTORS

Don't forget to call attention to the scale factor your graph uses (in a subtitle or footnote) so that your audience knows what values are being represented.

As you learned in Chapter 4, you use the Scale factor setting to scale the graphed values by a certain amount. The data element values will be divided by the number you type for the scale factor. For example, the data element value of 1000 would be displayed as follows:

SCALE FACTOR	VALUE DISPLAYED
100	10
10	100
5	200
1	1000
.5	2000

There are two other ways that you can use the Scale factor setting to adjust the data element values:

- To change the measurements graphed in the chart. For example, to change the data element values from inches to feet, type 12 in the Scale factor field. Since the scale factor tells Harvard to divide all values by 12, a value of 36 will appear as 3 on the graph.

- To ensure that Harvard does not change the values you enter. For example, if you enter 12000, Harvard displays the number 12 on the Y1 axis and adds the Y1-axis title Thousands. Type 1 in the Scale factor field to force Harvard to display the numbers just as you entered them.

ADJUSTING THE RANGE OF THE Y OR X AXIS

To adjust the range of the Y or X axis, enter the beginning value in the Minimum axis value field of the Axis Options box, and the ending value in the Maximum axis value field.

When adjusting minimum or maximum axis ranges, look at the values on your data-entry screen, not on your graph. The maximum range of 60 on a graph may really represent 60,000.

Remember, you can also choose which labels to display by changing the Major tick increment setting in the Axis Options box. For example, if you set the increment to 2 for the X axis, the number of labels will be cut in half, but all the data will still be graphed.

Most charts' scales should start at zero. Think twice before you reset the minimum and maximum values for your Y axis because scale changes can be confusing. If you have a good reason for changing the minimum or maximum value, make it clear in a footnote or explain it when you present the chart.

By increasing the minimum value of the Y axis, you change a graph's message. For example, you can change a graph that shows element values which are almost the same into one that focuses on their differences, as illustrated in Figure 6.11. In the figure, the top chart presents all the data, and the bottom chart shows a close-up of the variances. Just the opposite happens when you set a high maximum value without resetting the minimum: your data will appear to be more stable.

Harvard ignores maximum entries that are smaller than your largest data point, as well as minimum values that are larger than your smallest data point. Also note that you can't change the Y-axis range for 100% charts—they start at 0% and end at 100%. If you are changing the Y-axis values for logarithmic charts, do so in powers of 10, such as 1, 10, 100, 1000, and so on.

You might want to adjust the Minimum axis value or Maximum value setting for the X axis if you find that your X-axis labels overlap and you want to reduce the amount of data graphed in the chart. For example, if you decide to graph only the elements in rows 5 through 15 of your data-entry screen, enter 5 for the minimum value for the X axis and 15 for the maximum value.

SHOWING SELECTED LABEL VALUES

Grid lines, tick marks, and scales aren't always precise enough for your data. As you learned in Chapter 5, you can display the values of all your data elements by setting the Show data labels field in the Data Table/Data Labels box (press F8 and choose Data table/Data labels) to Yes.

When you add value labels in your graph, you do not need grid lines. You can even remove tick marks, scales, and full frames to create an effective, uncluttered chart. You'll make this type of chart in a hands-on session later in this chapter.

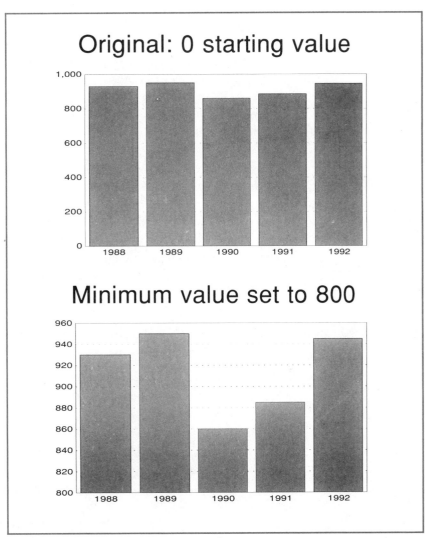

Figure 6.11: The effects of changing the minimum value of the Y axis

Set Show data labels to No when you want to label only a few elements within a series and use Draw to add the labels yourself. You can also use Draw to place the labels directly in the bars instead of above them.

If you want to label only certain series in the chart, set Show data labels to Yes, and then use the Series Options box to turn off the labels for each series you do not want marked with data values. Press F8, move the cursor to the Show series field in the column for the series you don't want labeled, and press the spacebar to change the setting to No.

CHANGING THE APPEARANCE OF A SERIES

Through the settings in the Series Options box, you can change the appearance of how a series is displayed in a chart, including its graph style; the style, pattern, and color of its fill; the fit, style, width, and color of its lines; or the style of its markers. Choose Series from the Options menu and adjust the settings as follows:

To display a series as High or Low, you must have a minimum of two series, with one defined as High and the other as Low.

- Show As: To change a particular series to another graph style, press F3 in the Show as field for that series and select from Bar, Line, Area, High, Low, Close, Open, or Point. For example, in a three-series bar chart, you might want to change the last bar to look like a line.

- Fill Style: In this field, you can select a different style for a series. Choose Color, Pattern, or Both.

- Fill Pattern: To change the pattern (bar shading) used for a series, enter the number for the pattern in its Fill pattern field. (Use the pattern charts in Chapter 4 as a guide when selecting patterns.)

- Fill Color: Select another color for a series by pressing F3 in its Fill color field and choosing the new one.

- Line Fit: To change the type of line used for a series, press F3 in the Line fit field in its column and choose from Normal, Trend, Curve, Average, Step, Exponential, Log regression, and Power regression. Figure 6.12 shows how each Line fit setting affects the line. You may want to use several types of line fits to present the same data. For example, you might create two series with the same identical data and show one series as a normal line and the other as a trend line.

- Line Style: To change the style of the line used for a series, move to the Line style field in its column and type 1 for a solid line, 2 for a dotted line, or 3 for a dashed line. Figure 6.13 shows the three line styles in different widths. You might want to use the Dotted or Dashed style for estimated or predicted values to show that they do not represent actual figures.

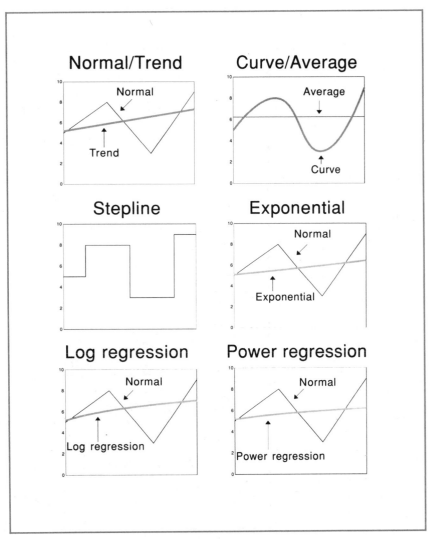

Figure 6.12: Line fit settings

When your line chart graphs more than one series, choose a different style, thickness, or color for each. A thick line should be used for your most important series. Dotted and dashed lines should be your secondary choices.

- Line Width: To set a different width for the line used to graph a series, type a number from 0 to 250 in the Line width field in its column. Figure 6.13 shows some widths you can choose from. Use heavier lines to make them darker than your grid lines. You can also adjust the Line width setting to darken lines that need emphasis.

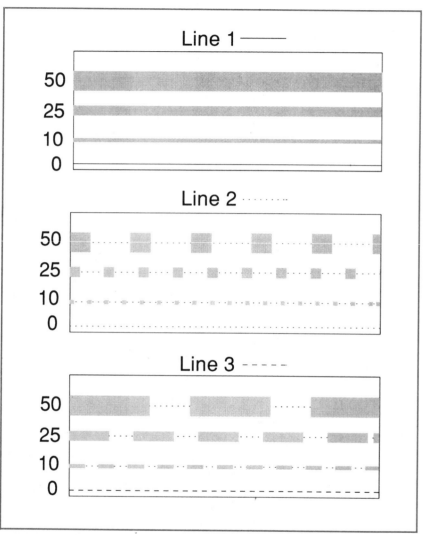

Figure 6.13: Line styles and widths

- Line Color: When you want to distinguish the lines used to graph each series in a chart by making them different colors, press F3 in the Line color field and select from the list that appears.

Set the marker number to zero when you want to display lines without markers, which is our preference.

- Marker Style: A *marker* is the character that represents a dot in point or line charts. To change the markers, type the number of the marker you want to use in the Marker style field in the column for the series. Table 6.1 shows the 13 different marker styles that are available and the number that represents each one.

Table 6.1: Harvard Marker Styles

MARKER STYLE SETTING	MARKER	MARKER STYLE SETTING	MARKER
0	None	7	△
1	•	8	⊠
2	+	9	○
3	✳	10	▽
4	✕	11	☆
5	□	12	⊠
6	◇	13	✝

DESIGNING REFINED CHARTS

In the following hands-on sessions, you will apply some of the techniques described in this chapter and also learn some more ways to fine-tune your charts. We will create a drop-grid graph to show many data elements, a "no-frills" chart that uses data labels instead of a grid and scale, and a customized 3D area chart.

HANDS-ON: CREATING A DROP-GRID GRAPH

Constructing a chart that graphs a large amount of data can be difficult. Along with fitting all the values in the chart, you must try to identify them, while keeping the elements readable.

In this section, you will create the life-expectancy chart shown in Figure 6.14, which shows how many more years a person at a given

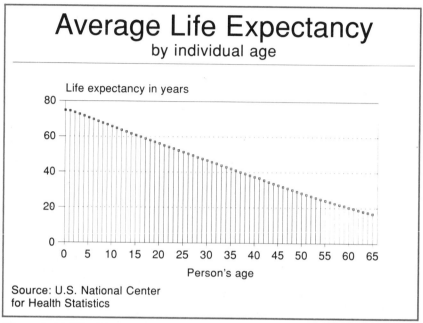

Figure 6.14: The life-expectancy chart in a drop-grid style

age can expect to live. The chart will graph ages from 0 (newborn) to 65. Thus, you have 66 data elements to display.

To show all this data clearly, we will create a *drop grid*, which is a vertical grid extending from the X axis to the data value but not through the whole graph. You create a drop-grid style chart by selecting Bar as the XY chart type and Numeric as the X-axis data type.

Follow these steps to create the life-expectancy chart:

1. From the Main menu, press **1**, then **3**, then **1** to create a bar chart.

2. Press **N** to select Numeric as the X data type, and then press Enter. For the Starting with value, type **0** and press Enter. At the Ending with prompt, type **65**. Press Enter twice to move to the data-entry screen.

3. Type the following title and subtitle:

   Average Life Expectancy

   by individual age

4. Harvard has already entered the 66 X-axis labels for you. Move the cursor to the Series 1 column and enter the values listed in Table 6.2.

5. Press Ctrl-T and type the following footnote in the Titles\ Footnotes box:

   Source: U.S. National Center

   for Health Statistics

6. For your X and Y1 axes titles, type

   Person's age

   Life expectancy in years

7. Press F10, then F8 to display the Options menu.

8. Press **7** to display the Legend Options box and set Show legend to No.

9. Press PgDn twice to reach the Axis Options box and set both the X and Y1 Major tick mark style fields to Out. This will make it easier to see the labels that the drop-grid lines point to.

10. Press F2, and you will see that it's difficult to identify the values along the X and Y axes. Also notice the gap between 65 and 70. Press Esc to continue.

11. Return to the Axis Options box and type **66** as the Maximum axis value in the X Axis column. Then type **5** in the Major tick increment and Minor tick increment fields in the X Axis column. Set the Y1 axis Minor tick increment field to **5**. These changes will help make your chart more readable.

12. Press Ctrl-S and save your chart as **DROPGRID**, and then print it. Your finished chart should look similar to the one shown in Figure 6.14.

You must enter a two-line footnote in the Titles/Footnotes box because you can only type one line in the Footnote field on the data-entry screen.

HANDS-ON: CREATING A NO-FRILLS CHART

Some data is suitable for a no-frills chart style, which uses value labels and does not include grids, frames, tick marks, or scales. In the

Table 6.2: Data for the Drop-Grid Chart

X Axis	Name Series 1	X Axis	Name Series 1
0	74.7	33	43.8
1	74.5	34	42.9
2	73.6	35	42.0
3	72.6	36	41.0
4	71.7	37	40.1
5	70.7	38	39.2
6	69.7	39	38.2
7	68.7	40	37.3
8	67.7	41	36.7
9	66.8	42	35.5
10	65.8	43	34.5
11	64.8	44	33.6
12	63.8	45	32.7
13	62.8	46	31.8
14	61.8	47	31.0
15	60.9	48	30.1
16	59.9	49	29.2
17	58.9	50	28.3
18	58.0	51	27.5
19	57.0	52	26.6
20	56.1	53	25.8
21	55.1	54	25.0
22	54.2	55	24.2
23	53.3	56	23.4
24	52.3	57	22.6
25	51.4	58	21.8
26	50.4	59	21.1

following steps, you will create the chart shown in Figure 6.15, which compares the United States population in the years 1986 and 1990.

1. From the Main menu, press **1**, then **3**, then **1** to create a bar chart. If you see the Keep current data prompt, press **N** for No and press Enter.

2. When the X Data Type box appears, press F10 to accept Name as the X data type.

3. On the data-entry screen, type the following title, subtitle, and footnote:

   U.S. Resident Population

   1986 and 1990

   Source: U.S. Bureau of the Census

4. Type the following X-axis labels and Series 1 and 2 values:

Northeast	South
50000000	83000000
50600000	87300000

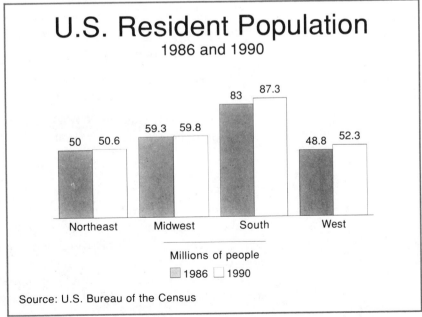

Figure 6.15: U.S. population chart in the no-frills style

Midwest	West
59300000	48800000
59800000	52300000

5. Press Ctrl-T to display the Titles/Footnotes box. Move the cursor to the Legend title field, type **Millions of people**, and then press Enter.

6. Move the cursor to the Series 1 label field and type **1986** to replace the Series 1 label for the first series. Press Tab and type **1990** to replace the Series 2 label.

7. Press F8 and type **7** to choose Legend. Press Tab twice to move to the Location field, and then press the spacebar three times to center and position the legend beneath the axis frame.

8. Press PgDn to move to the Axis Frame box and set the Axis frame style to X. Then change the Frame fill color setting to Background (it's the first color on the list).

9. Press PgDn to display the Axis Options box and change the Grid line style for the Y1 axis to None. In the Scale factor field in the Y1 column, type **1000000**.

10. Press PgDn to display the Format Options box, and in the Y1 axis column, set Show axis labels to No.

11. Press PgDn to move to the Data Table/Data Labels box and set Show data labels to Yes.

12. Save your chart as **NOFRILLS** and print it. It should look like the completed chart shown in Figure 6.15.

HANDS ON: CREATING A 3D AREA CHART

If you want to emphasize proportions rather than present exact numbers, a 3D area, stacked bar, or single-series chart can be effective. You can minimize 3D distortions by changing the floor depth and 3D object size.

In the last hands-on session of the chapter, you will create the 3D area chart shown in Figure 6.16, which graphs the United States

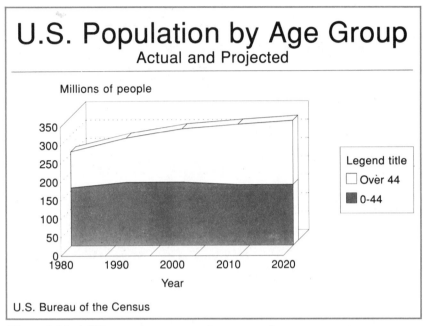

Figure 6.16: A 3D area chart comparing proportions

population by age group. Follow these steps to create the 3D chart:

1. From the Main menu, press **1**, then **3**, then **6** to create a
   XY Area chart. If you see the Keep current data prompt,
   type **N** and press Enter.

2. Press **Y** to select Year as the X data type and press Enter. For
   the Starting with value, type **1980** and press Enter. At the
   Ending with prompt, type **2020** and press Enter. At the Increment prompt, type **10** and press Enter.

3. The data-entry screen will appear with the years already
   entered on the X axis. Type the following title, subtitle,
   and footnote:

   U.S. Population by Age Group

   Actual and Projected

   U.S. Bureau of the Census

4. Move the cursor to the Series 1 title field, type **0-44**, and press Tab. Move to the Series 2 label and replace it with **Over 44**.

5. Move the cursor to the 0-44 column and enter these values:

   158

   172

   172

   165

   165

6. Move the cursor to the Over 44 column and enter the following values:

   98

   120

   145

   164

   174

7. Press Ctrl-T to display the Titles/Footnotes box and type the following X axis, Y1 axis, and legend titles:

   Year

   Millions of people

   Age Group

8. Press Esc, then F8 to display the Options menu.

9. Press **5** to select Style and change the Chart style setting to 3D.

10. Press F2, and you will see that the top of the 3D bar makes the Over 44 group look larger than it really is. Press Esc to continue.

11. Return to the Style Options box and set 3D object depth to **20** and 3D floor depth to **20**. These changes will help make your chart less distorted.

12. Save your chart as **3DAREA**, and then print it.

SUMMARY

In this chapter, you have learned how to customize XY charts. You can control features such as bar characteristics, frame styles, legends, axis labels, grid lines, tick marks, value labels, markers, patterns, and line styles. Through hands-on experience, you learned how to create a drop-grid chart, design a no-frills chart, and adjust 3D chart characteristics.

In the next chapter, you will learn how to use formulas and calculate statistics in your charts.

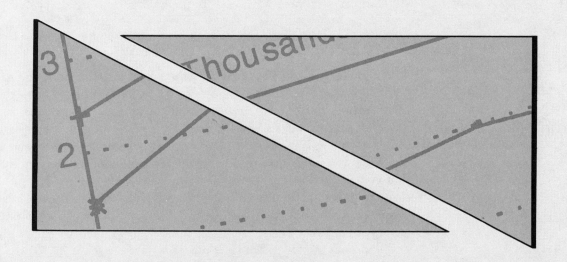

Working with Statistics, Calculations, and Formulas

CHAPTER 7 _____

IN THE PREVIOUS CHAPTERS, YOU HAVE LEARNED
about some of the calculations that Harvard does for you. For
example, Harvard will compute and plot a trend line. This chapter
describes the other types of calculations that you can use with the data
in your XY charts.

WORKING WITH STATISTICS IN YOUR CHARTS

When you need to show minimum and maximum statistical values, use a high/low/ close chart, as described in Chapter 5.

Statistics are often used in charts to help the audience get a quick
overview of the data presented. The following sections introduce
some basic statistics that are useful in presentations: populations versus samples, the three M's, and frequency-distribution shapes.

POPULATIONS VERSUS SAMPLES

When you show values for every single element of a study, you are
using a *population*. If the values are for a random number of the elements rather than all of them, you are using a *sample*. This distinction
is important in statistics.

For example, if you are trying to find the percentage of people who
purchase a certain product in a town, a population study requires
that you talk to each resident within that town. However, a sample
study requires that you communicate with a random number of people to see if they buy the item. A sample study assumes that the percentage of buyers in your randomly selected group approximates the
population of the town, which is not necessarily true.

In your charts that show frequency distributions, use a subtitle or
footnote to let your audience know whether you're portraying a population or a sample.

USING THE THREE M'S

In statistics, the three M's are often used to help analyze data: the mean, median, and mode. Harvard does not provide built-in functions to calculate these statistics, but you can easily compute them yourself, as follows:

The Harvard @AVG function averages a row on the data-entry screen, which contains data from a group of series. It does not average the values in a series column.

- The *mean* is simply an average, obtained by adding all your individual measurements and dividing it by the number of values you have added.

- To find the *median*, or the middle value in the given sequence of values, order the values numerically and find the middle number.

- The *mode* of a group of numbers is the peak of a distribution— the most common occurrence. As with determining the median, sort your values and then see which one occurs most often.

For example, suppose that you want to determine the mean, median, and mode of the test scores 40, 50, 60, 70, 80, 90, 90, 100, 100, 100, and 100. The 11 test scores added together total 880. Divide this by 11, and the mean is 80. Since there are 11 test scores, the middle number—the median—is the sixth score, or 90. There are four scores of 100, more than any other score, so the mode in our collection of test scores is 100.

You can show the mean, median, and mode in your charts by using Draw or by presenting them in a footnote.

UNDERSTANDING FREQUENCY DISTRIBUTION SHAPES

Frequency distributions follow certain patterns since there are always a mean and a median. Figure 7.1 shows the four terms that are used to describe frequency distribution charts. The first graph is skewed to the left; this is called a *negative skew*. When a graph is skewed to the right, it has a *positive skew*. Graphs that are approximately normal have a *symmetrical distribution*. *Bimodal* graphs are less common; they occur when your data shows two distinct modes.

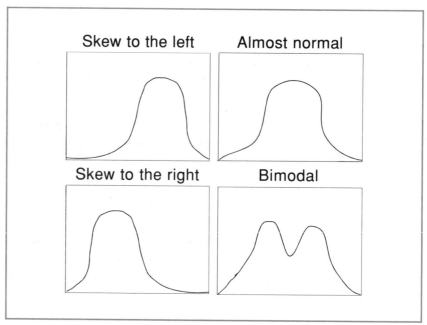

Figure 7.1: Frequency distribution shapes

For example, a population study showing human intelligence has a symmetrical distribution. However, a population study of income has a positive skew because the median figure is less than the mean.

GETTING STATISTICS INSTANTLY

Harvard calculates some statistics on each series in your XY charts for you automatically. To see the statistics for a series, move the cursor to the column for that series and press F9 to display the XY Data menu (in Chapter 5, we described how to use this menu to change the X-axis data type). Press **6** to select Show series statistics. You will see the statistics for that series in the Show Series Statistics box, which will look similar to the one shown in Figure 7.2.

The total number of data points is the number of values (excluding blank data elements) contained in the series. The minimum value is the smallest data element in the series, and maximum value is the largest. The average (mean) and median values are the statistics

Refer to a book on statistics for more information about these and other statistical calculations.

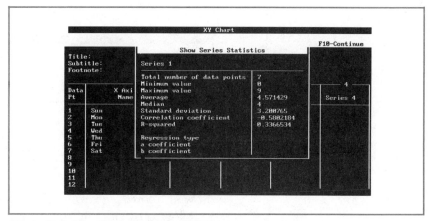

Figure 7.2: The Show Series Statistics box

described earlier in the chapter. To compute the standard deviation, correlation coefficient, R-squared, and regression statistics, Harvard uses special formulas (refer to the Harvard user's manual for the specific formulas and variables). You will only see regression data if you set the Line fit field in the Series Options box to trend, log regression, power regression, or exponential.

USING HARVARD'S CALCULATOR

You can use Harvard's built-in calculator to perform arithmetic on a single data element. It can add, subtract, multiply, or divide numbers. You can use integers, decimal numbers, or scientific notation in your calculations.

The calculator is accessed through the XY Data menu. Follow these steps to use the built-in calculator:

1. On the XY chart data-entry screen, move the cursor to the element you want calculated and press F9 to display the XY Data menu.

2. Press **4** to select Use calculator. The Calculator box will appear, with the cursor in the Calculation field, as shown in Figure 7.3.

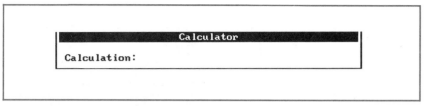

Figure 7.3: The Calculator box

3. Type the calculation and press Enter. Use a plus sign (+) for addition, a minus sign (−) for subtraction, an asterisk (*) for multiplication, and a slash (/) for division. When you want to use a column calculation, enter the pound sign (#) followed by the column number. Otherwise, Harvard will change only a single data element.

⊙ Computer experts beware: Harvard doesn't use the mathematical ordering that you usually find in programming. Instead, it calculates in the order you would verbally say the equation, from left to right.

For example, if you enter 3*2 + 1, Harvard will change the value at the current cursor location. It interprets this equation as 3 times 2 plus 1 and places the value 7 in that data element. Harvard always calculates in the order you enter your equation, working from left to right.

If you type #1*3 + 2 for the calculation, Harvard will interpret the #1 as meaning column 1. The calculation is column 1 times 3 plus 2. If you entered this calculation in the Series 2 column, it will change the data element's value, as shown in Figure 7.4.

```
                                    XY Chart                           ◄►▲▼
      F1-Help          F2-Show chart                 F4-Draw         F5-Mark
      F6-Main Menu     F7-Spell/Text    F8-Options   F9-XY data      F10-Continue

   Title:
   Subtitle:
   Footnote:

                            ─────── 1 ─────── 2 ─────── 3 ─────── 4 ───
   Data      X Axis
   Pt        Name            Series 1    Series 2    Series 3    Series 4

   1       Sun             7           23
   2       Mon             8
   3       Tue             4
   4       Wed             2
   5       Thu             9
   6       Fri             0
   7       Sat             2
   8
   9
   10
   11
   12
```

Figure 7.4: Computing a column's data

USING FORMULAS FOR CHART CALCULATIONS

In Chapter 5, you learned how to use the Enter formula option on the XY Data menu. In that chapter, we described the functions you can use to move, swap, and clear columns of series. You can also use this option to enter formulas and functions to perform calculations. Harvard provides functions for row and series calculations.

To enter a formula, follow these steps:

Remember to move the cursor to the row or column in which you want the results of the formula to be entered before you press F9.

1. On the XY chart data-entry screen, move the cursor to the column where you want the results of the formula to appear. When you are using row or series calculation functions, described in the next section, move the cursor to an empty column.
2. Press F9 to display the XY Data menu, then **3** to select Enter formula. The Enter Formula box will appear, as shown in Figure 7.5.
3. Type your formula using 40 characters or less. Use the same arithmetic operators that work with the calculator (described in the previous section) and any of Harvard's

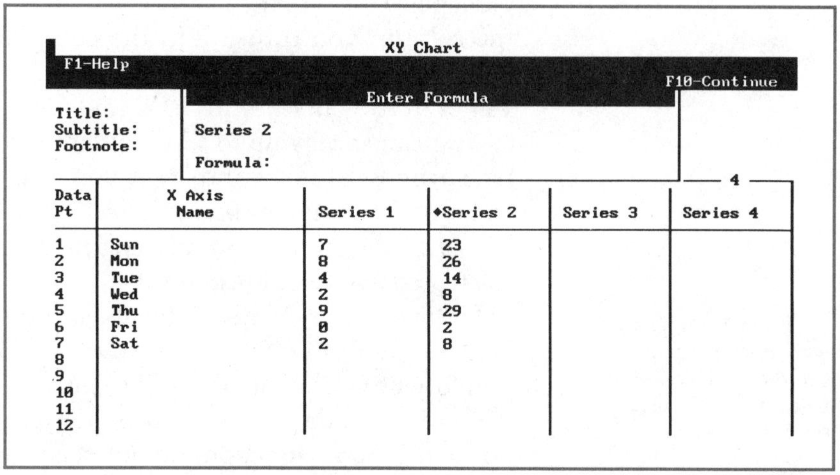

XY Chart
F1-Help
F10-Continue
Enter Formula
Title:
Subtitle:
Footnote:
Series 2
Formula:
4
Data Pt
X Axis Name
Series 1
◆Series 2
Series 3
Series 4
1 Sun 7 23
2 Mon 8 26
3 Tue 4 14
4 Wed 2 8
5 Thu 9 29
6 Fri 0 2
7 Sat 2 8
8
9
10
11
12

Figure 7.5: The Enter Formula box

built-in functions. If you make a mistake and want to cancel the formula entry, press Esc.

4. Press F10 to process your formula and continue.

Data elements that are entered as zeros (0) are used as zeros in calculations. However, a missing, or blank, data element does not have a value, and it will not affect the calculation.

You can tell when a formula has been used in a series because the diamond shape (♦) appears in the heading for the series (see Figure 7.5).

USING ROW AND SERIES CALCULATION FUNCTIONS

Harvard has four built-in functions that perform calculations on rows of data for the columns you designate:

@AVG(*#n*,*#n*)	Computes the average value of the row
@MAX(*#n*,*#n*)	Finds the largest number in each row
@MIN(*#n*,*#n*)	Finds the smallest number in each row
@SUM(*#n*,*#n*)	Adds the designated values in each row

You can't change the order of a calculation by using parentheses ( ).

Replace the *n* in the row calculation functions with the number of the column you're using in the computation. For example, type @SUM(#1,#2,#5) in the Enter Formula box to add together the values in rows in columns 1, 2, and 5.

You can specify up to seven different column numbers within the parentheses. For example, if you want to find the averages of columns 1 through 4, position the cursor in column 5, type @AVG (#1,#2,#3,#4) in the Formula field, and press Enter. You'll find the calculated averages in column 5.

You must have at least one empty column for Harvard to place the results of a series calculation function.

Unlike row calculation functions, series calculation functions use values only from one column. Harvard provides the series calculation functions listed in Table 7.1. Replace the *n* in the functions with the number of the column you want used in the calculation. You will notice that some functions do not need a column number.

FUNCTION	PURPOSE
@ABS($\#n$)	Converts any negative number into a positive (absolute) number
@CLR	Erases elements from the current column (where you pressed the F9 key)
@COPY($\#n$)	Copies a series from the designated column
@COS($\#n$)	Calculates the cosine of elements in a series
@CUM($\#n$)	Shows cumulative totals
@DIFF($\#n$)	Shows the difference between the current element and the preceding element
@DUP($\#n$)	Duplicates the specified series
@EXCH($\#n$)	Exchanges data between columns
@MAVG($\#n$)	Calculates moving averages
@MOVE($\#n$)	Moves the specified column to the current cursor location
@NEG($\#n$)	Works like @COPY but copies only negative data element values
@PCT($\#$)	Shows the percentage value of each element when compared to the series total
@POS($\#n$)	Works like @COPY but copies only positive data element values
@POWER($\#n$, p)	Raises the data elements to the specified power (p)
@REDUC	Sorts and combines duplicate X-axis labels in all columns

Table 7.1: Series Calculation Functions (continued)

FUNCTION	PURPOSE
@RECALC	Updates calculations in all columns to account for any change made in column values
@REXP(#*n*)	Calculates exponential regression curves
@RLIN(#*n*)	Calculates linear regression curves
@RLOG(#*n*)	Calculates logarithmic regression curves
@RPWR(#*n*)	Calculates power regression curves
@SIN(#*n*)	Calculates the sine of data values within a series

For example, you can use the @DUP function to save your series' values before you start working with them. This way, you will still have the original column in case you make a mistake in your calculations. Use the @REDUC function to consolidate and remove duplicates after importing data.

EDITING AND RECALCULATING FORMULAS

Most formulas remain linked to the series in which they were computed. In other words, the formula becomes part of the series. The only formulas that do not stay with the series are those that contain the function @CLR, @COPY, @EXCH, @MOVE, @RECALC, or @REDUC.

To edit a formula, move the cursor to the series that contains the formula, press F9, and then type **3**. The formula you originally entered is displayed in the Enter Formula box. You can change the formula or retype a new formula over it. Press Esc if you want to return to the data-entry screen without changing the formula.

The Recalculate option recalculates every formula. Use the @RECALC function to recalculate the results for a single series.

When you edit a chart and add, delete, or change the values of data elements that are used in formulas, the formulas need to be recalculated so their results are based on the different values. To have Harvard automatically recalculate all the formulas used in a graph, press F8 from the data-entry screen, and then type **5** to select the Recalculate option from the XY Data menu.

HANDS-ON: PERFORMING CALCULATIONS ON CHART DATA

If you produce charts with calculated values, you will find Harvard's formula options valuable. As an example, in the following steps, you will create a bar chart and have Harvard compute average and percentage values:

1. From the Main menu, press **1**, then **3**, then **1** to create a bar chart.

2. When the X Data Type box appears, press F10 to accept Name as the X-axis data type.

3. Type **1991 Home Video Sales** for the chart's title.

4. Type in the following data (Harvard will convert the large numbers into scientific notation):

X Axis	Units Shipped	Retail Sales
Camcorders	1090000	1210000000
B&W TVs	3730000	364000000
VCRs	12685000	5070000000
Color TVs	18855000	7630000000

When you enter a calculation function, think of each series as a sequential column number starting with one. For example, Units Shipped is column 1, Retail Sales is column 2, and Series 3 is column 3.

5. To see the statistics Harvard has automatically calculated for the retail sales data (Series 2), with the cursor in column 2, press F9 and type **6**. You will see the Show Series Statistics box, listing the minimum and maximum values, average, median, and other statistics, as described earlier in the chapter.

6. Press F10 to continue and move the cursor to column 3, where we will compute the average sales price. You calculate the average sales price of a unit by dividing retail sales by the units shipped.

7. Press F9, then **3** to display the Enter Formula box.

8. Type **#2/#1** and press Enter. This tells Harvard to divide column 2 by column 1. The results appear in column 3. For example, you will see that $1,110.092 is the average retail price of a camcorder.

9. Move the cursor to column 4, press F9, and then press **3**.

10. In the Formula field, type **@PCT(#2)** and press Enter. This formula calculates the percentage of each element in column 2 compared to the column's total amount. Your data-entry screen should look similar to the screen shown in Figure 7.6.

Calculated columns have a diamond character (◆) next to their series label.

11. Set the fourth column to display the figures as whole numbers with decimal points (use the Format Options box and set the number of decimal places to 2).

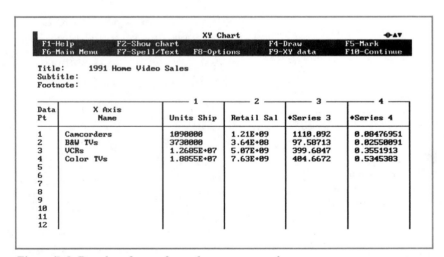

Figure 7.6: Results of your formulas appear on the screen

12. To create another column to show the data in column 4 as percentages, press Tab to move the cursor to column 5, press F9, and type **3** to enter a formula for this column.

13. Type **#4*100** and press Enter. You will see the percentage values.

You have now doubled the amount of information your chart can provide by creating the average price and percentage columns. This short hands-on exercise demonstrates how you can use Harvard to help generate statistics for a more informative presentation.

SUMMARY

In this chapter, you've learned how to use Harvard's calculation features in XY charts. You can take advantage of the statistics that Harvard automatically calculates for you (in the Show Series Statistics box) or use Harvard's built-in calculator or a formula to compute your own statistics.

Organizational statistics are important to many presentations. In the next chapter, you will learn how the organization itself can be graphed and put into a chart.

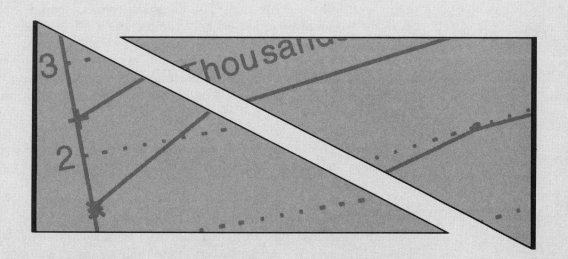

8

Creating Organization Charts

CHAPTER *8*

ORGANIZATION CHARTS SHOW THE FORMAL STRUC-ture of hierarchical groups. A well-designed organization chart can clearly illustrate even the most complicated organizational schemes. These charts are ideal for all types of groups, including clubs, companies, governments, and family trees. This chapter describes how to create organization charts with Harvard.

UNDERSTANDING ORGANIZATION CHARTS

Figure 8.1 provides an example of an organization chart for the United States government. Each box represents a branch or department within the organization. The lines that connect these boxes show the hierarchy of authority. For example, the legislative, executive, and judicial branches have the same level of responsibility, as shown by the horizontal line connecting them. The top box shows that each branch is invested with its authority by the Constitution. The boxes for departments and independent agencies beneath the executive branch show that these branches are all under the control of the president.

Figure 8.2 shows a typical organization chart for a business. In this case, the chart is organized by the controlling individuals' names and titles.

Harvard uses some special terms for parts of an organization chart. A *manager box* is one that has others beneath it. The boxes beneath a manager box are called *subordinate boxes*. For example, in Figure 8.2, Ray Bowen and Mary Yammatto are both manager boxes because they have subordinate boxes beneath them. A manager box and its subordinates are called a *group*. Our sample chart has two groups: one headed by Ray Bowen and the other by Mary Yammatto. Two or more boxes on the same level are *peers*. Referring to

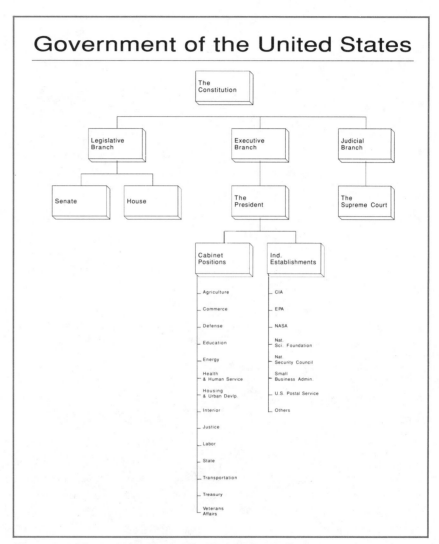

Figure 8.1: The organization of the United States Government

our sample chart again, Karl Cheroff and Bertha Smith are peers—their boxes are on the same level. A box on a level by itself beneath a manager box is called a *staff position box*. In Figure 8.2, Maxine Byrd holds a staff position.

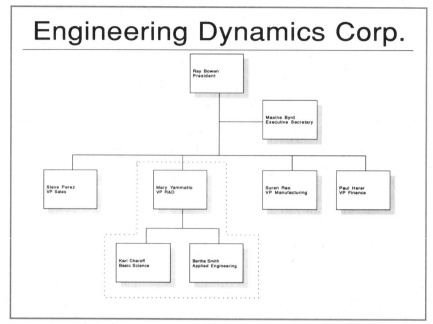

Engineering Dynamics Corp.

Ray Bowen
President

Maxine Byrd
Executive Secretary

Steve Perez
VP Sales

Mary Yammatto
VP R&D

Suren Rao
VP Manufacturing

Paul Herer
VP Finance

Karl Cheroff
Basic Science

Bertha Smith
Applied Engineering

Figure 8.2: A business organization chart

SETTING UP AN ORGANIZATION CHART

You can create an organization chart containing up to 210 boxes. You can place all the boxes first, and then go back to fill in the fields, or enter the data for each box as you create it.

Each box in an organization chart holds three fields: Name, Title, and Comment. Each field can contain up to 22 characters. You do not have to use all three fields in each box. For example, you can enter just the person's name or just type text in the Title or Comment field. By default, the text you enter in the Comment field does not appear on the chart, but you can select to show it, as described later in the chapter.

To create an organization chart, press **1** from the Main menu to choose Create chart, and then press **4** to select Organization. You will see the organization chart data-entry screen, with the first three boxes already placed, as shown in Figure 8.3.

Type the title, subtitle, and footnote for your chart. You can use up to 100 characters for each line. Then press Tab to move the cursor into the organization box chart area (press Shift-Tab to move back to the titles and footnote area).

Although you can enter 100 characters on a title, subtitle, or footnote text line, you can see only the first 65 characters you type.

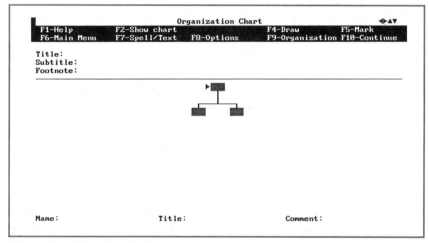

Figure 8.3: The organization chart data-entry screen

ENTERING TEXT AND ADDING BOXES

To enter information in the manager box displayed on the screen, use the arrow keys to highlight the box and press Enter. The Add/Edit Box Text box will appear, as shown in Figure 8.4. Fill in the Name, Title, and Comment fields. Remember, you do not have to use every field, and you can enter up to 22 characters in each one. You can use the Comment field for any type of information you would like to store with the chart. For example, you might specify the manager's office or telephone number. Enter all of the information you think the box should include as you create the chart. Later, you can edit the chart and delete text if space becomes a problem.

You can use Draw if you need to create extremely complicated structures.

The number of manager boxes you can fit in a chart depends on the organization's structural layout, although it's usually fewer than

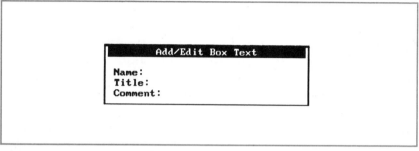

Figure 8.4: The Add/Edit Box Text box

16. Consider making two or more organization charts to show complex structures. For example, if you have more than four managers at the same level, divide them between two charts and present the charts together.

To add new manager, staff, or subordinate position boxes, press F9 to display the Organization menu, shown in Figure 8.5.

A manager box can have up to 50 subordinate boxes attached to it.

ADDING A MANAGER OR SUBORDINATE BOX To add a new manager or subordinate box, move the cursor to the manager box to which you want to attach the new box, press F9, then **2** to choose Add

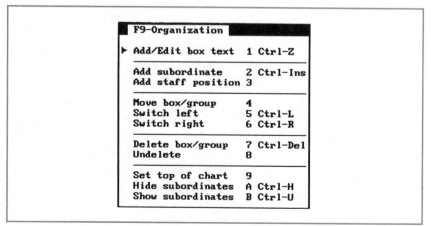

Figure 8.5: The Organization menu

subordinate from the Organization menu (any new manager boxes are actually subordinates to the manager box at the top of the chart). A shortcut is to move the cursor to the manager box and press Ctrl-Ins to add a subordinate to that position. Each time you press Ctrl-Ins, another subordinate position appears under that manager box. Move the cursor to that box, press Enter, and fill in the fields.

ADDING A STAFF POSITION BOX   You can add up to two staff position boxes to each manager box. Staff positions can't have subordinates assigned to them. To add a staff position box, highlight the manager box you want to assign the staff position to, and then press F9 to display the Organization menu. Press **3** to choose Add staff position. The new staff position box will appear on your chart under the manager box. Move the cursor to the new box, press Enter, and type in the information.

HANDS-ON: CREATING AN ORGANIZATION CHART

In the following steps, you will create the sample organization chart shown in Figure 8.6, which shows the structure of a hypothetical publishing company.

1. From the Main menu, press **1**, then **4** to create an organization chart. You will see the organization chart data-entry screen.

2. Type the following title and subtitle:

   American Publishing Cooperative

   Books for Enlightenment

3. Press Tab twice to move the cursor to the top manager box and press Enter.

4. In the Add/Edit Box Text box, type **John Booker** in the Name field and **President** in the Title field. Then press F10 (we will not use the Comment field).

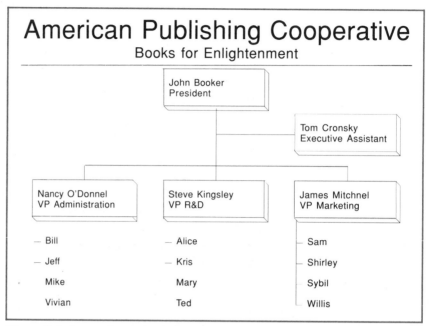

American Publishing Cooperative
Books for Enlightenment

John Booker
President

Tom Cronsky
Executive Assistant

Nancy O'Donnel
VP Administration

Steve Kingsley
VP R&D

James Mitchnel
VP Marketing

— Bill

— Jeff

Mike

Vivian

— Alice

— Kris

Mary

Ted

Sam

Shirley

Sybil

Willis

Figure 8.6: A sample organization chart for a publishing company

5. Press Ctrl-Ins to add a third subordinate box to the two that are already displayed. Press F9, then **3** to add a staff position box.

You can only designate two staff position boxes for a manager box, and staff position boxes cannot have subordinate boxes.

6. Press the down-arrow key to move the cursor to the staff position box, and then press Enter to add text to it. Type **Tom Cronsky** for the name and **Executive Assistant** for his title. Press F10 to continue.

7. Press the down-arrow key, then the left-arrow key to highlight the first box, and press Enter. Type **Nancy O'Donnel** for the name and **VP Administration** for her title. Then press Enter twice.

8. Press Ctrl-Ins four times to give Nancy O'Donnel four subordinates. Type the names **Bill**, **Jeff**, **Mike**, and **Vivian** in the subordinate boxes.

9. Highlight the manager box on the right of Nancy's and assign it to **Steve Kingsley**, whose title is **VP R&D**.

By default, only names appear in the boxes on the last level of the chart. However, you can turn on the display of the titles and comments, as described later in the chapter.

10. Highlight Steve Kingsley's box and press Ctrl-Ins four times. Place his subordinates names, **Alice**, **Kris**, **Mary**, and **Ted**, in the boxes that are assigned to him.

11. Move to the remaining empty box, press Enter, and enter the name **James Mitchnel** and the title **VP Marketing**.

12. Add the final four subordinate boxes with the names **Sam**, **Shirley**, **Willis**, and **Sybil**.

13. To change the order of the last group of subordinate names so that they are alphabetical, highlight Sybil's box and press Ctrl-L. Sybil will switch places with Willis. You will learn about the other ways to edit your chart in the next section.

14. Save your organization chart as **MYORG** and print it.

Your organization chart should look like the one shown in Figure 8.6. Later in the chapter, we will use some of Harvard's customization options to refine this chart.

EDITING ORGANIZATION CHARTS

You can change the text in any part of your organization chart. If you want to edit the text in the titles or footnote, press Shift-Tab to return to that area of the chart and make your correction. You can also press F5 to choose Mark and change the text format, or press F7 to check your spelling.

If you have a mouse, simply move the pointer to the box you want to edit and click the left mouse button.

To edit the text in a box, move the cursor to the box you want to change. This box will be highlighted and become the current one, and its name will be displayed at the bottom of the screen. Press Enter, and your original entries will appear in the Add/Edit Box Text box. Now you can add or delete text or make corrections.

MOVING AROUND THE ORGANIZATION CHART

You can easily move up and down the organization chart by using the up-arrow and down-arrow keys. You move between peers by pressing the left-arrow and right-arrow keys.

As your chart becomes more complex, you can use other keys to move to different parts of it quickly:

PgUp/PgDn	Moves the cursor up or down one page at a time
Ctrl-PgUp/Ctrl-PgDn	Moves the cursor to the extreme top or bottom edge of the organization box area
Home/End	Moves the cursor to the far left or the far right of the organization box area

CHANGING THE POSITIONS OF BOXES

The structure reflected in your organization chart is very likely to change with time. For example, if it is a company organization chart, there will be promotions and demotions; new employees will be hired and others will go elsewhere. When you need to change the structure of your organization chart, you can use the commands on the Organization menu to move, switch, and delete boxes. Press F9 and select the appropriate option:

- Move Box/Group: Use this option to move a manager box with or without its subordinates. For example, to demote a group to a lower level or assign it to a different manager, highlight the top box (the manager) in the group you want to move. Press F9, then **4** and choose whether the whole group or just the subordinates are to be moved. Use the arrow keys to move the group to their new manager, and then press F10.

- Switch Left and Switch Right: Use these options (press **5** or **6** from the Organization menu) to rearrange the order in which peers appear on the same level. You can also use the shortcuts from the data-entry screen: highlight the box and press Ctrl-R to move it to the right, or press Ctrl-L to move it to the left. For example, in Figure 8.2, you could highlight Steve Perez and press Ctrl-R to move him to the right and switch places with Mary Yammatto.

Move any subordinates you want to keep before deleting a position. Subordinates are deleted along with the manager.

- Delete Box/Group: Use this option to remove boxes from the chart. Highlight the manager, subordinate, or staff position box you want to delete, press F9, and then press **7**. The box you selected and all the subordinate boxes will be removed from your chart. To use the shortcut, highlight the box you want to delete and press Ctrl-Del.

- Undelete: Use this option if you change your mind and want to restore the box or boxes you most recently deleted. Press F9, then **8**, and the boxes will reappear.

DISPLAYING SELECTED BOXES

For certain presentations, you may want to show only a certain portion of the organization chart, especially if it is very large, with many boxes. Two options on the Organization menu allow you to print or display a subset of the organization chart.

To show only a particular manager and subordinate group, highlight the manager box for the group, press F9, and then press **9** to select Set top of chart. All the boxes on your chart except the chosen manager and subordinate boxes, will be dimmed. When you print the chart, only that group will appear on the chart, with the selected manager box at the top. To redisplay all the boxes in your chart, move the cursor to the top box on the organization chart data-entry screen, press F9, and then press **9** to turn the option off.

You can't edit subordinates who are hidden. You'll have to unhide them before editing or changing them.

You can choose to display just the higher levels of your organization chart by hiding the subordinate boxes in certain groups. For example, you might need a chart that shows only top executive positions. Move the cursor to the manager box, press F9, and then press **A** to remove all the subordinate boxes in that group (or highlight the manager box and press Ctrl-H). A dotted line appears beneath the manager box on the screen (not on the printed chart) to indicate that the boxes below it will not be on the printed output. To redisplay the subordinate boxes, move to the manager box, press F9, and then press **B** (or press Ctrl-U from the data-entry screen).

CUSTOMIZING ORGANIZATION CHARTS

As with other types of charts, you can customize your organization chart by making selections from the organization chart Options menu. Press F8 from the data-entry screen to see the Options menu, shown in Figure 8.7.

Use the first four options to modify your chart as follows:

Box names, titles, and comments are easiest to read in the Swiss 721 font (in either roman or bold). However, if you are using color in your presentation, you might want to try other fonts or styles.

- Titles/Footnotes: As with other types of charts, you can use this option to add an extra subtitle and two additional footnote lines to the chart.

- Text Attributes: Use this option to change the characteristics of the text on the organization chart, including its title, subtitle, and footnotes, as well as the names, titles, and comments in the boxes. You can set the type style, font, color, and size.

- Appearance: Use this option to modify the appearance of various regions of the organization chart. The title region refers to the title and subtitle section of your chart. The organization region contains the manager and subordinate boxes. The footnote region refers to the three footnote lines that can appear on a chart.

- Notes: Use this option to attach a note to your chart. You can enter up to 11 lines with 60 characters per line.

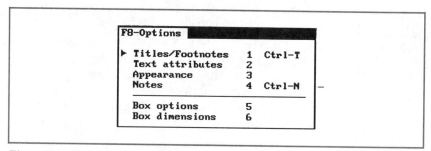

Figure 8.7: The organization chart Options menu

CUSTOMIZING BOX FEATURES

To customize features of the boxes on your organization chart, press F8, then **5** to choose Box options from the Options menu. You will see the Box Options box, as shown in Figure 8.8.

Through this box, you can change the settings for the box style and colors and the color of the lines that connect the boxes. You can also control how the text is placed in the box by choosing to split names, setting the alignment of the text in the boxes, and turning off the display of titles and comments. Move the cursor to the box option you want to change and press F3 to see a list of choices. Highlight your choice and press F10 to continue.

CHANGING BOXES AND COLORS   You can choose from the same 16 different box styles that are available for legend boxes (see Chapter 6). Choose None to show the text without a box. You can also change the box fill color and outline color, and the color of the line used to connect subordinate boxes. The selections you make affect all the boxes in your chart.

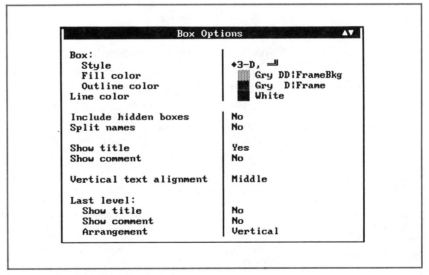

Figure 8.8: The Box Options box

CONTROLLING THE TEXT IN THE BOXES   The Include hidden boxes field in the Box Options box allows you to show all the subordinate boxes that you have hidden without unhiding each one. Change this setting to Yes when you want to display or print boxes you have hidden.

By default, Harvard displays the names within boxes on one line. To split names on two different lines, set the Split names field in the Box Options box to Yes.

The names and titles that you type are normally displayed with your chart. If your boxes are crowded and you don't want to include the titles, change the Show title field setting to No. On the other hand, if you have extra room on the chart, you may want to include comments, which Harvard does not display by default. Change the Show comment setting to Yes to add that line to your boxes.

By default, the text appears in the middle of each box. In the Vertical text alignment field of the Box Options box, you can choose to move the text to the top or bottom of the box, or to place the name at the top and the title at the bottom (Spread).

Figure 8.9 shows how some of the settings in the Box Options box affect the display of text in the organization chart.

CUSTOMIZING THE LAST LEVEL   By default, the last level of your chart appears with only names. To display titles and comments for this level, change these settings to Yes under the Last level heading in the Box Options box.

You can also change the setting in the Arrangement field under the Last level heading. Select Horizontal to list the last level's names horizontally rather than vertically. However, you should be aware that you can fit a maximum of six subordinate boxes in a horizontal display.

ADJUSTING BOX DIMENSIONS   Harvard automatically sets the dimensions of the boxes on your chart, but you can adjust them by choosing the Box Dimensions option on the organization chart Options menu. Press F8, then **6** to change the box dimensions. Set the Automatic sizing field to No, and then enter the values for the new dimensions.

You can control where a text line splits by pressing Ctrl-Enter before you enter the text you want to appear on another line.

Use the Comment field to display phone numbers or office numbers when space isn't a problem.

All the boxes in an organization chart are the same size.

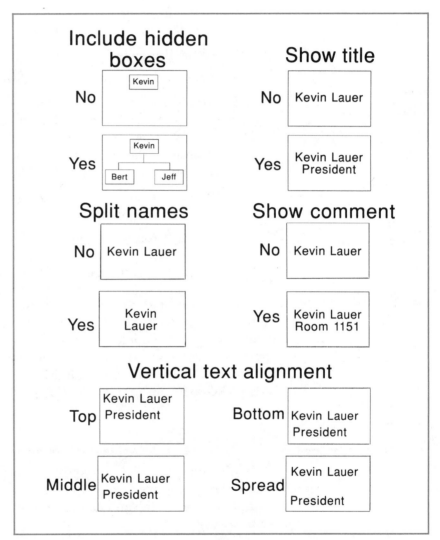

Figure 8.9: Box options that affect text in the chart

HANDS-ON: CUSTOMIZING
YOUR ORGANIZATION CHARTS

Now you will enhance the organization chart you created earlier in the chapter:

1. Use the File menu's Get chart option and select MYORG.

If you are not using the default Swiss 721 font, different font styles might be available.

2. Press **2** from the Main menu to select Edit chart. Then press F8 and **5** to display the Box Options box.

3. Set the Box style field to Shadow, and then press F10.

4. Press F8, then **2** to display the Text Attributes box.

5. Press Tab four times, then the down-arrow key three times to move the cursor to the Box name's Font Style field; press F3, and choose Bold. Move the cursor to the Box title field by pressing the down-arrow key and change the Box title's Font Style field to Bold Italic. Then press F10.

6. Press F2 to see how your chart looks. Press Esc to return to the data-entry screen.

7. Use the arrow keys to highlight Steve Kingsley's box, press F9, and type **9** to select Set top of chart. Press F2 to display the chart. Now it includes only Steve Kingsley's group.

You can continue experimenting with your organization chart on your own. Try adding some symbols or other features to your chart using Draw. For example, you can draw lines showing informal communications (the grapevine) within the organization. If you want to save your chart when you are finished working with it, save it as **NEWORG** so it won't replace MYORG.

SUMMARY

You've now rounded out your graphing experience by creating and customizing organization charts. In the next chapter, you'll learn how to use templates and macros to streamline the chart creation process.

9

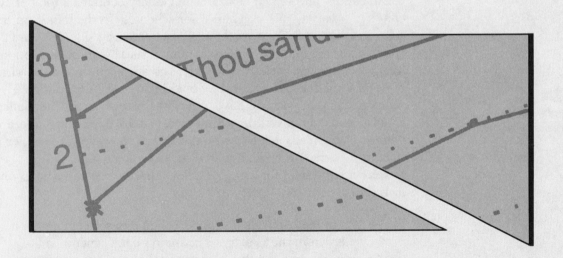

Saving Time with the Gallery, Templates, and Macros

CHAPTER 9

AFTER YOU HAVE BECOME FAMILIAR WITH HARVARD, you will find that you select certain chart styles and Harvard options more frequently than others. This chapter describes how to streamline the process of creating charts by using Harvard's time-saving features.

You will learn how to use Harvard's Gallery to choose predefined chart styles, create your own templates and apply them to charts that are already created, and create macros to automate Harvard tasks.

QUICK CHARTS FROM THE GALLERY

By using Harvard's Gallery, you can quickly make text, pie, XY, organization, and mixed charts. The Gallery contains a total of 164 charts in a variety of styles and color schemes. In the hands-on sessions in Chapter 2, we used the Gallery to create a title, list, and pie chart. You saw that the Gallery contains charts with preset options. You select the type of chart you want to create, clear the Gallery chart of its existing data values, and then add your own information.

Appendix D shows a sampling of the charts in the Gallery.

It is likely that you will have to adjust the settings for the Gallery chart to make them suit the actual data you are presenting. If a predefined chart needs just a few modifications, however, it is easier to start from it than to begin a new chart from scratch.

Here are the steps for using a Gallery chart as the pattern for your own chart:

1. From the Main menu, press **1** then **6** to select to create a chart from the Gallery. The main Gallery menu will appear, showing the main types of charts from which you can select.

2. Press the number associated with the type of chart you want to create, such as **3** for a bar chart. Harvard will display the choices for that type of chart. Figure 9.1 shows the

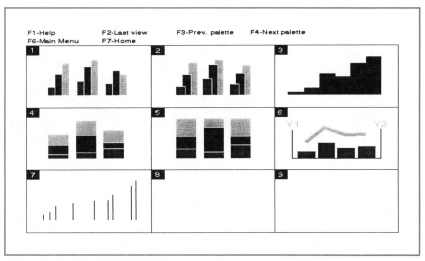

Figure 9.1: The Gallery bar chart selection screen

selections for bar charts. If you decide to choose a different chart type, press F7 to return to the main Gallery menu.

3. Press the number for the chart style that you want to use. For example, press **1** from the bar chart screen to choose a cluster style.

4. Depending on the type of chart you selected, the predefined chart will appear on the screen, or you will see another menu of style types. If you choose a clustered bar chart, for example, you will see the menu displayed in Figure 9.2. Press the number that corresponds with the enhancements you want in your chart, such as 1 for a 2D style bar chart.

5. To see the palette (color combination) choices, press F4 to cycle through them; press F3 to move back to the previous palette. Your palette selection is saved with your chart.

6. Press F10 when you are satisfied with how the template looks. This clears the template data so you can enter your own data on the data-entry screen. If you want to leave the data so that you can study the design of the chart, press F5.

Gallery palettes work with only EGA and VGA monitors. Also, many of the palette color choices are not appropriate for high-quality color presentations. See Appendix E for information about using colors in your charts.

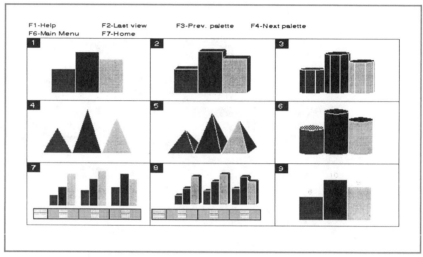

Figure 9.2: The Gallery bar chart styles

Some Gallery charts, such as the line charts, were designed for color. You will have to adjust their settings if you are going to output them in black and white.

After you follow these steps, you can continue creating the chart as you would any other Harvard chart. You can change the settings to modify the chart and use Draw to add elements. See Chapter 10 for details on placing text and modifying symbols with Draw.

CREATING AND USING TEMPLATES

Rather than using the Gallery's predefined charts, you can develop your own chart patterns, or *templates*. A template can contain preset features, specifications, symbols (such as a company logo), color schemes, and any data that you would like to keep. After you create and save a template, you can use it to quickly create new charts with the settings you already specified.

Harvard comes with the following built-in templates for each chart type:

TITLE	Title charts
BULLET	Bullet charts
TABLE	Table charts
PIE	Pie charts
BAR	Bar charts

STACKBAR	Stacked bar charts
OVERBAR	Overlapped bar charts
BARLINE	Bar and line charts
LINE	Line charts
AREA	Area charts
HLC	High/low/close charts
POINT	Point charts
ORG	Organization charts

These hold the Harvard default settings used for the new charts you create. If you create a template and save it with one of the built-in template's names, and store it in the \HG3\DATA directory, it will replace the Harvard template. Then its settings will become the defaults used for all new charts of that type. However, it is best to give your templates other names and keep Harvard's default settings as backups.

SAVING A CHART AS A TEMPLATE

You create a template by creating a new chart that contains all the settings and features you will want to use in other charts. After setting up the chart exactly as you want it, you save it as a template.

To save your chart as a template, press **4**, then **5** to choose Save as template from the File menu. The Save Template box will appear, as shown in Figure 9.3. Complete the fields as follows:

- The Directory field is already filled in with the path and name of the current directory. You can enter a different one to save the template in another directory.

- In the Filename field, specify a name of eight characters or less that matches the type of template you are creating. For example, you might enter DROPGRID for a numeric drop grid template, or 3DBAR for a 3D bar graph template.

- In the Description field, you can enter an explanation (of up to 40 characters) of the template. For example, you

If you decide to create your own default templates to replace those supplied with Harvard, be sure to keep their edited versions in the \HG3\DATA directory, or Harvard may not find them. If you are not satisfied with your new default template, delete it using the DOS DEL or ERASE command, and Harvard will once again use its own built-in default settings.

Place illustrations you use regularly, such as your company's logo, in your template.

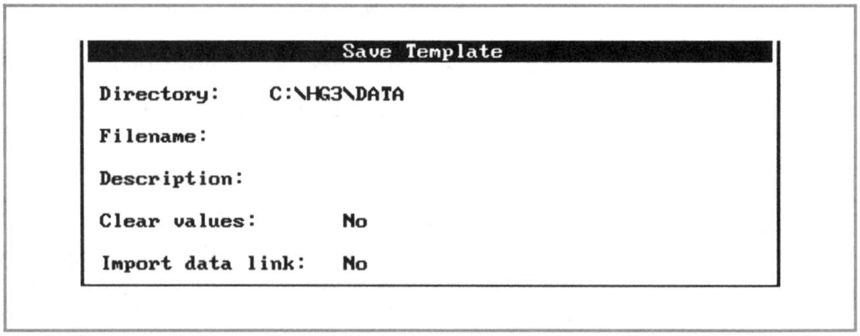

Figure 9.3: The Save Template box

could enter Quarterly Sales for a template that will be used to create charts showing sales figures for each quarter.

Save the template values if you regularly compare chronological data, such as monthly or yearly sales. Then you won't have to reenter these values for subsequent charts.

- The Clear values field is set to No by default. With this setting, your chart's data values and labels are saved with the template, and it will retain the title, subtitle, footnotes, series values, axis labels, and any other labels you created. If you will want to use entirely different labels each time you create a chart with this template, change the Clear values settings to Yes.

- The Import data link field is also set to No by default. As you will learn in Chapter 13, you can create a Harvard chart using data imported from other programs, such as Lotus 1-2-3, Excel, or dBASE. If you frequently work with data from other programs, making a template that preserves the data link speeds up the chart creation process considerably. To do this, set Import data link to Yes.

Move between the fields in the Save Template box by using the Enter, Tab, and arrow keys. Press F10 when you're finished. If you set the Clear values field to Yes, the warning shown in Figure 9.4 will appear after you press F10. To continue saving your template, press Enter.

Harvard will automatically store the following information in your templates:

- Draw symbols, drawings, and text

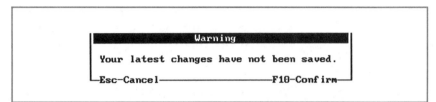

Figure 9.4: Harvard displays a warning before clearing values

- Text attribute settings
- Chart appearance options, including the orientation, palette, and background drawing
- Menu options and pop-up box settings
- The titles, footnotes, and all the labels (if you left Clear values in the Save Template box set to No)

USING YOUR TEMPLATES

To use a template as the basis for a new chart, press **4**, then **2** to select Get template from the File menu. Choose the template you want to use from the list displayed and press F10. Then you can proceed to add the data and make any of the necessary modifications. Save the new chart under its own name.

If you have already entered data and created a chart, you can fit that existing chart to an existing template. This is especially handy when you are collecting charts from many sources and you want them to have a uniform design for your presentation.

Templates include all the Options menu settings (displayed by pressing F8). If you apply a bar chart template to a line chart, for example, the lines will be replaced by bars.

To apply a template to the current chart, press **3** from the File menu to select Apply template. Harvard will display a list of your templates. Select the one you want to use and press F10. Harvard will replace the existing settings for the chart with those of the template.

HANDS-ON: CREATING AND APPLYING A TEMPLATE

Suppose that you plan to use a no-frills style chart like the one you created in Chapter 6 for several XY charts. If you save that chart as a template, you can easily make similar charts by using the template and typing new labels and values. You wouldn't have to reset the options for the axis-frame style, labels, grids, tick marks, or values.

In the following steps, you will create a template from the NOFRILLS chart and apply that template.

1. Get the NOFRILLS chart that you created in Chapter 6.

2. From the Main menu, press **4** to choose File, then **5** to choose Save as template.

3. Type **FRILLESS** and press Enter.

4. Type **Bar chart without frills** and press Enter three times.

You have just created a template based on the NOFRILLS chart. Now you will see how easy it is to apply a template to an existing chart.

5. From the Main menu, press **1**, then **6**, then **3**, then **1**, then **1** to create a 2D clustered bar chart using the Gallery.

6. Press F2 to see what it looks like (don't clear the values), and then press Esc until you see the Main menu.

7. Press **4** to select File, then **3** to choose Apply template.

8. Highlight FRILLESS and press F10.

9. Press F2 to view your chart now that the template has been applied.

In this example, all the settings from the existing chart you saved as a template were applied to the one you created from the Gallery. When you use existing charts for your own templates, be sure to change them as necessary so they are suitable for use with other charts before saving them as a template. For example, you might need to delete text and symbols that were created with Draw.

EDITING AND DELETING TEMPLATES

You can retrieve and edit a template as if it were a chart. To retrieve a template, select Get template from the File menu. Then use Harvard's

Edit chart option to change it. When you have finished editing the template, choose Save as template from the File menu.

If you will not be using a template, you can delete the template file using DOS commands, as follows:

1. Press **9** to choose the Applications option from the Main menu, then press **1** for the DOS shell.

2. From the DOS prompt, type **CD C:\HG3\DATA** and press Enter.

3. To see the templates in your subdirectory, type **DIR *.TP3** (Harvard gives template files a .TP3 extension). Note the file name of the template you want to delete.

4. Type **DELETE** *filename.* **TP3,** replacing *filename* with the name of the template file your want to delete, and press Enter.

5. Type **EXIT** to return to the Main menu, and then press Enter.

The template has been removed, and its name will not appear in any of Harvard's template listings.

CREATING AND USING MACROS

A *macro* is a recording of your keystrokes that you can play back to perform functions in Harvard. As you work with Harvard, you will find yourself using particular sets of keystrokes repeatedly. For example, you use the same series of keystrokes to send your current chart to the printer. You can save time by creating a macro to accomplish the task. To make your work even quicker, you can assign a speed key to the macro so that you can play it back with a single keystroke.

RECORDING A MACRO

Before you start to create a macro for some function, think through the steps you will take *before* you begin recording it. There are several points to keep in mind when you are recording a macro:

Press Esc five or six times when you first start recording a macro. The macro will then include enough Esc keystrokes to return to the Main menu from anywhere in Harvard, so you can run your macro from any location.

- Record the macro from the menu or screen that you plan to use it from, or it may not work as you intended. For example, if you recorded a macro from the Main menu and played it back from the File menu, the keystrokes would have different results.

- You cannot use a mouse when recording macros.

- You cannot use the Alt key when recording macros.

- Avoid using the Tab and arrow keys in macros. Instead, use numbers or letters to select menu and options whenever possible.

- When you must use the arrow keys, do not press and hold them down. To move the cursor, press and release the key for each increment.

Additionally, you cannot start recording, load, or run a macro from the Draw, DOS shell, or Palettes screen, or when a chart is displayed. You can however, start a macro at the Main menu and have the macro select and operate within Draw. However, this may not be very useful since you cannot record mouse movements.

When you are ready to record a macro, press **7** from the Main menu to choose Macros. You will see the Macros menu shown in Figure 9.5. Press **3** to select Record macro and display the Start Recording box, shown in Figure 9.6.

Complete the fields in the Start Recording Box as follows:

You erase unwanted macro files from the DOS prompt by using the ERASE or DEL command. When you delete a macro file, all of its associated macros are also erased. You might want to edit a macro file rather than delete it, as described later in the chapter.

- The Directory field shows the default drive and data subdirectory where Harvard plans to save the macro. You can change it by typing over it, or press Enter to continue.

- In the Filename box, type in a file name of eight characters or less. Harvard will automatically add the .MA3 extension to the file name.

- In the Macro name field, type a descriptive name for your macro, using up to 12 characters. Use a name that will remind you what your macro does. For example, enter Print Chart as the name for a macro that prints charts.

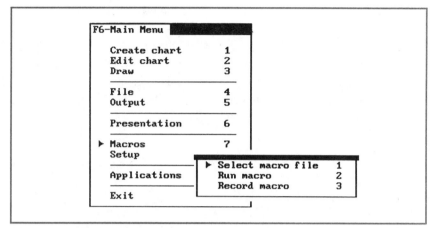

Figure 9.5: The Macros menu

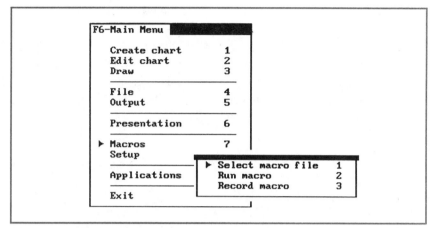

Figure 9.6: The Start Recording box

This name is stored with the macro file. Press Enter after you type a name.

- By entering a letter in the Speed key field, you will be able to run your macro by pressing the Alt key and that letter at the same time. Use a letter that will be easy to remember, such as P for a printing macro. Then you will be able to print your charts by pressing Alt-P.

After you complete the fields in the Start Recording box, press F10 to begin recording. Then type the keystrokes you want to store in the macro.

When you are finished with the keystrokes that you want to record, press Alt-0 (the number zero). You will see the Recording

If you create less than 35 macros, put them all into one file. That way, you will need to load only one macro file to have access to all your macros.

Options box, shown in Figure 9.7, which includes a Stop recording option. Select it to save your macro.

A macro file can hold as many as 35 macros, provided it hasn't reached the file limit of 1000 keystrokes. For example, you could have the Print, Directory, Color Zap, and DOS Shell macros all stored in the MYMACROS.MA3 file. This makes it easy to quickly load a group of your favorite macros.

STOPPING OR PAUSING MACRO RECORDING

You may want to pause a macro while you are recording it, either to test it or to have it stop and wait for user input. While recording the macro, press Alt-0 to display the Recording Options box.

To test each keystroke individually before recording it, select the first option, Pause recording. You can then experiment with your keystrokes until you find the right combination you need. When you are ready to resume recording, return to the position where you paused the macro and press Alt-0. Harvard will begin recording your keystrokes again.

You cannot continue a macro when a chart is displayed. Press Esc and then choose to continue the macro.

When you want the macro to pause and wait for you (or someone else) to enter keystrokes, select Pause for user input from the Recording Options box. This is useful when you want to enter a file name or execute some keystrokes from within the macro. After you enter the keystrokes during the pause, press Alt-0 and choose Continue recording to resume recording the macro.

LOADING AND RUNNING MACROS

Before you can play back a macro, the macro file that contains it must be loaded. From the Main menu, press **7**, then press **1** from the Macros menu to choose Select macro file. A list of your macro files will appear.

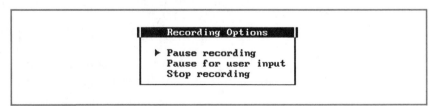

Figure 9.7: The Recording Options box

Unload the macros if you run out of memory in Harvard. This may happen when you have many symbols, illustrations, or elements in your chart. You have to exit Harvard to unload macros.

Change the drive and subdirectory if the macro file you want is stored elsewhere. Highlight the name of the macro file you want to load and press Enter. If you want to unload the macros from memory, you will have to exit Harvard and restart the program.

After loading the macro file, you can run the macros in it from the Macros menu. Press **8** from the Main menu, then **2** to select Run macro. You will see a list of the macros that are available. Highlight the name of the macro you want to run or type the macro's name. Press F10, and Harvard will play back the macro.

If you assigned a speed key to your macro, it is even easier to run it. Just press the Alt-key combination, and your macro will run. You do not have to return to the Main menu or go through the Macros menu.

INTERRUPTING A RUNNING MACRO

If necessary, you can interrupt a macro that is being played back. When you press Alt-0 while a macro is running, you see the Playback Options box, as shown in Figure 9.8. Select to suspend, step through, or cancel the macro, as follows:

- If you want to suspend the macro temporarily so you can enter your own keystrokes, select Pause playback. When you want the macro to continue running, press Alt-0 and choose Continue playback.

Use the Step play-back option in the Playback Options box (press Alt-0 while the macro is running) to test and debug your macros.

- If you want to stop the macro because it is not working correctly (or you want to learn how it works), choose Step playback. Then press a key to play back the macro keystrokes one at a time. Each time you press any key, the macro will process the next keystroke.

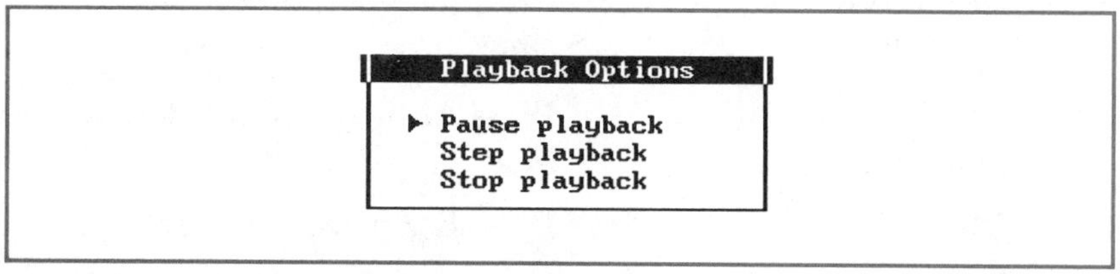

```
              ╔══════════════════════╗
              ║   Playback Options   ║
              ╠══════════════════════╣
              ║ ▶ Pause playback     ║
              ║   Step playback      ║
              ║   Stop playback      ║
              ╚══════════════════════╝
```

Figure 9.8: The Playback Options box

- To cancel the macro (stop the rest of it from running), select Stop playback.

HANDS-ON: RECORDING AND RUNNING A PRINTING MACRO

A common task for macros is printing. In the following steps, you will create a printing macro and give it a speed key to streamline the procedure for producing your charts.

1. From the Main menu, press **7**, then **3** to select Record macro from the Macros menu.

2. Press Enter to accept the default drive and subdirectory for your macro file.

3. Type **MACRO1** as the Filename for your macro and press Enter.

4. When you are prompted for the macro name, type **Quick Print** and press Enter.

5. Press **P** to designate Alt-P as the speed key and press Enter. You will see the recording message on the top-left side of the screen, indicating that Harvard will now record all your keystrokes.

6. Press Esc five times to ensure that your macro will start from the Main menu, regardless of where you are in Harvard when you run it.

7. Press **4**, then **1** to retrieve a chart.

8. Press Alt-0 (zero) to display the Recording Options box. Select Pause for user input and press Enter.

9. Press the appropriate keys to retrieve any chart. When the chart appears, press Esc.

10. Press Alt-0 and select Continue recording to resume the macro.

11. Press Esc twice to return to the Main menu.

Harvard may appear to have ignored your entry, but it hasn't; the pause will occur when the macro runs so you can choose a chart to print.

12. Press **5**, then **1**, then **D** to select draft quality printing from the Output to Printer menu.

13. Press Alt-0 and select Stop recording. You stopped the macro here so that you can either press F10 to print the chart, or reset the printing options before printing. Now let's test the macro.

14. To run your macro, press Alt-P. You will see the Select File list. Select the chart you want printed and press Esc.

15. Press Alt-0 and select Continue playback. The macro will bring you to the Output to Printer box.

You can see that it is much easier to run a macro than it is to repeat all the keystrokes each time you want to perform the same task. You can enhance your macros by editing them. For example, you might want to add a message box telling the user to press Alt-0 after selecting a chart to print. The next section explains how to edit macros.

EDITING YOUR MACROS

You can create macros from a word processor by typing in the commands. Save the file as an ASCII file.

Harvard saves your macro as an ASCII file. This means that if your macro does not work properly, you can use a word processor or DOS's EDLIN program to edit it. By editing a macro, you can add extra commands, as well as correct mistakes. Harvard has a sophisticated programming language that you can use to make your macros extremely efficient. For example, you can run a macro within the current one, include programming commands, insert text messages, provide menus, and insert time delays.

THE STRUCTURE OF A MACRO FILE

When you view your macro file in a text editor, you will see how Harvard has translated your keystrokes. Figure 9.9 shows an example of the text in a macro file.

Two commands that are required in every macro are #MACRO and #END_MACRO, which Harvard automatically inserts in your macro. These commands tell Harvard where to start and end your macros, as

```
#macro("Quick Print")
{This macro prints a draft of your chart.}

#escape 4
{Use several escapes to return to }
{the Main Menu before running a macro. }

#textbox("Draft",5,20)
#text("The macro will print a draft chart")
#text("using the Printer 1 default settings")
'51D'

#textbox("Printing, please wait.")
#f10

#end_macro()
```

Figure 9.9: A sample macro file

well as separate each macro from the others. Never delete one of these commands from the macro file.

The #MACRO command uses the syntax

#MACRO(*"macro-name"*,*"speed-key"*,*autostart*)

where *macro-name* is the name you assign the macro, *speed-key* is the assigned Alt-keystroke, and *autostart* is set to Yes or No. By default, autostart is set to No. If you set it to Yes, the macro will automatically start and run when you load it. The macro name is a required, but the speed key and autostart settings are optional.

Examples of valid #MACRO commands are:

    #MACRO("Quick Print")
    #MACRO("Quick Print","P")
    #MACRO("Quick Print","P",Yes)

It does not matter whether you type your macro commands in uppercase or lowercase letters.

All macros must end with the **#END_MACRO()** command. The commands for each macro come between the #MACRO and

#END_MACRO commands. There is a 1000-keystroke limit on the macros you create, and Harvard will automatically insert the #END_MACRO command when a macro reaches that limit.

You can add comments to explain your macro. Surround the text with curly braces, {}. Harvard will ignore this text when running the macro. For example, the second line in Figure 9.9 is a comment that reads

{This macro prints a draft of your chart.}

Use comments to remind yourself of what the macro is supposed to do.

ADDING KEYSTROKES TO A MACRO FILE

You enter keystrokes into a macro file by surrounding them with a single quotation mark. For example, if you want to enter a command for pressing 5, 1, and D to print a draft chart from the Main menu, you would type **'51D'** into your macro (as on the ninth line in Figure 9.9).

Special keys, such as the function keys, are entered by preceding them with a pound sign (#). For example, if you want to add the F10 keypress, enter **#f10** (see the eleventh line of Figure 9.9). Table 9.1 shows the commands for some of the special keystrokes you might need to use in your macro files.

You can repeat keystrokes by following the key command with a space and a number. For example, to enter the command to press the Esc key four times, type **#escape 4**.

Do not put spaces between the # and the keystroke. For example, type **#enter**, not **# enter**.

INSERTING PAUSES IN MACROS

There are two commands you can enter in a macro file to insert a pause in your macro:

#PAUSE()   Causes the macro to pause and display the Playback Options box. To resume processing, select Continue playback if the macro is paused; otherwise, press Esc to leave the box and continue the macro.

Table 9.1: Keystroke Commands in Harvard Macro Files

KEYSTROKE	MACRO COMMAND
F1–F10	#f1–#f10
Esc	#escape
Enter	#enter
Backspace	#backspace
Del	#delete
Ins	#ins
Spacebar	#space
End	#end
←	#left
→	#right
↓	#down
↑	#up
PgUp	#pgup
PgDn	#pgdn
Tab	#tab
Shift-Tab	#backtab
Ctrl-Del	#ctrldel
Ctrl-Ins	#ctrlins
Ctrl-Home	#ctrlhome
Ctrl-End	#ctrlend
Ctrl-←	#ctrlleft
Ctrl-→	#ctrlright
Ctrl-↓	#ctrldn
Ctrl-↑	#ctrlup
Ctrl-PgUp	#ctrlpgup
Ctrl-PgDn	#ctrlpgdn
Ctrl-(any letter)	#ctrl[*letter*]

#WAIT(*n*) Pauses the macro for *n* seconds before continuing, at the point in the macro where it appears. You can specify from 1 to 36,000 seconds. For example, the command #WAIT(60) pauses the macro for 60 seconds.

INSERTING MESSAGES TO USERS

You can use the #TEXTBOX and #TEXT commands to supply messages and instructions for users of your macros. The syntax for the commands are

#TEXTBOX("*title*",*left-margin*, *top-row*, *right-margin*, *bottom-row*)
#TEXT("*text-lines*")

The *title* can be a title for the message or a simple one-line message. For example, you could add the command

#TEXTBOX("printing")

to have Harvard place the word *printing* in a box in the center of your screen.

To place the box in a different position, follow the title with the *left-margin*, *top-row* parameters. To place a box with the word *printing* in the top-left corner of the screen, for example, you would type

#TEXTBOX("printing",1,1)

It's usually easier to enter just the left-margin and top-row positions for your message boxes. Let Harvard compute the other positions based on the space you need for the following lines of text.

You can define the other bottom-right corner of the box by including the *right-margin*, *bottom-row* parameters. Type a value from 0 to 79 for the left and right margins. Values from 0 to 24 can be entered for the top and bottom rows.

The *text-lines* parameter of the #TEXT command is the text you want inserted in the message box. You can add up to 15 #TEXT ("*text-lines*") statements following the #TEXTBOX command. Figure 9.9 shows two message boxes: one that uses #TEXT commands, and one that has just a #TEXTBOX command.

MACRO PROGRAMMING

If you're familiar with creating DOS batch files or other types of programming, you will be able to program complex macros to automate your work. By using Harvard's macro programming language, you can section off macros into blocks to assign labels and subroutines. Your macros can then use branching techniques with #GOSUB, #RETURN, or #GOTO statements to control the flow of the macro program. You can nest macros within each other using #CALL. All of these programming techniques can be combined with a #MENU command to add new features, commands, and tutorials to Harvard Graphics.

If you have some programming experience, refer to the Harvard Graphics user's manual for details on using advanced macro techniques. You might also want to print the SAMPLE.MA3 file that comes with Harvard Graphics 3.0, which provides examples of labels and branching statements.

ERROR HANDLING IN MACROS

There are several problems you might want to watch for when editing or using macros. Harvard stores the macros you load in memory. If you load more than one macro with the same name, you will see a warning message telling you that only the first macro will run. This can happen if you load the same macro twice (just ignore the message) or if you have two different macros that you have assigned the same name (edit the file and change its name).

The following are other errors that can cause problems in macros:

- A command does not start with the pound sign (#).

- A command has spaces in it.

- A command does not have opening and closing parentheses (). All commands, even those without parameters, must include a pair of parentheses.

- You have more than 30 #GOSUB statements in a single macro.

- There are incorrect commas, single quotation marks, or double quotation marks.

- A command is spelled incorrectly.

Finding problems can be difficult. Use the command

#STEP(Yes)

in your macro to help find an error or troublesome command. The keystrokes will be played back one at a time so you can catch any mistakes. After you have found and corrected any errors, either delete the #STEP command from your macro or set it to #STEP(No).

SUMMARY

As you have learned in this chapter, Harvard's Gallery and templates can help save time in creating and printing your graphs. You have also learned that macros can execute a wide variety of keystrokes, making routine procedures for Harvard, DOS, and other programs quick and effortless.

In the next chapter, you'll learn how to create custom charts with Draw.

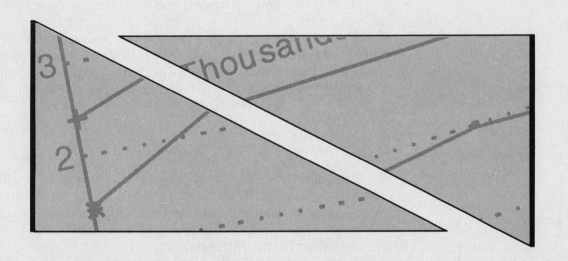

Designing Custom Charts

CHAPTER **10** _____

YOU CAN USE HARVARD'S DRAW OPTION TO CREATE
(*draw*) a custom chart from scratch or to add illustrations and text to
an existing graph. Using Draw, you can create more than just charts:

- Maps
- Signs and posters
- Personal greeting cards
- Flow charts and diagrams
- Floor plans and layouts
- Letterheads and stationery
- Brochures, announcements, and cover designs

Use Draw to enhance your charts with text, boxes, lines, circles,
and polygons. Add special symbols or objects such as arcs, wedges,
freehand drawings, and circular text. The chart itself is an object that
you can move, resize, rotate, or convert into a symbol.

FEATURES OF THE DRAW SCREEN _____

From any chart
data-entry screen,
press F4 to access Draw.
To return to the data-
entry screen, press F4
from the Draw screen.

If you want to create a custom chart from scratch, press **1**, then **5** to
choose a drawing chart. If you want to work on an existing chart,
retrieve it and then choose Draw. It will appear in the *drawing area* on
the right. The drawing area will match the orientation you chose for
your chart, either landscape or portrait.

Figure 10.1 shows the Draw screen. The tool icons appear on the
left side of the screen, the function-key commands are along the top,
and a status box appears on the left above the drawing area.

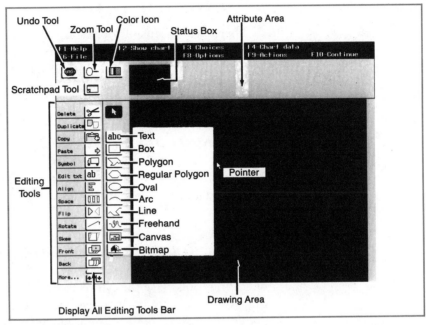

Figure 10.1: The Draw screen

It is much easier to use a mouse with Draw. Without one, it takes a long time and a lot of effort to use tools. The instructions provided in this and the following chapter are for the mouse. If you must use a keyboard, substitute these commands:

ACTION	KEYBOARD	MOUSE
Select an item	Use the arrow keys to move the pointer and press Enter	Move your pointer to an item and click the left button
Complete a task or exit a menu	Press F10	Click the right button
Drag an item	Press the spacebar, use the arrow keys to move the pointer, and press Enter	Press and hold the left mouse button, move the pointer with the mouse, and release the button

TOOLS OF THE TRADE

There are dozens of tools you can use to create and edit objects. You select a tool by moving the pointer to that tool's icon and pressing the left mouse button. A tool that is currently selected will be highlighted. You can also use speed keys for quick tool selection. Press Ctrl-F1 to see a list of these keys.

DRAWING TOOLS There are ten *drawing tools* you can select to add text, boxes, polygons, ovals, arcs, lines, and freehand drawings. You can also use drawing tools to add background drawings and import bit-map images. You will learn how to use the drawing tools shortly.

EDITING TOOLS *Editing tools* are labeled on the drawing screen so you can readily distinguish their functions. There are two columns of editing tools. Use the More... ↓ and ↑ icons on the bottom left of the Draw screen to move between these columns. If you select the bar above these icons, both columns of editing tools will be displayed, but you will not be able to read their descriptions. You might want to view the editing tools this way once you become familiar with their functions.

Use the editing tools as follows:

NAME	*ICON*	*FUNCTION*
Selection tool		Places you in selection mode so that you can choose icons or objects for modification. To stop using a drawing or editing tool, move the pointer to the selection tool and click the left mouse button.

Undo tool		Reverses your last action (such as restoring an object you just deleted). If you change your mind again, you can keep the previous action by selecting Undo again. Undo only works with options that affect objects in your drawing.
Zoom tool		Magnifies parts of your drawing. Use it for fine detail work.
Scratchpad tool		Displays a separate drawing area that you can use without affecting your chart. You can copy items from the scratchpad to your drawing.

THE STATUS BOX AND ATTRIBUTE AREA

The *status box* lets you see the objects you are working with. When you pick a drawing tool, for example, you will be able to get an idea of what your object will look like. If you select an object for editing, that object will appear in the status box. This is useful when editing complex objects because it's often difficult to see which object is selected on the Draw screen.

The attributes of the selected object shown in the status box are represented by icons in the attribute area. The attributes shown include color, line width, and style options. Figure 10.2 shows an

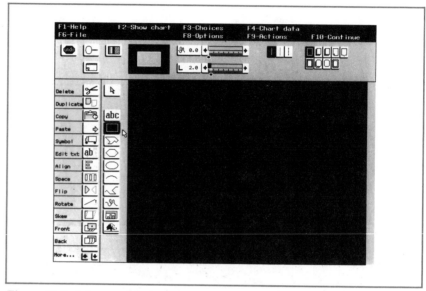

Figure 10.2: A box and its attributes

example of how the status box and attribute area appear when a box is selected.

Attributes can appear as icons or *slider bars*. You use a slider bar to change attributes that can vary in dimension, size, or shape. To change line width, for instance, you can click the mouse button over the numbers on the slider bar and type in new values, or you can drag the slider to the left or right until the numbers reflect the values you want to use.

Move the pointer to the slider bar and click on plus (+) to increase or minus (–) to decrease the increment value of the slides as you move them.

GETTING THE POINTER

The pointer is used to select icons, objects, and function keys, as well as to create, move, and resize objects. The pointer's position can change depending on the Draw function you are performing. For example, when you first enter Draw, the pointer will be in an arrow shape. When you select an object and hold the mouse button down, the pointer will change to a four-tipped arrow, indicating that you can now move the object. Figure 10.3 shows the pointer shapes you may see when working with Draw.

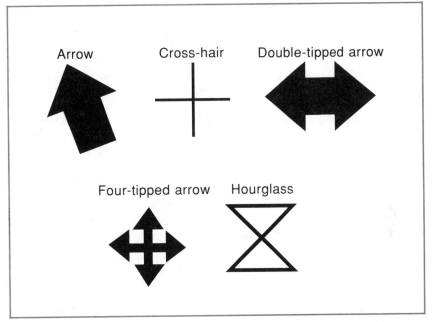

Figure 10.3: Pointer shapes in Draw

CREATING OBJECTS WITH THE DRAWING TOOLS

When you select a drawing tool, that tool's icon becomes highlighted, and the object drawn by that tool is displayed in the status box. Once you move the pointer into the drawing area, the pointer assumes a cross-hairs shape, indicating that it is ready to add an object.

DRAWING BOXES

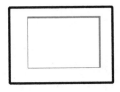

Use the Box tool to emphasize text and create symbols and pictures. Follow these steps to draw a box:

1. Select the Box tool icon.

2. Move the pointer to the drawing area and anchor the starting corner of the box by clicking the left mouse button.

3. Move the pointer to where you want the box to end. As you move it, Harvard outlines the box to show you its current dimensions. When you are satisfied with the size and position of the box, click the mouse button. If you make a mistake, select the Undo tool in the top-left corner of the screen, and the box will disappear.

4. When you have finished drawing, press the right mouse button to turn the drawing function off. The box will remain selected. (Draw automatically selects the last object you placed.)

You can make a box square by pressing the Shift key while you move the pointer after anchoring the corner of the box. Keep the Shift key depressed until you click the mouse.

ASSIGNING ATTRIBUTES TO OBJECTS

To save time, select attributes for your object immediately after you select the tool and before placing the object.

The default settings for your object's attributes are highlighted in the attribute area. To change its attributes, move your pointer to the attribute area. From here, you can change the thickness and style of the outline that surrounds the box, as well as the object's colors, style, and size. You can always change the attributes later by choosing the selection tool and reselecting the object.

BOX STYLES   You can choose from a variety of styles for your boxes, including different types of shadowing, 3D, page, with a pointer (a caption box), and framed. Figure 10.4 shows the box styles.

Select the icon in the attribute area that resembles the box style you want to apply. If you select a shadow, 3D, page, caption, or rounded shadow box, you will see additional icons for specifying the style. For example, if you choose a shadowed box, four more icons appear so that you can select the direction you want the shadow to fall.

ADJUSTING STYLE FEATURES   The slider bar with the shadowed box icon is used to change the size of a style features, not the size of the box itself. You enlarge the features as you increase the size.

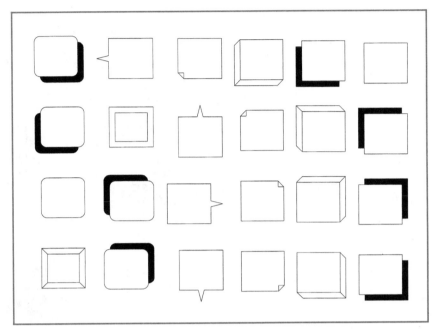

Figure 10.4: Box style options

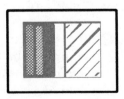

If you want to adjust the roundness of the corners of a rounded shadowed box, first give it the rounded corner attribute. Use the slider bar with the shadowed box icon to change the rounding of the corners. Then select the icon to change it to a shadow box style. Use the slider bar again to adjust the shadow so that it fits the corners.

For example, if you choose a larger size for a rounded corner box, the corners will be rounder. Valid ranges for this slider bar are from 0 to 25, with a default value of 2. Figure 10.5 shows the effects of changing the size of style features.

CHANGING LINE STYLES AND WIDTHS   The line style and outline width attributes apply to boxes, lines, ovals, arcs, freehand shapes, and polygons. You can select a solid, dotted, or dashed line style.

By default, thin lines are used for objects. To increase the line width, use the slider bar that shows a freehand (squiggly) line icon. Its default setting is 0. You can set line widths of up to 25. Figure 10.6 shows examples of different line styles and widths.

CUSTOMIZING THE FILL, OUTLINE, PATTERN, AND COLORS   The pattern and color attributes apply to boxes, text, lines, ovals, arcs, freehand shapes, and polygons. To assign a pattern

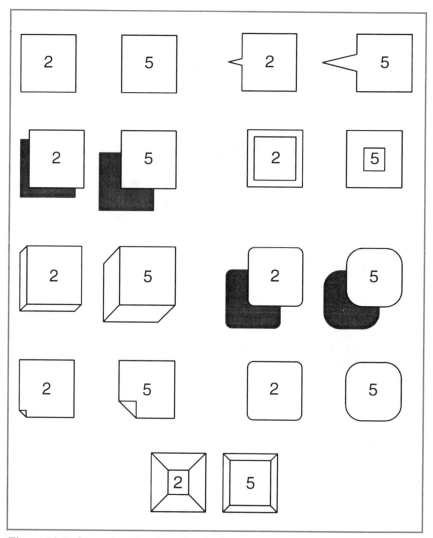

Figure 10.5: Changing the size of style features

By default, the black-and-white areas on your screen are reversed in the printed output—the white areas on your screen will be printed black, and black screen images will not print since they represent the white of the paper. You can, however, reverse this effect when printing.

or color to an object, select the color icon. The color and pattern choices will appear, as shown in Figure 10.7.

First select whether you want to apply the color or pattern choice to the object's fill, line/text, pattern, or shadow by clicking on the appropriate box above the colors and patterns. For example, to

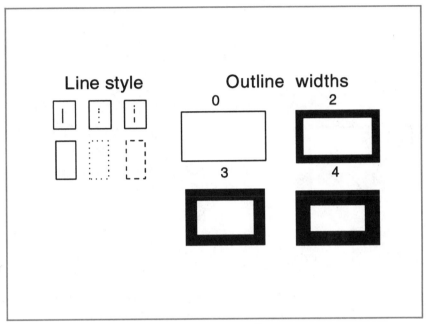

Figure 10.6: Outline widths and line style attributes

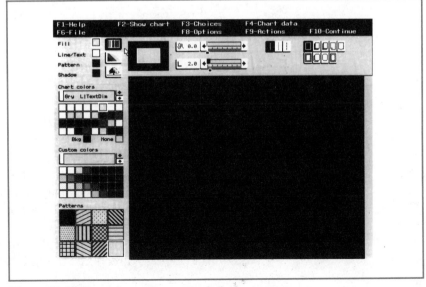

Figure 10.7: The color and pattern choices

change the fill color of your object, click on the small box next to Fill. A white line will appear around the selected object. Then click on the new chart color, custom color, or pattern and press the right mouse button.

DRAWING IRREGULAR POLYGONS

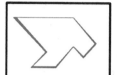

Use the Polygon tool to draw irregularly shaped objects. They are as easy to create as boxes but give you more flexibility for unusual shapes or designs.

To use the Polygon tool, follow these steps:

1. Select the Polygon tool.

2. Move the cross-hairs pointer to the drawing area and click where you want the polygon to start.

3. Move the pointer to where you want the line to end and click. If you make a mistake, press the Backspace key and reposition the line.

4. Repeat steps 2 and 3 until you have added all the lines you want.

5. Press the right mouse button when you are finished drawing the polygon.

To draw straight polygon lines, press the Shift key while moving your mouse horizontally, vertically, or diagonally.

APPLYING ATTRIBUTES TO POLYGONS The color, line width, and line style attributes that are available for boxes can also be selected for polygons. In addition, you can draw polygons with sharp or curved lines. When you choose the sharp attribute for the line shape, angular lines connect each point on the shape where you clicked. Selecting the curved attribute results in sloping lines.

When you draw a polygon with curved lines, the number of times you click determines the shape of the object. When you click at short intervals to change directions, the lines will be more angular. If you just click once to change directions, the lines will change gradually. To ensure that a curved polygon line touches a point in your chart, click three times.

Figure 10.8 shows examples of polygons that you can draw and some of the attributes you can apply.

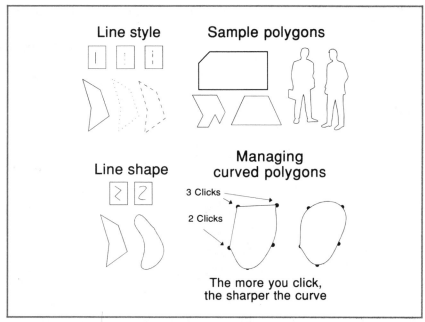

Figure 10.8: Drawing polygons

DRAWING REGULAR POLYGONS

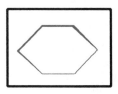

Unlike irregularly shaped polygons, regular polygons have uniform sides. Use the Regular Polygon tool to draw regular shapes, such as triangles, pentagons, and octagons, as follows:

1. Select the Regular Polygon tool.

2. Move the pointer to the attribute area and click in the Number of sides box.

3. Enter a value from 3 to 15 for the number of uniform sides you want your polygon to have. For example, enter 3 for a triangle, 4 for a square, 5 for a pentagon, and so on.

4. Move the pointer to where you want to position the center of the regular polygon and click.

5. Draw the polygon by moving the cursor. You will see an outline of the polygon that moves with the cursor. When the object is positioned where you want it, click again. The outline disappears, and the polygon takes its place.

You can change the shape's color, line width, line style, and line type. Figure 10.9 illustrates some of the attributes you can apply to regular polygons.

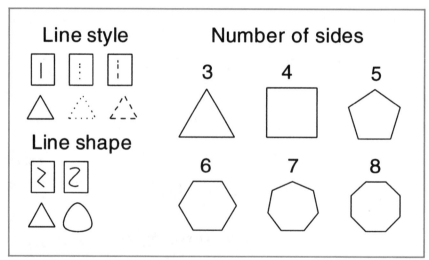

Figure 10.9: Regular polygon attributes

DRAWING OVALS AND CIRCLES

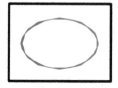

To draw either an oval or a circle, select the Oval tool, move the pointer to where you want to position the center of the oval, and click. If you want to draw a circle, press the Shift key while moving the pointer. Move the pointer until the outline shows the shape as you want it, and then click.

You can change the attributes of the oval or circle by selecting the appropriate icons in the attribute area. For example, you can change the style and thickness of the line that forms the shape, or you can select the color icon to change its color or pattern. Figure 10.10 shows examples of the attributes you can apply to circles and ovals.

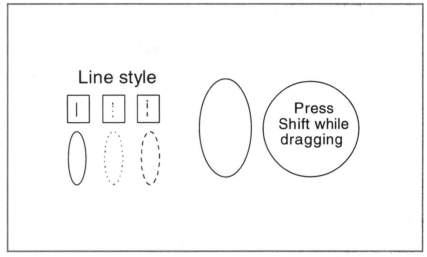

Figure 10.10: Attributes for ovals and circles

DRAWING ARCS

Use the Arc tool to draw arcs, with or without arrows. Follow these steps to draw an arc:

1. Choose the Arc tool.

2. Move the pointer to where you want the arc to start and click the left mouse button.

3. Move the pointer to where you want the arc to end and click the left mouse button again.

4. Move the pointer in the direction you want the arc to curve and click again.

As with other objects, you can change the attributes of the arc, such as the line width or color. Another attribute you can give to an arc is arrows, which you can add to one or both ends. To use arrows, click on the single- or double-arrow icon to highlight it. To remove the arrow points from an arc, click on the highlighted icon to turn it off. Figure 10.11 shows some of the attributes you can apply to arcs.

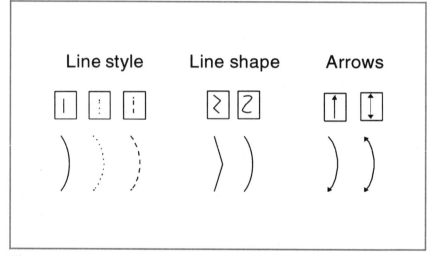

Figure 10.11: Arc attributes

DRAWING LINES

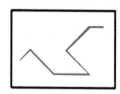

To draw straight lines, use the Line tool. Follow these steps to add a line:

1. Choose the Line tool.

2. Move the cross-hairs pointer to where you want the line to start and anchor it by clicking.

3. Move the pointer to where you want the line to end and click. If you make a mistake, press the Backspace key and try again.

4. Press the right mouse button or Esc when you are finished using the Line tool.

To draw a horizontal, vertical, or diagonal line, press the Shift key and hold it down while moving the pointer.

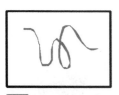

Set Fill to Background (select the color icon) when you want to place text inside a wide arrow. Then use the Text tool to label the arrows.

As with the other objects, you can apply different attributes to lines, including line thickness, line style, line type, and arrows. To draw a curved line, select the curved attribute. As when you draw irregular polygons, you can control how angular the curved lines are by the number of points you click on to change directions. You can force a curved line to touch a given point by clicking three times before moving the pointer. Figure 10.12 shows some of the attributes you can choose for lines.

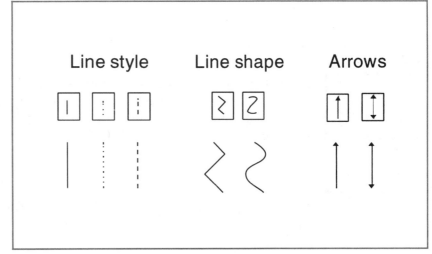

Figure 10.12: Drawing lines

DRAWING FREEHAND SHAPES

You can add a freehand drawing to your charts. Working with the Freehand tool is similar to drawing with a pen or pencil. Follow these steps to use the Freehand tool:

1. Choose the Freehand tool.

2. Move the pointer to where you want to start the freehand line.

3. Press the left mouse button while dragging the pointer to draw. A tracing of the line you are creating appears as you

Use a mouse for maximum flexibility in freehand drawing. If you use the keyboard, your drawings will look like polygons.

drag. When your line is finished, release the mouse button, and the new line will appear.

4. Repeat steps 2 and 3 until your freehand drawing is complete.

The attributes you can select for freehand drawings are similar to those available for lines (see Figure 10.12). If you want to fill your drawing with a color or pattern, first convert into a polygon. Converting objects is discussed in Chapter 11.

SETTING A CANVAS AREA WITH THE CANVAS TOOL

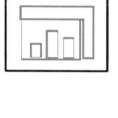

The Canvas tool works a little differently than the other drawing tools. With it, you can control the chart's position in a background drawing. You create a canvas area to regulate the amount of space that your chart occupies in a drawing chart, as illustrated in Figure 10.13.

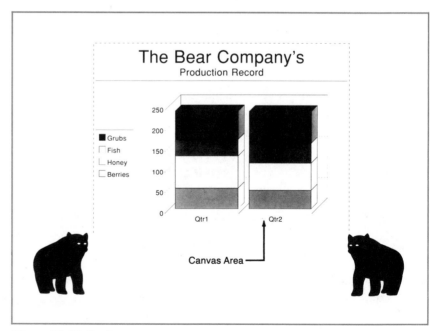

Figure 10.13: Setting a canvas area

Creating a canvas area is useful if the border in your background drawing runs into the chart area.

You draw the canvas area with the Canvas tool in the same way that you use the Box tool to draw a box. Position the pointer in drawing area where you want the top-left corner of the chart to appear and click. Drag the pointer to the opposite corner and click again. If you want the chart to maintain its proportions, press the Shift key while you drag to the opposite corner of the canvas area.

HANDS-ON: CREATING A BACKGROUND DRAWING WITH THE DRAWING TOOLS

As mentioned earlier in the book, adding a good background drawing to your charts is an efficient way to give them uniform elements, such as borders. In the following steps, you will create a background drawing similar to the one shown in Figure 10.14.

1. From the Main menu, press **1**, then **5** to create a new drawing chart. You will see the Draw screen.

The Bear Company

Figure 10.14: The sample background drawing

2. Press F8 to display the Options menu for drawing charts shown in Figure 10.15, and then press **8** to select Appearance. The Appearance Options box settings work the same for drawing charts as they do for the other types of charts. Make sure that chart orientation is set to Landscape and that the Background drawing field is empty, and then press Esc.

3. Select the Box tool. You will draw a box as a frame for the background drawing.

4. Move to the attribute area and click on the 0.0 value for the line width icon. A cursor will appear in the number box. Type *.3* and press Enter.

5. Change the box style by selecting the shadowed box icon to highlight it. Four directional boxes will appear. Select the icon that has the shadow on the bottom-right side of the box.

6. Click on the color icon to display the color and pattern choices. Highlight the Fill box and then click on the Bkg chart color. Setting the fill of the box to the background

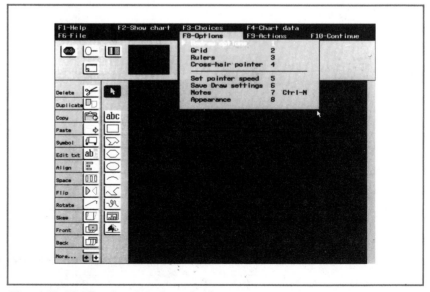

Figure 10.15: The drawing chart Options menu

color ensures that it will not interfere with the chart you place on it. Change the Line/Text and Shadow options to white.

7. Press Esc twice. Then reselect the Box tool.

8. Move the pointer to the drawing area and anchor the starting point of the box in the top-left corner of the chart by clicking the left mouse button.

9. Drag the mouse pointer to the bottom-right corner of the chart and click. Your box will appear as a chart frame.

10. Select the Text tool (the tool under the Selection tool in the right column, with the letters *abc*). Change the text size to 4.0. Then move the cursor to the bottom-right corner inside the frame and type **The Bear Company**.

Because the canvas area outline disappears after you place the canvas (although the canvas area remains defined), it is a good idea to add it last.

11. Select the Canvas tool, and the screen will change colors. Position the pointer in the top-left corner of the drawing area and click. Press the Shift key while dragging the mouse to the opposite corner at the bottom-right area of the drawing area and click again.

12. Click on the Selection tool.

13. Press Ctrl-S and save the drawing chart as **MYBACK.CH3**. Give it the description **My background drawing**.

You can now assign other charts you create to use this file as your background drawing. The charts will automatically be positioned in the canvas area.

ADDING BIT-MAP DRAWINGS

Bit-map drawings can add interest to your charts. You can create bit-map drawings using a program such as PCPaint or Window's Paintbrush, and then bring them into your Harvard drawing chart.

You can also use the CAPTURE utility provided with Harvard to copy images from your screen (in any program) and save them as .PCX bit-map files. To run the utility, at the DOS prompt, type

C:\HG3\CAPTURE

Harvard provides two sample bit-map images in the \HG3\DATA subdirectory: FLOOR.PCC and ROCKTOP.PCC.

Press the Print Screen (sometimes labeled PrtSc) key to save a screen in a .PCX file.

To insert a bit-map image, select the Bitmap tool. Harvard will display the Get Bitmap File list. Select the name of the bit-map file that contains the image and press F10 to continue. The bit-map image will appear in the drawing area of the screen.

CUSTOMIZING THE DRAWING AREA

Some of the options listed on the drawing chart Options menu (press F8 from the Draw screen) are similar to those for other charts. The options for drawing charts include the following:

- Appearance
- Notes
- Redraw
- Grid
- Rulers
- Cross-hairs pointer
- Set pointer speed
- Save Draw settings

The Save Drawing settings option allows you to save your Options menu settings so that they will be used with each new drawing chart you create. If you will want to use your customized settings regularly, press **6** from the Options menu to save them. The following sections describe how to adjust drawing chart options.

REDRAWING OPTIONS

To redraw your screen at anytime, press Ctrl-D.

By default, each time you change a chart, Harvard redraws the screen to show you all the details. It may take some time for the screen to be redrawn, especially when the chart has bit-map images, gradient fills, and subcharts. You can adjust the redrawing settings by choosing

Redraw from the Options menu. This displays the Redraw Options box, shown in Figure 10.16.

You can save redrawing time by keeping Harvard's Quality field set to Draft and setting the remaining options in the Redraw Options box to No. To view all the details in the chart, set the Quality field to High and the other options to Yes.

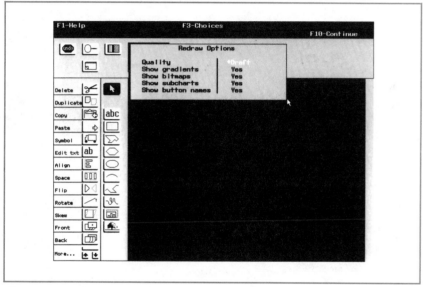

Figure 10.16: The Redraw Options box

USING GRIDS AND RULERS FOR PRECISE DRAWINGS

A grid helps you draw and align the different objects in your chart. When you select Grid from the Options menu, you see the Grid box, as shown in Figure 10.17.

To display the grid in your chart, set the Show grid field to Yes. Harvard's grids are composed of dotted lines. To adjust the *density* of the dots, or how closely the dots are spaced, enter values in the Horizontal spacing and Vertical spacing fields. By default, Harvard sets the grid in 1-inch blocks. You can change the unit of measurement to inches, centimeters, or percent of the chart's size by changing the Units setting.

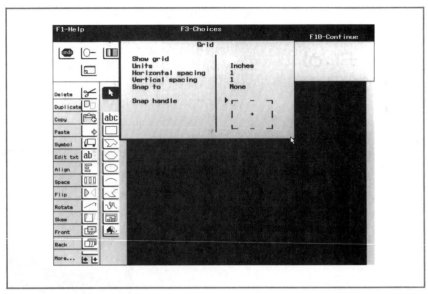

Figure 10.17: The Grid box

Because Snap to restricts the placement of your lines, set Horizontal spacing and Vertical spacing to .25 inch for greater drawing flexibility.

If you set the Show grid field to No and forget to reset Snap to None, your objects will snap to invisible grid dots.

By turning on Draw's Snap to feature, you force the objects you create to start and end on a grid dot. This is handy for precise, symmetrical drawings, such as flow charts and other diagrams.

By default, the Snap to field in the Grid box is set to None. Change the setting to suit how you want the objects aligned. The choices are Horizontal, Vertical, and All. Snap to does not affect existing objects unless you modify them after turning it on.

The Snap handle setting in the Grid box establishes which part of the object aligns on the grid. The box outline in the Snap handle field represents your object, and the pointer shows which part will snap to the grid. The default position for the snap handle is the upper-left corner. To change the position, use the arrow keys to move the pointer. For example, if you pick the center for the snap handle, the center of each object will snap to a grid point.

Figure 10.18 shows how drawing over an image on paper and using Harvard's Grid settings can help in reproducing the image in Harvard. Concentrating on one grid box at a time makes it easier to draw precise illustrations.

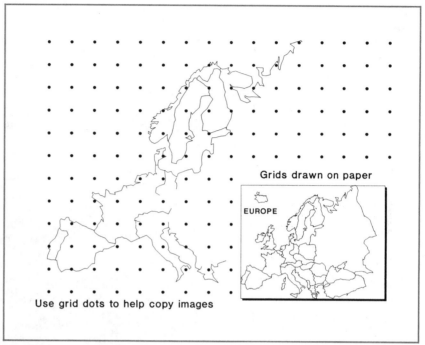

Grids drawn on paper

EUROPE

Use grid dots to help copy images

Figure 10.18: Reproducing an illustration by using Harvard's grid

Rulers help you determine the position of objects or the pointer and to align your objects in your charts. Press **3** from the Options menu to display the Ruler box, which contains two settings. The Ruler field is set to No by default. Change it to Yes to display rulers along the top and left side of the drawing area. The Units field setting controls the measurement increments on the ruler. The default is Inches; you can change it to Centimeters or Percent.

ADJUSTING POINTER SETTINGS

Harvard allows you to view and change the pointer coordinates, adjust the size of the cross-hairs cursor, and slow down or speed up pointer movement on the Draw screen.

VIEWING AND SETTING POINTER COORDINATES To see the coordinates of your pointer, press Ctrl-X anywhere in the

You can press Ctrl-X for the pointer coordinates at any time, even in the middle of a drawing operation.

drawing area (or press F9 to choose Actions, and then press **2**). This displays the Pointer Position box, shown in Figure 10.19, which indicates the unit of measurement and the horizontal and vertical position of the pointer.

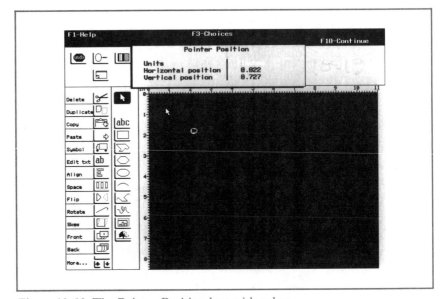

Figure 10.19: The Pointer Position box with rulers

You can change the settings in the Pointer Position box to place the pointer on exact ruler coordinates. Enter new coordinates in the Horizontal and Vertical position fields and click the right mouse button. The pointer will then move to the position you specified.

ADJUSTING THE SIZE OF THE CROSS-HAIRS POINTER

You can set the cross-hairs pointer to extend to the top and left rulers so you can easily see the positioning and dimensions of objects. To change the pointer size, choose Cross-hair pointer from the Options menu, and change the setting from Small (the default) to Large. However, you should be aware that a large cross-hairs pointer makes it difficult to work with and position small objects.

SETTING THE POINTER SPEED   The Set Pointer Speed selection on the Options menu is for keyboard users. Choose it to change the speed in which the pointer moves when you press an arrow key. You can also use the shortcuts, Ctrl-+ and Ctrl-−. to speed up and slow down the pointer speed, respectively.

WORKING WITH
THE EDITING TOOLS

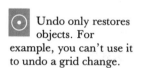 Undo only restores objects. For example, you can't use it to undo a grid change.

Draw's editing tools allow you to modify the layout and design of your charts. Figure 10.20 illustrates what some of the editing tools do, as well as other editing techniques.

CHOOSING OBJECTS TO MODIFY

In order to change an existing object, you must select it first. Use the Selection tool to select a single object or groups of objects, as described in the following sections.

Remember to save your chart before modifying it, so that you can retrieve the original version if you make a serious mistake during the editing process.

You can't modify objects that weren't created with Draw. Instead, save them as symbols and then modify them after you bring them back into your chart, as described later in the chapter.

SELECTING AN INDIVIDUAL OBJECT   The Selection tool changes the cursor to the pointer so you can select an object. To select just one object in the drawing area, move the cursor to the object and click. You should see eight small squares (three for lines), called *handles*, surrounding the object. You will also see the image appear in the status box above the drawing area. If the handles are not around the object you wanted to select, click again. Keep clicking until they surround the correct object.

Reselect an object to see other parts, and carefully view the status box. Sometimes, several objects appear as one, especially stacked lines and polygons.

After an object is selected, you can choose an editing tool to work with it. Press the right mouse button or Esc if you want to cancel your selection.

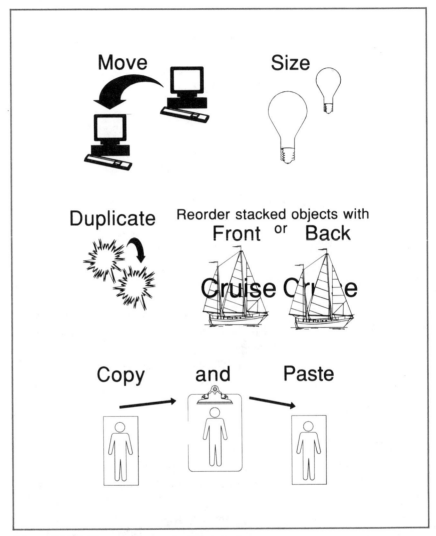

Figure 10.20: Frequently used editing tools

SELECTING A GROUP OF OBJECTS   To select groups of objects, use one of the following methods:

- Box in your selection: To enclose them in a box, move the pointer to an empty corner, click to anchor the box, move the pointer until all the objects are inside the box, and click again. Each object in the group will then be surrounded by eight handles to show that the group is selected.

- Select each individual object: To select multiple objects one at a time, press the Shift key as you select each individual objects for a group. The status box will show the multiple selections. This method lets you select objects that aren't within a physical group.

- Use the Select Objects box: Press the F9 key and then press 3 to choose Select objects. Then choose All to select every object in your drawing, Similar to select only objects that are of the same type and with attributes identical to your selected object, or Buttons to select all button objects (you will learn about buttons in Chapter 11).

DESELECTING AND RESELECTING OBJECTS If you have selected a group of objects, you can "deselect" an object within that group. Press the Shift key and click on the object you want deselected. That object's handles will disappear, and the object will be removed from the status box. To deselect all objects, move the pointer to a blank section of the drawing area and click.

You can recall an object's attribute icons and then change them by reselecting that object. You might see additional attribute icons if you choose a group of objects. Changes to attributes in groups affect all objects in that group with similar attributes. For example, if you select an arc, an oval, and a line object, changing the arrow attribute will affect the arc and line objects.

MOVING OBJECTS

Use the Ctrl-X shortcut to display the Pointer Position box and move an object to an exact position.

To move an object, follow these steps:

1. Select the object or objects that you want to move. The object is ready to move when you see handles surrounding it.

2. Click in the middle of the object (don't touch any handles) and keep the mouse button depressed. The pointer will change to a four-tipped arrow.

Press the Shift key while dragging to move an object horizontally, vertically, or diagonally.

3. Drag the object to move it into its new position. You will see a box surrounding the object as you move it.

4. When the object is in its new position, release the mouse button. The box outline will then be replaced with the object. Select the Undo tool and try again if you are not satisfied with the new layout.

RESIZING OBJECTS

You can increase or decrease the size of an object by following these steps:

1. Move your pointer to the Selection tool and click. Select the object or objects that you want to resize, and you will see handles surrounding your selection.

2. Click on one of the handles and keep the mouse button depressed, as follows:

   • Select a corner handle to change both the length and width of an object.

   • Select a top or bottom handle to stretch the object's length.

   • Select a side handle to resize the object's width.

3. A box will surround the object. Change the size by dragging the mouse. If you select a corner handle and you want to maintain the object's original proportions, press the Shift key as you move the mouse.

4. When you are satisfied with the new size, click the mouse button. The box outline will be replaced with the resized object. If you make a mistake and want to start over, select the Undo tool and try again.

DELETING OBJECTS

As you learned in Chapter 3, you can delete an object from the drawing area by first selecting it with the Selection tool and then using the Delete tool. If you make a mistake, choose the Undo tool to restore your objects.

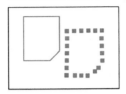

You cannot delete a data chart nor its regions from a drawing. If you attempt to delete all objects, including the data chart, you will see a warning message, and all objects except for the data chart will be deleted. To get rid of the data, simply create a new chart.

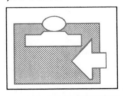

If you use the Copy and Paste tools for an object in the same chart, the pasted object will sit on top of and hide the original object. Remember to move the copied object to where you want it.

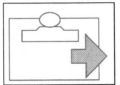

To delete all the objects, press F9, then **3**, then Enter to select all of them. Then select the Delete tool to erase them.

DUPLICATING OBJECTS

To make an exact copy of an object, first select it, and then choose the Duplicate tool. You will see a copy of the object on your screen, which is slightly off center from the original. Drag the object to its new location.

Select the Duplicate tool again for another copy. The next duplicate will be in the same direction and at the same distance from the previous duplicate as the previous duplicate was from the original. When you have positioned all the copies you want, press the right mouse button.

COPYING AND PASTING OBJECTS

By copying and pasting objects, you can move outside the drawing area of the current chart. Use the Copy and Paste tools for this editing procedure.

COPYING OBJECTS   The Copy tool lets you copy an object to the *clipboard*, which is a temporary holding area in the computer's memory. An object that is in the clipboard can be pasted onto other drawings, charts, or to the scratchpad area. Copied objects remain in the clipboard until you copy a different object to it.

PASTING OBJECTS   Use the Paste tool to insert the contents of the clipboard in the drawing or scratchpad area you are currently working with. You can paste a clipboard object as many times as you like.

You can't view the contents of a clipboard. To see its contents, paste it onto the scratchpad.

MOVING OBJECTS TO THE FRONT OR BACK

Objects are placed on your chart in transparent layers in the order you create them. The first object you created is on the bottom layer, the last object created sits on the top layer, and all other objects are

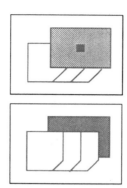

layered between them. The Front tool and the Back tool let you rearrange the layers and thus the order in which objects are placed. You will need to move objects to the front or back when an object covers another one that you want to be visible.

To reorder an object's layer, first select the object you want to change. To bring a selected object forward, select the Front tool. To push an object to the back, select the Back tool. You will see another group of icons, from which to select whether to move the object just one layer or all the way to the front or back.

HANDS-ON: CREATING A SIGN WITH THE DRAWING TOOLS

In the following steps, you will use the drawing tools to create the sign shown in Figure 10.21. If you have a color monitor, follow the instructions for creating this sign in color and also use patterns so you can produce it with any printer.

If you make a mistake, use the methods you have learned in this chapter to correct it. For example, press the Backspace key and reposition an object, delete it and try again, or use the Undo tool to restore the previous version.

1. From the Main menu, press **1**, then **5** to create a drawing chart.

2. Press F8, then **8** to display the Appearance Options box. Set the Chart orientation to Portrait and press Esc. The shape of the Draw screen changes to reflect the portrait orientation.

3. Select the Irregular Polygon tool. You will use this tool to create the large clock case.

4. Select the color icon and set Fill to Brown. Press F10 to return to the Draw screen.

5. Reselect the Irregular Polygon tool and, using Figure 10.21 as a guide, move the pointer to the lower-left corner of the screen and click to begin drawing the clock case.

6. Move the pointer to the right while pressing the Shift key. At the right corner, click. Continue drawing the clock case; when you are finished, click the right mouse button or press Esc several times until you see the drawing tools again.

7. Select the Oval tool, which you will use to add the clockface.

8. Select the color icon and change the circle's fill to white.

Figure 10.21: A sample sign

9. Position the Oval tool inside the clock case polygon, and hold down the Shift key while you drag to create a circle. When you are finished drawing the clockface, press Esc or the right mouse button until you see the drawing tools.

10. You can use a shortcut to change the color attribute for similar types of objects when that color is present in your

drawing. Select the brown polygon clockface. Now select the Box tool (notice that the box uses the color of the last selected object), and use it to create a brown base for the clock case.

11. Choose the Text tool to add numbers to the clockface. Set the text size to 5.5 and the Line/Text color to purple. Place the numbers **3**, **6**, **9**, and **12** on the clockface.

12. Use the Text tool to add the sign's other text. Change the text size of 8 and the Line/Text color to white. Click in the center of the chart, below the clock, and type **Clocks for Sale** and **$5 to $20**. Place them below the clock. Return to the drawing tools when you're finished.

Copying a symbol is easier and quicker than trying to recreate it.

13. The missing numbers on the clockface are represented by bullets. Choose the Text tool and add a bullet (by pressing Ctrl-B and selecting one from the special characters list). Set Line/Text color to blue. Place a bullet at the one o'clock position and then press the right mouse button or Esc twice to return to the drawing tools. Use the Duplicate tool to duplicate the bullet. Place a duplicated bullet at the next hour that is missing a number. Continue duplicating and placing bullets to fill in the remaining clockface positions.

14. Add the two clock hands in your chart using the Line tool. Set the line attributes to use an arrow and a line thickness of 1.5.

15. Add a circle on the top of the clock and make it look like a sun by setting both the Fill and Line/Text color to yellow.

16. To create the mountains in front of the sun, select the Regular Polygon tool. Set the number of sides to 3 (for a triangle) and the color to green.

17. Select the Freehand tool and draw the wood carvings in the clock case. Try adding some scrollwork or other decorative touches.

18. Save the drawing chart as **SIGN** and print it.

In making this sign, you used most of Harvard's drawing tools. You are now ready for more advanced drawing techniques.

TRANSFORMING DRAWINGS INTO SYMBOLS

After you create a complex drawing, you should turn it into a symbol and save it for future use. To do this, you use the Group tool.

This tool is in the second column of tools. Before selecting it, you need to locate it by clicking on the More... ↑ icon in the bottom-left corner of the screen.

GROUPING AND UNGROUPING SYMBOLS

To group your objects into one symbol, you must first select the objects that you want to include in the group. Use one of the methods described earlier in the chapter for selecting groups of objects. For example, you can move the cursor to the edge of your drawing, click to anchor a corner, drag the pointer across the other objects you want included, and click.

When you group objects, the entire group assumes the layer of the foremost object.

Each of the objects within the group should have handles around it. To group these objects, click on the More... ↑ icon and select the Group tool. (If you did not select the correct objects, press the right mouse button to deselect them.) Once you've grouped the objects, a single set of handles surrounds them. Click on the right mouse button when you are finished grouping objects.

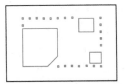

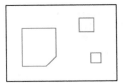

To reverse the grouping process and change a symbol back into separate objects, choose the symbol to be separated. Handles will surround your choice. Now select the Ungroup tool. The symbol will be divided into its individual components. You may have to use the Ungroup tool several times if a symbol is composed of several groups of objects.

You can ungroup a data chart into its chart regions. For example, if you ungroup a text chart, you can move and treat the title, text body, and footnotes as separate objects.

WORKING WITH SYMBOLS

When you select the Symbol tool (the one with a truck), you will see another menu of tools, which you can use to get, save, or delete a symbol from your files. You can also assign your company's logo to an icon called Logo.

GETTING A SYMBOL   In Chapter 3, you added symbols to your chart when you created your Harvard diploma. To bring a symbol into a drawing chart, select the Symbol tool and click on the Get symbol icon. From the list of available files, choose the one you want to open, and then select a symbol from that file.

You can press F8 to sort the list of files that you're viewing.

If you want to work with the individual components of the symbol, use the Ungroup tool. Then you can delete the symbol's objects you do not want or change them as necessary.

SAVING YOUR SYMBOLS   If you will want to use a drawing you created with Draw in other charts, group its objects, data charts, and chart regions and save them as a symbol. This way, you can retrieve it later by selecting Get symbol. Here are the steps for saving a symbol:

1. Select the object you want saved as a symbol.

2. Select the Symbol tool.

3. Click on the Save icon. You will see the Save Symbol File box.

4. The current drive and subdirectory appear in the Directory field. If you want to store the symbol file in another location, change the entry in this field.

5. In the Filename field, type the name of the file in which you want to save the symbol. Harvard adds an .SY3 extension to all symbol files.

6. In the Description field, enter a description of this symbol file. Use one that will remind you of what the file contains.

7. Give the symbol itself a name.

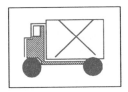 Sometimes symbols are reduced, or the palettes are changed so you cannot easily see what they look like. Use symbol names so you can readily identify your symbols.

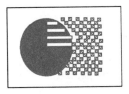 Save time by pressing Esc when the symbols start to appear. Then only the names will be listed.

8. Click the right mouse button when you are finished. The symbol will be saved as the last symbol in the file.

You can place up to 32 symbols in a file. Symbol files store a symbol's shape, screen location, and the options used for its objects. It is a good idea to store symbols that you use with different output devices separately. For example, store the symbols that you will produce with color and PostScript printers in one file and those for black-and-white printers in another file.

DELETING SYMBOLS   If you will no longer be using an existing symbol, you can delete it from the symbol file.

1. Select the Symbol tool

2. Select the Delete icon. A list of symbol files will appear.

3. With the left mouse button, click on the file that contains the symbol you want to remove. You will see all the symbols that are in that file.

4. Click on the right mouse button. Harvard will display a warning box telling you that you cannot undo this command. Click on F10 to delete the symbol (click on Esc if you decide to keep it).

If you delete the last symbol in a file, the file itself will be removed. To transfer a symbol into a different file, use the Symbol tool to get the symbol, place it in your chart, and resave it to a new chart.

GETTING A LOGO   If you create a symbol and save it in the location

C:\HG3\HG3LOGO.SY3

you can use the Symbol tool's Logo icon to quickly place it in your chart. You will not have to list the file and select the symbol. Harvard will use the first symbol that it finds in the HG3LOGO.SY3 file as the logo.

HANDS-ON: CREATING
A MAP CHART WITH SYMBOLS

Although Harvard sells an accessory program called Geographics that helps you make map charts, you can also use Harvard 3.0 to create simple map charts.

In the following steps, you will create a United States map chart template containing labeled states. You will then use the template to create a chart that identifies the North, South, Midwest, and West regions of the country.

Map charts show at a glance the geographical composition of your statistical data, such as acres in forests, sales revenue, or average income levels. For example, you can show population composition by shading each state based on the number of people within it.

1. Choose to create a text bullet chart. Type the following placeholders for the title, subtitle and footnote (they will be cleared when you save the chart as a template):

   Title

   Subtitle

   Footnote

2. Press F4 to display the Draw screen

3. Select the Symbol tool.

4. Select the Get icon, and then click on the file name MAPS1.SY3. Figure 10.22 shows what your screen should look like.

5. Move the pointer to the U.S. map chart and select it by pressing the left mouse button. Confirm your choice by pressing the right button. You will see the map symbol in the drawing area.

6. Press the right mouse button until you see the drawing tools. Using the techniques you learned in this chapter, move and resize the map. Keep the map's proportions by pressing the Shift key while moving the cursor to the opposite corner. Your map should fill most of the chart.

7. Select the color icon to change the map symbol's colors. Set Fill to Bkg and Line/Text to White. Click the right mouse button when you are finished so that you can choose an editing tool.

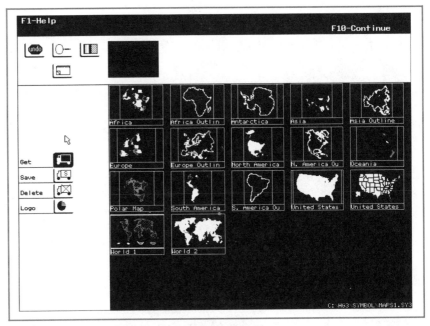

Figure 10.22: The maps in the MAPS1.SY3 file

Harvard does not display a message to let you know that the symbol is ungrouped. To check, choose to ungroup the symbol again. If you see an error message, the symbol is already ungrouped.

Ungroup the map symbol and edit it to create regional map templates. For example, you might want a template that only shows the northern states.

8. With your map symbol selected, click on the More . . . ↓ icon to see additional editing tools, and then choose the Ungroup tool.

9. Select the Text tool. Change the text size to 2.5.

10. Place the two-letter abbreviation on each state, using Figure 10.23 as a guide. If the state is too small to label, place its label next to it and add a line to connect the label to the state.

11. To turn the map chart into a template, press the right mouse button until you see the Main menu. Select File, then Save as template, and type **USMAP** for the template's file name. Press F10 to accept the other default values.

12. To use this template, return to the File menu and select the Get template option.

13. From the Get template box, choose USMAP.TPL and press Enter.

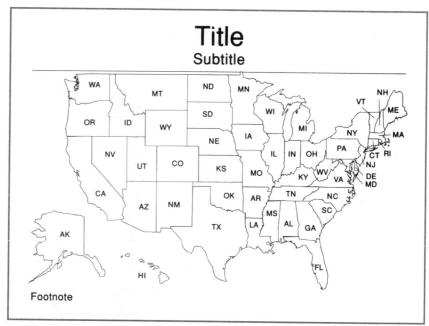

Figure 10.23: Your map template

14. Type the following title, subtitle, and footnote:

    U.S. Map Chart

    showing census regions

    Source: U.S. Bureau of the Census

For uniform legend box sizes, draw one and use the Duplicate tool to create the others.

15. Press F4 to return to the Draw screen and then select the Box tool.

16. Using Figure 10.24 as a guide, create a legend box for each of the four regions. Use the color icon to give each box a different color or pattern. Press the right mouse button when you are finished.

17. Select the Text tool and change the size to 3.5. Add a legend label to each of the four boxes: **North, South, West**, and **Midwest**.

18. Select a state and give it a color or pattern representing the legend it uses. For example, if West uses a red legend, make California red.

19. Repeat step 18 for all 50 states. You might want to practice selecting multiple objects and changing their colors in one step.

20. Save your chart as **MYMAP** (not as a template) and print it. It should resemble Figure 10.24.

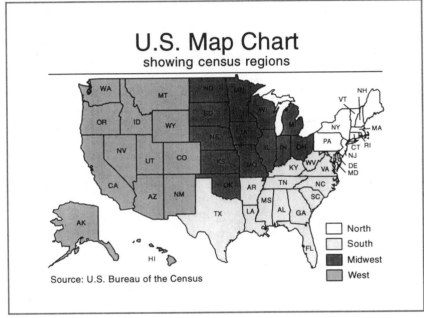

Figure 10.24: Regions in the United States

The map chart you created came from a symbol where each state was a polygon. This allows you to change each state's pattern to match the statistics you want to display. Unfortunately, other symbols cannot be modified easily. You might want to trace these symbols using polygons and save your drawing as a map template.

A problem with tracing a symbol is that you cannot always tell which is the original and which is the tracing. To give yourself a way to distinguish them, before tracing the symbol, add a small object (like a box), and group it with the original symbol. Then when you are finished tracing, you can select the small object and delete it along

You might want to try the To-Poly tool discussed in Chapter 11 before going through all the work of tracing a symbol.

with the original symbol, so that it does not interfere with your tracing or take up too much memory. If your drawing disappears, press F1, then 1 to redraw it.

SUMMARY

In this chapter, you have learned how to draw circles, boxes, lines, and polygons to create your own illustrations. You can even turn your illustrations into symbols and modify them so they can be printed on any type of printer. You also modified symbols to create a map chart.

The next chapter describes how to use the more advanced features of Draw to create all types of illustrations.

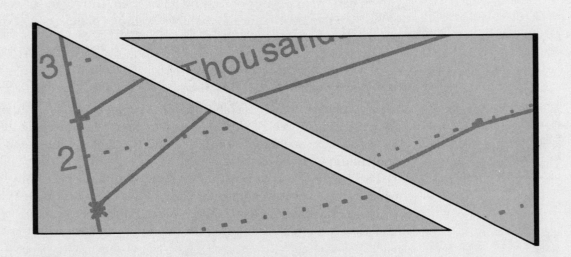

Designing with Draw

CHAPTER *11* _____

HARVARD'S DRAW PROVIDES MANY OF THE TOOLS offered by sophisticated drawing programs. After you become familiar with the basic drawing techniques, which were introduced in the previous chapter, you can begin using Draw's other tools to create all types of special effects.

This chapter describes how to use gradient and bit-map fills, modify text and shapes, magnify chart areas, add buttons, animate objects in a single chart, and insert subcharts.

FILLING OBJECTS WITH GRADIENT TONES AND BIT-MAPS

You can enhance your objects by filling them with gradient colors or bit-map patterns. Figure 11.1 shows examples of objects that contain gradient and bit-map fills.

USING GRADIENT FILLS

Gradient fills consist of color tones that progress from dark to light from one side of an object to another. For example, you might fill an object with tones of blue, beginning with the lightest blue at the top and ending with the darkest.

The gradient icon (a box that graduates from black to white) sits beneath the color icon and to the right of the Line/Text box. When you select the gradient icon, the Gradient Fill box appears.

To select a gradient fill instead of a pattern, follow these steps:

You can assign a gradient fill to any object. To assign gradient fills to chart parts, save them as symbols and then ungroup the symbol.

1. Select the object you want filled with a gradient. You can skip this step if you are creating a new object that will have the gradient fill.

2. Click on the color icon and then on the gradient icon.

Figure 11.1: Objects with gradient and bit-map fills

3. If you want to begin with a color instead of a white, click on the starting color box and select the color you want to use.

4. If you do not want the ending color to be black, click on the ending color box and select a color.

5. You can change the angle in which the gradient starts by using the slider bar or by entering a number from 0 to 180 for the starting angle.

6. The view color window in the Gradient Fill box shows what your selections will look like. Press the right mouse button when you are satisfied with the fill.

If you use an editing tool to change an object's shape or rotation, the gradient angle will remain the same (unless you change it).

Gradient fills take longer than other types of fills to appear on your screen. If you change a gradient's starting angle, it will take even longer to display.

USING BIT-MAP FILLS

In the previous chapter, you learned how to include a bit-map image in your drawing to easily import .PCX, .PCC, and .TIF files. You can also use these images to make fill patterns for boxes, ovals, and polygons. When you select the bit-map fill icon, Harvard displays the Bitmap box in the bottom-left corner of your screen.

Bit maps should be limited to 512K file sizes, or Draw will start dropping some of the pixels to import it.

To use a bit-map fill, follow these steps:

1. Select the object you want to fill with a bit-map. Skip this step if you are creating a new object.

2. Click on the color icon and then on the Bitmap tool.

3. Select the bit-map image you want from the displayed list. If you already used a bit-map image, you will not see a file list. The name of the file you are using will appear next to the bitmap label icon on the bottom of the screen. Click on the bitmap label icon if you want to see the list and change the file name.

4. Click the right mouse button.

Check the bit-map fill after it is in Draw. Bit-map images look best when you do not change their shape or size.

Save a chart as a symbol, and then ungroup the chart frame (see Chapter 10) and use bit-map images as a background for your bars, lines, and other chart elements.

FINE-TUNING BIT-MAP IMAGES

You can adjust bit-map images by using the icons in the Bitmap box as follows:

- Bitmap: Displays the file name of the bit-map image you are using. Click on this icon to change to another bit-map file.

- Anchor pt: Moves the bit-map image around within the object. Click on the anchor point and drag the illustration until it is properly positioned in the object.

You can tint black-and-white bit-map images. The color in the Fill box at the top left of the chart colors section will be used in the black areas of the chart. The color in the Pattern box is used for the white areas of the chart.

- Colors: Assigns colors to the bit-map image. When you import a .PCX file, the resulting file uses dithered (patterned or dotted) colors to represent the original RGB colors. Give the bit-map solid colors by clicking on the solid color icon.

- Fill: Lets you choose between tile or scale bit-maps fills. A *scale* bit-map is one that is scaled down to fit inside an object. *Tile* bit-maps are full sized and can be used to create a wallpaper effect when the objects they fill are larger than the bit-map image.

To select bit-map patterns easily, copy patterns from the PATT-VIEW.CH3 chart into the scratchpad and then paste them into your current chart.

Figure 11.2 shows Harvard's C:\HG3\DATA\PATT-VIEW.CH3 chart. Each box in this chart uses a different bit-map file that you will find in the C:\HG3\SYMBOL directory under the file name PATT#.PCC, where # represents the three-digit pattern number. The pattern numbers are in increments of ten. For example, the bit-map file for the first box is called PATT010.PCC, and the file for the second box is called PATT020.PCC.

WORKING WITH TEXT IN DRAW

As with other Draw objects, you can assign various attributes to your text. You can also edit, the text, resize the text box, and connect text to shapes for special effects.

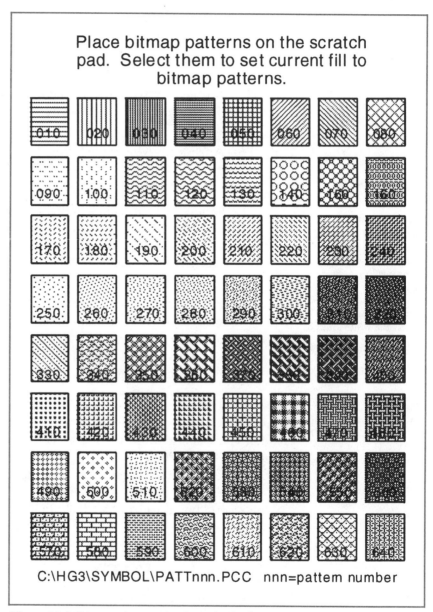

Figure 11.2: Bit-map images in the C:\HG3\SYMBOL subdirectory

CHANGING TEXT ATTRIBUTES

See Chapter 3 for information about text sizes, fonts, font styles, and text overflow. The options for text charts also apply to objects you create with the Text tool. Also, the information in Chapter 10 about box styles applies to the boxes that surround text.

When you select the Text tool, you see the first of three attribute groups. To move between text attribute groups, press the ↑ or the ↓ icons at the right edge of the attribute area. Figures 11.3, 11.4, and 11.5 illustrate the attributes you can select from the three groups. You can also select the color icon to change text colors.

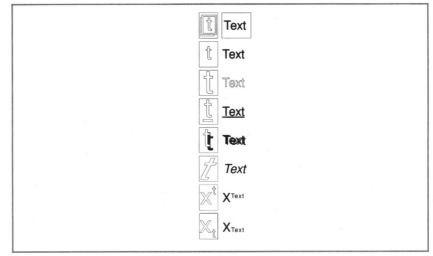

Figure 11.3: Using text box and text style attributes

The alignment attribute icons allow you to select horizontal and vertical alignment for text.

Line spacing values, between 0 and 200, are based on a percentage of the text size. Click on the values and type new ones or use the slider bar to change line spacing. A line spacing of 85 is usually suitable for single-spaced text. Use 170 for double-spaced text. If you're using international characters or your g's and p's start running into your capitalized letters, try setting single-spaced text to 100 and double-spaced text to 200.

Change the text block margin attribute to adjust the amount of space between the text and the box that optionally surrounds it. For example, use this attribute to add space between the sides of the box and the text inside it.

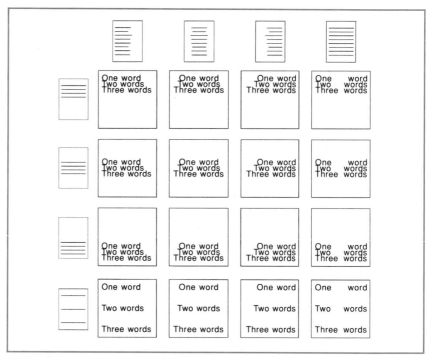

Figure 11.4: Using text alignments

The third text attribute group controls the appearance of the box that surrounds your text. These attributes function like the Box tool's attributes.

EDITING TEXT IN DRAW

Draw provides a separate tool for editing text objects. You do not use the Text tool to edit text you created in Draw. To edit text, follow these steps:

1. Select the block of text you want to edit with the Selection tool.

2. Select the Edit Text tool from the editing tools column. You will see the edit text icon (it looks just like the Edit tool) and the size block icon on your screen.

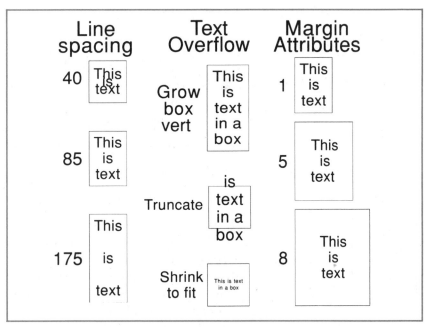

Figure 11.5: Using line spacing, text overflow, and margin attributes

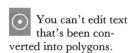 You can't edit text that's been converted into polygons.

3. Select the edit text icon. The original text you typed will appear in the Edit box.

4. Move the cursor to the Edit box and insert text, delete text, or type in your correction. You can press F5 to mark some of the words and assign text attributes to them. You can also press F7 or Ctrl-B to see the special characters list while editing text.

5. Press F10 or click the right mouse button when you are finished.

RESIZING THE TEXT BLOCK AND BOUNDARY

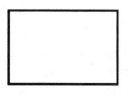

You resize text in the same way that you change the size of any other object. Click on the text object, and its handles will appear. Drag on the handles to change the text size. Press Shift while dragging on a corner handle if you want to maintain the text block's proportions.

To resize the *boundary*, which is the frame in which the text is placed, follow these steps:

1. Select the Edit Text tool.

2. Select the size block icon. Triangle-shaped handles will appear on the screen.

3. Drag on one of the handles. Press the Shift key while dragging to maintain the original proportions.

4. Click the right mouse button when you are finished.

CONNECTING TEXT FOR SPECIAL EFFECTS

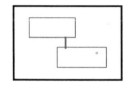

By using the Connect tool, you can create special text effects. This tool makes your text conform to the shape of the object to which it is connected. For example, you can create a polygon, regular polygon, oval, arc, line, or a freehand object and then fit a block of text around it using the Connect tool. Although the Connect tool can be used to connect all types of objects, it is especially useful when working with text, as illustrated in Figure 11.6.

When you connect text to a regular polygon or oval, the text starts at the 270-degree location and continues clockwise. This means that you will probably have to group the two objects together and rotate them for the text to appear right side up.

You can often correct connected text alignment problems by using the Flip tool twice: once to flip text horizontally, and again to flip it vertically.

For polygons, lines, arcs, and freehand drawings, text starts at the point in which you started drawing the object and continues in the direction you drew it. For example, if you drew the line clockwise, the text will sit on top of the line. If the line was drawn counterclockwise, the text sits below the line.

The text alignment attribute also affects how connected text appears. For example, left-aligned text starts at the point you first started the line, centered text is placed in the center of your line, and right-aligned text ends at the point you finished drawing your line.

HANDS-ON: CREATING A LOGO WITH CIRCULAR TEXT

In the following steps, you will create a sample company logo that consist of text connected to a circle with a pentagon inside it, as shown in Figure 11.7.

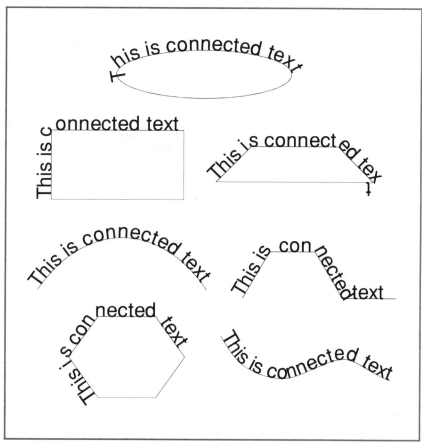

Figure 11.6: Connecting text to objects

1. Select the Oval tool.

2. Select the color icon and change the circle's fill color to Red and Pattern to Solid.

3. Move the pointer to the drawing area and click to anchor the center of your circle.

4. Move the pointer while pressing the Shift key until the circle outline is about 2½ inches in diameter, and then click. You will see the red circle in the center of your screen. Press the right mouse button until you see the drawing tools.

If you're using a monochrome graphics monitor, color will appear in varying shades of gray.

Figure 11.7: Sample logo with circular text

5. Use the arc tool to draw two arcs to serve as temporary guides for connecting the text. Place one arc slightly above and the other slightly below the circle. Start the arc line by clicking on the left side of the circle and then on the right side. Move the cursor and click on the top of the circle to form the arc. Your drawing should now look similar to Figure 11.8.

6. Select the Text tool.

7. To set text attributes, select the color icon and set Line/ Text to White. Click on the size slider bar and set it to 5. Click on the ↓ icon in the attribute area and set both vertical and horizontal alignment to center (as in the second box in the second row in Figure 11.4).

8. Move the pointer to the drawing area and click above the top arc. You will see the text box, with the cursor inside it.

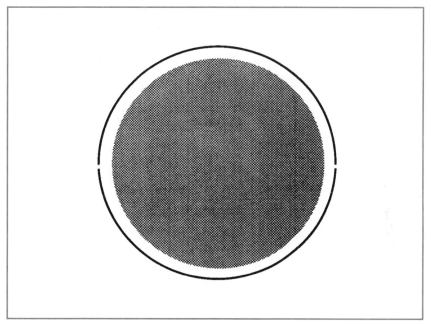

Figure 11.8: Getting ready for circular text

9. Type **American Publishing** and press F10.

10. Move the pointer below the bottom arc and click. Type **Cooperative** and press F10.

11. Select the *Cooperative* text block and the bottom arc by holding down the Shift key while you select both of them.

12. Select the Connect tool. *Cooperative* will be connected to the bottom arc.

13. Select the top arc and the *American Publishing* text block, and then select the Connect tool to connect them.

14. Use the Delete tool to remove the two arc guides from the drawing. If necessary, adjust the curved text blocks by moving them.

15. Use the Regular Polygon tool to draw a white pentagon (five sides) in the center of the red circle. Your logo should look like Figure 11.7.

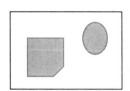

Before saving a logo symbol, position it where you'll usually want it to appear, such as in the bottom-right corner.

You now have a completed symbol that you can save. If you created an actual logo, you could group the objects and save the file as C:\HG3\HG3LOGO.SY3 so that you could insert it with the logo icon.

WORKING WITH OBJECTS

There are a number of other editing tools you can select to change the objects you create. The following sections describe how to match attributes, rearrange objects in many ways, and use the other special Draw tools to customize your drawings.

MATCHING ATTRIBUTES

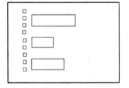

If you use the Matching Attributes tool to copy attributes from a text block containing marked text, you may have unexpected color changes in some of your characters.

Use the Matching Attributes tool to transfer one object's attributes to another, as follows:

1. Select all the objects that are to receive the attribute changes. Press the Shift key to select multiple objects.

2. After selecting the object whose attributes you wish to change, with the Shift key still depressed, select the object whose attributes you want the other objects to match.

3. Select the Matching Attributes tool. All objects will take on the attributes of the last object selected. If you are not satisfied with the results, select the Undo tool.

ALIGNING OBJECTS

Using the Align tool, you can easily align objects in your chart. You can even align objects on top of one another. Figure 11.9 shows the various alignment options.

To align objects, first select the objects you want to align and then select the Align tool. A menu of alignment icons will appear on the left side of your screen. Choose the alignment icon that represents the alignment you want and press Enter. For example, click on the Top icon if you want your objects to align vertically at the top of the topmost object. Draw will reposition the objects to conform to your selection.

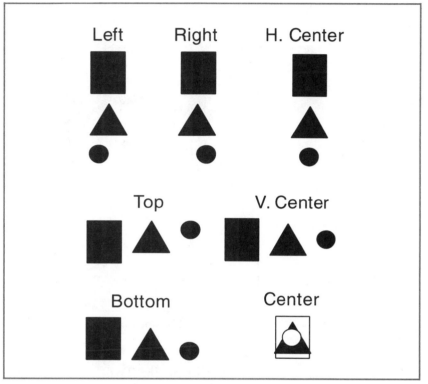

Figure 11.9: Aligning objects

SPACING OBJECTS EVENLY

The Spacing tool saves you the time and effort of evenly spacing your objects manually. Figure 11.10 illustrates the effects you can achieve with the Spacing tool.

Select three or more objects that you want evenly spaced, and then select the Spacing tool. Then choose between horizontal or vertical spacing. Click on your choice, and the objects will be spaced apart evenly.

FLIPPING OBJECTS

The Flip tool allows you to change the orientation of objects. Select the object you want flipped, click on the Flip tool, and then click on

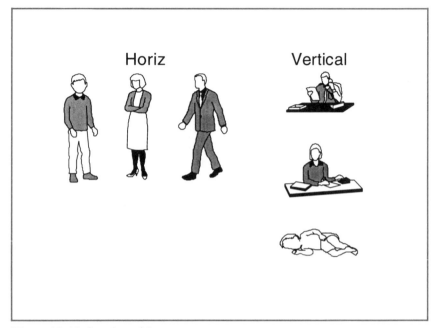

Figure 11.10: Spacing objects

one of the icons that appear to the left of the chart to indicate the direction of the flip. To flip an object from left to right or from right to left, click on Horizontal. When you want the object turned upside down, click on Vertical. Figure 11.11 show the effects of flipping an object.

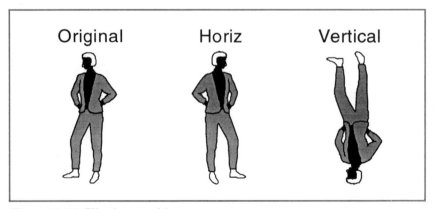

Figure 11.11: Flipping an object

You can give the effect of a reflection of an object or text by using the Duplicate and Flip tools. Use the Duplicate tool to create a copy. Then select the Flip tool and click on the Horizontal icon. Move the flipped object under the original.

ROTATING AN OBJECT

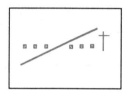

Another way to change an object is to rotate it to a different angle using the Rotate tool. Figure 11.12 shows the effects of rotating an object from 45 to 225 degrees.

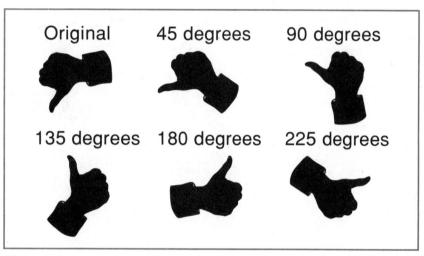

Figure 11.12: Rotating an Object

There are two ways you can rotate an object. One way is to select the object you want to rotate and then select the Rotate tool. The Rotate box appears on the left side of the screen. Click on the Degrees field and type the number of degrees (0 to 360) you want the object to be rotated, and then press the right mouse button. Click on the clockwise or reverse icon to rotate the object. Continue entering the number of degrees and rotating the object until you are satisfied with the position. When you are finished, click the right mouse button.

If you do not know the number of degrees to enter for the rotation, you can use the other method to rotate an object. Move the pointer to the object you want rotated and click to select it. Select the Rotate tool,

Fine-tune the rotation by clicking on the clockwise or reverse icons.

and you will see an outline with a handle appear around the object. Press the left mouse button and drag the handle to rotate the object. When you release the mouse button, the rotated object will replace the outline.

SKEWING AND CHANGING PERSPECTIVES

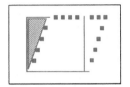

Use the Skew tool to change an object's slant or perspective. Figure 11.13 shows some of the effects of skewing an object.

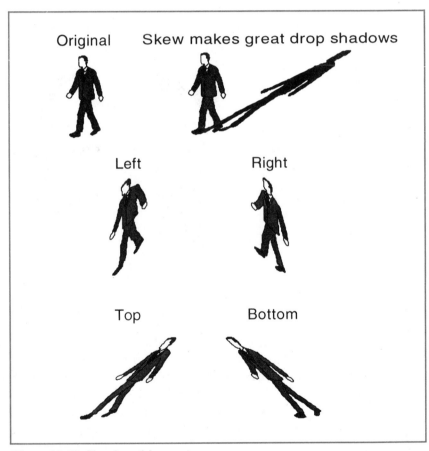

Figure 11.13: Skewing objects

Select the object you want to skew and click on the Skew tool. Four diamond-shaped skew handles will surround the selected object, and several skew icons appear on the left side of the screen. Drag on one of the skew handles until you're satisfied with the new outline, and then press the right mouse button.

Another way to skew an object is to select it, click on the Skew tool, and then click on the Degree icon. Enter the number of degrees you want the object skewed and click a skew edge icon to make the change. Press the right mouse button when you are finished. If you are not satisfied with the way it looks, select the Undo tool and start over.

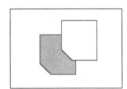

Make cast shadows by copying the object and using the Skew tool to make the copy look like a shadow.

ADDING OR DELETING A DROP SHADOW

Adding a shadow is similar to copying an object. Figure 11.14 shows some effects you can achieve with the Shadow tool.

Select the object you want shadowed and then click on the Shadow tool. Click on one of the shadow icons that appear on the left to indicate which direction you want the shadow to fall. A drop shadow will appear under the object. To change the distance between the object and its shadow, use the slider bar or type a number from 0 to 25. Press the right mouse button when you are finished. To delete a shadow from an object, select the Shadow tool and then click on the remove shadow icon.

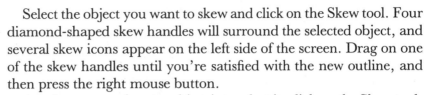

You can select shadow attributes for box and text objects when you draw them, as explained in Chapter 10.

SWEEPING OBJECTS WITH THE EVOLVE TOOL

The Evolve tool allows you to create a variety of special effects. With it, you can ''sweep'' an object to gradually change its color, size, shape, position, and rotation. For example, if you select a blue square and a red circle, evolve will gradually change the blue square into the red circle in the specified number of steps. Figure 11.15 shows some special effects you can create with the Evolve tool. The three-dimensional ball in the figure was created by selecting a large, dark-colored circle as the object to begin with and a small, light-colored oval as the ending object.

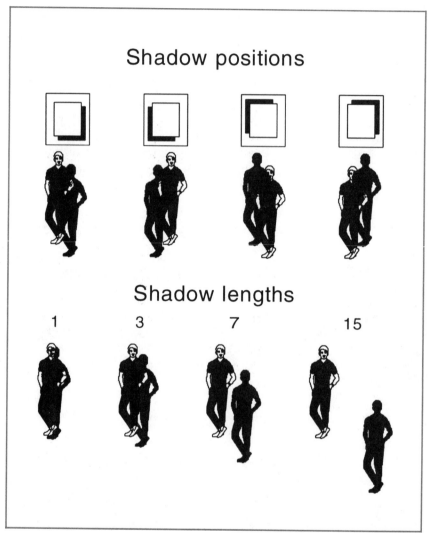

Figure 11.14: Adding shadows

Get special effects by rotating, skewing, or changing the size and color of an object.

Follow these steps to use the Evolve tool:

1. Select the starting and ending objects. Remember to press and hold down the Shift key when selecting both objects.

2. Select the Evolve tool, and the evolve icons will appear on the left side of your screen.

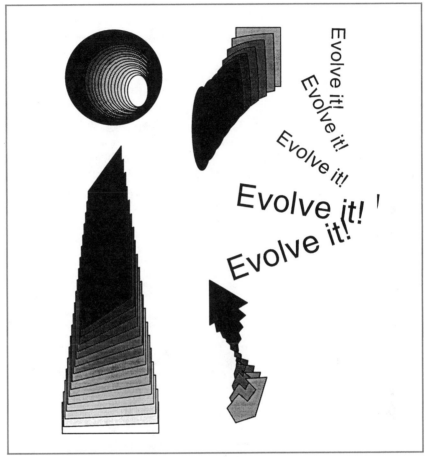

Figure 11.15: Special effects created with the Evolve tool

3. Click on the number of steps icon, and enter a number from 3 to 50 to designate how many objects you want inserted between the first and last objects.

4. Click on the forward icon for a clockwise rotation or the reverse icon for a counterclockwise rotation. Click the right mouse button when you are finished.

CONNECTING AND DISCONNECTING OBJECTS

Earlier in the chapter, you used the Connect tool to create a logo with circular text. As we mentioned, this tool can be used to connect

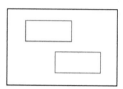

To create a porthole effect, use the Connect tool to connect a circle that sits on a rectangle.

any objects, not just text. For example, you can connect open-line objects such as lines and freehand drawings. Figure 11.16 shows the effects of connecting open-line and closed-line objects.

Select the two objects you want to connect and click on the Connect tool. The endpoints of open-line objects must touch in order to be connected. The second object will assume the colors and attributes of the first object you selected. Closed-line objects merge into a single polygon. The overlapping sections will appear as openings.

If you change your mind about connecting closed line objects (which become polygons), select the object you want disconnected and click on the Disconnect tool. The objects will no longer be connected, and you can treat them as separate objects.

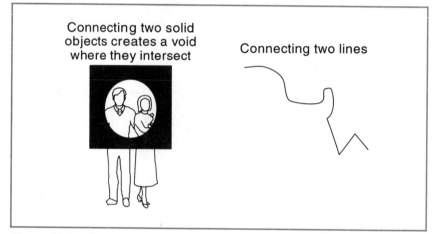

Figure 11.16: Connecting objects

EDITING POINTS TO TRANSFORM OBJECTS

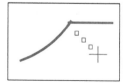

You can change the shape of polygons, lines, arcs, and freehand objects by editing their points. Select the object whose points you want to edit and click on the Edit points tool to display the four point-editing icons. Choose the appropriate icon to add, move, delete, or change the direction of a point. Figure 11.17 shows the effects of editing the points in a four-point line.

To edit the points of another type of object, first convert it to a polygon or line, as explained later in this chapter.

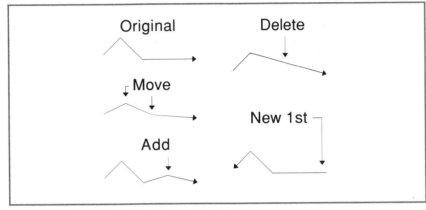

Figure 11.17: Editing the points of an object

To delete a point from an object, click on the delete point icon. Move the cross-hairs cursor to the point you want to delete and click with the left mouse button. Continue deleting any points you want to remove, and then press the right mouse button to continue.

You can change the direction in which a line runs by selecting the new first icon. For example, you could use this option to move an arrow to the other side of a line (arrows are automatically placed at the end of the line). After you click on the new first icon, move the cross-hairs cursor to the end of your object's line and click the left mouse button. This will become the object's first point.

HANDS-ON: ADDING AND MOVING A POINT

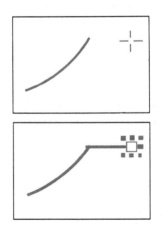

The add point and move point icons displayed when you select the Edit Points tool allow you to add more points to an object and rearrange the order of those points. In the following steps, you will learn how to use these icons by adding a point to the five-sided regular polygon in the logo you created in the last hands-on session.

1. Retrieve the logo and select the five-sided regular polygon.

2. Click on the Edit Points tool, then on the add point icon. You will see an asterisk (*) and four hollow circles (°) at the five corners of the polygon.

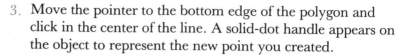

When you select to add points to curved objects, a direction lever will be attached to the handle. Move the direction lever to change the curved shapes.

3. Move the pointer to the bottom edge of the polygon and click in the center of the line. A solid-dot handle appears on the object to represent the new point you created.

4. Click on the move point icon and drag the new handle toward the bottom of the circle. As you move the cursor, notice the elastic, or rubberbanding, effect of the outline that appears.

5. When your screen looks like Figure 11.18, release the left mouse button. The object will conform to the outline's shape. Press the right mouse button when you are finished. If you do not like the point-editing effect, press Backspace to restore the original object.

CONVERTING OBJECTS INTO POLYGONS OR LINES

In Draw, a polygon is the most flexible type of object because you can alter its shape by editing its points, as well as fill it with colors,

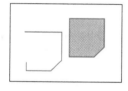

Figure 11.18: Adding a point to a shape

gradients, or bit-maps, as you have learned in this chapter. You can convert ovals, boxes, text, and regular polygons into irregular polygons with the To-Poly tool. Select the object you want to change and then click on the To-Poly tool. When you use the To-Poly tool on text, each character becomes a separate polygon. Lines, arcs, and freehand drawings may change shape when unconnected lines are joined to form a polygon object.

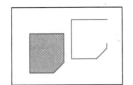

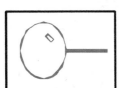
If you make an error in converting an object to a polygon or line, use the Undo tool immediately because there is no other way to reverse the effects.

You can also convert text, boxes, polygons, regular polygons, and ovals into lines by using the To-Line tool, and then edit the line points if desired. Select the object you want to convert and then click on the To-Line tool. If you convert a text object into lines, you will no longer be able to edit it or change its attributes.

Figure 11.19 shows examples of the effects you can achieve with the To-Poly and To-Line tools.

ZOOMING IN TO SEE DETAILS

In Draw, you can magnify part of your chart for precision detailing. To do this, select the Zoom tool. Several zoom icons will appear on the left side of the screen.

Click on the zoom-in icon to magnify your drawing. Move to the center of the object you want to magnify and click the left mouse button. The area you selected will become enlarged to twice its original size. Continue clicking to double the object's size until you are satisfied with the level of detail. Then press the right mouse button.

Another way to zoom in is to click on the zoom-in icon, click while holding the left mouse button to anchor a corner, and then drag the mouse to draw an outline box around the area you want magnified. Release the left mouse button and press the right mouse button to continue.

Zoom out reverses the effects of zoom in. Click on the zoom-out icon, move to the center of the object whose size you want to decrease, and click the left mouse button. Continue clicking until you see the view you want, and then press the right mouse button.

Click on the actual size icon to view the actual size in which your drawing will appear when you send it to an output device. If your chart's actual size is larger than your screen, you can click in different sections of your chart to view its actual size appearance. If you are

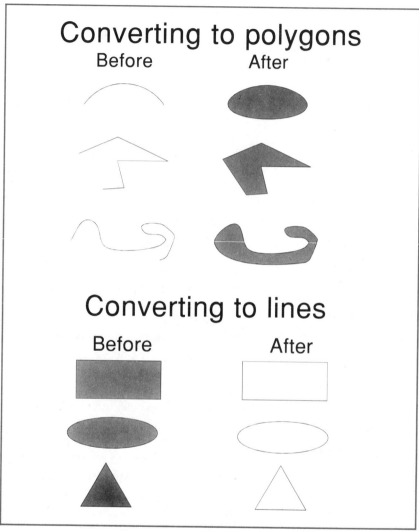

Figure 11.19: Converting objects into polygons or lines

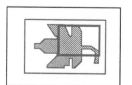

working on slides, since 35mm is too small to see on the screen, the actual size becomes proportional instead of actual. Press the right mouse button when you are finished.

You can only see part of the drawing when you zoom in on a portion of it. Click on the pan icon to slide your zoom window to another part of the drawing. The miniview window appears in the status box.

Press the left button and drag the mouse to move the window in the status box, and release the button when it is in the area of the chart that you want to work with. Continue panning to refine your work area, and press the right mouse button when you are finished.

To quickly return to the chart's full size, click on the full page icon and press the right mouse button.

CREATING BUTTONS
TO DIRECT SCREEN SHOWS

Screen shows are on-line computer presentations. You will learn how to create them in the next chapter. A *button* is a designated object on a chart that links it to another chart so that you can move between charts in a presentation.

For example, if you have a bar chart showing monthly sales, you can add a button to the bar for each month to display another chart that gives additional information for that month. You could point to the bar for May with your mouse, click on the button, and jump to the chart showing the May sales breakdowns by salesperson. Figure 11.20 illustrates how buttons can be used in a screen show.

You create buttons with Draw. You will find the Button tool with the other editing tools in Draw. You can use up to 100 buttons per chart, assigning each button a unique name of up to 12 characters. Button names are placed on the objects with which the buttons are associated. These names are visible only within Draw; they will not appear when you print the charts or run the screen show.

To create buttons for objects, follow these steps:

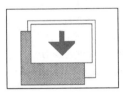

Use a button to add interest to your presentation. For example, create a button that jumps to an identical chart that has animation (the next section explains how to animate a chart).

To see a list of names that you've already designated in your chart, click on the Button name box label. Click on one of the names if you want to reuse it, but remember that a given button name can only point to one chart.

1. Select the object you want designated as a button.

2. Select the Button tool. You will see a box appear on the screen.

3. Click in the Button name box and type in a name using 12 characters or less. (If you want to delete a button, click on the remove button icon.)

4. Press the right mouse button when you are finished.

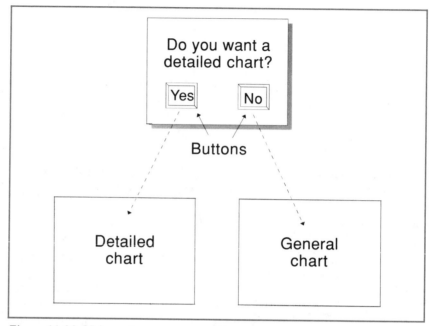

Figure 11.20: Using a button

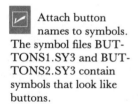 Attach button names to symbols. The symbol files BUTTONS1.SY3 and BUTTONS2.SY3 contain symbols that look like buttons.

If you assign buttons to objects and then group those objects with the Group tool, Harvard will recognize only the button name that you gave to the front object. Ungroup the objects to regain their individual button names.

You will learn more about the use of buttons in screen shows in Chapter 12. Just keep in mind that you add the buttons to your chart with Draw.

ANIMATING A CHART

 Draw's Animate tool allows you to animate objects in your chart. For example, to animate a drawing of a car so that it looks like it is driving across the screen, start by placing several car symbols in your chart and arrange them as you would have them move across the screen. Then pick the first symbol to be displayed and animate it to appear for only a few seconds before it disappears. Animate each of the other car drawings in the same manner, but don't animate the last car if you want it to remain on the screen.

To animate objects, follow these steps:

1. Select the object you want to animate.

2. Select the Animation tool. You'll see the animate icons appear in the left side of your screen, as shown in Figure 11.21.

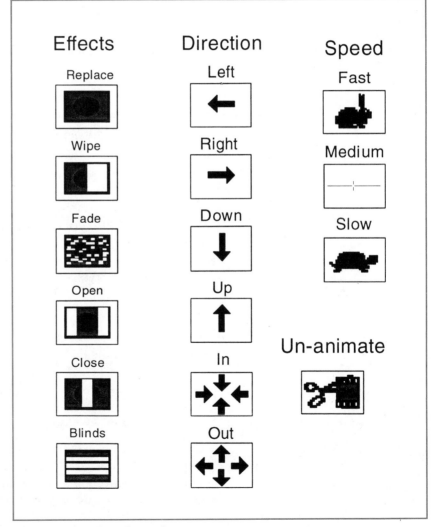

Figure 11.21: The animate icons

You can select different effects for displaying and removing the same object. Select the Animate tool to set the effect in drawing the object. Then reselect the Animate tool and the same object to set the effects for erasing it. See Chapter 12 for more animation techniques, including growing bars and running lines.

3. Select a drawing effect for your object by clicking on one of the following icons:

   • Choose the replace icon (the default) to simply replace or draw the object without effects.

   • Select the wipe icon to display the objects in a sweeping motion.

   • Click on the fade icon to have the object appear to fade away, using dots for this effect.

   • Choose the open icon to draw the object from its center and work toward the outer edge.

   • Click on the close icon to draw the object from the outer edge to its center.

   • Select the blinds icon to have the object appear as if you were opening blinds, drawing objects in stripes for this effect.

4. Click on the Draw box near the slider bar to gradually build selected objects and then quickly remove them, or click on the Erase box to use a special effect for removing objects. You can also use the slider bar and enter the number of seconds (0 to 100) you want the object displayed before erasing it. To temporarily display an object and then erase it when you press a key, select the Wait for key box. Do not select the Draw or Erase box if you simply want to animate the object on the screen and leave it there.

5. Click on the icon for the transition direction. The arrows on the icons point in the direction in which the object will be drawn (see Figure 11.21). Note that some drawing effects do not use all the transition directions. For example, the in and out directions are not used with a wipe effect, and replace does not use any directions.

You can override the transition time while displaying the chart by pressing any key to continue.

6. Click on the transition speed icon that matches your choice. Pick the rabbit for fast, the middle mark on a line for medium, or the turtle for slow. Since complicated objects usually take a long time to draw, use a fast transition speed

to display them. Small objects are often drawn quickly, so you might want to set their transition speed to slow.

7. Press F2 to see the effects of your animation, and then press Esc to continue.

8. Adjust the settings as necessary. Press the right mouse button when you are finished.

To remove animation effects from a selected object, click on the Animate tool, select the remove animation icon (the one in the lower-left corner), and press the right mouse button. All the animation effects will be deleted.

In the next chapter, you will learn how animation can be used in screen show presentations.

INCLUDING CHARTS WITHIN CHARTS

Although you can put a number of subcharts in a chart, you should avoid cluttering your chart with subcharts. Instead, use only one or two subcharts when you need them to present your information.

You can bring another chart into your drawing chart as a subchart object. Figure 11.22 shows an example of a drawing chart that contains a subchart. Subcharts can be moved, sized, copied, rotated, and skewed like other Draw objects. However, you cannot edit the data in a subchart. To make changes to the subchart's data, you must get the subchart and edit it as you would any other chart.

To add a subchart, from the Draw screen, press F6 to display the File menu, and then press 3 to select Create subchart. Select the file name of the chart that you want to use as a subchart from the list. It will appear in your chart at 25 percent of its original size. You can then use the drawing and editing tools to modify the subchart's appearance.

SUMMARY

This completes our discussion of Draw. You have learned that Draw can import bit-map images and create gradient fills. You also

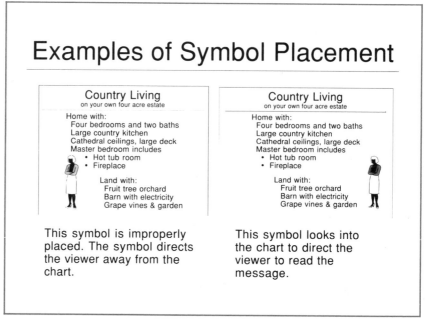

Figure 11.22: Including a subchart

know how to modify objects, add buttons, and animate individual drawings. As you experiment with the many Draw options, you will see that you can create other types of special effects in your charts.

Now you're ready to learn about Harvard's options for designing entire presentation.

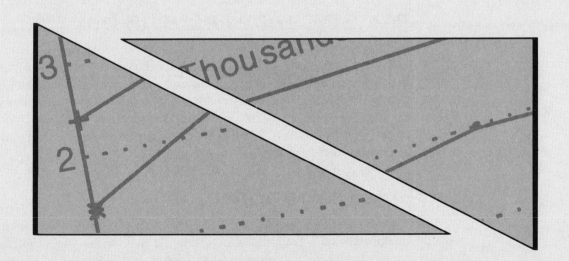

Creating Presentations

CHAPTER 12

YOU ARE NOW FAMILIAR WITH ALL OF HARVARD'S capabilities and can create well-designed charts quickly and effectively. In this chapter, you will learn how to tie all your charts together into a highly professional presentation.

You can organize and plan your presentation by using Harvard's Presentation options. As with any presentation, you specify the order in which the charts are presented. You can include either Harvard Graphics chart files or bit-mapped files from other programs. A presentation can store up to 175 files. By using the Presentation feature, you can produce output for your presentation with just one command—all the files included in the presentation will be printed, plotted, or recorded on film together. Alternatively, you can present a *screen show*, on your computer's screen, complete with special effects, and even make the show interactive.

PLANNING YOUR PRESENTATION

Planning your presentation is essential. As you review your charts and decide which ones to include, think about your presentation's goal, both for you and your audience. Choose charts that will contribute to that goal. Consider how many charts you can show in the time allotted for your presentation. Be selective and do not include too many charts or you will overwhelm your audience, and perhaps run out of time before showing them all.

OUTLINING YOUR IDEAS

While selecting the charts for your presentation, start outlining the speech that will accompany it by listing the main ideas. For example, you might use the following outline structure:

1. Introduction

   a. Purpose

      b. Goals

  2. Points and Arguments

      a. Point 1

      b. Point 2

      c. Point 3

      d. Optional Point 4

  3. Summary or Conclusion

CHOOSING CHARTS

Along with the charts that make the main points of your presentation, you should include transitional charts to help you move from one idea to another.

Text charts dominate most presentations. Typically, at least half of the presentation will consist of text charts. Build charts, which hold the audience's attention by gradually revealing the message, are good choices for presentations. As described in Chapter 3, you can create a series of build charts with any type of text chart, including title, bullet, list, and table charts.

A single chart can be animated as a build chart. Do this by adding text using Draw. Then use Draw's Animate tool to reveal or animate the build parts.

Break the monotony of a text-oriented presentation by using pictorial charts whenever possible. Like text charts, bar and line charts can be set up as a series of build charts that show one series of data at a time. Make a master chart, and then make copies with the series' color set to background to hide the bars or lines for the other charts in the series. For example, to make three charts displaying a three-series bar chart, on the first chart, hide the bars for Series 2 and 3. In the second chart, hide the bars for Series 3. Use the last chart to show all the series and reveal the complete picture.

You can hide a slice within a pie chart by setting a slice to the background color or by using the chart as a symbol and deleting the slices to be hidden. Use the build technique to create a sequence of charts for one pie. With Draw, enter any labels, values, or percentages you want to show. Hide all the slices but one in the first chart. Then display an additional slice in each subsequent chart, with the last chart showing the completed pie.

If you are creating a presentation to be shown on a computer screen, you can add animation to the build charts by using special effects, as discussed later in the chapter.

Whether you are using text or pictorial charts, always double-check them to make sure they are effective and accurate. Redesign them or modify their content if necessary.

It is also a good idea to select a background drawing chart to use for your presentation. This will unify the charts. (See Chapters 3 and 11 for more information about creating background drawings.)

USING A STORYBOARD

You can fill in a *storyboard* to show the sequence of your charts. You can sketch rough layouts and write notes on the storyboard to visualize the presentation. Photocopy the storyboard in Figure 12.1 and use it to plan your own presentations. This will save you a lot of time, expense, and frustration in excessive editing and changes.

A storyboard also serves as a draft of your presentation that others can review. Your coworkers can write their comments on their copies, and you can submit a copy for any approvals or authorizations you may need.

After you have a plan for your presentation, you are ready to create it with Harvard.

CREATING A PRESENTATION

To set up your presentation in Harvard, press **6** from the Main menu to select Presentation. You will see the Presentation menu, shown in Figure 12.2. Press **1** to choose Create presentation and display the Edit Presentation screen, shown in Figure 12.3. As on other Harvard screens, the function-key commands appear across the top of the screen, and there are fields to be filled in.

See Appendix E for information about using Harvard's palettes.

Add the background drawing and palette for your presentation first. Press F8 to display the Options menu for presentations and choose Presentation appearance. You will see the Presentation Appearance box. If you want to use a palette, change the Use presentation chart palette field to Yes and enter the file name of your palette

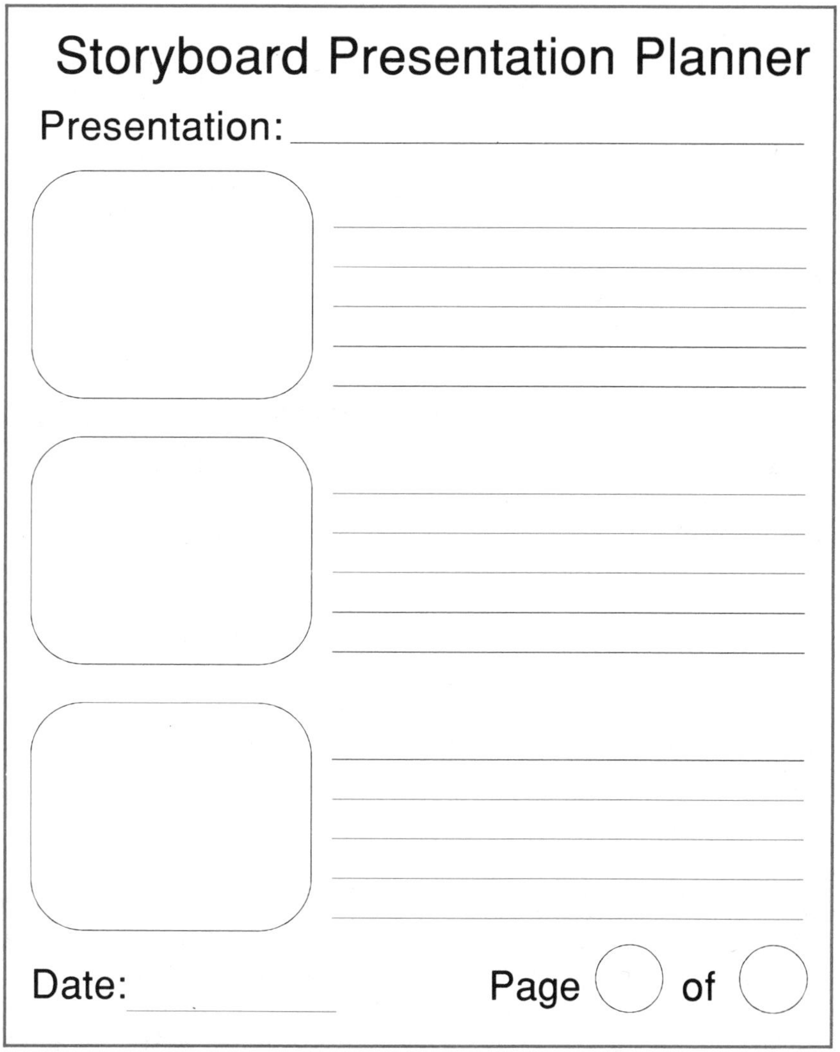

Storyboard Presentation Planner

Presentation: _____

Date: _____   Page ◯ of ◯

Figure 12.1: Use storyboards for presentation planning

in the Presentation chart palette field. To use a background drawing, change the Use presentation background drawing field to Yes and enter the file name of your background drawing in the Presentation background drawing field. When you include a background drawing or palette in your presentation, Harvard uses it for the files that follow in the presentation list.

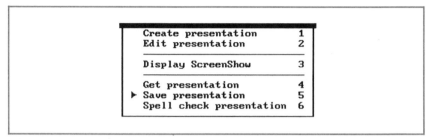

```
        Create presentation      1
        Edit presentation        2

        Display ScreenShow        3

        Get presentation          4
      ▶ Save presentation         5
        Spell check presentation  6
```

Figure 12.2: The Presentation menu

```
                            Edit Presentation
 F1-Help         F2-Preview                  F4-Effects      F5-Mark block
 F6-Main Menu    F7-Add/Edit    F8-Options   F9-HyperShow    F10-Continue

  #    Filename     Type            Description/Directory

  ▶                 DRAW   Background drawing for presentation

  1
  2
  3
  4
  5
  6
  7
  8
  9
 10
 11
 12
 13
 14
 15
 16
```

Figure 12.3: The Edit Presentation screen

You can include up to 175 charts in a presentation.

To add a chart to a presentation, press Ctrl-Ins (or press F7 and choose Add file from the Add/Edit menu). You will see a list of the files in the current directory. If necessary, change to another directory by highlighting the Directory field and entering a new directory. Then highlight the name of the file you want and press Enter. The chart's file name, type, and description (by default, the chart's title) will appear in the list on the Edit Presentation screen.

If you want to add several charts to your presentation at a time, select the file you want and press F5 to mark it for addition. Continue scrolling through the file list and pressing F5 to mark each chart you want to include. When you are finished selecting charts, press F10. All the charts you marked will be added to the Edit Presentation screen.

You can't print .PIC, .PCX , or .PCC files from a presentation. You must import the file as a bit-map image and save it as a chart. See Chapter 10 for details on using bit-map files.

You can also add screens and files from other programs. For example, you can include bit-mapped files that you created with Windows Paintbrush, PC Paintbrush, Publisher's Paintbrush, PC Paint, and many other programs; or screen images you captured with Harvard's CAPTURE utility. These files must have a .PIC, .PCC, .PCX, or .TIF extension.

You might want to add blank charts and templates to the list with a chart description as you are planning the presentation. Then you can create the other charts you need and replace the blank charts and templates. From the Edit Presentation screen, press F7, then **A** to select Add a blank chart, or **B** to select Add a template. Then press F7, then **9**, then **1** to enter its description.

USING PRESENTATION OPTIONS FOR A UNIFORM PRESENTATION

Design your charts so that you can use them more than once. Maintaining consistency in their elements allows you to reuse charts in other presentations.

The presentation Options menu is similar to the Options menus for the chart types. It contains selections that can help unify your presentation. You can use this menu to add consistent titles, subtitles, and footnotes; and control the style, font, and size of the text used in them. Keep the color combinations in the presentation uniform by specifying a palette to be used by all the files in the presentation (working with color palettes is described in Appendix E).

PREVIEWING A PRESENTATION

After you have added the charts for your presentation to the Edit Presentation screen, you will want to preview it to check its sequence and contents. On the Edit Presentation screen, highlight the name of the file that you want to begin the preview with and press F2.

The highlighted chart will appear. Press the right mouse button (or the Enter, down-arrow, or right-arrow key) to display the next chart. To view the previous chart, press the left button (or the Backspace, up-arrow, or left-arrow key). If you want to start the show over again from the first chart, press Home. Press End to display the last chart. When you press Enter from the last chart in the presentation, you will return to the Edit Presentation screen. You can also press Esc to return to the Edit Presentation screen.

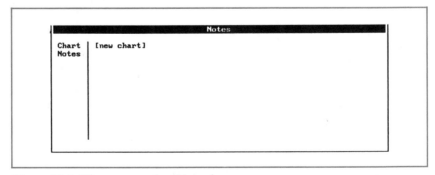

Use the Ctrl-E shortcut from a chart display or the Edit Presentation screen to see the chart's data-entry screen. Edit the data as necessary. Press Esc to return to the Main menu (unfortunately, you cannot simply pick up where you left off in the presentation preview).

If you see that a chart has a mistake in it or needs some type of modification, return to the data-entry screen for that chart and edit it as necessary. To edit the order or elements in your presentation, return to the Edit Presentation screen and make your changes using the techniques described shortly.

TAKING NOTES FOR YOUR PRESENTATION

When you are satisfied with the general structure of your presentation, you might want to take notes for your speech. These notes are Harvard's version of old-fashioned index cards. You can fill in any information to guide you through your speech.

To add a note from the Edit Presentation screen, highlight the file name of the chart that you want to attach the note to and press Ctrl-N (or press F7 and choose to add a note from the Add/Edit menu). As when you select to add notes to individual charts, you will see the Notes box. This Notes box contains the file name for the current chart in your presentation, as shown in Figure 12.4. Enter your notes, key words, outline, or the other information you will need for your presentation. Press Esc to return to the Edit Presentation screen. To edit a note, highlight the name of the file it is attached to, press Ctrl-N, and make your changes in the Notes box.

To print your notes, set Print notes to Yes when you print your presentation from the Output menu (producing your presentation is discussed later in the chapter). Harvard will print the chart and its

Figure 12.4: The presentation Notes box

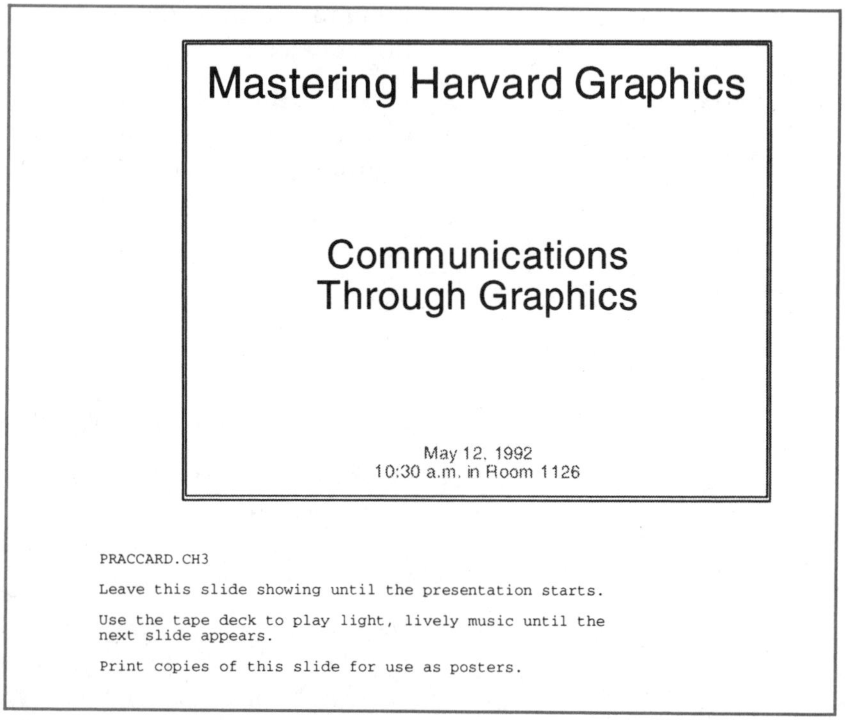

Mastering Harvard Graphics

Communications
Through Graphics

May 12, 1992
10:30 a.m. in Room 1126

PRACCARD.CH3

Leave this slide showing until the presentation starts.

Use the tape deck to play light, lively music until the
next slide appears.

Print copies of this slide for use as posters.

Figure 12.5: A note prints with its associated chart

associated note on the same page, as shown in the example in Figure 12.5 (they print on an entire 8½-by-11-inch sheet of paper).

SAVING YOUR PRESENTATION

To save your presentation, return to the Presentation menu (press **6** from the Main menu) and then press **5** to choose Save presentation.

In the Save box, type the file name you want to give your presentation, using eight characters or less. You can also enter a description for the presentation. When you are finished, press F10.

HANDS-ON: CREATING A PRESENTATION

In the following steps, you will create your own presentation with some of the charts you created in earlier chapters.

If you don't have these chart files, choose other ones.

1. From the Main menu, press **6**, then **1** to display the Edit Presentation screen.

2. Press Ctrl-Ins and highlight the names of the following files. Press F5 after highlighting each chart to tag it for your presentation list.

   MYPIE

   MYTITLE

   MYHIGH

   MYAREA

3. Press F10 to continue, and you will see the charts you selected listed on the Edit Presentation screen.

4. Press F2 to preview your presentation. You will see the first chart appear on the screen. Move through the presentation by pressing Enter at each screen. When you reach the last chart, press Enter to return to the Edit Presentation screen.

5. In an actual presentation, the title chart would come first. Highlight the MYTITLE chart and press Ctrl-up arrow to make it the first slide. Harvard will move that chart up in the list. You will learn about other presentation-editing techniques shortly.

6. Press Ctrl-N to add a note to the first chart and type the following reminders.

   Show until the meeting starts.

   Introduce yourself and the topic.

7. Press F10 when you are finished.

8. Continue and add notes for the other charts. For example, you could type a few comments about each type of graph and how it is used.

9. Press Esc to return to the Main menu.

10. Press **6**, then **6** to check the spelling in each of the charts in your presentation. Spell checking a presentation is similar to checking individual charts, except that you are prompted to save the file if spelling errors are found.

Chapter 3 describes how to have Harvard check the spelling in individual charts.

11. Press **6** and **5** to save the presentation and the notes you added. Type the name **MYSHOW** and the description **My first presentation**. After saving your presentation, you will be returned to the Main menu.

EMBEDDING PRESENTATIONS WITHIN PRESENTATIONS

To set up a continuous presentation that reruns by itself, place the presentation's file name after the last chart's file name on the Edit Presentation screen. This is useful for exhibits and trade shows.

Although Harvard limits presentations to 175 files, you can still create larger presentations. To include more charts in a presentation, group them into two or more presentations. Then add the name of the presentation file, which should have a .SH3 extension, to the Edit Presentation screen list. Harvard will continue the primary presentation with the charts in the secondary presentation file whenever it finds an .SH3 file in place of a .CH3 chart file. You can only embed presentations in the master (the first) presentation file. Any .SH3 files in a secondary presentation list will be ignored.

Embedding presentations is a great technique for organizing presentations into modules. For example, you could have modules describing your company's products or services, arranged in a separate presentation for each product. It would then be easy to quickly create a presentation tailored for your client by simply linking presentation files.

EDITING A PRESENTATION

Before you can edit a presentation, you must first select it. Press **4** from the Presentation menu to select Get presentation. You will see a list of your presentation files. Highlight the one you want to work with and press Enter. To edit a current presentation, from the Main menu, press **6**, and then press **2** to choose Edit presentation. You will see the Edit Presentation screen for that presentation.

As you saw in the last hands-on session, you can have Harvard check the spelling in your presentation by choosing Spell check presentation from the Presentation menu. The other techniques for editing your presentations are described in the following sections.

MOVING, COPYING, AND DELETING CHARTS IN A PRESENTATION

As when you are adding new files to your presentation list, you can mark groups of files for deletion, moving, or copying. Highlight each file you want the action to affect and press F5. Press F10 when you're finished.

If you want to reorganize the order of the charts in the presentation, just change the order of the charts in the list. Highlight the file name of the chart you want moved and press Ctrl-down arrow to move it down one chart or Ctrl-up arrow to move it up one chart.

Move between pages of chart listings by pressing PgUp or PgDn. To quickly jump to another chart, press Ctrl-J and then type the number of the chart you want to go to.

If you need to show a chart twice in the same presentation, you can duplicate it. Highlight its file name on the Edit Presentation screen, press F7, and then press **3**. To delete a chart from a presentation list, move to the chart you want removed and press Ctrl-Del.

EDITING PRESENTATION CHART DESCRIPTIONS

Maintaining the descriptions of the files in your presentations will help you organize your files. If you have a number of presentations and chart files, file descriptions help you find the charts you want to edit or use within other presentations.

From the Edit Presentation screen, press F7, then **9** to display the Edit description box. Then choose from one of these options:

- Edit Description: Use this option to edit the description for the highlighted chart.

- Update All Descriptions: Select this option to have Harvard scan your charts and use the chart's title as the description. This is the same title Harvard uses as the default description when you save your chart. Instant description updating can help you find charts that undergo frequent revision.

- View Description/Directory: This option toggles between the description directory and drive and subdirectory listing. Select it once to replace the description directory with the location of your chart by drive and subdirectories. Choose it again to return to the description directory.

PRODUCING YOUR PRESENTATION

After you have organized your presentation, you are ready to produce it. You can use Harvard's Output menu to send the presentation to a printer, plotter, or film recorder. If the presentation will be displayed on a computer monitor or LCD panels, you can display the screen show from the Presentation menu.

PRINTING A PRESENTATION

Chapter 2 discusses the advantages of producing charts as paper copies, plotters, transparencies, and 35mm slides.

You can print or plot your entire presentation using the Printer 1, Printer 2, or Plotter option. Harvard's printing options for presentations save you the time of printing, recording, or plotting each chart individually. Follow these steps to output your presentation:

1. From the Main menu, press **5** to select Output.

2. From the Output menu, press **5** to select Presentation.

3. Choose the output device you want to use to print your presentation. If you want to produce your show on 35mm slides, use the Output menu's Film recorder option. An Output box similar to the one you see for printing individual charts will appear.

4. Select the printing options you want for your presentation. For example, set Quality to High.

5. To print the notes, change the Print notes field setting to Yes.

6. Press F10, and your notes and charts will start printing.

7. When your charts and notes finish printing, you will return to the Main menu. Press **5**, then **6**, select the printer, and press F10 to print the presentation list. This sends a list of the charts in your presentation to the printer.

Use the printed notes and list to double-check your presentation's organization.

PRESENTING A SCREEN SHOW

If your audience will be 10 to 20 people, you can present your screen shows on 19-inch monitors or LCD overhead panels. If you are working with a larger group, you can give your screen shows on video projectors or 33-inch to 37-inch monitors.

If your presentation is designed to be displayed on a monitor screen, you can give it by selecting the Display ScreenShow option on the Presentation menu. Press the right mouse button or Enter to display the next chart and the left button or Backspace to return to the previous chart. Press Esc to stop a show and return to the Main menu.

Large (33- to 37-inch) monitors are suitable for presentations to larger audiences, but are costly. Many of these monitors have input and output jacks that let you put your presentations on a VCR tape. However, don't bother hooking up your computer to a television set because a television monitor does not provide the resolution that a high-quality presentation needs.

If you need the flexibility to show your screen show on other computers, you may want to purchase the Harvard add-on program called ScreenShow Utilities. This utility allows you to transfer a presentation to a computer that isn't running Harvard Graphics. This means you are less restricted in when or where you present your screen show; you can even use a portable laptop computer.

There are many special effects you can add to screen shows. These are described later in the chapter.

WORKING WITH LCD PANELS AND VIDEO PROJECTORS

PC Viewer is an LCD panel that stores graphs in memory, so you don't need a computer for your shows. This product comes with an infrared remote control, special effects generator, and battery memory backup.

LCD panels function much like transparencies but offer the additional advantage of screen shows. The LCD panel sits on the overhead projector and is connected to your computer. When you use the panel with the Display ScreenShow option, the images are displayed on the panel instead of the monitor. The overhead projector then transfers the images to a screen.

You should be aware that LCD panels do not show color well. Panels with CGA resolutions are blurry and difficult to read. Some VGA color panels are now available, but they still lack the crisp resolution and colors of a monitor. Also, LCD panels will not work on inexpensive view projectors with overhead lighting. Light must come from the base of the projector.

PC Emcee lets you hook up sound from a tape deck to your show and also works as a remote control device. Alternatively, you can use a mouse with a long cord to control the screen show.

There are several commercial companies that make video projection units. Although the projected images aren't as crisp as 4000-line resolution charts, they are adequate for most screen shows.

USING A SLIDE SERVICE

Slide service firms can give you professional 35mm slides and overhead transparencies. Harvard includes the AGX communications software, accessed from the Applications menu, to order slides and send your charts to the Autographix slide service by using a modem. Or you can mail a disk to the slide service company for processing. Harvard's AGX program will ouput your slides onto a disk if you like.

Chapter 13 explains how to export your charts to a slide service.

ADDING SPECIAL EFFECTS TO SCREEN SHOWS

You can add special effects to a presentation created for display on a monitor, an LCD panel, or a video projector. For example, you can show a chart that fades in while the old one fades out, or you can present a chart that opens from the center of the screen, enlarging to replace the previous one. You can select from dozens of effects.

To add special effects to a screen show, display the Edit Presentation screen for that presentation and press F4 to see the Effects screen, shown in Figure 12.6.

You can't change the data in the first two columns of the Effects screen.

The first column on the Effects screen shows the chart number, and the second column contains the chart's file name. The remaining columns categorize the effects you can specify for each chart, as follows:

- Draw: Turns on a screen effect for drawing the chart
- ←↑↓→: Determines the direction of chart drawing
- Speed: Sets the drawing speed for the effect (slow, medium, or fast)
- Time: Sets the length of time that the chart is displayed
- Erase: Turns of a screen effect for erasing the chart

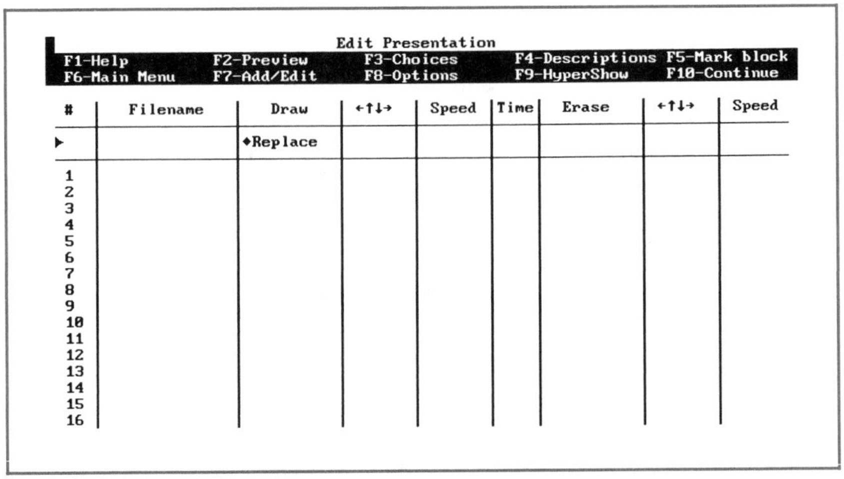

Figure 12.6: The Effects screen

- ←↕→: Determines the direction of chart erasing
- Speed: Sets the erasing speed for the effect (slow, medium, or fast)

Move the cursor to the column you want to select from and press the F3 key to see a list of the effects. Use the Tab and arrow keys to move among the columns and rows and add effects to each chart in your presentation. To remove an effect, highlight the chart's file name and press Ctrl-Del.

You can change the order of the charts in your presentation through the Effects screen in the same way that you rearrange the charts from the Edit Presentation screen: highlight the chart you want to move and press Ctrl-up arrow or Ctrl-down arrow.

One file stores all the information for a particular chart show, including its notes and special effects. Thus, when you make changes on the Effects screen, you change the other lists as well.

SETTING DRAW AND ERASE EFFECTS

Whenever you select a Draw effect for a chart, you can also specify how the chart is displayed and how it is erased. If you don't specify a time period, the chart will stay on the screen until you press Enter. If you don't specify how it's erased, Harvard will quickly clear the screen and show the next chart.

The default effect in the Draw column is Replace, which simply clears the screen and replaces the old chart with a new one, as if you pressed F2 to view your graph.

When your press F3 in the Draw column, you will see the following choices:

Not all monitors and video adapters will display all of Harvard's special effects.

- Overlay: Superimposes a new chart over the old one. In other words, the old chart isn't erased while the new chart is drawn on top of it. For example, you can use it to overlay Harvard charts on .PCX files drawn with drawing programs such as PC Paintbrush.

- Wipe: Removes the old chart by pushing it off the screen and sliding the new one onto the screen from left to right (default direction). To slide the chart from right to left, press L in the ←↕→ column.

- Scroll: Similar to Wipe, but pushes the old chart off the top of the screen as the new one scrolls up from the bottom. You can reverse the default up scroll direction by pressing D in the ←↕→ column.

- Fade: Slowly removes (when erasing) or gradually adds pixels that appear as small dots until your chart is erased or drawn.

- Blinds: Works like venetian blinds. The screen is divided into horizontal planes that reveal your chart in sections.

It doesn't matter if you choose Left or Right when selecting a direction in the ←↕→ column for charts with the Open or Close effect because these directions work the same.

- Open: Draws charts starting from the center of the screen while working towards the top and bottom borders. You can open from the center to the side borders by pressing L or R in the ←↕→ column.

- Close: Works like Open, except that it draws the chart from the border to the center of the screen. The default direction is from the top and bottom borders. Press L or R in the ←↕→ column to close from the left and right borders to the center.

- Iris: Displays charts diagonally, working from the center of the screen towards the four corners. Choose Out (the default direction) or In in the ←↕→ column.

The ←↑↓→ column
on the Effects screen
does not apply to the
Replace, Overlay, and
Fade effects.

Figure 12.7 illustrates these special effects.

When you add a Draw effect to a chart, you can also specify the direction it moves in and the speed in which it moves. For example, if you choose Scroll, you can specify Left in the ←↑↓→ column so that the chart scrolls on the screen from right to left. If you don't specify the direction, Harvard uses the default direction for the chosen effect. The speed in which the effect moves can be set to Slow, Medium (the default), or Fast.

Similarly, you can decide how you want your chart erased. Before the next chart is displayed, Harvard removes the current chart using the effect you specified in the Erase column. For example, if you specify Wipe in the Erase column, Fast in the Speed column, and Down in the ←↑↓→ column, the chart will be quickly wiped off the screen horizontally, starting at the top.

You can set default values for effects by entering them in the top row of the Effects screen (between the column headings and the file

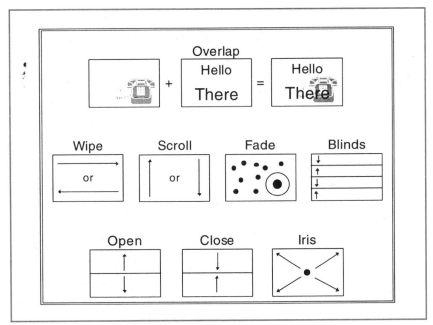

Figure 12.7: Harvard's special effects for screen shows

Some Draw effects work together better than others. For example, if you erase a chart using Scroll from one direction, display the next by scrolling from the opposite direction. Similarly, if you erase a chart using Iris Out, show the next one using Wipe Right. Experiment and see which combinations are best for your charts.

Do not set times for live presentations because your timing might not always match your trial run. Use the keyboard or mouse to change charts manually.

names). You can then vary some of the charts by setting just their rows to other effects; leave the columns for the other charts blank to accept the default settings in the top row.

ADDING TIME DELAYS

The Time column on the Effects screen allows you to add time delays to automate your presentation. For example, you might want to set times for a trade booth or convention presentation, or one that is presented using a tape recorder or other audio device.

To set a display time for a chart, move the cursor to the Time column for that chart and enter the time in minutes or seconds. For example, you can type 30 for 30 seconds or 1:30 (or 130) for 1 minute and 30 seconds.

To create an ongoing presentation—one that continually repeats itself (for example, for a trade booth)—move the cursor to the last chart file name on the Effects screen and press F9. You will see the HyperShow menu. Press **1** to choose Edit keys. Move the cursor to the Go To column, press **1**, and then press Esc (do not type anything in the Key column). Now you won't have to restart the show every time it ends. The HyperShow menu options are described later in the chapter.

HANDS-ON: PRODUCING A PRESENTATION WITH SPECIAL EFFECTS

Now you can try out some of Harvard's special effects by adding a few embellishments to the simple presentation you created in the last hands-on session.

When you first get a presentation, you will automatically go to the Edit Presentation screen.

1. From the Main menu, press **6**, then **4** to choose Get presentation. Highlight the MYSHOW file and press Enter.

2. Press F4 to display the Effects screen.

3. Move the cursor to the top (unnumbered) row in the Time column. Press **3**, then Enter to set the default time to three seconds. This sets up a self-running show.

CH. 12

4. Move to the Draw column for your first chart (MYTITLE) and type **S** for Scroll. Press Tab and type **L** for Left in the ←↑↓→ column. Move the cursor to the Erase column and type **S** for Scroll again. Press Tab to move the cursor to Erase's ←↑↓→ column and type **R** for Right. When the presentation runs, Harvard will erase your chart by scrolling it to the right.

5. Enter effects and directions for the other charts in your show until your Effects screen looks like Figure 12.8.

6. Press F6, then **6**, then **3** to select Display ScreenShow, and watch your show run by itself.

SIMULATING ANIMATION WITH SPECIAL EFFECTS

> Individual chart animation can also add interest, as you learned in the last chapter.

You can create spectacular presentations by using special effects to simulate animation. For example, you could create a series of build charts, as discussed earlier in the chapter, and then use effects like Wipe and Scroll to animate the building process.

#	Filename	Draw	←↑↓→	Speed	Time	Erase	←↑↓→	Speed
▶		◆Replace			0:03			
1	MYTITLE .CH3	Scroll	Down			Scroll	Up	
2	MYPIE .CH3	Iris	In			Iris	Out	
3	MYHIGH .CH3	Wipe	Left			Wipe	Right	
4	MYAREA .CH3	Fade	Up			Fade		
5								
6								
7								
8								
9								
10								
11								
12								
13								
14								
15								
16								

Edit Presentation
F1-Help F2-Preview F3-Choices F4-Descriptions F5-Mark block
F6-Main Menu F7-Add/Edit F8-Options F9-HyperShow F10-Continue

Figure 12.8: Choosing your special effects

Consider saving the master chart as a symbol. Create a drawing chart for the copy. Put the master chart symbol in your drawing, ungroup the symbol, and then delete the bars or objects that you do not want initially displayed.

CHEATING RISING-BAR AND RUNNING-LINE EFFECTS

You can make the bars in bar charts rise and look as if they're growing (for example, to show stock prices or sales figures). First create a master bar chart that contains all your data. Make a copy of the master chart and hide the bars by setting the series' Color columns to background or by setting the Series options so that the bars are not displayed. This copy becomes the first chart in your presentation and sets the stage for animation.

The animation occurs when you show the master chart (with visible bars) using the Scroll effect in an Up direction (the default). Follow these steps to create the rising-bar effect:

1. Create the two or more charts you need for animation. The master chart has the series values visible, and the series in the copies are hidden.

2. Display the Edit Presentation screen.

3. Insert the chart copy—the one without the bars.

4. Insert the master chart, which shows the series values.

5. Press F4 to add effects. In the Draw column for the copy, set the Overlay effect.

6. In the Draw column for the master chart, choose the Scroll effect.

7. Continue with steps 3 to 6 until you have added all the charts you want with rising-bar effects.

Show falling or shrinking bars by setting Scroll to Down.

You can show lines and horizontal bars that run from one side of the screen to another, using the same techniques you used to make bars grow. Set the stage by displaying a chart with hidden lines. The animated running lines appear when you display the next chart (with visible lines) using the Wipe effect.

Set X and Y axis Grid Lines to None when you hide bars and lines. This way, you will not see grid lines with gaps. If you must have grids, use Draw to add them.

USING BIT-MAP IMAGES AS CHART BACKGROUNDS

As mentioned earlier in the chapter, you can add bit-mapped images as .PCX files to your presentations. This means that you can use scanned images, such as photographs and other illustrations, as backgrounds for your charts. Superimpose your charts over the .PCX file chart by selecting the Overlay effect for Draw on the Effects screen.

For example, you could place a scanned image of a city skyline as the background of a bar chart about sales in that city. Figure 12.9 shows an example of this type of chart.

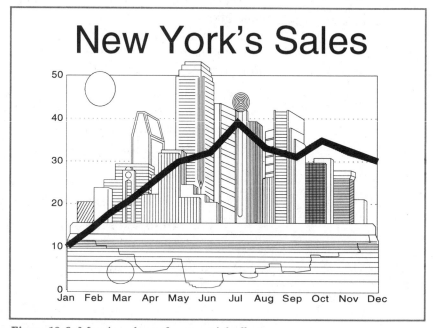

Figure 12.9: Merging charts for a special effect

CREATING AN INTERACTIVE SCREEN SHOW

Even if your screen show needs to be seen from beginning to end, an interactive design allows those who have already seen your presentation to review a particular section.

Through Harvard's HyperShow options, you can set up an interactive presentation, which can be controlled by the viewer. The choices for the viewer are provided through a menu system, and selections are made through keypresses or through buttons. In effect, you can divide your screen show into independent sections and let the audience decide the order in which these sections are presented.

SETTING UP MENUS

Figure 12.10 shows an example of a menu for an interactive screen show. To set up this type of menu system for your show, create a text chart containing the menu and make it your show's first chart, and then follow these steps:

1. Press F4 from the Edit Presentation screen to display the Effects screen and highlight the first file name (the menu chart).

2. Press F9, then **1** to select Edit keys, and you will see the Edit HyperShow Keys box, shown in Figure 12.11.

3. Specify the keystroke associated with each chart in the show by entering the key to press in the Key column and the number of the chart it displays in the Go To column. For the sample menu shown in Figure 12.10, for example, you would enter 1 in the Key column and 1 in the Go To

Interactive Menu

Press	To See
1	Introduction
2	Quality assurance
3	Features for comfort
4	Products prices

Figure 12.10: Using a menu for an interactive show

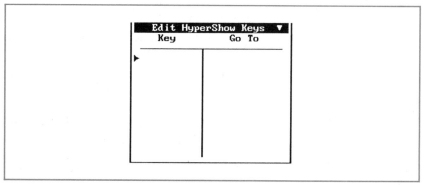

Figure 12.11: The Edit HyperShow Keys box

column for the Introduction chart. If you enter 2 in the Key column and 10 in the Go To column, Harvard will display the tenth chart when the user presses 2.

4. Continue typing Key and Go To instructions until you have covered all your menu choices.

You can enter keystrokes other than numbers in the Key column. Assign any letter key or function key (except F1) to control your show. You can even include mouse clicks in the Key column by typing Rmouse for the right mouse button or Lmouse for the left mouse button.

If you leave the Key column blank and enter a number in the Go To column, Harvard jumps to that chart if the viewer does not press any of the other keys listed in the Key column. This way, your chart show will always run; you have created a default order. This technique also lets you enter unconditional jumping instructions. For instance, you can jump to the first chart at the end of every section by highlighting the last chart, pressing F9, typing **1** in the Go To column and leaving the Key column blank for each section's last chart.

You can assign more than one key for each chart.

The Edit HyperShow Keys box can handle up to 100 sets of instructions per chart. When you add branching instructions for a chart, a check mark appears to the left of the file name on the Effects screen. Use this screen as a reference when you are checking or adding HyperShow key commands.

*CONTROLLING THE SHOW WITH BRANCHING INSTRUC-
TIONS* Instead of entering chart numbers in the Go To column of
the Edit HyperShow Keys box, you can insert the following words to
control branching:

Next	Displays the next chart in the list
Prev	Displays the previous chart in the list
LastView	Displays the last chart that was viewed (not necessarily the previous one)
First	Displays the first chart in the list
Last	Displays the last chart in the list
Notes	Displays the notes for the chart
Chart	Gets the chart data so the viewer can edit it
Template	Gets a chart's template but not its data
Nextpal	Displays the chart using the next palette in the palettes directory
Prevpal	Displays the chart using the previous palette in the palettes directory
Exit	Exits HyperShow and returns to the Main menu

ADDING BUTTONS TO INTERACTIVE SHOWS

Create a chart of default buttons to be used throughout your presentation by creating a background drawing with buttons. From the Edit Presentation menu, press F8, then **3** to select Presentation Appearance. Then set the presentation to use the background drawing by providing the chart's complete file name in the Presentation background drawing field.

As explained in Chapter 11, you add buttons to chart objects by
using the Button tool in Draw. You can activate the buttons for your
screen show, so that clicking on the object with a button displays the
chart assigned to that button.

Press F9, then **2** to display the Edit HyperShow/Edit Buttons box,
shown in Figure 12.12. A list of the buttons you created in Draw will
appear in the Button column. The Go To column in this box works
the same as the Go To column in the Edit HyperShow keys box,
described in the previous section, to provide branching instructions.
Enter a chart number or one of the special instructions listed above in
the Go To column beside each button. Then, when the chart with

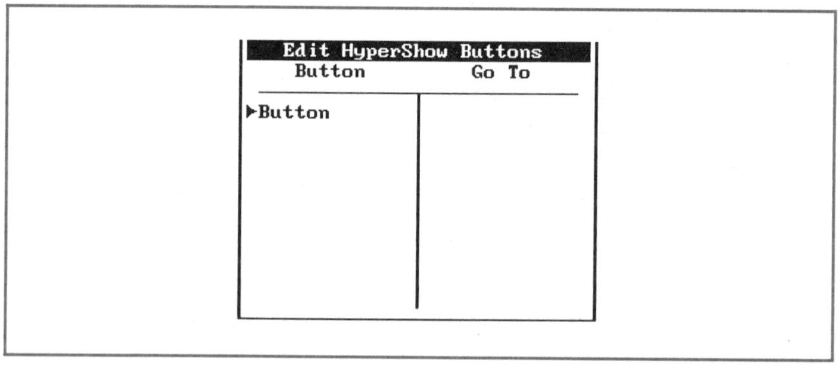

Figure 12.12: The Edit HyperShow/Edit Buttons box

that button appears, Harvard displays an arrow on the screen that can be moved to select a button and view the chart associated with it.

For example, suppose that you used the Button tool in Draw to assign the name Introduction to an invisible area (a box object using background colors and line fill) around the Introduction option (1) in the menu chart shown in Figure 12.10. When you display the Edit HyperShow Buttons box, you will see the Introduction label in the Button column. If you enter the number 10 in the Go To column next to Introduction, when Harvard displays the menu chart, a small arrow will appear on the screen. When you move the arrow to Introduction and press Enter, the tenth chart will appear. Using this technique, you can assign buttons and branching instructions to a menu chart to create the interactive show.

If you move, delete, or insert charts in your presentation, Harvard will automatically rearrange the branching instructions to match the new order. However, you can disable this feature so that the branching instructions are not affected. To do this, from the Edit Presentation screen, press F9, then *3*, and set Automatic recalculation to No.

If you turn off Automatic recalculation, screen show branching may take some unexpected routes.

GIVING YOUR PRESENTATION

With your presentation planned and produced, you're ready to show it to an audience. Most of the hard work is finished, but you still have to present the show effectively.

In many ways, you're an entertainer; you must capture your audience's attention using a variety of techniques—including acting. Change your vocal intonation, move your arms and hands for gestures, smile, stand up straight, and be enthusiastic. You might want to rehearse your show in front of a mirror or with a friend, or tape it and listen for ways to improve it.

When you display a new chart, wait a few seconds before you explain it. This gives you a chance to refresh your memory and your audience a chance to absorb the data. Show the chart for as long as it takes to explain the idea—and not a second longer. Keep the presentation flowing and energetic.

If time allows, encourage the audience to participate. Ask them questions and get them involved. Present your ideas to them—not to the screen or projector. Also, watch for their response. If they get restless or if your presentation lasts for more than an hour, take a ten-minute break to stand and stretch or get a cup of coffee.

If your presentation elicits action, strike while the iron is hot. Get volunteers and assign tasks while you have a captive audience. If you let them get away, the excitement of your presentation can subside, and you won't get the results you're looking for.

Here are some other suggestions for giving an effective presentation:

- For maximum audience participation, time your presentation to be accessible to as many people as possible. Don't schedule it during a holiday week, near lunchtime, or after 3:30 p.m.

- Set your equipment up early and make sure everything works— *before* your audience arrives. Murphy's Laws certainly apply to presentations.

- Have your title screen ready and displayed so the audience members see it when they enter the room.

Depending on the size of your audience, the seating arrangement (and thus your audience's view of the charts) can also be an important factor in the success of your presentation. Figure 12.13 shows some seating arrangements you may want to consider.

If you don't have much time, don't let the audience ask questions that interrupt your presentation. Ask them to hold all questions until you're finished.

Respect the efforts of those who arrive on time by starting your show on time.

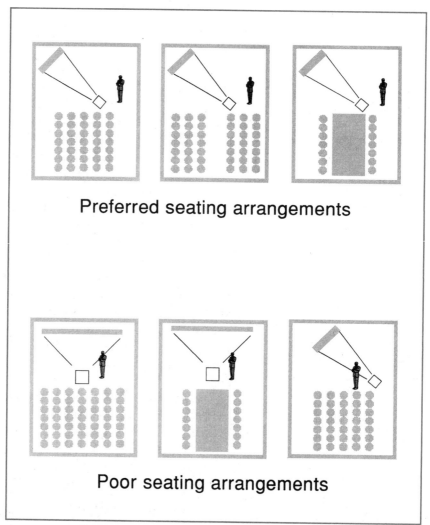

Figure 12.13: Seating arrangement possibilities

SUMMARY

This chapter pulled together all the techniques and enhancements that you learned throughout this book. By combining charts you create in Harvard, charts you import from other programs, and templates to ensure consistency, and adding special effects, you can create presentations worthy of a Harvard Graphics master.

13

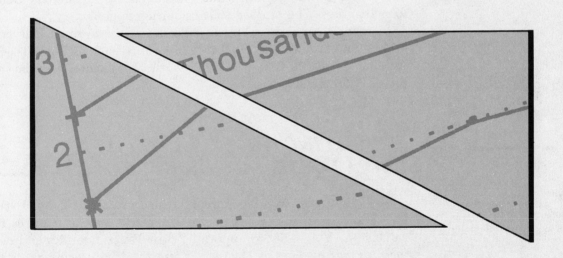

Transferring Information Between Harvard and Other Programs

CHAPTER **13** _____

WHEN YOU WORK WITH SEVERAL PROGRAMS, IM-
porting and exporting data can save you a considerable amount of
time. By using Harvard's Import and Export options, you avoid
having to retype data from other programs. For example, you can
import a Lotus 1-2-3 spreadsheet to Harvard and use its data in a
chart. You also can export a Harvard graph for use in other
programs.

Harvard provides you with eight importing options so that you can
import data from almost any program. If you work with Lotus 1-2-3,
Excel, or dBASE, you can select the option for importing the specific
files produced by these programs. If you work with other programs,
you can save your work in either the standard or delimited ASCII
format and use Harvard's ASCII importing options.

Harvard's Applications menu provides access to some Harvard
utilities and also lets you run other programs, such as Lotus 1-2-3,
Excel, and dBASE, from within Harvard. This menu is described at
the end of this chapter.

_____ *IMPORTING GRAPHS AND DATA*
FROM LOTUS 1-2-3 OR EXCEL _____

You cannot import
Lotus .PIC files as
graphs.

You might want to bring a graph created in Lotus 1-2-3 or Excel
into Harvard so that you can use Harvard's special features to
enhance it. You can also import 1-2-3 or Excel data files and use
them to create charts in Harvard. From the Main menu, press **4**,
then **7** to choose Import from the File menu. You will see the Import
menu, shown in Figure 13.1.

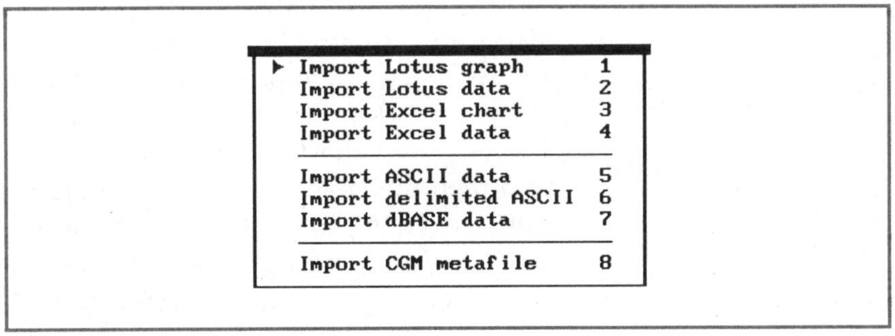

```
       ► Import Lotus graph      1
         Import Lotus data       2
         Import Excel chart      3
         Import Excel data       4

         Import ASCII data       5
         Import delimited ASCII  6
         Import dBASE data       7

         Import CGM metafile     8
```

Figure 13.1: The Import menu

IMPORTING SPREADSHEET GRAPHS

To bring in a 1-2-3 graph, press **1** to choose the Import Lotus graph option. You will see a list of files that you can select, including those with .WKS, .WK1, .WRK, and .WR1 extensions. Highlight the name of the file that you want to import and press Enter.

Next, you will see a list of the graphs within that file, as shown in Figure 13.2. The Import data only field at the top of the screen determines which settings are used for the imported chart. When it is set to No, the default, all the Lotus 1-2-3 chart settings are imported with the graph. If you want Harvard to use its own default settings in creating the chart, set Import data only to Yes.

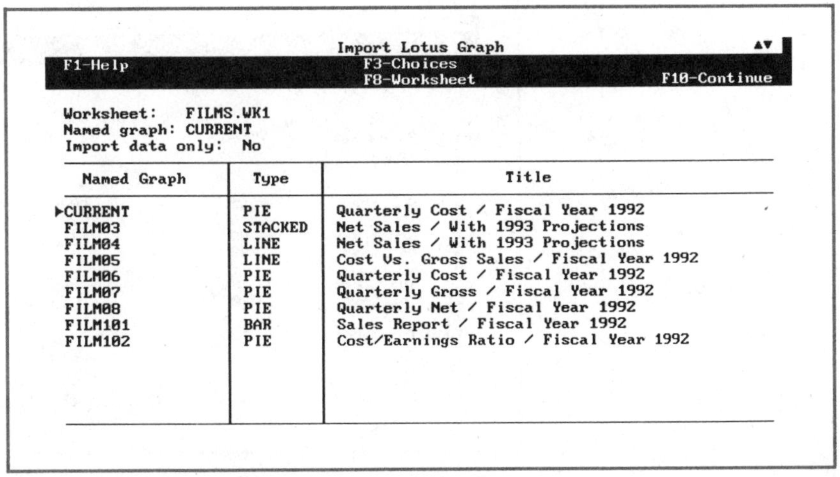

Press Tab to toggle between the Named graph field and the Import data only field.

```
                          Import Lotus Graph                    ▲▼
    F1-Help                     F3-Choices
                                F8-Worksheet              F10-Continue

    Worksheet:    FILMS.WK1
    Named graph: CURRENT
    Import data only:  No

    ┌─────────────────┬───────────┬──────────────────────────────────────┐
    │  Named Graph    │   Type    │              Title                   │
    ├─────────────────┼───────────┼──────────────────────────────────────┤
    │ ►CURRENT        │ PIE       │ Quarterly Cost / Fiscal Year 1992    │
    │  FILM03         │ STACKED   │ Net Sales / With 1993 Projections    │
    │  FILM04         │ LINE      │ Net Sales / With 1993 Projections    │
    │  FILM05         │ LINE      │ Cost Vs. Gross Sales / Fiscal Year 1992 │
    │  FILM06         │ PIE       │ Quarterly Cost / Fiscal Year 1992    │
    │  FILM07         │ PIE       │ Quarterly Gross / Fiscal Year 1992   │
    │  FILM08         │ PIE       │ Quarterly Net / Fiscal Year 1992     │
    │  FILM101        │ BAR       │ Sales Report / Fiscal Year 1992      │
    │  FILM102        │ PIE       │ Cost/Earnings Ratio / Fiscal Year 1992 │
    └─────────────────┴───────────┴──────────────────────────────────────┘
```

Figure 13.2: The Import Lotus Graph screen

Highlight the name of the graph you want to import and press F10. Your imported graph will appear on the screen, and you can now edit, save, and print it in Harvard.

Save time hunting for files. Let Harvard know where you keep your spreadsheet files by the Import directory field on the Program Default screen of the Setup menu.

To import an Excel graph, press **1**, then **7**, then **3** to select the Import Excel chart option from the Import menu. Choose the file, and then the chart you want to bring in, set the Import data only option to No if you want to use the Excel settings or Yes if you want to use Harvard's settings, and then press F10. The Excel graph will appear on your screen, and you can modify and save it in Harvard.

IMPORTING LOTUS 1-2-3 OR EXCEL DATA

The Lotus options also import charts and data files created with Symphony.

The Import Lotus data and Import Excel data options on Harvard's Import menu allow you to transfer a data file from 1-2-3 or Excel into Harvard. You can then use the data to create Harvard charts. This takes a few more steps than when you import the graph itself, but it is still faster than retyping all the data. If you regularly create charts from a Lotus 1-2-3 or an Excel file, you should create a template, as described later in the chapter.

Before you import data from a spreadsheet program into Harvard, you should be familiar with the structure of a spreadsheet so that you can specify the location of your data. As shown in the sample 1-2-3 worksheet in Figure 13.3, a spreadsheet is organized by lettered

```
                          View Lotus Worksheet                    ◄►▲▼
  F1-Help                                    F4-Import form   F5-Mark
                                             F9-Jump to      F10-Continue

  Current location: A1: Sales Rpt
          ▼
            A         B       C       D       E       F       G       H
  ►1      Sales Rpt
   2      In mil $
   3
   4                                  1991
   5      Quarter            Q1      Q2      Q3      Q4
   6      Cost               16      26      30      18
   7      Gross Rev          69      82      77      58
   8      Net Rev            53      56      47      40
   9
  10      Tot Gross          286             Net %   68.53
  11      Tot Cost           90              Cost %  31.47
  12                         =========
  13      Total Net          196
  14
  15
  16                                  1992
  17      Quarter            Q1      Q2      Q3      Q4
```

Figure 13.3: Sample Lotus 1-2-3 spreadsheet data

columns (A to D in the figure) and numbered rows (1 to 17 in the figure). The intersection where a column and row meets is called a *cell*. Cells hold the values or data for your charts. For example, the element *16* is in cell C6 (column C and row 6) and the word *Cost* is in cell A6 (column A and row 6). Cell A1 contains the spreadsheet's title.

Print a copy of the spreadsheet file you are going to import and determine the location of the cells, or the *ranges*, that contain the data you want to transfer.

Before bringing in the data, you must set up a Harvard chart to receive it. When you are ready to import your 1-2-3 or Excel data file, follow these steps:

> You must choose a chart or template before importing Lotus 1-2-3 or Excel data. If you do not, Harvard will display an error message when you try to import the data.

1. Start Harvard and choose the type of chart you want to create and the X-axis data type. For example, you might create a bar chart and specify Year as the X data type. Alternatively, you can retrieve an existing Harvard chart to which you want to add the imported data.

2. From the chart data-entry screen, press F10 to return to the Main menu. Your newly created chart is still active and is ready to receive the spreadsheet data.

3. From the Main menu, press **4**, then **7** to display the Import menu. Then press **2** to import 1-2-3 data, or **4** to import Excel data.

4. When the list of data files you can import appears, highlight the name of the file you want and press Enter.

> If you have already used the Import Lotus (or Excel) data option, you will see the Import Lotus Data screen with the data from the previous file you imported, instead of the file list. Harvard assumes that you want to make changes to the previous file you imported. To see the file list, press F8, then **1**.

The files in the list are either the ones that you specified through the Setup menu's Program defaults option or, if you didn't specify any, the ones in the current data directory. If you don't see the file you want, move the cursor to the Directory field and type the name of the subdirectory where you keep your spreadsheet files. Or click on a subdirectory file name if it's listed on the screen, and you will see the names of the files that are in your home directory.

Next, you will see the screen for defining how you want to import the data into the Harvard chart. Figures 13.4, 13.5, and 13.6 show the Import Lotus Data Into XY Chart, Pie Chart, and Table Chart

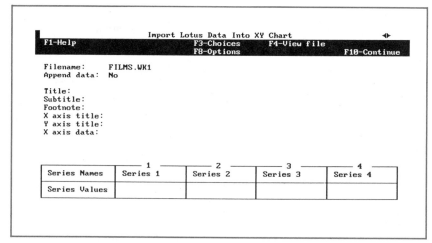

Figure 13.4: The Import Lotus Data Into XY Chart screen

screens, respectively. No matter which type of chart you are importing data into, the procedures for designating the data ranges are the same.

5. Fill in the fields for the Title, Subtitle, Footnote, and axis titles (for an XY chart) by using one of three methods:

- Type in the text that you want to appear.

- If you want to use the text on the spreadsheet and know the range it is in, enter its location. Precede a single cell with a slash, and use two dots for a group of cells. For example, you could enter **\A1** to use the value in cell A1 or **B3..D3** to specify the values in cells B3 through D3.

- Select the range of the spreadsheet by pressing F4 to view the spreadsheet you are importing. To designate a single cell, move the cursor to the cell that contains the text for the field. To specify a range, move to the first cell of the range, mark it by pressing F5, and then use the arrow keys to highlight the rest of the range. After selecting the cell or range, press F4 again to return to the data-entry screen.

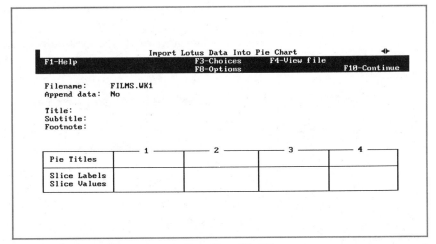

Figure 13.5: The Import Lotus Data Into Pie Chart screen

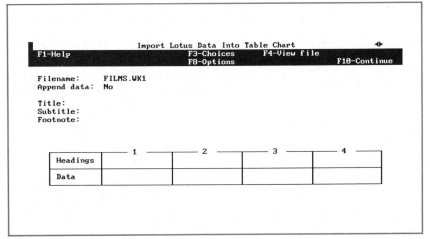

Figure 13.6: The Import Lotus Data Into Table Chart screen

6. If you are creating an XY chart, continue by designating the x-axis data range. Move your cursor to the X axis data field, press F4 to view the spreadsheet, and mark the data range using the third method described in the previous step.

7. Identify each series on your spreadsheet and specify its label and data range on the data-entry screen (press F4 to select the ranges on the spreadsheet, or type in the locations).

8. When you are creating an entirely new chart from the imported spreadsheet data, the Append data field at the top of the data-entry screen should be set to No. If you are adding the data to an existing Harvard chart, set the Append data field to Yes.

9. Press F10 to return to the Main menu, and then save your chart.

HANDS-ON: CREATING AND USING A TEMPLATE FOR LOTUS 1-2-3 DATA

Harvard also includes an Excel file called FILMS.XLS.

As mentioned earlier, if you work with Lotus 1-2-3 or Excel frequently, you should create a template for importing data. In the following steps, you will set up a template using the practice 1-2-3 file provided with Harvard. This file is named FILMS.WK1, and it is on the C:\HG3\IMPORT directory.

1. From the Main menu, press **1** to select Create chart.

2. Press **3**, then **2** to select a stacked bar chart, and then press F10 until you return to the Main menu.

3. Press **4**, then **7**, then **2** to choose Import Lotus data.

4. Highlight FILMS.WK1 and press Enter. You will see the Import Lotus Data Into XY Chart screen (Figure 13.4).

5. Press F4 to view the spreadsheet. The Current location field shows that the cursor's position is A1: Sales Rpt. This is the text you will use for the title, so press F4 to import the cell. On the data-entry screen, you will see \A1 in the Title field, showing that Harvard will use the contents of cell A1 for the chart's title.

If you see highlighted columns while moving to cell D4, you pressed F5 or another key accidentally. Just press Esc and start over.

6. Press Enter three times to move to the X axis title field and press F4 to see the spreadsheet. Use the arrow keys to move the cursor to cell D4. Watch the Current location field to see which cell is selected. Press F4 again to import the 1991 value.

7. Press Enter to move to the Y axis title and type **\A2**. (The title you will use for the Y-axis is in cell A2.)

8. Press Enter to move to the X axis data field and press F4. Move the cursor to cell C5, press the F5 key, and move the cursor to cell F5. The Current location field should contain C5..F5, and the values Q1 to Q4 should be highlighted. Press F4 to define this range for the X-axis values. The X axis data field should read C5..F5.

9. Press Enter to move the cursor to the Series 1 label. Press Ctrl-Del to delete the label, type **\A6**, and press Enter. Type **C6..F6** to define the cost figures for Series 1.

10. Press the up-arrow key, then Tab to move the cursor to the Series 2 label. Type **Net Income** and press Enter. Press F4, move the cursor to cell C8, press F5, and then move the cursor to cell F8 to highlight the C8..F8 range. Press F4 again to import it. Your data-entry screen should look like Figure 13.7.

11. Press F10. The data you imported will appear on the XY chart data-entry screen. You can now modify this chart as necessary. After viewing the chart, press F10 until you see the Main menu.

You do not have to enter ranges or cells from the spreadsheet. Replace the labels or titles with those you like better.

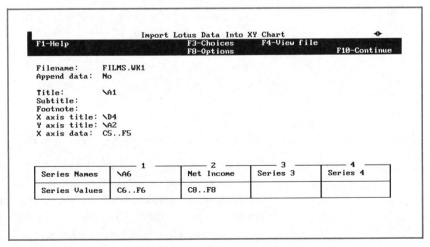

Figure 13.7: The completed Import data-entry screen

> ☑ To keep your completed graph, save it as a chart before you save it as a template.

Now that you have created a chart of imported data, you will save it as a template so that you do not have to go through these steps every time you want to use imported data in your Harvard charts.

12. From the Main menu, press **4**, then **5** to choose the Save as template option from the File menu.

13. In the Save Template box, type **QUARTER** as the template's name and press Enter. Type **Sales, costs, and profits (Lotus 1-2-3 import)** as the description.

14. Change the Clear values field to Yes. Clearing the values saves the importing procedure without the actual data. This way, when you modify the Lotus 1-2-3 file (for next year's reports, for example), the revised data will be imported to Harvard automatically.

15. The Import data link field is set to Yes. Since this is just what you want, press F10 to continue.

You will now see the Main menu. You have created a template that can automatically find your Lotus 1-2-3 file and import its data. For example, if you make changes to the FILMS.WK1 spreadsheet using Lotus 1-2-3, you can update the Harvard chart by using your template. Choose the Get template option from the File menu, highlight QUARTER.TP3, and press Enter. If you did not save the last chart you created with the template, you will see a message indicating that your latest changes have not been saved; just press F10. You will see that the chart is already updated, and the data is formatted according to the specifications in your template.

IMPORTING ASCII FILES

Dozens of programs, including database, word processing, graphics, and communications software, use the ASCII format for data portability. You may find that your programs refer to ASCII formats as DOS, text, or nondocument files. Harvard's Import menu provides options for importing standard and delimited ASCII files.

IMPORTING STANDARD ASCII DATA

At the DOS prompt, enter **TYPE** *d:\path\filename* when you want to see if a file uses the ASCII format. If you can easily read the text on the screen, you're probably working with an ASCII file.

You can easily import standard ASCII data into Harvard charts. As with spreadsheet data, you must define the ranges of the ASCII data you are importing, so you should be familiar with the structure of the ASCII file.

Figure 13.8 shows a sample standard ASCII file, and Figure 13.9 shows how the imported file looks in Harvard. The numbers along

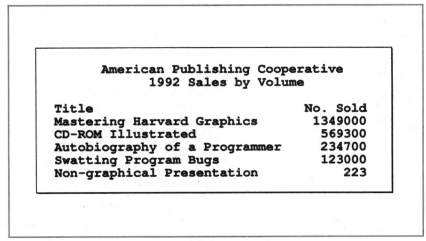

Figure 13.8: Sample standard ASCII file

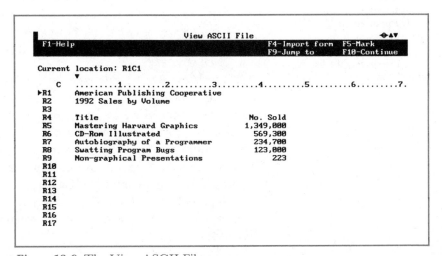

Figure 13.9: The View ASCII File screen

the left margin on the View ASCII File screen are row numbers. For example, R6 is the row that contains the CD-ROM Illustrated data.

Immediately above the data are the column numbers ....1, ...2, and so on. The first period (.) represents column 1, the second period is column 2. The numbers represent groups of ten, such as 1 for column 10, 2 for column 20, and so on.

For example, if you wanted to import the ASCII file shown in Figure 13.8, you would follow these steps:

1. Start by creating a text table chart (you can use a template to create the table chart).

2. Return to the Main menu and press **4**, then **7**, then **5** to select the Import ASCII data option from the Import menu and press Enter.

3. When the list of the files in your current directory appears, choose the ASCII file you want to import and press Enter. You will see the Import ASCII Data Into Table Chart screen, shown in Figure 13.10.

4. Complete the fields on the Import ASCII Data screen in the same way that you fill in the Import Lotus Data screen. You can type in your own titles and headings, type in the locations of the values, or press F4 to view the file (see Figure 13.9) and select ranges. As with spreadsheets, specify ranges using two dots. For example, type R1C1..R1C45 when you want the range from R1C1 to R1C45.

On the View ASCII File screen, the cursor's position appears in the Current location field expressed as R#C# for row number and column number. Move between rows by pressing the down-arrow key. You cannot move past the last row in your ASCII file. For example, our sample file has nine rows, so you can only move to R9. To move quickly to a given row and column number, press F9. When the Jump To box appears, type R#C# (row number and column number) and press Enter. Harvard will position your cursor at that location.

Figure 13.11 shows the completed screen for importing the sample ASCII file.

If you need an ASCII file to practice importing, create the sample shown in Figure 13.8. From the DOS prompt type **COPY CON: C:\HG3\IM-PORT\TOPBOOK.ASC** and press Enter. Then type each line in Figure 13.8, taking care to line up the spaces exactly. When you are finished, press F6, then Enter. You will return to the DOS prompt, and you can restart Harvard from there.

As when you reselect the Import Lotus Data option, you will see the Import ASCII Data screen instead of the file list if you have previously imported an ASCII file. If you want to select a different file, press F8, then **1** to display the list and choose another file.

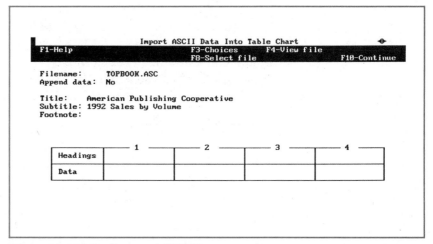

Figure 13.10: The Import ASCII Data screen

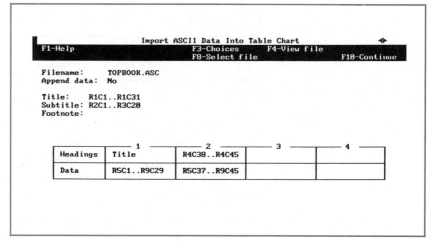

Figure 13.11: Working with imported ASCII table data

After you are satisfied with the ranges you have defined, press F10. You will then see the chart data-entry screen. Edit, print, and save the chart with the imported ASCII data as you would any other chart.

IMPORTING DELIMITED ASCII DATA

In a *delimited* ASCII file, each individual segment of data is set off from the rest of the data by certain marks. Traditionally, text is enclosed in double quotation marks (''), and elements are separated by commas (,), known as *end-of-field delimiters*. Records usually end with a carriage return and line feed (#13 #10), so that each record starts on a new line. For example, Figure 13.12 shows how the sample ASCII file presented in the previous section would look if it were delimited.

```
"American Publishing Cooperative"
"1992 Sales by Volume"

"Title","No. Sold"
"Mastering Harvard Graphics",1349000
"CD-ROM Illustrated",569300
"Autobiography of a Programmer",234700
"Swatting Program Bugs","123000"
"Non-graphical Presentation","223
```

Figure 13.12: Sample delimited ASCII file

To import this type of data, first create a Harvard chart for it. Then, from the Main menu, press **4**, then **7**, then **6** to select Import delimited ASCII from the Import menu. Highlight the name of the delimited file in the file list and press Enter. You will see the ASCII Delimiters box, shown in Figure 13.13.

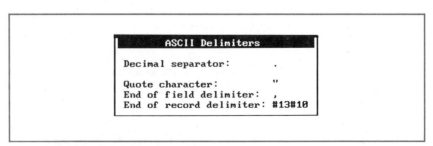

Figure 13.13: The ASCII Delimiters box

If your delimited ASCII file follows the conventional formats listed in the ASCII Delimiters box, just press F10 to continue. If not, reset the delimiters and then press F10 to see the Import Delimited ASCII Data screen. If you press F4, you will see your data arranged in cells, like a Lotus 1-2-3 or Excel spreadsheet. Define the data ranges in the same way as you select them when importing a Lotus 1-2-3 data file.

IMPORTING dBASE FILES

As in Lotus 1-2-3 files, the data in dBASE files is stored in cells, identified by a column letter and row number. The procedure for importing a dBASE file is essentially the same as the one for importing a 1-2-3 file.

After you select the type of chart you want to create, from the Main menu, press **4,** then **7,** then **7** to select Import dBASE data from the Import menu. In the list of files, highlight the .DBF file you want to import and press Enter. Complete the Import dBASE Data screen to define the data ranges, using the same techniques that are used to specify ranges in Lotus 1-2-3 data files. After the data is imported, you can edit, print, and save your chart.

IMPORTING METAFILES

The CGM (Computer Graphic Metafile) format is fast becoming the standard for vector graphic files. You can import a CGM metafile that was created in a page-layout program such as Freelance, PageMaker, and Ventura into a Harvard chart.

Some imported metafiles use the same color as your background. For example, if the metafile has black lines, importing it into a black background results in an invisible drawing. To solve this problem, change palettes to select a different background, or use Draw to change the line colors.

To import a metafile, first get or create a Harvard chart or template. Then, from the Main menu, press **4,** then **7,** then **8** to choose Import CGM metafile from the Import menu. When you see the file-selection menu, choose the directory that stores the CGM file you want to import, type the file name with the .CGM extension, and then press F10. Harvard imports the CGM file into Draw. You can edit the metafile using Draw options and save it as a chart or symbol. Be sure to review the chart created with the imported metafile. You may need to adjust the text, fonts, colors, or other features.

EXPORTING HARVARD CHARTS

You can easily transfer a Harvard graph into a word processing or desktop publishing program, perhaps to illustrate a report you are creating with that program.

To export a chart, first retrieve that chart, and then, from the Main menu, press **4**, then **8** to select the Export option from the File menu. You will see the Export menu, shown in Figure 13.14.

```
      ▶ Export Professional Write          1

        Export CGM metafile               2
        Export Encapsulated PostScript    3
        Export HPGL plotter file          4
        Export PCX bitmap file            5
```

Figure 13.14: The Export menu

Select the format in which you want to export the chart. Harvard provides five choices:

Print Professional Write documents that use exported charts in portrait orientation only if you use a Hewlett-Packard LaserJet printer.

- Export Professional Write: Use this option to transfer a chart to Pro Write or Office Writer. In the Export box that appears, enter the directory, file name, printer number, and output quality you want to use with the chart. The printer you will use to output the Pro Write or Office Writer document must match the printer number.

- Export CGM Metafile: Use this option to save your chart as a CGM file (see the section on importing metafiles). In the Export box, shown in Figure 13.15, set the options as necessary, and then press F10 to export the file. The Use CGM fonts option lets you use metafile fonts for text. Select No if you want to export text as polygons. Check the exported chart. Some programs, such as Ventura and Freelance, use white for the background, rendering CGM objects invisible (white objects on a white background).

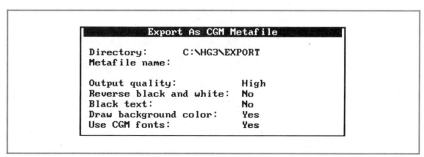

Figure 13.15: The Export as CGM Metafile box

Before you export your chart, use the Printer Setup options to change features such as paper size, chart size, reverse black and white, background color, and hardware fonts. They affect the way your Post-Script file appears.

- Export Encapsulated PostScript: Use this option to export your chart to programs such as Ventura Publisher and PageMaker. In the Export box, enter the directory, file name, printer number, and output quality you want for the chart. Then press F10 to export the chart.

- Export HPGL Plotter File: Use this option to export charts to programs that read HPGL formats, such as Ventura Publisher and PageMaker. HPGL (Hewlett-Packard Graphic Language) is a special set of instructions for plotters. The Export box that appears is similar to the one for exporting to an Encapsulated PostScript file, except that you enter a HP plotter instead of a printer number.

- Export PCX Bitmap File: Select this option to export a chart as a PCX bit-map file (see Chapters 10 and 11 for more information about bit-maps). In the Export box, enter the directory and file name. Set the Export for ScreenShow field to No unless you are using the chart for a screen show. Press F10 to export the file.

By default, Harvard sends your export files to the C:\HG3\EX-PORT directory. Use the Program Defaults option on the Setup menu to change the Export directory if desired. For example, you might want to send a Harvard drawing chart to the subdirectory where you keep desktop publishing files.

EXPORTING A SLIDE SHOW FOR PROCESSING

Harvard's AGX program lets you export and send a Harvard presentation to a slide service, such as Autographix, for processing. (See Chapter 12 for details on creating presentations.) Slide services can transform your charts into high-quality 35mm slides, view graphs, and color paper prints. If you have a modem, you can use Harvard's AGX option to send your presentation over the telephone lines, and get them back via express mail within 24 hours. If you do not have a modem, AGX will transfer your slide show onto a disk that you can mail to the service center.

To begin exporting your slides, press **9** from the Main menu to choose Applications. Then press **4** or highlight AGX Slide Service and press Enter. You will see the AGX Main menu, shown in Figure 13.16.

Figure 13.16: The AGX Main menu

Select Setup from the AGX Main menu and set the following parameters:

- Select your modem port, either COM1 or COM2.
- Set the modem rate to 300, 1200, 2400, or 9600.
- Indicate the type of telephone line (TouchTone or Rotary) you use.
- Insert the modem setup string that you need for your equipment.

- Specify the type of display you use, either monochrome or color.

Press F10 to return to the AGX Main menu. Select Enter delivery and billing info to see the screen shown in Figure 13.17. Type in the information to let the vendor know how to bill you and deliver your slides, and then press F10.

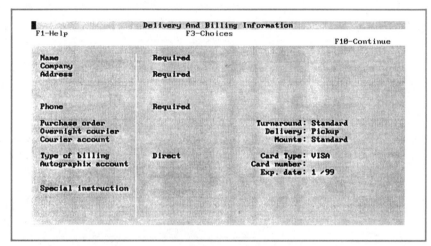

Figure 13.17: Delivery and Billing Information screen

You are now ready to order your slides. The procedure is described in the following hands-on session.

HANDS-ON: ORDERING SLIDES

If you change your mind and don't want slides, press Ctrl-C or Esc to exit AGX.

Before following the steps below, format a blank disk for your Order Disk and put it in the appropriate floppy disk drive. An *Order Disk* is a formatted disk that contains the files needed to produce your slides. AGX will not use disks that are unformatted or that contain files other than those with a .SH3, .CH3, or .PCX extension. Follow the instructions in the previous section to enter your setup and delivery and billing information.

1. From the AGX Main menu, choose the Select files option. If you have used this option before, you will see a small

box. If this is the first time you have ordered slides, you will see the Select Files screen, and you can skip to step 3.

2. Press **1** to create a new order, and you will see the Select Files screen, shown in Figure 13.18. (If you want to edit an old order, press 2 instead.)

3. Press F3 to add files to your order.

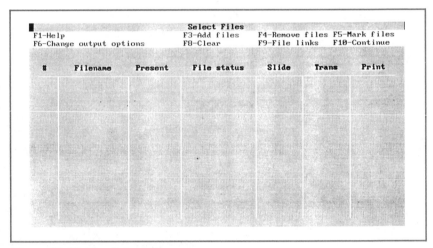

Figure 13.18: The Select Files screen

It's quicker and easier to include presentations than charts. You add all the charts in a presentation by selecting a single .SH3 file.

4. Highlight the subdirectory where you saved your presentation or charts and press F10. Press F5 to mark all the presentations and charts you want included and then press F10. The Output Options box will appear.

5. Type your order for the number of slides, transparencies, and prints you want. If you want extra copies of some slides, you can make minor revisions later. Press F10 to continue. All the charts you selected will appear on your order list.

If you made an error, highlight the file you want deleted and press Ctrl-Del and then F10 to confirm the deletion. You also can delete a highlighted file by pressing F4, then F10. To clear all the files from your list so that you can start over, press F8, then F10. Press F9 if you want to see the files that are linked to a slide.

To make changes to your order, highlight the slide you want to change and press F6. Select the media you want (color slides, overhead transparencies, or color prints), and type the number of copies you want. Press F10 when you are finished to return to the Select Files screen.

6. Examine your order carefully—mistakes can be costly. You don't want to be billed for 111 slides at $12 each when you only wanted 1. Press F10 when you are satisfied with your order.

7. Press **4** to select Create order on diskette. Press Enter to accept the default of drive A. Put your blank, formatted disk into drive A, and then press F10.

Harvard copies your charts and the palettes you used to your Order Disk, which you can then mail to the slide service center. If you want to send your order by modem, in step 7, select Send by modem from the AGX Main menu. Then your order will be transmitted over the telephone lines to the service company.

8. Press **E** to select Exit from the AGX Main menu and return to the Applications menu.

Although Autographix is Harvard's recommended slide service, other qualified vendors process Order Disks and modem transmissions to create slides.

USING APPLICATIONS MENU OPTIONS

The options on the Applications menu give you access to some useful utilities:

- DOS Shell: Provides the DOS shell for entering DOS commands. Perhaps the greatest use you will get from the Applications menu is to select DOS when you want to delete your files. You delete files by typing **DEL** *d:\subdir\ filename.ext* where *d:* is the drive name, *subdir* is the subdirectory, and *filename.ext* is the file's name and extension.

- HGcopy Utility: Lets you copy your screen shows to another disk or directory. It copies the presentation files, charts, subcharts, palettes, background drawings, bit-maps, and other files that are used in the presentation. When you choose this option, you are prompted for the presentation file name. Include the drive and subdirectory. When you are prompted for the destination drive and subdirectory, enter where you want the presentation copied.

- Convert 3.0 Files: Converts your .CH3 chart files into .CHT files used in earlier versions of Harvard. Select the file you want converted and press Enter. Those less fortunate than you can then use the older version of Harvard to see your charts.

- AGX Slide Service: Lets you order slide production from a slide service (see the preceding section for details).

Convert cannot transfer all the features that your .CH3 charts use. For example, you can't convert gradient or bit-map fills.

CUSTOMIZING THE HARVARD APPLICATIONS MENU

You can customize Harvard's Applications menu by adding options to run the programs you use most often. For example, you might want to select Lotus 1-2-3 or Excel from the Applications menu and return immediately to Harvard when you finish working in those programs. Or, you could add the DOS FORMAT command, so that you do not have to exit Harvard to format an Order Disk for a slide service.

To add an option to the Applications menu, from the Main menu, press **8**, then **3** to select the Applications option from the Setup menu. You will see the Applications menu customization screen, shown in Figure 13.19.

Press Tab to move the cursor to the first empty application slot (Application No. 5 if you have not already added options). Type the menu option that you want to appear on the Applications menu. For example, you might type **Format A:** if you are adding an option to format a disk in drive A.

Press Enter to move to the Command field, type the command that will be invoked by this choice on the Applications menu, and

Do not add any memory-resident programs to the Applications menu. They may cause Harvard to run poorly, or not run at all.

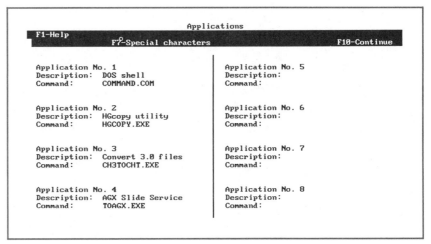

Figure 13.19: Applications menu customization screen

press Enter. For example, to format a disk in drive A, type **C:\DOS\ FORMAT A:**. Press F10 when you are finished, and your new option will appear on the Applications menu.

SUMMARY

You are now familiar with Harvard's importing and exporting capabilities. You can make a polished graph out of any program's data. In today's world, where computer users need to work with several programs and to present their data well, these are essential tools.

A

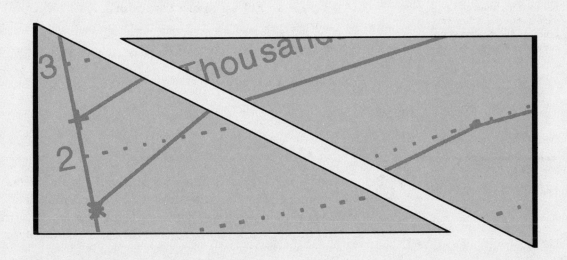

Installing Harvard

APPENDIX *A*

HARVARD GRAPHICS VERSION 3.0 IS DESIGNED TO run on an IBM or compatible computer with an 80286, 80386, or 80486 processor. To install Harvard Graphics version 3.0, your computer should be equipped with the following:

- A hard disk with a minimum of 3.8 megabytes (Mb) of available memory; 10.2Mb is required for all the files that come with Harvard Graphics 3.0

- At least one floppy disk drive

- A minimum of 640 kilobytes (K) of memory installed on your computer

- A VGA or an EGA graphics card with at least 256K of memory

- DOS version 3.0 or later; DOS 3.1 or later if you are using a network

Do not use memory-resident programs such as Side-Kick while running Harvard 3.0 because they can cause problems with your computer system.

PREPARING FOR INSTALLATION

Before you install Harvard Graphics 3.0, you should check the amount of memory your computer has available and make backup copies of all your program disks. Format a blank disk for each original Harvard Graphics disk you have, and then follow these steps:

1. Boot your computer by turning it on. You will see the DOS prompt, usually C>, indicating that DOS is ready for a command.

If the CHKDSK command did not work, you might not have established a path for the DOS files on your hard disk. Try typing **PATH C:\DOS** and press Enter. (Many systems use a subdirectory called \DOS to store DOS programs.) Then reenter the CHKDSK command. If it still doesn't work, you might not have booted your computer with a complete DOS disk. Find your original DOS floppy disk and reboot your computer from it.

2. At the DOS prompt, type **CHKDSK** and press the Enter key.

3. Read the line showing the number of bytes free on your disk. To install all of the Harvard software, including the program, tutorial, sample, and symbol files, you need 10,200,000 bytes of hard disk space. You need a minimum of 3,800,000 bytes to install just the program files. If you do not have enough memory available, you will have to delete or move files from your disk to provide enough space for the program to function.

4. Read the last line on the screen to see how much memory your computer has available. If you have at least 434,000 bytes of memory free, you can run Harvard Graphics. If not, you will need more memory installed in your computer.

5. Proceed by making backup copies of all your Harvard disks. Type **DISKCOPY A: B:** and press Enter. Take a Harvard Graphics disk and insert it into drive A. Place a blank, formatted disk in drive B. Then press Enter to continue. If you have only one disk drive on your computer, follow the copying instructions that appear on your screen. When the computer tells you to place a *source* disk in the drive, it is referring to the Harvard disks. The *target* disk means the blank disks you are using to copy Harvard.

6. After copying the disk, place an identifying label on it, including the disk number, disk name, and version number.

7. When you are asked if you want to copy another disk, press **Y**.

8. Repeat steps 5 through 7 until you copy all your disks. When you are finished, press **N** to indicate that you do not want to copy another disk.

Put your original Harvard disks away in a safe place. Use your backup disks to install the program.

INSTALLING HARVARD GRAPHICS 3.0 ▬

Because the files on the program disk for version 3.0 are combined and compressed, you cannot simply copy the Harvard Graphics files from the backup disks to your hard disk using the DOS COPY command. You must use Harvard's Install program, as follows:

1. Place the backup Install disk (Disk 1) in drive A. Type **A:** and press Enter to make A the default drive.

2. Type **INSTALL** and press Enter. The first screen you will see provides general directions on using Install. Read it, and then press Enter.

3. Install checks the drives you use and prompts you to select one for installation, as shown in Figure A.1. Highlight the drive on which you want to install Harvard Graphics and press Enter.

4. The next screen prompts you for the directory in which you want to install Harvard Graphics, as shown in Figure A.2. Press Enter to install Harvard in the \HG3 subdirectory, or type a new subdirectory name and press Enter.

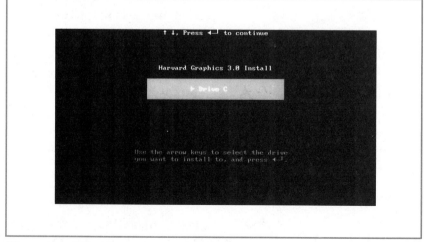

Figure A.1: Selecting a drive for installation

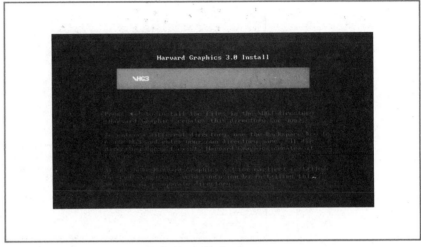

Figure A.2: Selecting a path for installation

You can reinstall
Harvard Graphics
later and add any of the
other files, as explained at
the end of this appendix.

5. The Harvard Graphics 3.0 Install Main menu will appear, as shown in Figure A.3. If you want to install all the files, including the program, tutorial, sample, and symbol files, and have at least 10,200,000 bytes of hard disk space available, press Enter to choose All files. If you have less hard disk space, but at least 3,800,000 bytes, select Program files. Allow plenty of time for installation. It takes 25 to 35 minutes on an 80286 computer, 15 to 20 minutes on an 80386, and 5 to 10 minutes on an 80486.

6. Next, you are prompted to insert the first program disk. Place Disk 1 in drive A and press Enter. You will see the files copied from drive A to your hard disk.

7. Read the instructions on the screen and insert Disk 2 into drive A when prompted. Press Enter. Repeat this step to copy all the backup disks If you insert the wrong disk, Install will ask if you want to retry. Insert the correct disk and press Enter to continue.

8. When you are finished installing Harvard Graphics, you will see the Install Main menu. Highlight Exit and press Enter to return to the DOS prompt.

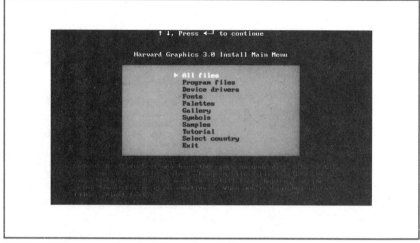

Figure A.3: Harvard Graphics 3.0 Install Main menu

Harvard created several subdirectories for you when you ran Install. The \HG3\GALLERY subdirectory contains the files you need to use Harvard's Gallery program, and \HG3\SYMBOL holds the symbol files. You're now ready to start using Harvard Graphics. Proceed to Chapter 1.

UPGRADING FROM AN EARLIER VERSION OF HARVARD GRAPHICS

If you are upgrading from version 2.3 of Harvard Graphics, you aren't losing version 2.3's symbols. Version 3's symbols are the same, except that they are in the advanced .SY3 format.

REINSTALLING HARVARD GRAPHICS

When you reinstall Harvard, it will not erase any existing charts you have created.

You can rerun the Install program at any time to install other files. For example, you might want to install the Tutorial so that another person can learn how to use Harvard Graphics. Just repeat the installation procedure described earlier in this appendix, and select only the Tutorial option from the Install Main menu.

Or perhaps you recovered some disk space and now want to install the symbols. If you select Symbols from the Install Main menu, you will see a menu of symbol (.SY3) files. Use the arrow keys to highlight the .SY3 files you want and press Enter; or choose All symbols. (See Appendix C for more information about symbol files.)

After you are finished installing additional files, choose Exit from the Install Main menu.

B

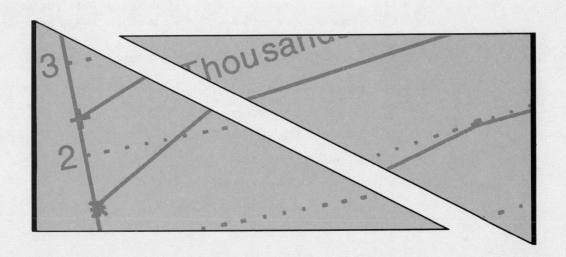

Supported Devices

APPENDIX **B** _____

THIS APPENDIX LISTS THE PRINTERS, PLOTTERS, film recorders, and video screen controllers that are supported by Harvard Graphics version 3.0. To avoid problems, use only these supported devices; other devices may not work properly with the program.

SUPPORTED PRINTERS

If you have a Hewlett-Packard (HP) LaserJet IIP or III printer, install 2 megabytes or more memory in it so that the Harvard Graphics driver can compress the data and print your charts faster. Choose the HP LaserJet III (HPGL/2) if you have a LaserJet III with at least 2 megabytes of memory. This outputs your chart into an HPGL/2 vector mode for quick printing at a high-quality resolution of 300 dots per inch.

Harvard Graphics 3.0 supports the following printers:

Apple	LaserWriter
	LaserWriter IINT, IINTX
	LaserWriter Plus
CalComp	ColorMaster
	ColorMaster Plus
	ColorMaster Plus PS
	PlotMaster
Canon	LBP4
	LBP8 II, III
DEC	LN03+

Epson	EX 800, 1000
	FX 80, 80+, 85, 100, 100+, 185
	JX-80
	LQ-800, 850, 950, 1050, 1500, 2500, 2550
	LX-80, 86, 800
	MX-80 III, 100 III
	RX-80, 100
HP	DeskJet
	DeskJet Plus
	LaserJet 500+
	LaserJet II, IIP
	LaserJet IID
	LaserJet III, IIISi, IIIDr, IIIp
	LaserJet+
	PaintJet
	PaintJet Transparency
	PaintJet XL
	PaintJet XL Transparency
IBM	Graphics Printer
	Laser Printer (HP Mode)
	Personal Page Printer
	Personal Page Printer II
	Proprinter
	Proprinter II, III, III XL
	Proprinter X24, X24E
	Proprinter XL, XL24, XL24E
	Quietwriter III, Model 2

Kodak	Diconix 150 Plus
NEC	CP6, CP7
	Colormate PS
	LC-860 (LaserJet)
	LC-890 (PostScript)
	P2200, P2200XE
	P5200, P5300
	P5XL
	P6, P7, P9XL
Okidata	MicroLine 182, 183, 192, 193, 292, 293, 294, 390, 391, 393, 393C, 92, 93
Olivetti	PG 208, M2, 306
Panasonic	KX P1080, P1080i, P1091, P1091i, P1124
QMS	ColorScript 100
	JetScript
Tektronix	4693D, 4693DX
	ColorQuick
	Phaser CP, II DX, PX
Toshiba	P321SL, P341, P351, P351C, P351SX
	P1350, P1351
Xerox	4045

Note that the medium and draft quality settings produce the same output on the following printers:

- HP PaintJet
- Okidata MicroLine 92 and 93
- Toshiba P341, P351, and P351C
- Xerox 4045

SUPPORTED PLOTTERS

Harvard Graphics supports the following HP plotters:

- ColorPro
- DraftPro
- DraftPro EXL
- 7470, 7475, 7550

SUPPORTED FILM RECORDERS

Harvard Graphics supports the following film recorders:

Agfa	Matrix ChromaScript
	Matrix SCODL
Lasergraphics	LFR
	PFR
PTI	Montage FR1
Polaroid	CI3000, CI5000
	Palette Plus (EGA)
VideoShow	File
	Preview

SUPPORTED INPUT DEVICES

You can use the following input devices with Harvard Graphics 3.0:

CalComp Drawing Board 23180-1 or 23120-11

Kurta Tablet

IBM-compatible mouse

Summa SummaSketch MM1201 or MM961

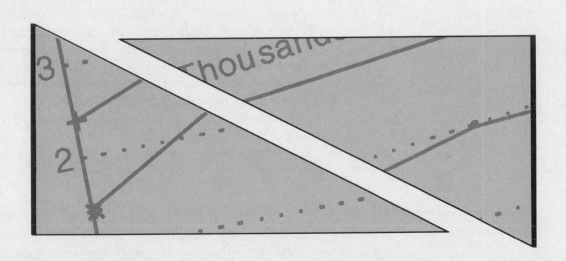

Symbols, Symbols, and More Symbols

APPENDIX C

THIS APPENDIX BRIEFLY DESCRIBES HOW TO WORK with symbols and presents the symbols available with Harvard Graphics 3.0. It also shows the symbols contained on the Enhancement Disk that comes with this book.

WORKING WITH SYMBOLS

As described in Chapters 10 and 11 of this book, you use Draw's Symbol tool to add symbols to your Harvard charts. After you have added a symbol to your chart, you can move it, copy it, and change its attributes—all the things you can do to your own drawings. If the symbol is made up of a group of objects, you can also use Draw's Ungroup tool and then select some of its parts.

For example, if you want to move a couple of objects from a symbol to another part of your chart, first select the Ungroup tool to separate the symbol's parts. Position the cursor on one of the symbol's objects, press Enter to select it, position the cursor on the next object you want, and press the Shift key while pressing Enter again. (Selecting the same object twice *deselects* it.) When you have finished selecting the objects, press Enter while moving the arrow keys to reposition the objects. You can also use some of the editing tools you learned about in Chapters 10 and 11 to modify the symbol. Delete the original symbol if you no longer need it.

Remember, you can print the symbols or record them on film. However, some symbols do not work well with plotters.

HARVARD GRAPHICS 3.0 SYMBOLS

True version 3.0 symbols differ not only in appearance but in name. For example, not only is a symbol contained in a given .SY3 file, but it also has its own unique name within the .SY3 file.

Figures C.1 through C.35 present all the symbols included in Harvard Graphics version 3.0. You can also use Harvard Graphics version 2.1 .SYM files with 3.0. When selected, a .SYM file is converted and brought into your drawing as a .SY3 file. Do not use Harvard Graphics version 2.3 symbols because they are the same as the ones in version 3.0, except that the ones in 3.0 are in the advanced .SY3 format.

Figure C.1: Harvard 3.0 ANIMALS.SYM file

Figure C.2: Harvard 3.0 ANIPLANT.SYM file

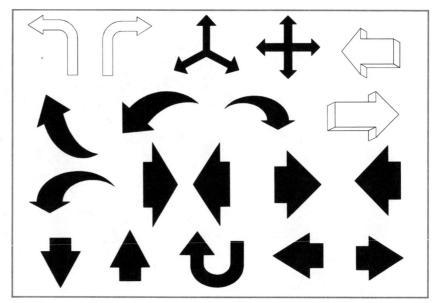

Figure C.3: Harvard 3.0 ARROWS2.SYM file

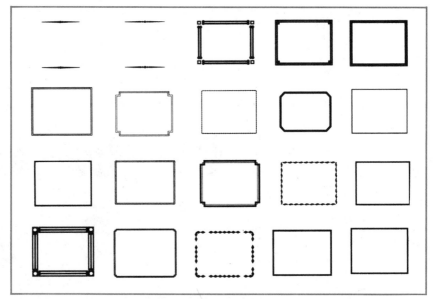

Figure C.4: Harvard 3.0 BORDERS.SYM file

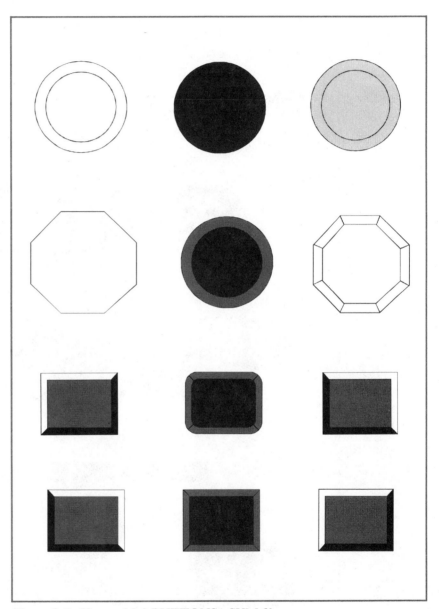

Figure C.5: Harvard 3.0 BUTTONS1.SYM file

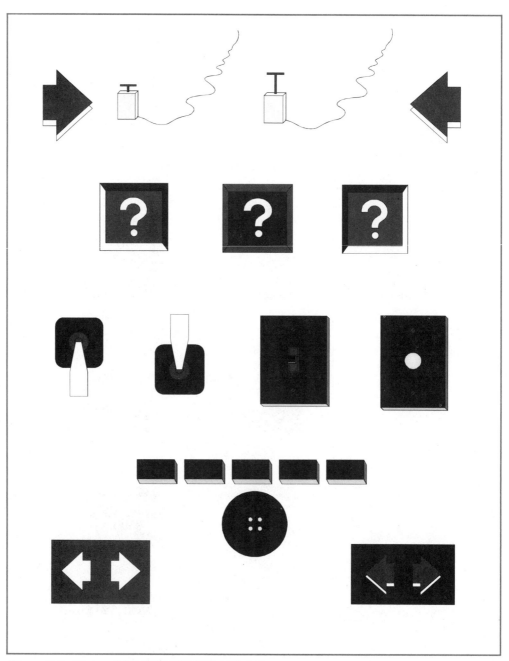

Figure C.6: Harvard 3.0 BUTTONS2.SYM file

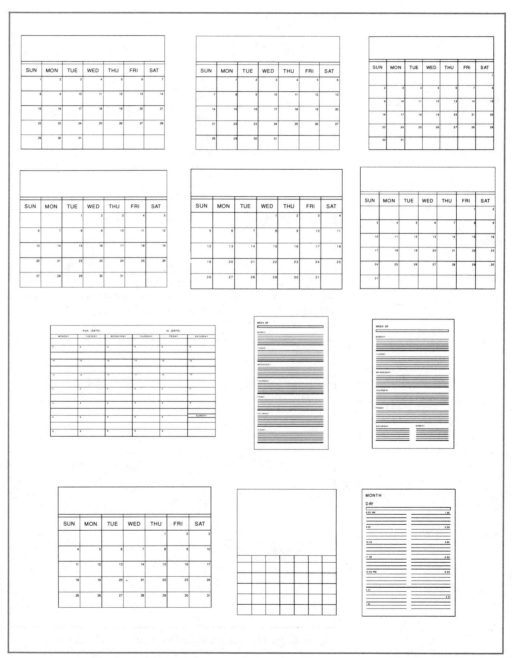

Figure C.7: Harvard 3.0 CALENDAR.SYM file

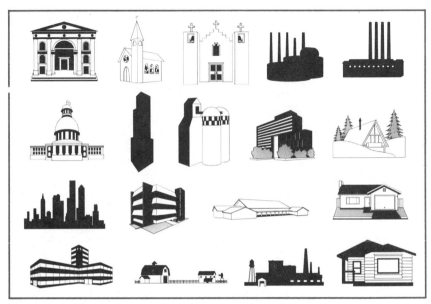

Figure C.8: Harvard 3.0 BUILD3.SYM file

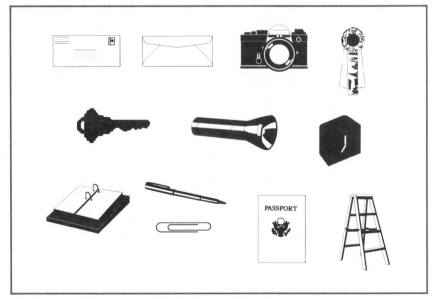

Figure C.9: Harvard 3.0 COMNOBJ1.SYM file

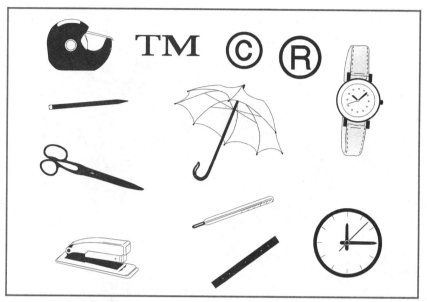

Figure C.10: Harvard 3.0 COMNOBJ2.SYM file

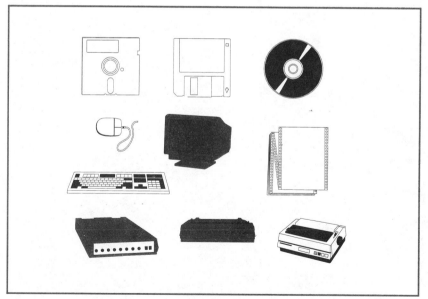

Figure C.11: Harvard 3.0 COMPUTR2.SYM file

Figure C.12: Harvard 3.0 COMPUTR3.SYM file

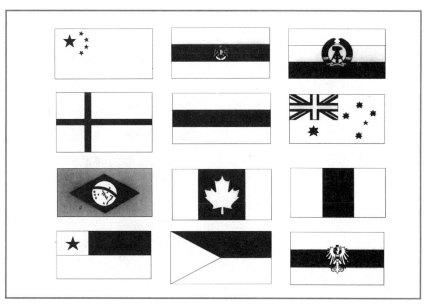

Figure C.13: Harvard 3.0 FLAGS1.SYM file

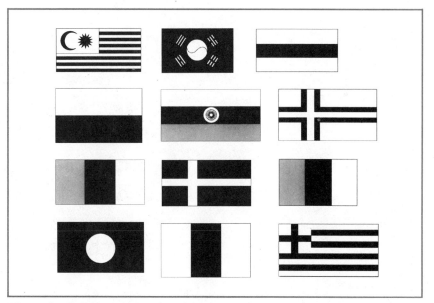

Figure C.14: Harvard 3.0 FLAGS2.SYM file

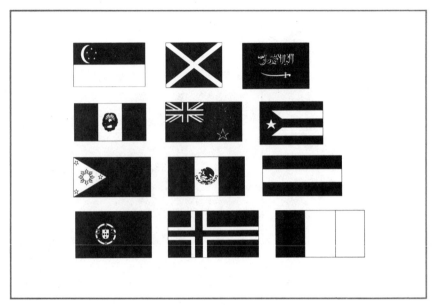

Figure C.15: Harvard 3.0 FLAGS3.SYM file

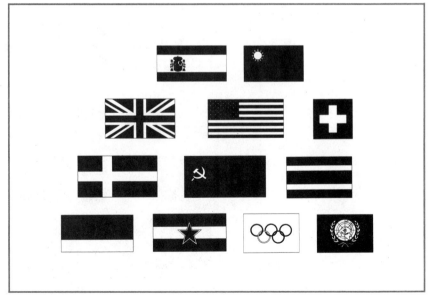

Figure C.16: Harvard 3.0 FLAGS4.SYM file

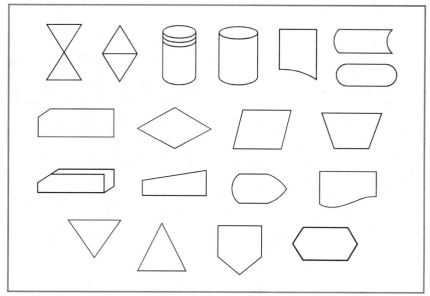

Figure C.17: Harvard 3.0 FLOWCHT.SYM file

Figure C.18: Harvard 3.0 GREEKLC1.SYM file

Figure C.19: Harvard 3.0 GREEKLC2.SYM file

Figure C.20: Harvard 3.0 GREEKUC1.SYM file

$$N \; \Xi \; O \; \Pi$$
$$P \; \Sigma \; T \; \Upsilon$$
$$\Phi \; X \; \Psi \; \Omega$$

Figure C.21: Harvard 3.0 GREEKUC2.SYM file

Figure C.22: Harvard 3.0 HUMANS4.SYM file

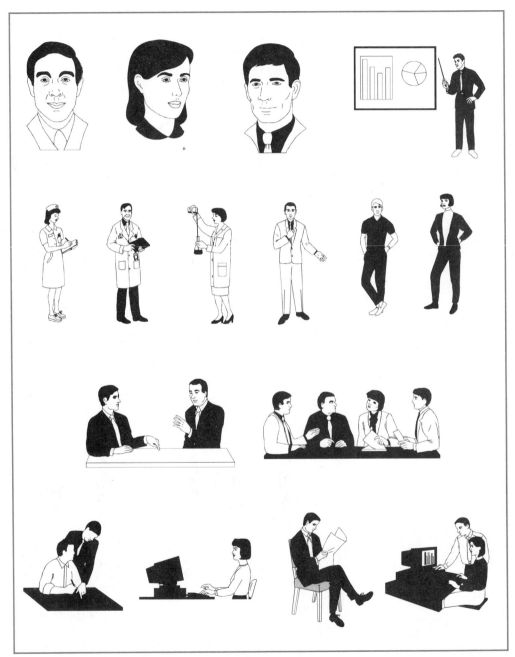

Figure C.23: Harvard 3.0 HUMANS5.SYM file

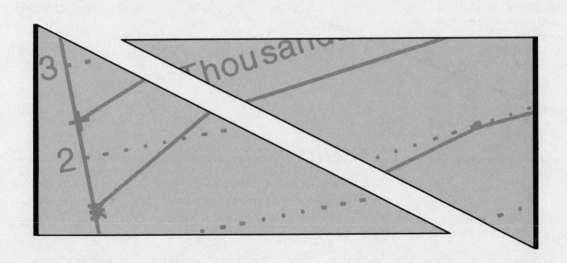

Installing Harvard

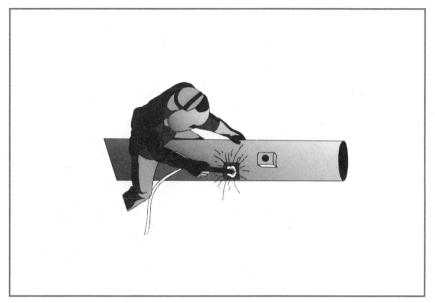

Figure C.69: MasterClips SYBX4-5.SY3 Welder symbol

Figure C.70: MasterClips SYBX4-5.SY3 Engineer symbol

Figure C. 71: MasterClips SYBX4-5.SY3 Farmer symbol

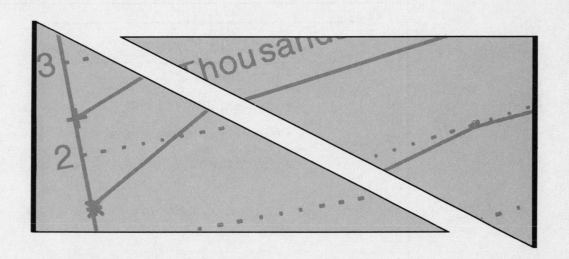

Touring the Gallery

APPENDIX D

THE HARVARD GRAPHICS GALLERY LETS YOU quickly select prepared charts to serve as templates. The Gallery also serves as a source of inspiration when you are dealing with difficult graphing problems. It provides many ways of expediting and improving your graphics presentations. However, in order to use the Gallery charts, you should know how to work with Harvard. Be sure to read the chapters in this book before selecting charts from the Gallery.

The figures in this appendix show 81 of the Gallery's 164 charts, with instructions for selecting them. We chose the chart designs that are the least likely to misrepresent data; however, even some of these should be used with caution.

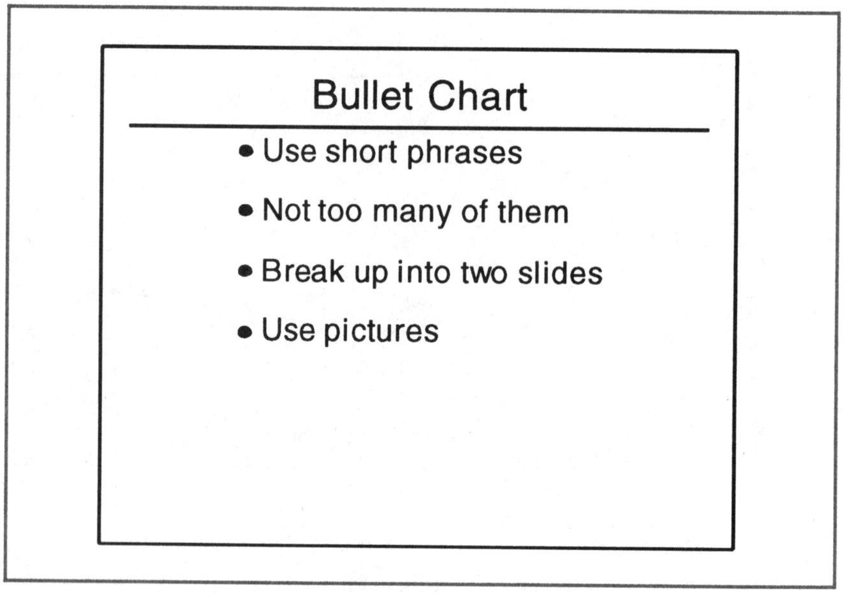

Bullet Chart

- Use short phrases

- Not too many of them

- Break up into two slides

- Use pictures

Figure D.1: Press 1, 6, 1, and 1

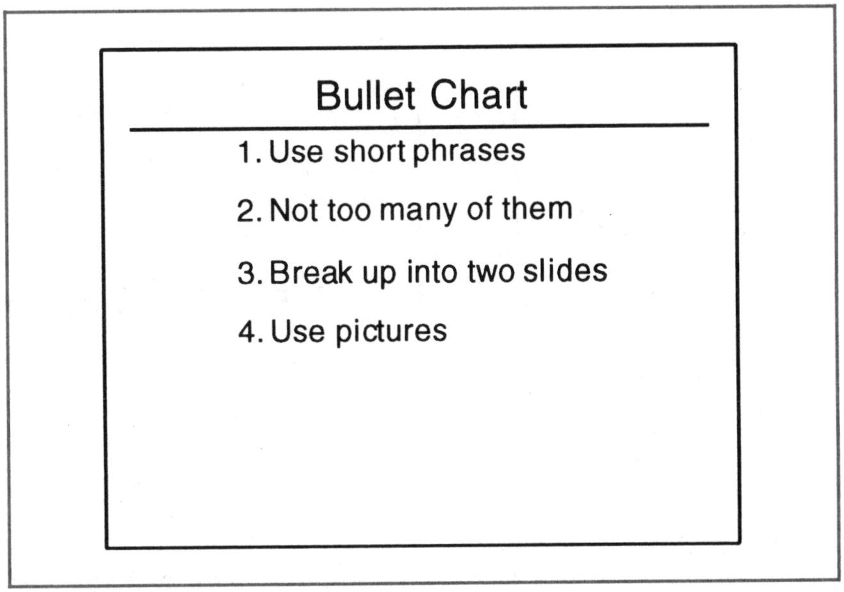

Bullet Chart

1. Use short phrases

2. Not too many of them

3. Break up into two slides

4. Use pictures

Figure D.2: Press 1, 6, 1, and 2

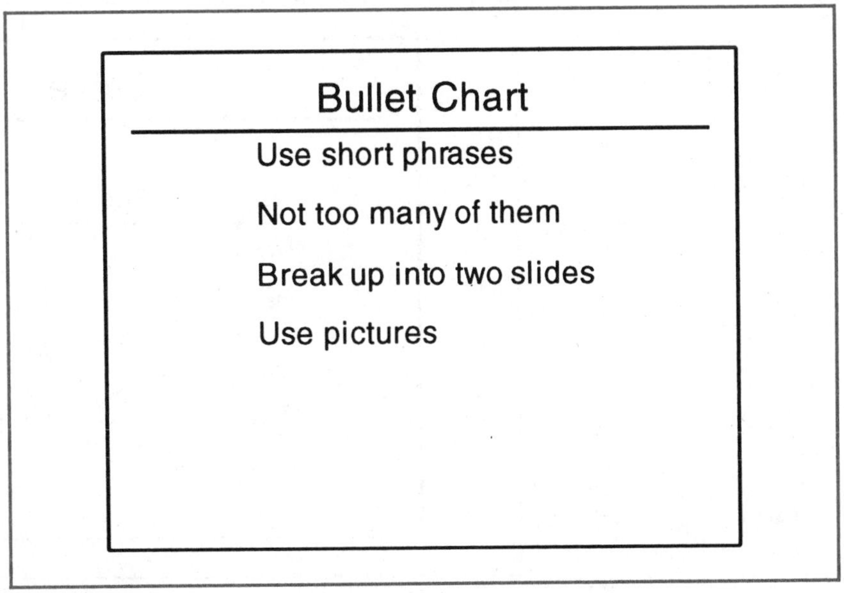

Bullet Chart

Use short phrases

Not too many of them

Break up into two slides

Use pictures

Figure D.3: Press 1, 6, 1, and 4

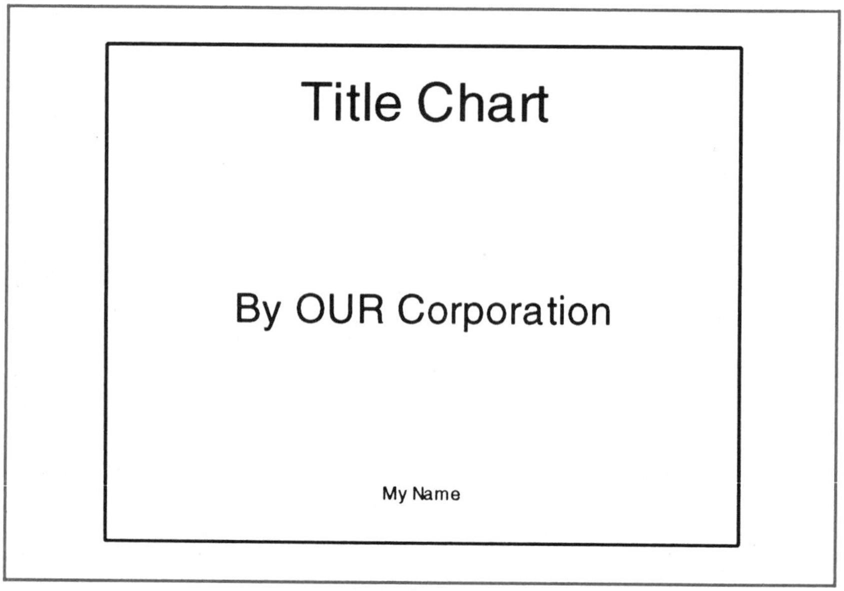

Title Chart

By OUR Corporation

My Name

Figure D.4: Press 1, 6, 1, and 5

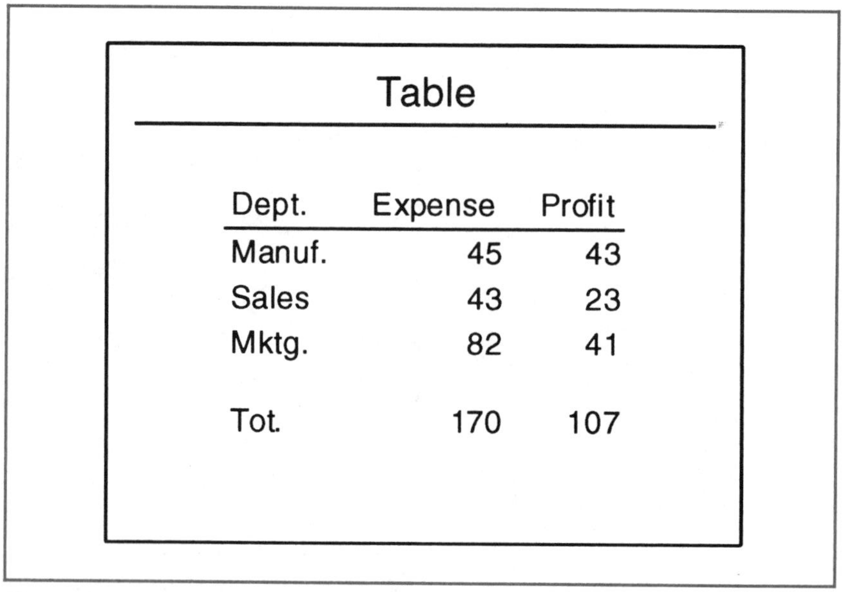

Table

Dept.	Expense	Profit
Manuf.	45	43
Sales	43	23
Mktg.	82	41
Tot.	170	107

Figure D.5: Press 1, 6, 1, and 7

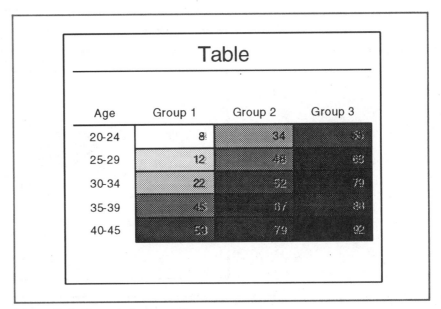

Figure D.6: Press 1, 6, 1, and 8

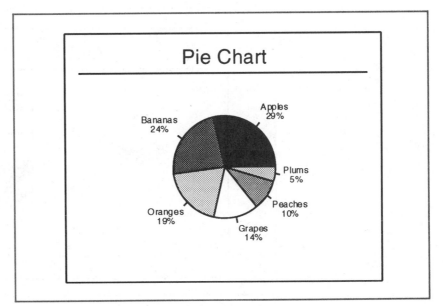

Figure D.7: Press 1, 6, 2, and 1

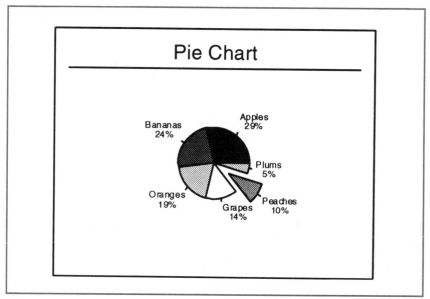

Figure D.8: Press 1, 6, 2, and 2

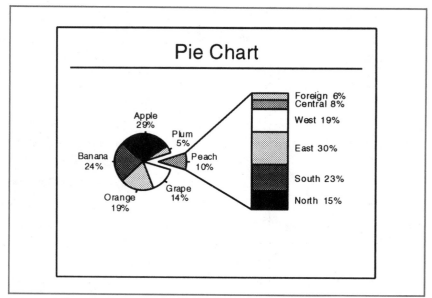

Figure D.9: Press 1, 6, 2, and 3

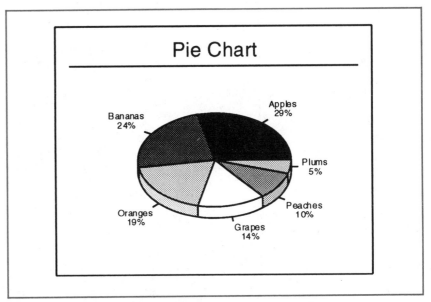

Figure D.10: Press 1, 6, 2, and 4

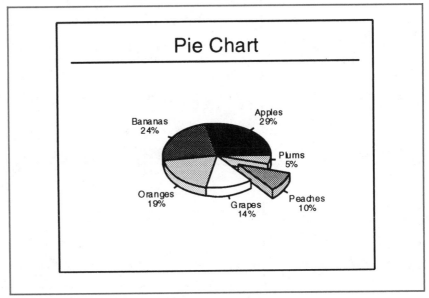

Figure D.11: Press 1, 6, 2, and 5

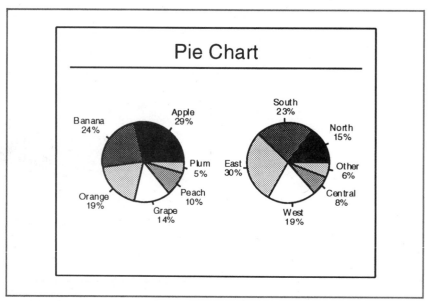

Figure D.12: Press 1, 6, 2, and 7

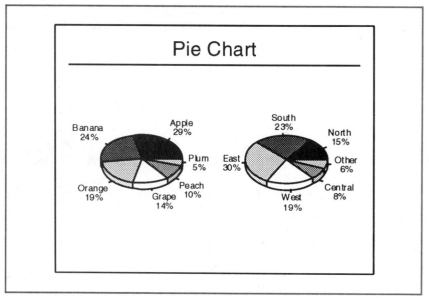

Figure D.13: Press 1, 6, 2, and 8

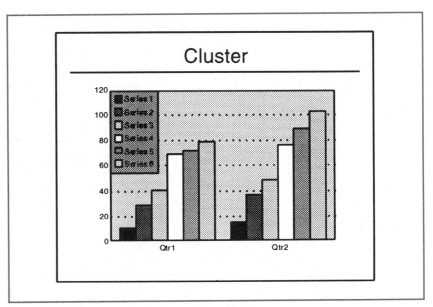

Figure D.14: Press 1, 6, 3, 1, and 1

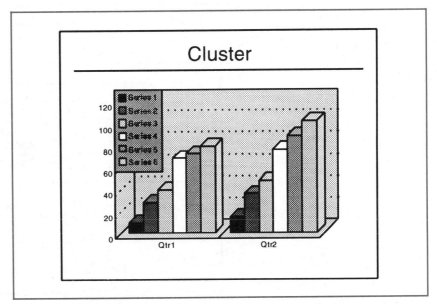

Figure D.15: Press 1, 6, 3, 1, and 2

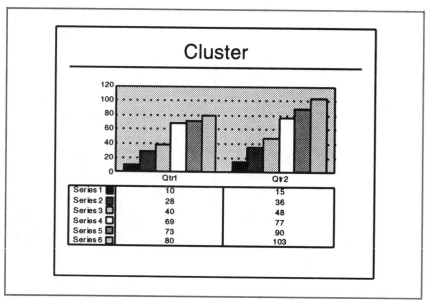

Figure D.16: Press 1, 6, 3, 1, and 7

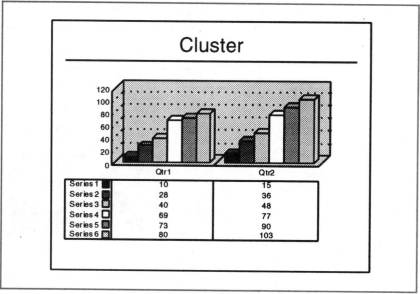

Figure D.17: Press 1, 6, 3, 1, and 8

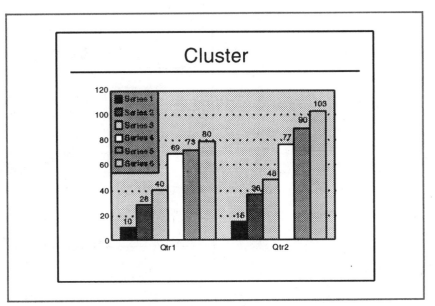

Figure D.18: Press 1, 6, 3, 1, and 9

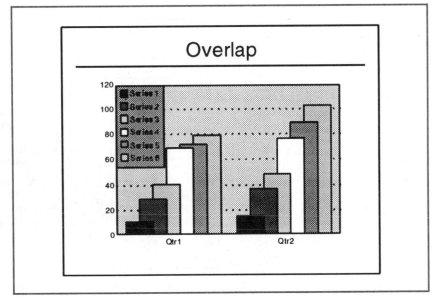

Figure D.19: Press 1, 6, 3, 2, and 1

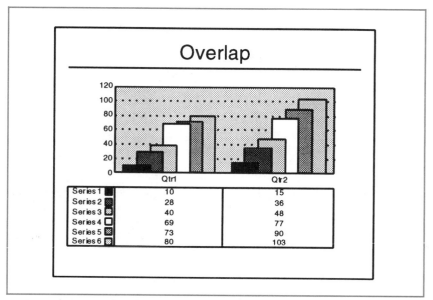

Figure D.20: Press 1, 6, 3, 2, and 7

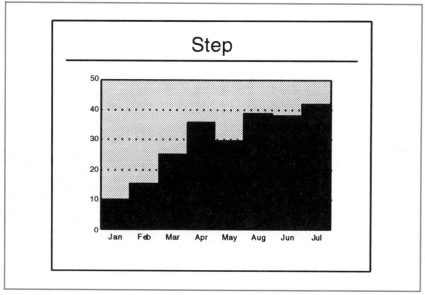

Figure D.21: Press 1, 6, 3, 3, and 1

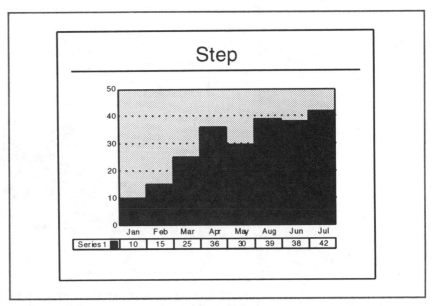

Figure D.22: Press 1, 6, 3, 3, and 7

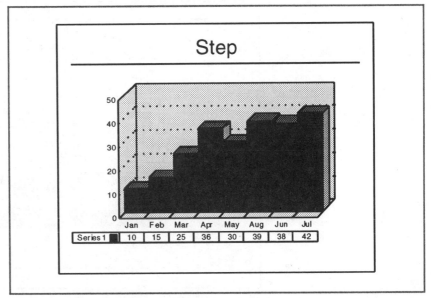

Figure D.23: Press 1, 6, 3, 3, and 8

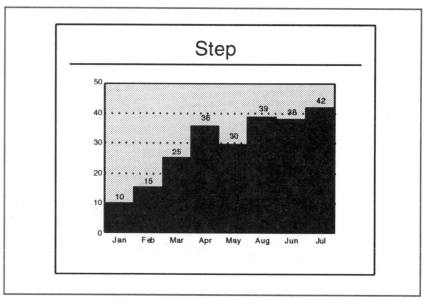

Figure D.24: Press 1, 6, 3, 3, and 9

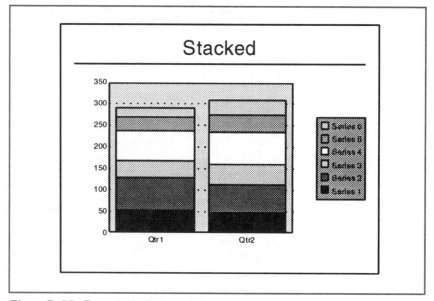

Figure D.25: Press 1, 6, 3, 4, and 1

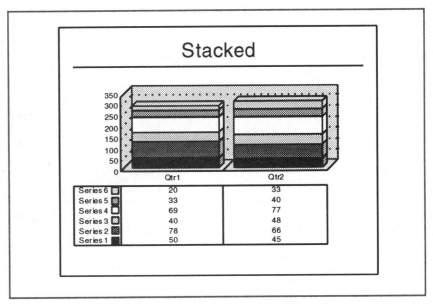

Figure D.26: Press 1, 6, 3, 4, and 5

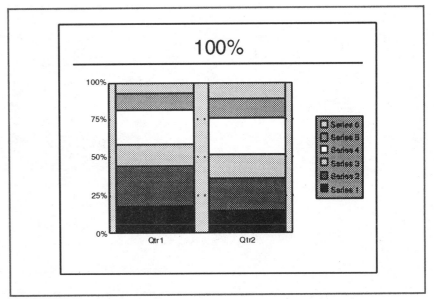

Figure D.27: Press 1, 6, 3, 5, and 1

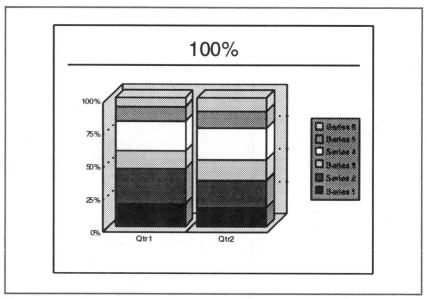

Figure D.28: Press 1, 6, 3, 5, and 2

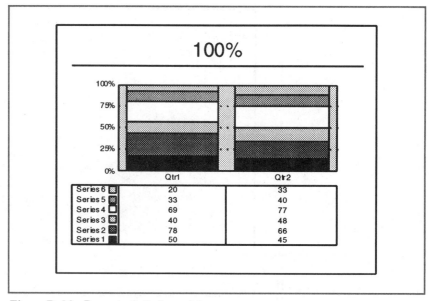

Figure D.29: Press 1, 6, 3, 5, and 4

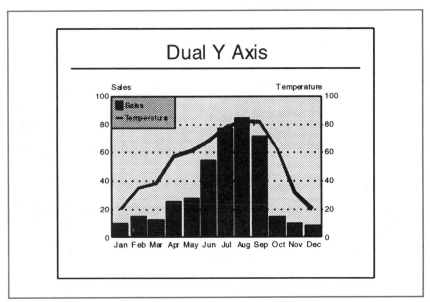

Figure D.30: Press 1, 6, 3, 6, and 1

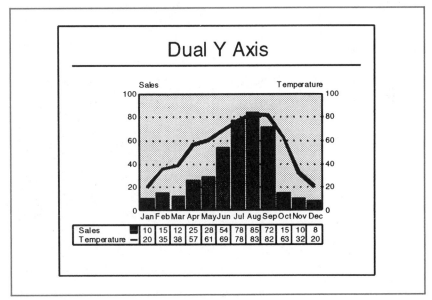

Figure D.31: Press 1, 6, 3, 6, and 7

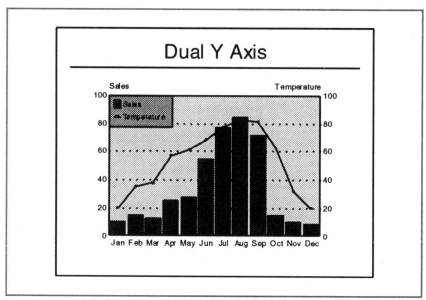

Figure D.32: Press 1, 6, 3, 6, and 9

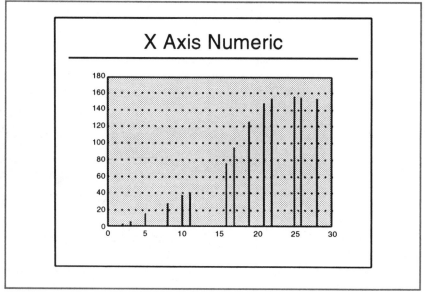

Figure D.33: Press 1, 6, 3, 7, and 1

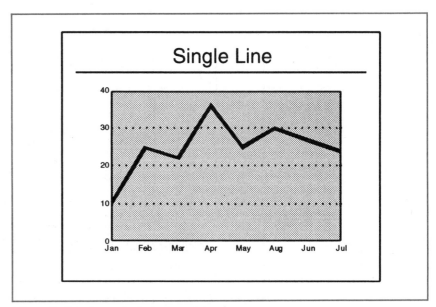

Figure D.34: Press 1, 6, 4, 1, and 1

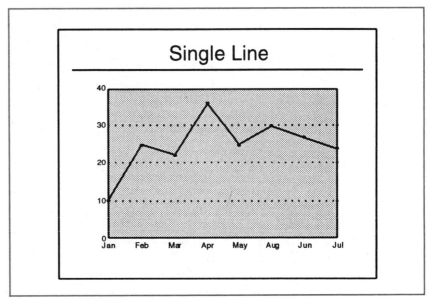

Figure D.35: Press 1, 6, 4, 1, and 3

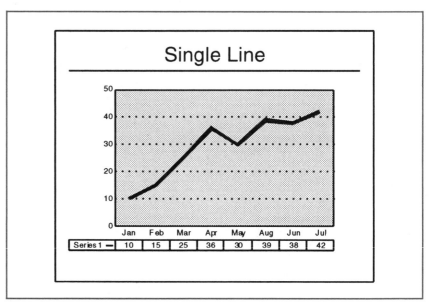

Figure D.36: Press 1, 6, 4, 1, and 4

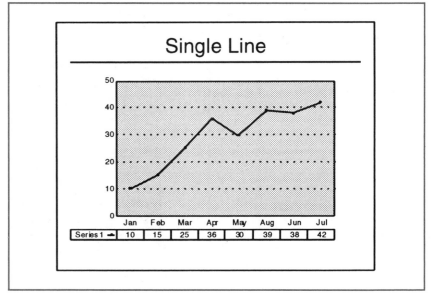

Figure D.37: Press 1, 6, 4, 1, and 6

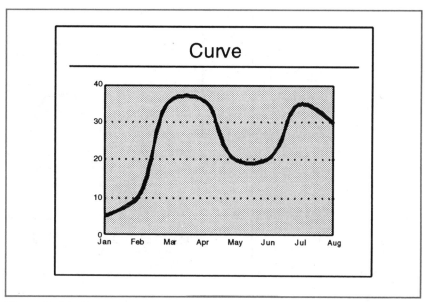

Figure D.38: Press 1, 6, 4, 2, and 1

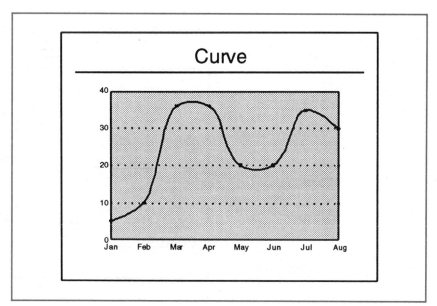

Figure D.39: Press 1, 6, 4, 2, and 3

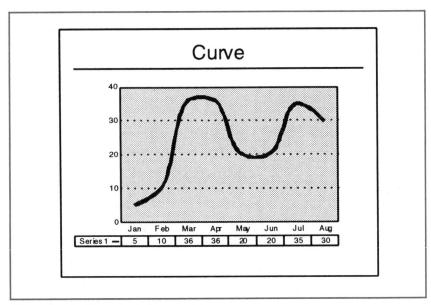

Figure D.40: Press 1, 6, 4, 2, and 4

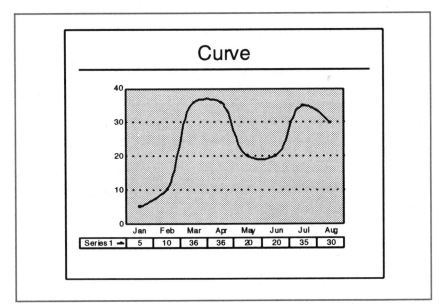

Figure D.41: Press 1, 6, 4, 2, and 6

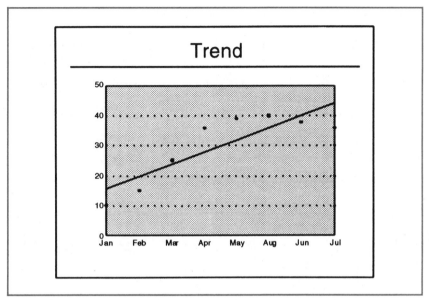

Figure D.42: Press 1, 6, 4, and 3

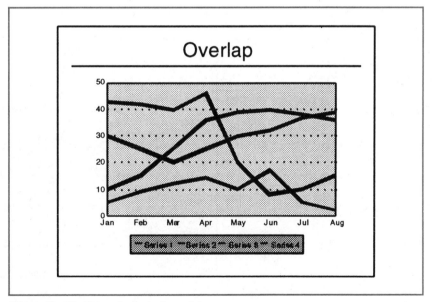

Figure D.43: Press 1, 6, 4, 4, and 1

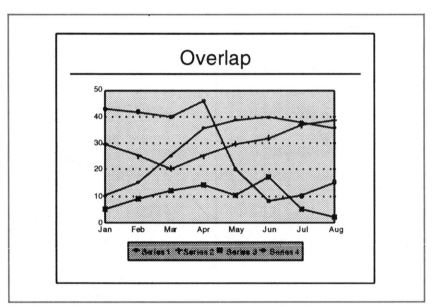

Figure D.44: Press 1, 6, 4, 4, and 3

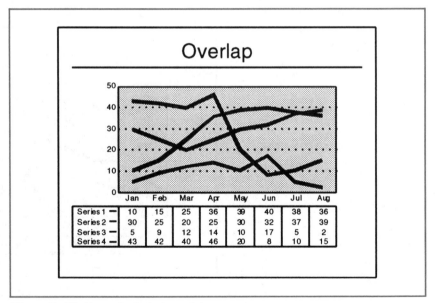

Figure D.45: Press 1, 6, 4, 4, and 4

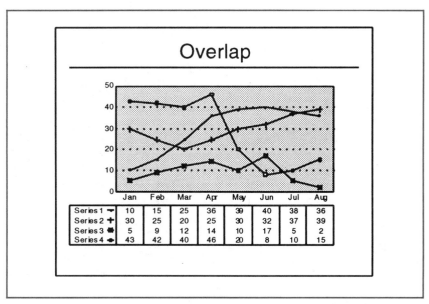

Figure D.46: Press 1, 6, 4, 4, and 6

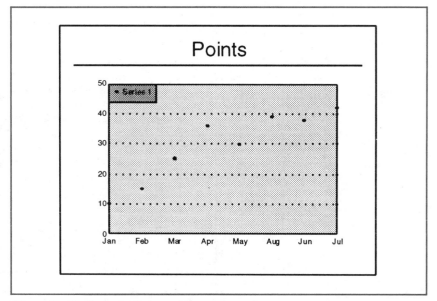

Figure D.47: Press 1, 6, 4, and 5

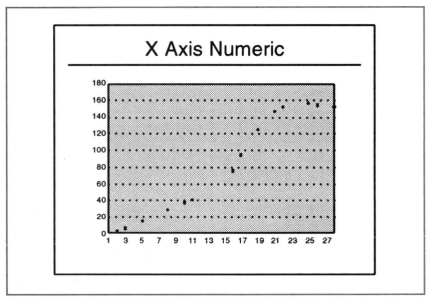

Figure D.48: Press 1, 6, 4, and 6

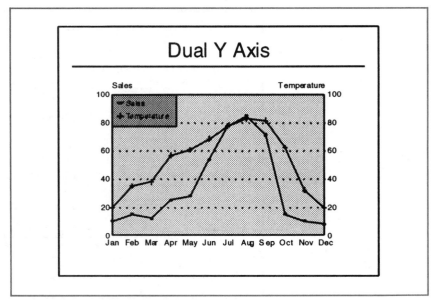

Figure D.49: Press 1, 6, 4, and 7

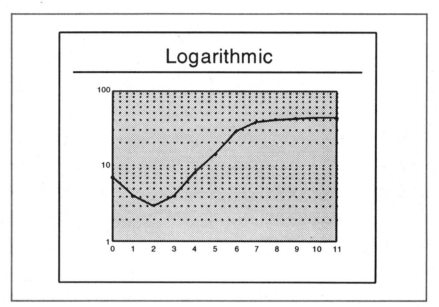

Figure D.50: Press 1, 6, 4, and 8

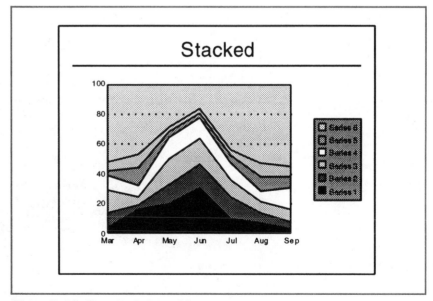

Figure D.51: Press 1, 6, 5, and 2

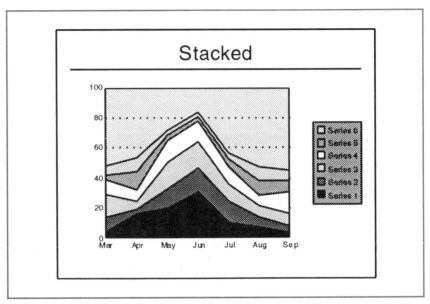

Figure D.52: Press 1, 6, 5, and 3

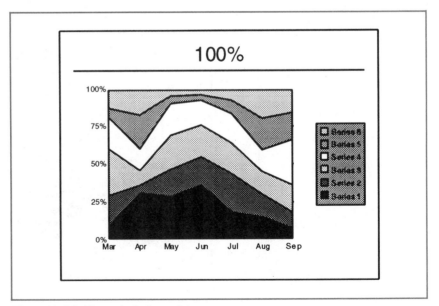

Figure D.53: Press 1, 6, 5, and 4

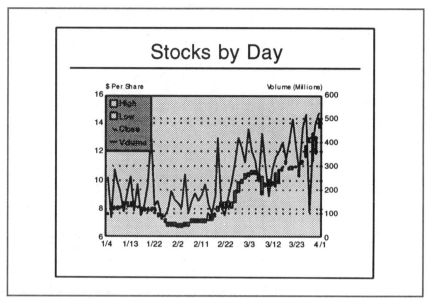

Figure D.54: Press 1, 6, 6, and 1

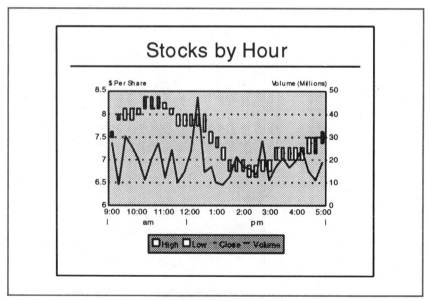

Figure D.55: Press 1, 6, 6, and 2

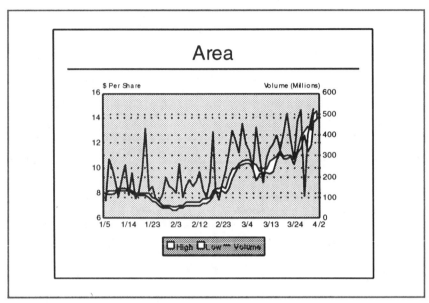

Figure D.56: Press 1, 6, 6, and 3

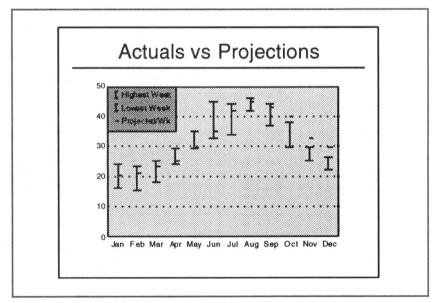

Figure D.57: Press 1, 6, 6, and 6

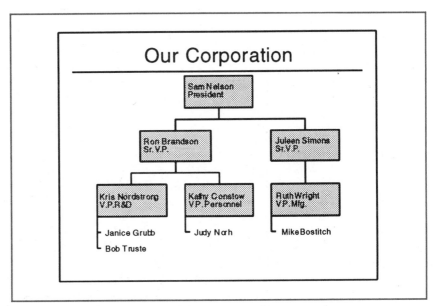

Figure D.58: Press 1, 6, 7, and 1

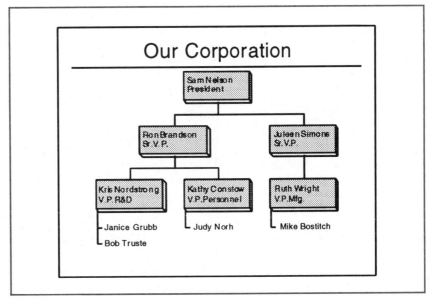

Figure D.59: Press 1, 6, 7, and 2

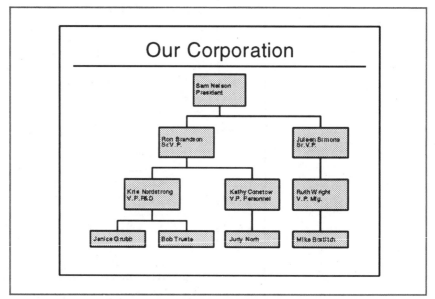

Figure D.60: Press 1, 6, 7, and 4

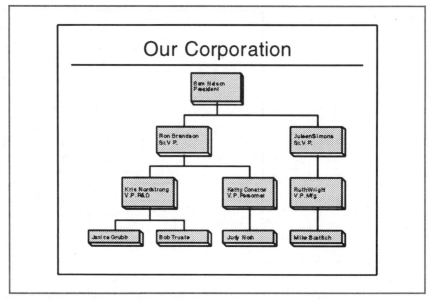

Figure D.61: Press 1, 6, 7, and 5

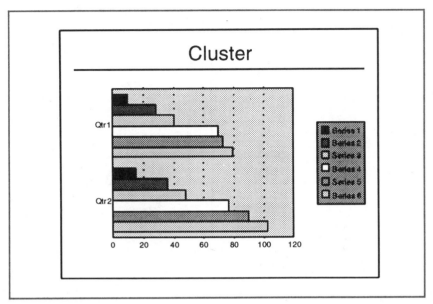

Figure D.62: Press 1, 6, 8, 1, and 1

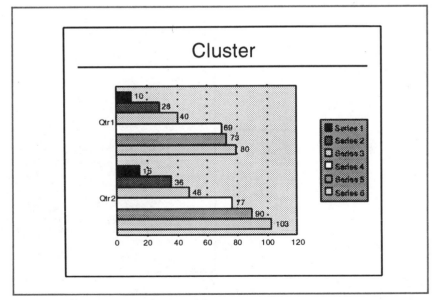

Figure D.63: Press 1, 6, 8, 1, and 3

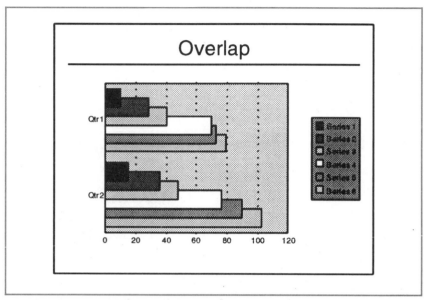

Figure D.64: Press 1, 6, 8, 2, and 1

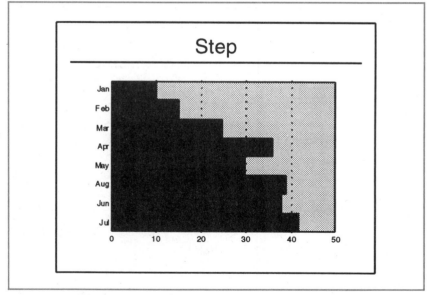

Figure D.65: Press 1, 6, 8, 3, and 1

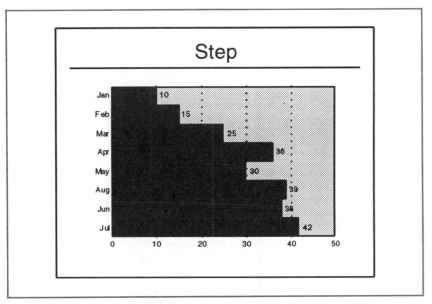

Figure D.66: Press 1, 6, 8, 3, and 3

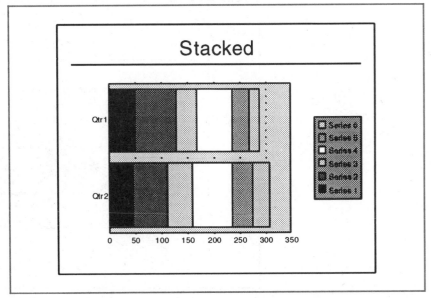

Figure D.67: Press 1, 6, 8, 4, and 1

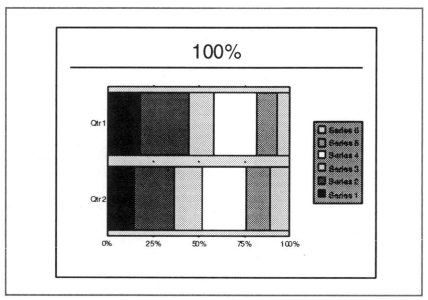

Figure D.68: Press 1, 6, 8, 5, and 1

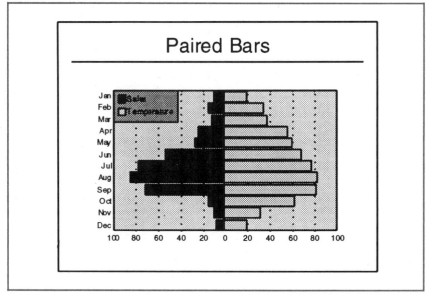

Figure D.69: Press 1, 6, 8, 6, and 1

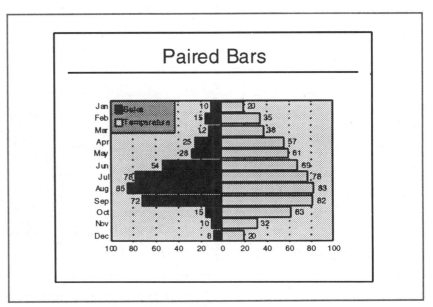

Figure D.70: Press 1, 6, 8, 6, and 2

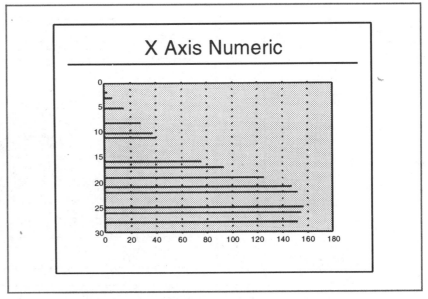

Figure D.71: Press 1, 6, 8, and 8

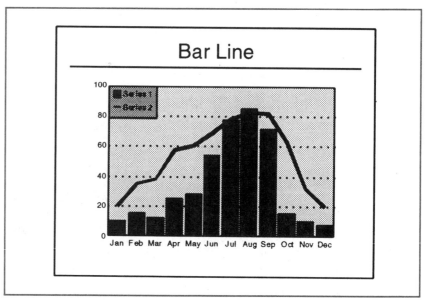

Figure D.72: Press 1, 6, 9, 1, and 1

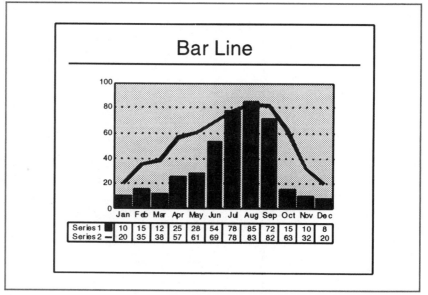

Figure D.73: Press 1, 6, 9, 1, and 7

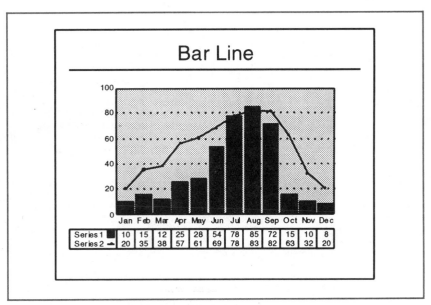

Figure D.74: Press 1, 6, 9, 1, and 9

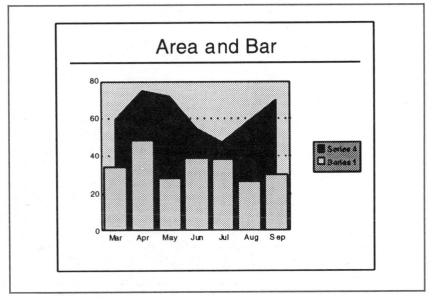

Figure D.75: Press 1, 6, 9, 3, and 1

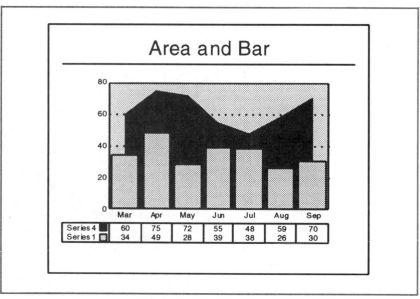

Figure D.76: Press 1, 6, 9, 3, and 7

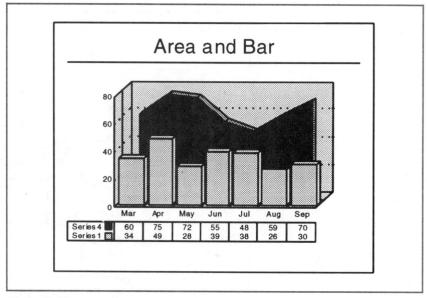

Figure D.77: Press 1, 6, 9, 3, and 8

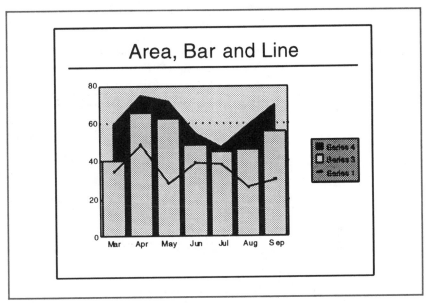

Figure D.78: Press 1, 6, 9, 4, and 1

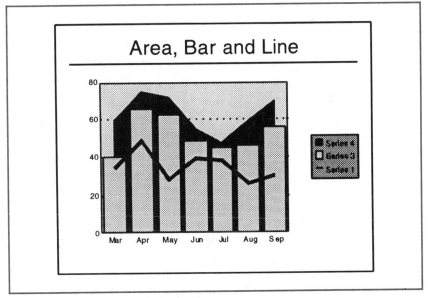

Figure D.79: Press 1, 6, 9, 4, and 3

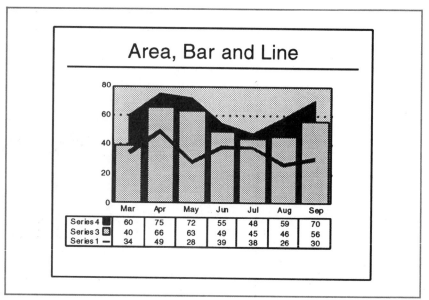

Figure D.80: Press 1, 6, 9, 4, and 4

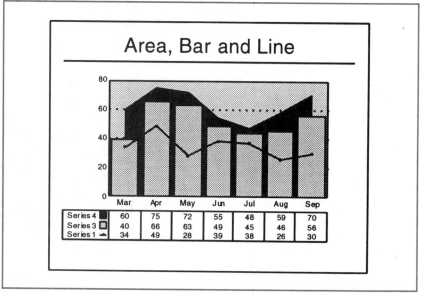

Figure D.81: Press 1, 6, 9, 4, and 6

E

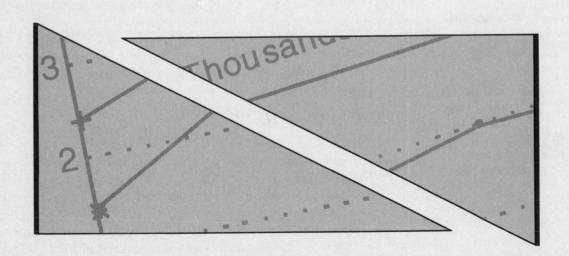

Working with Color and Selecting Palettes

APPENDIX E

THIS APPENDIX DESCRIBES HOW TO USE COLORS with your Harvard Graphics version 3.0 charts. It begins with a discussion of the proper use of color, which will help you to design attractive charts. Then it explains how to select and edit the palettes supplied with the program.

WORKING WITH COLOR

Color charts add a bright, fresh appearance to your presentations. Prices of color printers continue to drop, and more offices routinely produce color graphics. As color graphics find their way into everyday presentations, your understanding of color will become increasingly important.

Slide services can process your Harvard chart files into high-quality 35mm color slides at a reasonable cost. These slides can be reproduced as color view graphs and impressive color paper prints.

PostScript color printers reproduce the colors that you see on your screen if you press F8 and set Reverse black and white to No before printing.

THE COLOR WHEEL

The color wheel shown in Figure E.1 is a tool that artists use to interpret and combine colors. The solid line in the color wheel connects the three primary colors that all the other colors can be mixed from: red, yellow, and blue. A secondary color, such as green, violet, or orange, is one that you get by mixing two of the primary colors. For example, if you mix yellow and red you will see orange, which is a secondary color. Secondary colors are connected in Figure E.1 by dashed lines.

You will find complementary colors opposite from one another on the color wheel. Thus, there are three sets of complementary colors on

Your colors will vary depending on the palette you're using.

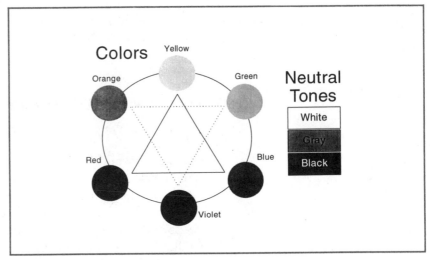

Figure E.1: The color wheel

our color wheel:

- Yellow and violet
- Orange and blue
- Red and green

When you use two complementary colors next to each other, you make each more vibrant and colorful. For example, red appears more intense when placed next to green. Complementary colors can thus be used for emphasis.

COLOR INTENSITY

Intensity refers to the brightness or amount of light in a color. The more intense a color is, the brighter it appears. For example, magenta is brighter and more intense than violet. They are actually the same color, but the difference in their intensity makes them look like two different colors. When you darken a color, you remove some of the light to make it less intense, or more subtle.

Use subtle colors for large areas. Use intense colors for thin lines and small graphic symbols.

When you create your charts, try to balance the intensity of the colors you use. The eyes are naturally drawn to pure, intense colors, so don't use too many of them or they will fight for your audience's attention.

CHOOSING AN EFFECTIVE COLOR SCHEME

Artists use the following traditional color schemes:

- **Analogous harmony**: In this scheme, you choose one color as the predominant color in your chart and use other colors that are next to it on the color wheel. For example, if you choose blue as the predominant color, you also can choose greens and violets. Another analogous scheme you can use is yellow supplemented with greens and oranges. You can choose differing degrees of intensity to emphasize parts of your chart.

- **Complementary**: There are three complementary color schemes: orange and blue, yellow and violet, and red and green. Your predominant color should be muted. For example, use a dark green background with green, red, and crimson. Use neutral tones—black, gray, and white—where necessary to separate intense colors and avoid garish effects.

- **Perfected harmony**: This scheme combines the analogous harmony and the complementary color schemes. For example, if your predominant color is blue, your analogous colors are violet and green. Orange is the complement of blue, so it is used for contrast and emphasis. Use this color scheme with care, since it is more complex than the previously discussed schemes.

Yellow or white on blue are good choices that many people find pleasing.

- **Triad harmony**: The triad harmony scheme uses any three colors on the color wheel that form an equilateral triangle. For example, you might choose red, yellow, and blue; or orange, green, and violet. Choose one color to dominate your chart, and let the other two take second and third place accordingly. You will probably need to use white and black to neutralize parts of your chart. If possible, use only one intense color.

The shaded colors of the color wheels in Figure E.2 show examples of color schemes you can use. Notice that you can use white, gray, and black in complementary or triad harmony color schemes.

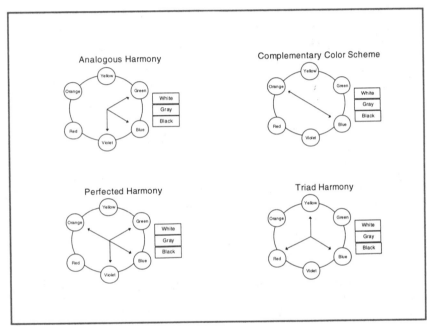

Figure E.2: Color schemes

> Imagine that the arrows in Figure E.2 are on a spinner. As the arrows spin, they will point to a color scheme you can use.

UNDERSTANDING COLOR PSYCHOLOGY

Because colors influence human emotions, you can control the impact of your chart's message by using color to help create a particular mood. You can see the application of color psychology in the advertisements produced by advertising agencies.

For example, use a bright and cheerful yellow to represent warmth, sunshine, and gaiety. In a chart about air conditioners, you might use blues, cyans, whites, and greens to suggest coolness. Colors and their psychological effects are summarized in Table E.1.

> The intensity of a color can change its psychological effect.

Table E.1: The Psychology of Color

COLOR	SYMBOLIZATION OR REPRESENTATION
White	Cold and cool; purity; innocence
Cyan	Cool; wintertime
Green	Cool and relaxing; jealousy; springtime; money
Blue	Calm and cool; justice; loyalty; honesty; tranquility; purity
Red	Warmth; fire; passion; love; courage; danger; anger; financial loss
Yellow	Warm; sunshine; festivity; merriment
Orange	Warmer than yellow; stimulating; decorative
Gold	Wealth; glamour
Violet	Royalty; splendor; anguish
Gray	Conservativeness; stability
Crimson	Cruelty; anger
Dark Green	Peacefulness; the great outdoors
Black	Death; mourning; despair

Note: Color psychology can vary among different ethnic groups, cultures, and countries. For example, red, white, and blue connote patriotic feelings in America, England, France, and Norway; in Mexico and Italy, red, white, and green inspire these feelings.

HARVARD GRAPHICS' COLOR SCHEMES

On monochrome monitors, colors are displayed as varying shades and patterns of gray.

The palettes you use for your Harvard Graphics charts affect the colors your monitor displays, as well as the shades or patterns your printer uses to print your charts. Color-capable printers will print in colors that are similar to those shown on the screen. However, some printers do not print all the colors on the palettes. For example, the Hewlett-Packard (HP) ColorJet prints only the first eight colors, which are then repeated for colors 9 through 16.

Harvard Graphics palettes are stored in files with .PL3 extensions. Chapter 4 of this book provides information about the default HG3.PL3 palette and the color numbers that are assigned to chart parts. When you save a chart file, Harvard also saves its palette file in the same drive and directory. If you are creating slides, the slide service can use this file to see which colors you want in your charts.

PALETTE SETUP

The Harvard Graphics palette setup screen, shown in Figure E.3, illustrates how palettes work. To see this screen, select Setup from the Main menu, and then select Color palette.

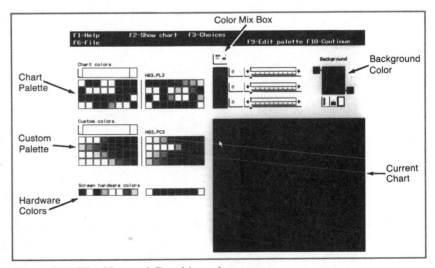

Figure E.3: The Harvard Graphics palette setup screen

Open the C:\HG3\ DATA\PAL-VIEW.CHT file before working with Setup's palette screen. This way, you can see the effects of color changes on text, range, pie, and XY charts.

If you output color charts or presentations, use the HG3.PC3 Custom colors palette. Use GRAYS.PC3 when you output to a black-and-white printer.

Changing the palette for the Custom colors can produce unexpected results because these colors are used for symbols. For example, if you create a yellow sun symbol and then change the Custom colors palette, your sun may turn green. Use a consistent Custom colors palette to avoid problems with symbol colors.

The palette setup screen contains a color mix box and the following four color areas to show the effects of the palette on your current chart:

- **Chart colors**: Controls the colors of your chart's parts (the subtitle, footnote, series, and so on).
- **Custom colors**: Controls the colors used for drawings, objects, and symbols. This palette should be reserved for symbols so that they are consistent no matter which chart palette you use.
- **Background**: Controls the background color in drawings. Use this area to create shaded backgrounds with two colors that fade into each other.
- **Screen hardware colors**: Controls the basic 16 colors used to mix chart and custom palettes.

If you want WYSIWYG (what-you-see-is-what-you-get) charts, select MONOCHRW.PL3 Chart colors palette and GRAYS.PC3 Custom colors palette when printing to a black-and-white printer. Any palette whose file name (not extension) ends with HDW or SHD is suitable for WYSIWYG color printing. Make sure to set your black-and-white or color printer to use these settings:

- Reverse black and white: No
- Black text: No
- Draw background color: Yes

You can change or create palettes for your screen display and output from the palette setup screen, as described in the following sections.

CREATING A CUSTOM SCREEN PALETTE

To create your own custom palette, first pick a palette to use as the basis for its design. For example, you might want to modify the MONOCHRW.PL3 file to show more variation in the shading.

Follow these steps to design a palette:

If you want to select a palette for just the charts you'll create in a specific working session, follow steps 1 and 2 only. These settings will not be retained when you exit Harvard; they do not automatically become the new defaults.

1. Get a chart so you can see the effects of your palette changes. The C:\HG3\DATA\PALVIEW.CH3 chart is a good choice because it shows the effects on a variety of chart types.

2. From the Main menu, press **8**, then **B**. You will see the current chart and its default palette on the palette setup screen.

3. Press F6, then **1** to select a palette to edit. Make sure the directory is set to C:\HG3\PALETTE; change it if necessary.

4. Highlight the palette whose pattern you want to use for the new palette and press Enter. For example, if you want to base your palette on the MONOCHRW.PL3 file, highlight that palette and press Enter. You will return to the palette setup screen.

5. You can now change the background color or edit the chart, custom, or hardware palettes, as explained in the following sections. Press Ctrl-D to redraw the chart and see the effect your changes have.

To make a temporary change without saving the palette, just press F10 in step 6.

6. When you are satisfied with the palette, press F6, then **2**, then **1** to save it as a Chart palette. Alternatively, you can press F6, **2**, and **2** to save it as a Custom palette (we suggest that you don't).

7. Type the name of the new palette and its description. Do not use the old name because you will overwrite the original file, and you will not be able to retrieve it if you want to use it again.

CHANGING THE BACKGROUND COLOR

To change the background colors of your palette, on the palette setup screen, click on the small box that is connected to the top-left corner of the Background box to highlight it. Then click on a color on the left side of the screen, and the color in the Background box will change. Press Ctrl-D to redraw the screen to see how your chart looks. If you don't like the effect, try a different color.

You can add another color to the background to create a shaded effect. Click on the small box that is connected to the bottom-right corner of the Background box. Then click on the color you want mixed with the one in the Background box. Next, click on one of the three shading boxes positioned below the background box. Choose either side-to-side or top-to-bottom shading. Click on the last box if you want to keep a solid color. Press Ctrl-D to see the effect on your chart.

CHANGING HARDWARE COLORS

Besides the 64 colors for your custom and chart palettes, there are 16 hardware colors available. You might want to change the hardware colors if you are working with a monochrome monitor. For example, you could change blue to dark gray. All the colors in your palette that have blue will be affected by the change. If you do not like the results, reset the original hardware colors by pressing Ctrl-U.

EDITING PALETTES

You can edit the chart, custom, and hardware palettes to get the precise colors you want. To edit a palette, from the palette setup screen, click to select the color you want to edit. Then press F9 to display the Edit Palette menu, shown in Figure E.4, and select the editing option you want to use. Alternatively, you can use speed keys to edit the palette, as follows:

- **Copying and pasting colors**: Click on the color box you want to copy and press Ctrl-C to copy the color to the clipboard. Then click on the box you want the color pasted to and press Ctrl-P.

- **Cutting a color**: Click on the color you want to delete and press Del. All the colors to the right of the box will move up one position. For example, deleting color 62 moves color 63

You cannot cut hardware colors.

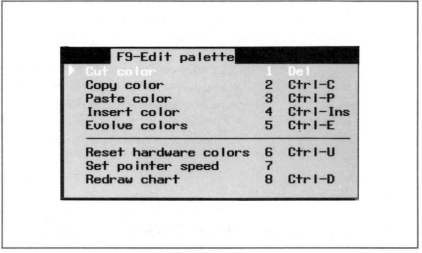

Figure E.4: The Edit Palette menu

to 62's old position, and color 64 takes 63's old position. The color you cut is moved to the clipboard, so if you change your mind, press Ctrl-Ins to reinsert it.

- **Inserting a color**: Move to where you want to insert the color and press Ctrl-Ins. All the colors at the point of insertion will shift one position to the right, and the inserted box will appear with the color that was last copied to the clipboard.

- **Evolving colors**: To evolve colors, press Ctrl-E. Enter the starting and ending box number and press F10. This creates a range of colored boxes based on the two colors you selected. For example, if you select box 2 (white) as the starting color and box 10 (dark blue) as the ending color, boxes 3 to 9 will range from a very light blue to a dark blue.

- **Creating new colors**: Click on the box that will get the new color. Slide the red, blue, and green slider bars at the top right of the screen, and the color in the mix box will change. Experiment to see the effect of your settings. In general, the higher the number, the lighter the color. To

You cannot undo the Evolve command, so make sure you use a new file name for your palette. If you make an error, just start over.

get a high-intensity white, for example, set the Red, Green, and Blue columns to 999. Set all three columns to 0 for black.

Another way to create a new color is to click on the mix icon that is located above the mix box (to the left of the slider bars). You will see a range of colors where the slider bars used to be. Click in the area of this box that best represents the color you want. Then use the slider bar that is above it to fine-tune the intensity of the color.

SELECTING A PALETTE FOR A SINGLE CHART

You can select an optional color palette by pressing F8 from any chart data-entry screen or from Draw, and then choosing the Appearance option from the Options menu. Click on the Chart palette field. If you know the name of the palette you want to use, type

C:\HG3\PALETTE*filename.***PL3**

where *filename* is the name of the palette file. To see a list of palettes to select from, press F3. Then move the cursor to the palette file you want and press Enter.

DESIGNATING A DEFAULT PALETTE

To change the Custom colors palette, press **1** and use the arrow keys to highlight the Custom color palette field. Type the new name of the .PC3 custom palette you want and press F10.

The default palette is always available for your charts when you start Harvard. If you have a favorite palette that you frequently select, follow these steps to make it the default palette:

1. From the Main menu, press **8** to display the Setup menu.

2. Press **2** to display your chart default settings.

3. Move to the Default palette field.

4. Type the palette name you want to use as your default and press Enter. For example, type C:\HG3\PALETTE\ HG3.PL3 if you want to reset the default palette back to HG3.

5. Press F10 when you are finished.

F

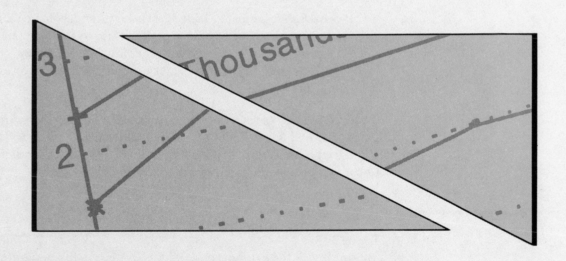

Installing the Harvard Graphics Enhancement Disk

APPENDIX **F** _____

You can copy the files from the 360K Enhancement Disk to a 3½-inch disk. Or Honey Tree Computers can do it for you. Just send a photocopy of the Enhancement Disk envelope along with a $10 check for postage and handling to Kristopher A. Larsen, Honey Tree Computers, General Delivery, Mechanicsville, MD 20659.

THE SYBEX HARVARD GRAPHICS ENHANCEMENT Disk contains additional software that you can use with Harvard Graphics to enhance your productivity and creativity. This valuable 360K disk (with 984K of compressed files) is bound in the envelope in the book's back cover. This disk is packed full with the following features:

- **Symbols Enhancement**: Includes 984K of compressed Master-Clips symbols for Harvard Graphics 3.0 (a $49 value), including color symbols with gradient shading and gradual changes in color backgrounds. Additionally, these color symbols look great when printed on black-and-white printers. The symbols on this disk are in Harvard Graphic's special .SY3 format.

- **Palette Enhancement**: Adds several additional color palettes and a black-and-white palette you can use to produce charts with professional-looking color schemes. Use these new palettes with the Harvard Gallery, or when creating your own charts.

MasterClips symbols are marketed by Masterclip Graphics, Inc., 5201 Ravenswood Road, Suite 111, Fort Lauderdale, Florida 33312-6004. (All rights are reserved.) See Appendix C for more information about the symbols available from this company.

INSTALLING THE ENHANCEMENT DISK

You can install the symbols and palette enhancements separately, depending on the amount of disk space you have available. It takes about 984K of space to install the .SY3 files and about 15K of space to install the palettes.

INSTALLING THE SYMBOL ENHANCEMENTS

The symbols on the 360K Enhancement Disk are in a compressed format. When you run the Enhancement Disk's Install program, the files will decompress into 984K of .SY3 files for easy access from within Harvard Graphics. To install the symbols, follow these steps:

If your 5¼-inch drive is connected to drive B, substitute **B** for A in the installation instructions.

1. Remove the Enhancement Disk from the back cover of this book and place it in drive A.

2. From the DOS prompt, type **A:INSTALL** and press Enter.

3. Read the opening screen, shown in Figure F.1, and press Enter to continue.

4. Type **A:** and press Enter when you are prompted for the drive you are installing from.

5. When you are prompted for the drive that you want to install the symbols on, type **C:** (or another drive) and press Enter. You will see the installation screen, which should look similar to Figure F.2. If you have enough room to install the symbols, proceed with step 6 or type R to select another drive. If you don't have enough room, press X to cancel the installation. You will have to make more room on your drive and repeat the installation process.

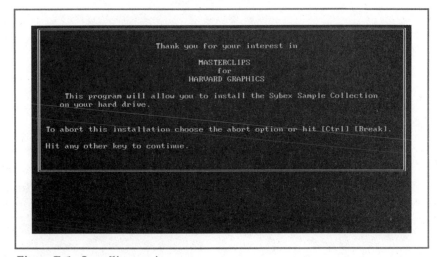

Figure F.1: Install's opening screen

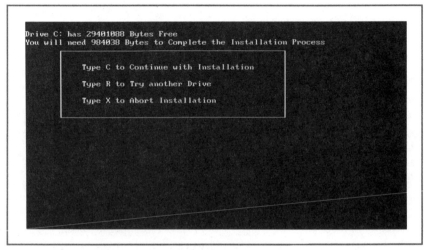

Figure F.2: Install to drive screen

To save time in accessing symbol files, install Master Clips symbols in C:\HG3\SYMBOL\MCLIPS.

6. Press **C** to continue with the installation process. You will see the menu shown in Figure F.3, which prompts you for the subdirectory to use for installation. Press **A** to install the symbols into the default \MCLIPS subdirectory.

The Install program lists each symbol file on the screen as it is decompressed. After all the symbols are decompressed, you will be returned to the DOS prompt.

INSTALLING THE PALETTE ENHANCEMENTS

You can copy the palette enhancements on the Enhancement Disk using the DOS COPY command. Place the Enhancement Disk in drive A and, from the DOS prompt, type

COPY A:\PALETTE*.* C:\HG3\PALETTE*.*

and press Enter. If you installed Harvard Graphics on a drive and directory other than C:\HG3, substitute that directory's name in place of C:\HG3. This copies the palette enhancement files into the proper subdirectory.

To save time in accessing symbol files, install Master Clips symbols in C:\HG3\ SYMBOL\MCLIPS.

6. Press **C** to continue with the installation process. You will see the menu shown in Figure F.3, which prompts you for the subdirectory to use for installation. Press **A** to install the symbols into the default \MCLIPS subdirectory.

These valuable additions from the SYBEX Harvard Graphics Enhancement Disk provide more tools that you can use to achieve the effects you need in your charts and presentations.

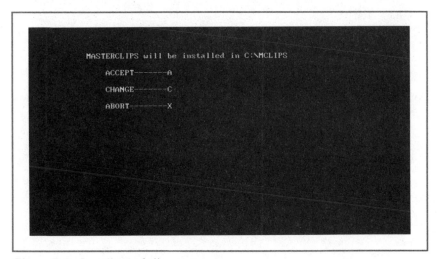

Figure F.3: Install to subdirectory screen

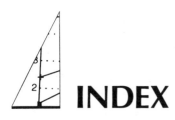

INDEX

Selections from The SYBEX Library

DESKTOP

Harvard Graphics Instant Reference
Gerald E. Jones
154pp. Ref. 726-6

This handy reference is a quick, non-technical answer manual to questions about Harvard's onscreen menus and help displays. Provides specific information on each of the program's major features, including Draw Partner. A must for business professionals and graphic artists who create charts and graphs for presentation.

Harvard Graphics 3 Instant Reference
(Second Edition)
Gerald E. Jones
200pp; ref. 871-8

This handy, compact volume is the single complete source for quick answers on all of Harvard's menu options and features. It's small enough to keep on hand while you work—and fast enough to let you keep working while you look up concise explanations and exact instructions for using Harvard commands.

Mastering Animator
Mitch Gould
300pp. Ref.688-X

A hands-on guide to creating dynamic multimedia presentations. From simple animation to Hollywood-style special effects, from planning a presentation to bringing it all to life—it's all you need to know, in straightforward, easy-to-follow terms.

Mastering Harvard Graphics
(Second Edition)
Glenn H. Larsen
375pp, Ref. 673-1

"The clearest course to begin mastering Harvard Graphics," according to *Computer Currents*. Readers master essential principles of effective graphic communication, as they follow step-by-step instructions to create dozens of charts and graphs; automate and customize the charting process; create slide shows, and more.

Teach Yourself Harvard Graphics 3
Jeff Woodward
450pp; Ref. 801-7

A graphical introduction to the hottest-selling presentation graphics program! This illustrated guide leads newcomers through the exact steps needed to create all kinds of effective charts and graphs. There are no surprises: what you see in the book is what you will see on your screen.

Up & Running with Harvard Graphics
Rebecca Bridges Altman
148pp. Ref. 736-3

Desktop presentation in 20 steps—the perfect way to evaluate Harvard Graphics for purchase, or to get a fast, hands-on overview of the software's capabilities. The book's 20 concise lessons are time-coded (each takes no more than an hour to complete), and cover everything from installation and startup, to creating specific types of charts, graphs, and slide shows.

Up & Running with Harvard Graphics 3
Rebecca Bridges Altman

140pp; Ref. 884-X

Come up to speed with Harvard Graphics 3—fast. If you're a computer-literate user who needs to start producing professional-looking presentation graphics now, this book is for you. In only 20 lessons (each taking just 15 minutes to an hour), you can cover all the essentials of this perennially popular progam.

DESKTOP PUBLISHING

The ABC's of the New Print Shop
Vivian Dubrovin

340pp. Ref. 640-4

This beginner's guide stresses fun, practicality and original ideas. Hands-on tutorials show how to create greeting cards, invitations, signs, flyers, letterheads, banners, and calendars.

The ABC's of Ventura
Robert Cowart
Steve Cummings

390pp. Ref. 537-9

Created especially for new desktop publishers, this is an easy introduction to a complex program. Cowart provides details on using the mouse, the Ventura side bar, and page layout, with careful explanations of publishing terminology. The new Ventura menus are all carefully explained. For Version 2.

Desktop Publishing with WordPerfect 5.1
Rita Belserene

418pp. Ref. 481-X

A practical guide to using the desktop publishing capabilities of versions 5.0 and 5.1. Topics include graphic design concepts, hardware necessities, installing and using fonts, columns, lines, and boxes, illustrations, multi-page layouts, Style Sheets, and integrating with other software.

Mastering CorelDRAW 2
Steve Rimmer

500pp. Ref. 814-9

This comprehensive tutorial and design guide features complete instruction in creating spectacular graphic effects with CorelDRAW 2. The book also offers a primer on commercial image and page design, including how to use printers and print-house facilities for optimum results.

Mastering Micrografx Designer
Peter Kent

400pp. Ref. 694-4

A complete guide to using this sophisticated illustration package. Readers begin by importing and modifying clip art, and progress to creating original drawings, working with text, printing and plotting, creating slide shows, producing color separations, and exporting art.

Mastering PageMaker 4 on the IBM PC
Rebecca Bridges Altman, with Rick Altman

509pp. Ref. 773-8

A step-by-step guide to the essentials of desktop publishing and graphic design. Tutorials and hands-on examples explore every aspect of working with text, graphics, styles, templates, and more, to design and produce a wide range of publications. Includes a publication "cookbook" and notes on using Windows 3.0.

Mastering Ventura for Windows (For Version 3.0)
Rick Altman

600pp, Ref. 758-4

This engaging, hands-on treatment is for the desktop publisher learning and using the Windows edition of Ventura. It covers everything from working with the Windows interface, to designing and printing sophisticated publications using Ventura's most advanced features. Understand and work with frames, graphics, fonts, tables and columns, and much more.

Mastering Ventura 3.0 Gem Edition
Matthew Holtz
650pp, Ref. 703-7

The complete hands-on guide to desktop publishing with Xerox Ventura Publisher—now in an up-to-date new edition featuring Ventura version 3.0, with the GEM windowing environment. Tutorials cover every aspect of the software, with examples ranging from correspondence and press releases, to newsletters, technical documents, and more.

Understanding Desktop Publishing
Robert W. Harris
300pp. Ref. 789-4

At last, a practical design handbook, written especially for PC users who are not design professionals, but who do have desktop publishing duties. How can publications be made attractive, understandable, persuasive, and memorable? Topics include type, graphics, and page design; technical and physiological aspects of creating and conveying a message.

Understanding PFS: First Publisher
Gerry Litton
463pp. Ref. 712-6

This new edition of the popular guide to First Publisher covers software features in a practical introduction to desktop publishing. Topics include text-handling, working with graphics, effective page design, and optimizing print quality. With examples of flyers, brochures, newsletters, and more.

Understanding PostScript Programming (Second Edition)
David A. Holzgang
472pp. Ref. 566-2

In-depth treatment of PostScript for programmers and advanced users working on custom desktop publishing tasks. Hands-on development of programs for font creation, integrating graphics, printer implementations and more.

Up & Running with CorelDRAW 2
Len Gilbert
140pp; Ref. 887-4

Learn CorelDRAW 2 in record time. This 20-step tutorial is perfect for computer-literate users who are new to CorelDRAW or upgrading from an earlier version. Each concise step takes no more than 15 minutes to an hour to complete, and provides needed skills without unnecessary detail.

Up & Running with PageMaker 4 on the PC
Marvin Bryan
140pp. Ref. 781-9

An overview of PageMaker 4.0 in just 20 steps. Perfect for evaluating the software before purchase—or for newcomers who are impatient to get to work. Topics include installation, adding typefaces, text and drawing tools, graphics, reusing layouts, using layers, working in color, printing, and more.

Your HP LaserJet Handbook
Alan R. Neibauer
564pp. Ref. 618-9

Get the most from your printer with this step-by-step instruction book for using LaserJet text and graphics features such as cartridge and soft fonts, type selection, memory and processor enhancements, PCL programming, and PostScript solutions. This hands-on guide provides specific instructions for working with a variety of software.

WORD PROCESSING

The ABC's of Microsoft Word (Third Edition)
Alan R. Neibauer
461pp. Ref. 604-9

This is for the novice WORD user who wants to begin producing documents in the shortest time possible. Each chapter has short, easy-to-follow lessons for both keyboard and mouse, including all the basic editing, formatting and printing functions. Version 5.0.

The ABC's of Microsoft Word for Windows
Alan R. Neibauer
334pp. Ref. 784-6

Designed for beginning Word for Windows users, as well as for experienced Word users who are changing from DOS to the Windows version. Covers everything from typing, saving, and printing your first document, to creating tables, equations, and graphics.

The ABC's of WordPerfect 5
Alan R. Neibauer
283pp. Ref. 504-2

This introduction explains the basics of desktop publishing with WordPerfect 5: editing, layout, formatting, printing, sorting, merging, and more. Readers are shown how to use WordPerfect 5's new features to produce great-looking reports.

The ABC's of WordPerfect 5.1 for Windows
Alan R. Neibauer
350pp; Ref. 803-3

This highly praised beginner's tutorial is now in a special new edition for WordPerfect 5.1 for Windows—featuring WYSIWYG graphics, font preview, the button bar, and more. It covers all the essentials of word processing, from basic editing to simple desktop publishing, in short, easy-to-follow lessons. Suitable for first-time computer users.

The ABC's of WordPerfect 5.1
Alan R. Neibauer
352pp. Ref. 672-3

Neibauer's delightful writing style makes this clear tutorial an especially effective learning tool. Learn all about 5.1's new drop-down menus and mouse capabilities that reduce the tedious memorization of function keys.

The Complete Guide to MultiMate
Carol Holcomb Dreger
208pp. Ref. 229-9

This step-by-step tutorial is also an excellent reference guide to MultiMate features and uses. Topics include search/replace, library and merge functions, repagination, document defaults and more.

Encyclopedia WordPerfect 5.1
Greg Harvey
Kay Yarborough Nelson
1100pp. Ref. 676-6

This comprehensive, up-to-date WordPerfect reference is a must for beginning and experienced users alike. With complete, easy-to-find information on every WordPerfect feature and command—and it's organized by practical functions, with business users in mind.

Mastering Microsoft Word on the IBM PC (Fourth Edition)
Matthew Holtz
680pp. Ref. 597-2

This comprehensive, step-by-step guide details all the new desktop publishing developments in this versatile word processor, including details on editing, formatting, printing, and laser printing. Holtz uses sample business documents to demonstrate the use of different fonts, graphics, and complex documents. Includes Fast Track speed notes. For Versions 4 and 5.

Mastering Microsoft Word 5.5 (Fifth Edition)
Matthew Holtz
650pp; Ref. 836-X

This up-to-date edition is a comprehensive guide to productivity with Word 5.5—from basic tutorials for beginners to hands-on treatment of Word's extensive desktop publishing capabilities. Special topics include style sheets, form letters and labels, spreadsheets and tables, graphics, and macros.

Mastering Microsoft Word for Windows
Michael J. Young
540pp. Ref. 619-7

A practical introduction to Word for Windows, with a quick-start tutorial for newcomers. Subsequent chapters explore editing, formatting, and printing, and cover such advanced topics as page design, Style Sheets, the Outliner, Glossaries, automatic indexing, using graphics, and desktop publishing.

Mastering Microsoft Word for Windows
(Second Edition)
Michael J. Young
550pp; Ref. 1012-6

Here is an up-to-date new edition of our complete guide to Word for Windows, featuring the latest software release. It offers a tutorial for newcomers, and hands-on coverage of intermediate to advanced topics, with an emphasis on desktop publishing skills. Special topics include tables and columns, fonts, graphics, Styles and Templates, macros, and multiple windows.

Mastering Microsoft Works on the IBM PC
Rebecca Bridges Altman
536pp. Ref. 690-1

Written especially for small business and home office users. Practical tutorials cover every aspect of word processing, spreadsheets, business graphics, database management and reporting, and basic telecommunications under Microsoft Works.

Mastering MultiMate 4.0
Paula B. Hottin
404pp. Ref. 697-9

Get thorough coverage from a practical perspective. Tutorials and real-life examples cover everything from first startup to basic editing, formatting, and printing;

advanced editing and document management; enhanced page design, graphics, laser printing; merge-printing; and macros.

Mastering WordPerfect 5
Susan Baake Kelly
709pp. Ref. 500-X

The revised and expanded version of this definitive guide is now on WordPerfect 5 and covers wordprocessing and basic desktop publishing. As more than 200,000 readers of the original edition can attest, no tutorial approaches it for clarity and depth of treatment. Sorting, line drawing, and laser printing included.

Mastering WordPerfect 5.1
Alan Simpson
1050pp. Ref. 670-7

The ultimate guide for the WordPerfect user. Alan Simpson, the "master communicator," puts you in charge of the latest features of 5.1: new dropdown menus and mouse capabilities, along with the desktop publishing, macro programming, and file conversion functions that have made WordPerfect the most popular word processing program on the market.

Mastering WordPerfect 5.1 for Windows
Alan Simpson
1100pp. Ref. 806-8

The complete guide to learning, using, and making the most of WordPerfect for Windows. Working with a mouse and the Windows graphical user interface, readers explore every software feature, build practical examples, and learn dozens of special techniques—for macros, data management, desktop publishing, and more.

Microsoft Word Instant Reference for the IBM PC
Matthew Holtz
266pp. Ref. 692-8

Turn here for fast, easy access to concise information on every command and feature of Microsoft Word version 5.0—for editing, formatting, merging, style sheets, macros, and more. With exact keystroke sequences, discussion of command options, and commonly-performed tasks.

Microsoft Word for the Macintosh Instant Reference
Louis Columbus
200pp; Ref. 859-9

Turn here for fast, easy access to precise information on every command and feature of Word version 4.0 for the Mac. Alphabetized entries provide exact mouse or key sequences, discussion of command options, and step-by-step instructions for commonly performed tasks.

Teach Yourself WordPerfect 5.1
Jeff Woodward
444pp. Ref. 684-7

Key-by-key instructions, matched with screen-by-screen illustrations, make it possible to get right to work with Word-Perfect 5.1. Learn WordPerfect as quickly as you like, from basic editing to merge-printing, desktop publishing, using graphics, and macros.

WordPerfect 5.1 On-Line Advisor Version 1.1
SYBAR, Software Division of SYBEX, Inc.
Ref. 934-X

Now there's no more need to thumb through lengthy manuals. The On-Line Advisor brings you answers to your Word-Perfect questions on-screen, right where you need them. For easy reference, this comprehensive on-line help system divides up each topic by key sequence, syntax, usage and examples. Covers versions 5.0 and 5.1. Software package comes with $3\frac{1}{2}$" and $5\frac{1}{4}$" disks. **System Requirements:** IBM compatible with DOS 2.0 or higher, runs with Windows 3.0, uses 90K of RAM.

Understanding Professional Write
Gerry Litton
400pp. Ref. 656-1

A complete guide to Professional Write

that takes you from creating your first simple document, into a detailed description of all major aspects of the software. Special features place an emphasis on the use of different typestyles to create attractive documents as well as potential problems and suggestions on how to get around them.

Understanding WordStar 2000
David Kolodney
Thomas Blackadar
275pp. Ref. 554-9

This engaging, fast-paced series of tutorials covers everything from moving the cursor to print enhancements, format files, key glossaries, windows and MailMerge. With practical examples, and notes for former WordStar users.

Up & Running with Grammatik 2.0
David J. Clark
133pp. Ref. 818-1

Learn to use this sleek new grammar- and style-checking program in just 20 steps. In short order, you'll be navigating the user interface, able to check and edit your documents, customizing the program to suit your preferences, and rating the readability of your work.

Up & Running with WordPerfect Office/Library PC
Jeff Woodward
142pp. Ref. 717-7

A concise tutorial and software overview in 20 "steps" (lessons of 15 to 60 minutes each). Perfect for evaluating the software, or getting a basic grasp of its features. Learn to use the Office PC shell; use the calculator, calendar, file manager, and notebooks; create macros; and more.

Up & Running with WordPerfect 5.1
Rita Belserene
164pp. Ref. 828-9

Get a fast-paced overview of telecommunications with PROCOMM PLUS, in just 20 steps. Each step takes only 15 minutes to an hour to complete, covering the essentials of creating, editing, saving and printing documents; formatting text; creating multiple-page documents; working with fonts; importing graphic images, and more.

Up & Running with WordPerfect 5.1 for Windows
Rita Belserene
140pp; Ref. 827-0

In only 20 lessons, you can start making productive use of the new WordPerfect 5.1 for Windows. Each lesson is pre-timed to take just 15 minutes to an hour to complete. As you work through the book, you'll pick up all the skills you need to create, edit, and print your first document—plus some intermediate and advanced skills for a more professional look.

Up & Running with Word for Windows
Bob Campbell
148pp. Ref. 829-7

This fast-paced introduction will have readers using Word for Windows in no time. The book's 20 lessons or "steps" first cover installation and program navigation, then move on to the essentials of text entry, editing, formatting, and printing. Styles, templates, glossaries, macros, outlines, pictures, and merge letters are also covered.

Up & Running with WordPerfect for Windows
Rita Belserene
140pp. Ref. 827-0

Get a fast-paced overview of telecommunications with PROCOMM PLUS, in just 20 steps. Each step takes only 15 minutes to an hour to complete, covering the essentials of creating, editing, saving and printing documents; formatting text; creating multiple-page documents; working with fonts; importing graphic images; more.

WordPerfect 5 Instant Reference
SYBEX Prompter Series
Greg Harvey
Kay Yarborough Nelson
316pp. Ref. 535-2

This pocket-sized reference has all the program commands for the powerful WordPerfect 5 organized alphabetically for quick access. Each command entry has the exact key sequence, any reveal codes, a list of available options, and option-by-option discussions.

The WordPerfect 5.1 Cookbook
Alan Simpson
457pp. Ref. 680-4

A timesaving goldmine for word processing professionals, this cookbook offers a comprehensive library of sample documents, with exact keystrokes for creating them, and ready-to-use templates on an accompanying disk. Makes full use of version 5.1 features, including PostScript and Laser Jet III support, and covers everything from simple memos to multi-column layouts with graphics.

WordPerfect 5.1 Instant Reference
Greg Harvey
Kay Yarborough Nelson
252pp. Ref. 674-X

Instant access to all features and commands of WordPerfect 5.0 and 5.1, highlighting the newest software features. Complete, alphabetical entries provide exact key sequences, codes and options, and step-by-step instructions for many important tasks.

WordPerfect for Windows 5.1 Instant Reference
Alan Simpson
200pp; Ref. 821-1

This complete pocket reference, tailored specifically for the Windows version of WordPerfect 5.1, provides quick answers to common questions, and step-by-step instructions for using every software features.

WordPerfect 5.1 Macro Handbook
Kay Yarborough Nelson
532pp, Ref. 687-1

Help yourself to over 150 ready-made macros for WordPerfect versions 5.0 and 5.1. This complete tutorial guide to creating and using work-saving macros is a must for every serious WordPerfect user. Hands-on lessons show you exactly how to record and use your first simple macros—then build to sophisticated skills.

WordPerfect 5.1 Tips and Tricks (Fourth Edition)
Alan R. Neibauer
675pp. Ref. 681-2

This new edition is a real timesaver. For on-the-job guidance and creative new uses, this title covers all versions of WordPerfect up to and including 5.1—streamlining documents, automating with macros, new print enhancements, and more.

OPERATING SYSTEMS

The ABC's of DOS 4
Alan R. Miller
275pp. Ref. 583-2

This step-by-step introduction to using DOS 4 is written especially for beginners. Filled with simple examples, *The ABC's of DOS 4* covers the basics of hardware, software, disks, the system editor EDLIN, DOS commands, and more.

The ABC's of DOS 5
Alan Miller
267pp. Ref. 770-3

This straightforward guide will haven even first-time computer users working comfortably with DOS 5 in no time. Step-by-step lessons lead users from switching on the PC, through exploring the DOS Shell, working with directories and files, using essential commands, customizing the system, and trouble shooting. Includes a tear-out quick reference card and function key template.

ABC's of MS-DOS (Second Edition)
Alan R. Miller
233pp. Ref. 493-3

This handy guide to MS-DOS is all many PC users need to manage their computer files, organize floppy and hard disks, use

EDLIN, and keep their computers organized. Additional information is given about utilities like Sidekick, and there is a DOS command and program summary. The second edition is fully updated for Version 3.3.

The ABC's of SCO UNIX
Tom Cuthbertson
263pp. Re. 715-0

A guide especially for beginners who want to get to work fast. Includes hands-on tutorials on logging in and out; creating and editing files; using electronic mail; organizing files into directories; printing; text formatting; and more.

The ABC's of Windows 3.0
Kris Jamsa
327pp. Ref. 760-6

A user-friendly introduction to the essentials of Windows 3.0. Presented in 64 short lessons. Beginners start with lesson one, while more advanced readers can skip ahead. Learn to use File Manager, the accessory programs, customization features, Program Manager, and more.

DESQview Instant Reference
Paul J. Perry
175pp. Ref. 809-2

This complete quick-reference command guide covers version 2.3 and DESQview 386, as well as QEMM (for managing expanded memory) and Manifest Memory Analyzer. Concise, alphabetized entries provide exact syntax, options, usage, and brief examples for every command. A handy source for on-the-job reminders and tips.

DOS Instant Reference
SYBEX Prompter Series
Greg Harvey
Kay Yarborough Nelson
220pp. Ref. 477-1

A complete fingertip reference for fast, easy on-line help:command summaries, syntax, usage and error messages. Organized by function—system commands, file commands, disk management, directories, batch files, I/O, networking, programming, and more. Through Version 3.3.

SYBEX ®

FREE CATALOG!

Mail us this form today, and we'll send you a full-color catalog of Sybex books.

Name _____

Street _____

City/State/Zip _____

Phone _____

Please supply the name of the Sybex book purchased.

_____

How would you rate it?

_____ Excellent   _____ Very Good   _____ Average   _____ Poor

Why did you select this particular book?

_____ Recommended to me by a friend

_____ Recommended to me by store personnel

_____ Saw an advertisement in _____

_____ Author's reputation

_____ Saw in Sybex catalog

_____ Required textbook

_____ Sybex reputation

_____ Read book review in _____

_____ In-store display

_____ Other _____

Where did you buy it?

_____ Bookstore

_____ Computer Store or Software Store

_____ Catalog (name: _____)

_____ Direct from Sybex

_____ Other: _____

Did you buy this book with your personal funds?

_____ Yes   _____ No

About how many computer books do you buy each year?

_____ 1-3   _____ 3-5   _____ 5-7   _____ 7-9   _____ 10+

About how many Sybex books do you own?

_____ 1-3   _____ 3-5   _____ 5-7   _____ 7-9   _____ 10+

Please indicate your level of experience with the software covered in this book:

_____ Beginner   _____ Intermediate   _____ Advanced

Which types of software packages do you use regularly?

_____ Accounting	_____ Databases	_____ Networks
_____ Amiga	_____ Desktop Publishing	_____ Operating Systems
_____ Apple/Mac	_____ File Utilities	_____ Spreadsheets
_____ CAD	_____ Money Management	_____ Word Processing
_____ Communications	_____ Languages	_____ Other _____
		(please specify)

Which of the following best describes your job title?

_____ Administrative/Secretarial	_____ President/CEO
_____ Director	_____ Manager/Supervisor
_____ Engineer/Technician	_____ Other _____
	(please specify)

Comments on the weaknesses/strengths of this book: _____

_____

_____

_____

_____

PLEASE FOLD, SEAL, AND MAIL TO SYBEX

– –

SYBEX, INC.
Department M
2021 CHALLENGER DR.
ALAMEDA, CALIFORNIA USA
94501

SYBEX ®

SEAL